the MODERN PIONEER PANTRY

the MODERN PIONEER PANTRY

A Complete Guide to Preserving Food

MARY BRYANT SHRADER

Publisher Mike Sanders
Art & Design Director William Thomas
Editorial Director Ann Barton
Senior Editor Brook Farling
Designer Lindsay Dobbs
Photographer Kimberly Davis
Food Stylist Susan Gebhard
Recipe Testers Thom England, Susan Gebhard
Copy Editor Megan Douglass
Proofreaders Lisa Starnes, Monica Stone
Indexer Michael Goldstein

First American Edition, 2025
Published in the United States by DK Publishing
1745 Broadway, 20th Floor, New York, NY 10019

The authorized representative in the EEA is Dorling Kindersley
Verlag GmbH. Arnulfstr. 124, 80636 Munich, Germany

Note: This publication contains the opinions and ideas of its author. It is intended to provide helpful
and informative material on the subject matter covered. It is sold with the understanding that the
author and publisher are not engaged in rendering professional services in the book. If the reader
requires personal assistance or advice, a competent professional should be consulted. The author
and publisher specifically disclaim any responsibility for any liability, loss, or risk, personal or
otherwise, which is incurred as a consequence, directly or indirectly, of the use and application of
any of the contents of this book. At the time of publication, this book contains the latest U.S.
Department of Agriculture recommendations for safe food preservation according to the Complete
Guide to Home Canning, Agriculture Information Bulletin No. 539, USDA, revised 2015.

A catalog record for this book is available from the Library of Congress.
ISBN 978-0-5939-6511-5

DK books are available at special discounts when purchased
in bulk for sales promotions, premiums, fund-raising, or educational use.
For details, contact SpecialSales@dk.com

Images © DK Books with the exception of following pages: 57, 59, 73, 77, 79, 83, 89, 105, 111, 117,
131, 135, 163, 165, 187, 195, 205, 209, 228, 233, 245, 285, 286, 292 © Mary Bryant Shrader

Printed and bound in China

www.dk.com

This book was made with Forest
Stewardship Council™ certified
paper – one small step in DK's
commitment to a sustainable future.
Learn more at
www.dk.com/uk/information/sustainability

DEDICATION

To my husband, Ted, the greatest love of my life and my constant source of strength. Your unwavering support has made all my hopes and dreams become a reality. And to Ben, my wonderful son, you are the light of my life. Watching you grow into the incredible man you have become fills me with such joy. I thank God every day for the two of you, and I will love you both with all my heart forever and ever!

Table of Contents

6 ALL ABOUT FERMENTATION 179

7 ALL ABOUT FROZEN FOOD PRESERVATION 221

INTRODUCTION

Greetings, sweet friend, and welcome to _The Modern Pioneer Pantry_!

I am so thrilled to be able to bring you this second book in my Modern Pioneer series. In this cookbook, I focus on what I like to call "The Four Corners Pantry," which includes the Working Pantry, the Refrigerator, the Freezer, and the Extended Pantry, or what we like to nickname the Prepper Pantry. Here, you'll learn all about the best methods of food preservation, including home canning—both water bath and pressure canning—drying and dehydrating, fermentation, freezing, and pickling. Once you learn these skills, all four corners of your pantry will be well stocked, and you will never be caught off guard, no matter what comes your way. You will always have nutritious food on hand to feed yourself and your family, as well as your friends and neighbors, during both good times and more challenging times, such as when severe storms hit, illness strikes, supply chains are disrupted, a job is lost, or budgets become tight. The good news is that you will be prepared and ready to weather it all.

My mother and father lived through the Great Depression of the 1930s and the shortages of World War II, but they made it through no matter how difficult circumstances became. And, when raising me, they shared everything they did to survive those eras. And just as I shared with you the traditional foods cooking skills my mom had taught me in my first book, _The Modern Pioneer Cookbook_, I have even more to share with you here. You'll learn what my mom taught me about how to always have a well-stocked pantry, as well as all I have learned on this subject over the course of my adult life. And I am anxious to share this with you!

Just as my first book was a road map, in essence, to guide you on how to create a traditional foods kitchen, it is my wish that this book will be your road map for how to successfully stock a pantry. I hope this book will be your reference book, tucked up on your kitchen bookshelf next to *The Modern Pioneer Cookbook*, that you will turn to time and time again as your resource for how to stock a traditional foods pantry.

Most importantly, I want to assure you that all the skills I share here are very attainable, even for the beginner. I walk you through step by step, so nothing is left to chance. And when you wish I was right there guiding you in your kitchen, I can be—at least virtually—thanks to the various QR codes you can scan throughout this book to watch my videos explaining many of the supplies and techniques in this book. In spirit, we'll be working together, and when you come to the end of this book, you will not only have valuable skills that will last you a lifetime, but you will also have a well-stocked Four Corners Pantry!

I'm so blessed you and I are continuing on this traditional foods journey together. Here's to self-sufficiency, learning to preserve more and waste less, and learning to be the best modern pioneers in the kitchen that we can be!

Love and God bless,
Mary

Chapter One
THE FOUR CORNERS PANTRY

THE FOUR CORNERS PANTRY

When we hear the word "pantry," we often think of a closet or cupboard in a kitchen where nonperishable foods are stored. These foods may be store-bought or home-preserved, but what they have in common is that they can last—unrefrigerated or unfrozen—for a fairly long time. But for me, pantry means much more. The pantry, or the Four Corners Pantry, as I call it, is a system I learned from my mom a long time ago for being prepared and storing a variety of foods.

My parents and I lived on what many today would refer to as a small homestead. My dad longed for the country life, so with my mom and me in tow, he left the suburbs behind and moved to what, back in the early 1970s, was the country. My father worked in New York City, so we could only move so far, but the far northern part of our county was perfect. My parents bought a home on three acres with a well for water and, like many country properties, a septic system. There was a lot of work to be done, but my parents were never afraid of hard work. My dad fought in the Korean War with the US Army 5th Regimental Combat Team, was badly wounded near the Yalu River, but was blessed to survive after a long recovery in a military hospital in Valley Forge, Pennsylvania. The entire experience toughened him. So unexpected events, like the well being hit by lightning or a malfunctioning septic system, were not going to defeat him!

My mom and dad had lived through the Great Depression of the 1930s and the rationing of World War II. Surviving those times taught them to be prepared for whatever may come their way. They never wasted anything and lived by the old Yankee saying, "Use it up, wear it out, make it do, or do without!" As the chief cook and bottle washer—as my mom often

jokingly referred to herself—she was going to ensure she could always feed and care for her family under even the most difficult of circumstances. Both my parents maintained the mindset that an economic depression or a major war could happen at any time, and they would not be caught off guard. When gas lines and stagflation came along in the 1970s, they were glad to have their little homestead. But most importantly, my mom felt secure knowing she had a well-stocked pantry.

As the years went by, no matter where my parents lived as they aged, they always made sure they were prepared. That's the beauty of having a well-stocked pantry. It doesn't matter where you live. You might have a large or small homestead or live in the suburbs or even the city. It doesn't matter. You can develop a Four Corners Pantry system to ensure you always have a good supply of food and related needs on hand.

Unfortunately, when life becomes comfortable, we can forget (or maybe we never knew in the first place) how to fully stock a pantry to make sure that we can cope with various calamities, whether they be illness, bad weather, job loss, supply chain problems that create shortages of food and medical supplies, or all of the above! When the worldwide pandemic hit in 2020 and grocery store shelves emptied, many were caught off guard. Suddenly, everyone wanted to know how to live a life of preparedness.

I had been humming along with a website and YouTube channel where I created videos, accompanying blog posts, and recipes for making homemade traditional foods, including how to preserve food and stock a pantry— a Four Corners Pantry. All of a sudden, in late March 2020, I was inundated with comments and emails. Those who wrote to me shared their stories of finding themselves utterly unprepared for the shortages they encountered, but my information was extremely helpful to them as they tried to cope with challenging situations. I was glad to be able to help my viewers create recipes with what they had available and start them on what I call a Traditional Foods Journey to recapture the skills of our ancestors. Eventually, my first book, *The Modern Pioneer Cookbook*, was born, and many home cooks added it to their kitchen bookshelf to have a printed copy of everything they needed to know for how to make homemade traditional foods, sometimes from nothing more than scraps!

In *The Modern Pioneer Cookbook*, I wrote about the importance of what I refer to as Multiple Streams of Food to ensure that we have a variety of foods from different sources that we keep in our pantries. Some food may come from our local grocery store already prepared and packaged for us. For example, many of us know how to take individual ingredients and make soup, but is it also okay to keep canned soup on hand? Definitely! In situations where you are not able to cook, maybe because of illness or a tight budget that doesn't allow you to buy your usual supply of fresh food, canned soup can be a lifesaver!

However, we also want to ensure we find other food sources during good times. We can then take this food in its whole form and preserve it in various ways to store in our Four Corners Pantry. Stocking up on food in season and in bulk, whether it's imperfect (fresh food that is unblemished but often referred to as misfits or ugly food), from the grocery store, from a local farmer's market, or even harvested from your own kitchen garden, and then preserving it in your kitchen, will allow you to save money and have a full pantry with lots of variety.

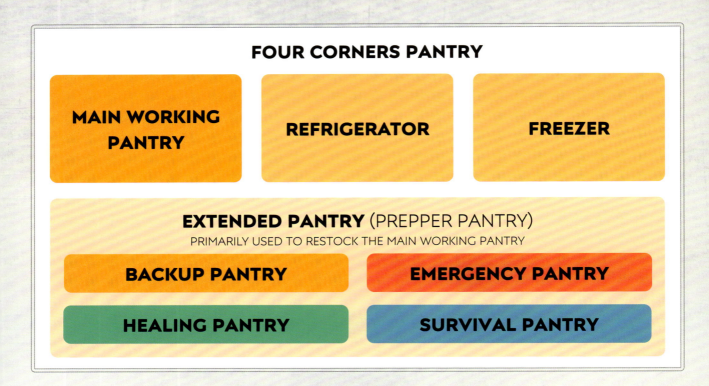

FOUR CORNERS PANTRY

MAIN WORKING PANTRY

REFRIGERATOR

FREEZER

EXTENDED PANTRY (PREPPER PANTRY)
PRIMARILY USED TO RESTOCK THE MAIN WORKING PANTRY

BACKUP PANTRY

EMERGENCY PANTRY

HEALING PANTRY

SURVIVAL PANTRY

What Is a Four Corners Pantry?

So, what exactly is a Four Corners Pantry? As I shared above, it's actually the way my mom ran her household and the way many mothers and grandmothers of her generation ran theirs. The Four Corners Pantry system makes sure you have sufficient food and supplies to carry your household through a period of time when food, water, and other supplies might be in short supply or difficult to obtain because of bad weather, illness, job loss, a tight budget, or rapid inflation. Over time, my mom built up her Four Corners Pantry to see us through 1 year of such difficult times. With the ebbs and flows that life often throws your way, my mom's Four Corners Pantry saw us through many a rough, snowy winter, power outages, lightning striking our well, and a variety of maladies from colds and coughs to upset tummies and poison ivy!

Today, I run the same Four Corners Pantry system in my home. No matter what comes our way here in central Texas, from rising grocery prices, ice storms, power outages, to the occasional cold or flu, I can make sure that I am prepared to take care of my sweet family, including my husband, Ted; our son, Ben; and our pup, Indy. Now let's review all the areas that make up a well-stocked Four Corners Pantry.

A Four Corners Pantry includes four main areas:

- **Corner 1 (The Working Pantry)** is where home cooks store the nonperishable foods they access on a daily basis. You'll find home-canned goods, dried or dehydrated food, and store-bought goods in this pantry.

- **Corner 2 (The Refrigerator)** is where the home cook stores perishable foods, including fermented foods.

- **Corner 3 (The Freezer)** is where the home cook stores perishable foods for long-term storage.

- **Corner 4 (The Extended Pantry)**, or what many nickname the Prepper Pantry, is where home cooks primarily store nonperishable foods that are used to restock the Working Pantry when food runs low. As with the Working Pantry, these include home-canned goods, dried or dehydrated foods, and store-bought goods.

The Extended Pantry deserves more explanation since it is made up of four sub-pantries: the Backup

Pantry, the Emergency Pantry, the Survival Pantry, and the Healing Pantry.

The main focus of an Extended Pantry, and the largest part of this pantry, is the Backup Pantry, where you store the bulk of your food to restock your Working Pantry when supplies run low.

Maintaining a well-stocked Backup Pantry ensures you don't have to run out at the last minute to find missing ingredients in your Working Pantry to make a meal. When you can turn to your Backup Pantry for what you need, you save yourself a trip to the grocery store where items may be overpriced or not available at all.

When we can buy food on sale or in bulk at a discount, preserve it, and stock it in our Backup Pantry, we automatically save money. Running out to buy one or two ingredients for a recipe or having to restock a Working Pantry when we have to pay full price can often, as my mom used to say, "bust the budget." And sometimes, as we have learned from recent history, the foods we may need are simply out of stock.

Next thing you know, we find ourselves wandering the aisles of the grocery store, looking for substitutes and possibly even buying other foods we did not plan or budget for. The less time we spend in the grocery store shopping outside our grocery list, the more money we can save!

Beyond the Backup Pantry, the Extended Pantry has three additional sub-pantries that are important for preparedness through food preservation:

- **The Emergency Sub-Pantry** is where you will want to store 2 weeks worth of food you can prepare without electricity or clean running water. Sometimes, we find ourselves in situations where we are isolated at home instead of evacuating. When we have to shelter in place because of bad weather, we are also likely to lack power and water. In these cases, home-preserved foods can be a boon to your Emergency Pantry.

- **The Survival Sub-Pantry** is where you will store foods that many home cooks refer to as Forever Foods—foods that the United States Department of Agriculture (USDA) has classified as having an indefinite shelf life. The good news is that you don't have to purchase specially prepared foods, like a factory-packaged freeze-dried meal. Many simple foods available at your local grocery store are considered Forever Foods. And better yet, once you learn how to preserve certain foods, they are perfect for your Survival Pantry.

- **The Healing Sub-Pantry** is a critical area of your Extended Pantry and one that my mom always kept well stocked. You will want to ensure that you have the ingredients you need to prepare a variety of natural remedies and a supply of over-the-counter products that you like to keep on hand for treating common maladies. Learning how to home preserve certain basic healing ingredients will come in handy when you stock this area of your Extended Pantry.

Now, don't worry. You don't need to stock your Four Corners Pantry overnight. Just like learning how to make traditional foods from scratch, stocking your pantry is also a journey. In this book, you will discover five different ways to preserve fresh food, including home canning, drying and dehydrating, fermentation, freezing, and pickling, so as to have a variety of foods on hand for the long haul.

HOW LONG CAN YOU STORE SHELF-STABLE FOODS?

The USDA guidelines for storing shelf-stable food vary, but here is what the website says: "Most shelf-stable foods are safe indefinitely. In fact, canned goods will last for years as long as the can itself is in good condition (no rust, dents, or swelling). Packaged foods (cereal, pasta, cookies) will be safe past the 'best by' date, although they may eventually become stale or develop an off flavor. You'll know when you open the package if the food has lost quality. Many dates on foods refer to quality, not safety."

Getting Started with Preserving Food at Home

Once you decide you are ready to begin preserving food to stock your pantry, start by inventorying what you already have on hand. Even if you have never preserved food before, you will have some store-bought foods in your pantry. Taking this inventory will give you an insight into what type of foods you stock and which ones you might be able to make homemade and preserve.

Over time, you will want to stock more of your home-preserved foods and less of the store-bought varieties. You're not going to eliminate all store-bought food since you want to have multiple streams of food. However, in time, you will be amazed to learn how much you can make homemade and home preserve to have an abundance of food for maintaining a well-stocked Four Corners Pantry.

Best of all, once you have a well-stocked Four Corners Pantry, you will be able to feed and care for yourself, your family, and others. Chances are you will be one of the best prepared home cooks in your neighborhood, making you a blessing to your neighbors during times of difficulty, whether large or small. Being able to put together a blessing basket, as I call them, of home-preserved foods to share with friends and neighbors will be much appreciated when they may be going through short-term setbacks, such as illness or job loss.

For the home cook, there are five easy and efficient ways to home preserve foods:

- **Home Canning** allows high-acid foods to be water bath canned and low-acid foods to to be pressure canned. Home-canned foods allow you to control what ingredients you want to have in your jams, jellies, condiments, fruits, pickled vegetables, and more. You can easily store these foods in your Working Pantry and Extended Pantry. Once opened, you'll consume them or move them to your refrigerator.
- **Drying and Dehydrating** uses air, a low-temperature oven, and in some cases, an electric dehydrator to preserve food. This form of food preservation is perfect for storing in your Working Pantry and Extended Pantry.
- **Fermentation** relies on a simple brine of salt and water to create probiotic-rich foods that are good for our digestive health and lead to good overall health. Thanks to the good bacteria in fermented foods, they store well in the door or top shelf of your refrigerator for up to 6 months.
- **Freezing** preserves both individual ingredients, as well as complete meals that you can easily defrost or pop into the toaster or the oven at a moment's notice.
- **Pickling** is similar to fermentation since food is preserved in a brine. However, this form of preparation gives you the option of refrigerating or water bath canning your pickled food. Pickling food enables you to preserve a lot of fresh food you bought in season or on sale from the grocery store or farmer's market, or food you harvested from your kitchen garden. And the process is relatively quick and easy. Due to the high-acid content of pickled food, these foods have an extended shelf life when stored in the refrigerator or an even longer shelf life when home canned.

As you learn each form of food preservation, you will build upon your skills and discover how each method will provide a bounty of food to stock in one or more areas of your Four Corners Pantry.

Why Preserve Food to Stock in Your Pantry?

Nowadays, we enjoy all the conveniences of popping down to the grocery store and buying pretty much any type of food, bottled water, over-the-counter remedies, and more. So why would anyone want to take the time and energy needed to make foods homemade and then go on to preserve them? If we learned anything from the pandemic in 2020, it's that we can't take the ability to pop down to the grocery store for granted.

Not only might there be situations where our ability to even enter the grocery store is limited, but once we do get into the store, we may find a limited availability of food. Let's hope those times don't return anytime soon, but other calamities may come our way. We never know when we might be ill and unable to head out to the store. Or we might find ourselves unemployed and living on a tight budget. And most of us, at one time or another, have found ourselves stranded at home during a bad weather event. How comforting it will be to know that our pantries are well stocked with everything we need to get through whatever situation we are dealing with!

Being able to stock our pantry goes well beyond convenience. When you make food homemade and then preserve it, you control every ingredient that goes into the making of that food. Whether it's sugar, salt, or other ingredients, you decide what to include in your recipe. Best of all, your homemade and home-preserved food will be free of most of the chemicals contained in modern pre-prepared and packaged foods sold at the grocery store.

In recent times, we have been able to choose from a wide variety of natural foods or organic foods prepared and marketed as having been made with fewer chemicals and preservatives. Having these more natural options enables us to supply another stream of food in our Four Corners Pantry. But are these foods we want to rely on 100 percent? Most likely not, because they are often considerably more costly than conventionally grown and commercially prepared foods. When we make food homemade and then preserve it, we not only have a more natural food, but we often have a food that costs us considerably less to make.

How Much Food Do You Need to Preserve?

When it comes to home preserving food to stock in your Four Corners Pantry, you might be wondering how much food you need to preserve. This boils down to personal preference, but for me, I learned from my mom that making sure to have 1 year of food on hand would basically see me through any difficulties I may encounter in life.

If you look at various food storage calculators online, you can easily become overwhelmed. Sometimes the amount of food these calculators recommend you have on hand can be daunting. A better and simpler approach is to save your grocery store receipts, record what you buy each week, and determine how much you use in a week. Over time, you will have a clear picture of how much food you need to stock to see you through 1 week. From there, it's easy to calculate how much food you need for 2 weeks, a few months, or even a year. Then you can decide how much food you want to stock.

Some people I know were comfortable only keeping 2 weeks of food on hand. That was before the pandemic. Most of those people now keep at least 2 months of food in their pantries, while others have worked toward making sure they have at least 6 months or a year of food on hand at all times. You can never go wrong with building up a supply of food that can see you through 1 year. You just want to make sure that you keep track of what you stock, especially in your Working Pantry and Backup Pantry. You want to make sure that you use the food you stock in the proper order, which brings us to the First-In First-Out (FIFO) method.

USING THE FIFO METHOD

When you stock food in your Working Pantry, it can be easy to stay on top of what you have and to use those foods to create nourishing meals. Generally, most home cooks access their Working Pantry daily or at least on a weekly basis. However, forgetting about the food you've stored in your Backup Pantry can be easy. This is why you always want to ensure you are practicing the FIFO method. Whatever you put into your Backup Pantry first also needs to be accessed and used before you use foods that were put in last (the more recent additions).

When you follow the FIFO method, you won't discover that some of your home-canned (or store-bought) foods that you added to your Backup Pantry 10 years ago weren't used and have now degraded significantly in nutritional value or have spoiled or gone stale and may need to be discarded. Traditional foods cooks like ourselves hate to waste food because it's a precious commodity. It also hits us in the pocketbook because we are essentially discarding money—the money it took to buy those foods, not to mention the time and effort it took in many cases to preserve those foods!

When you take the time to put your food away in a manner that makes sure that those newer additions go behind the older ones found in your Backup Pantry, it will be easy to follow the FIFO method, and nothing will go to waste. Plus, having an organized pantry system and taking a few extra minutes to put your food away properly also helps you create a mini inventory. You will start to see patterns in what you use the most, what you use the least, and when and what foods should be restocked. As each season passes, you learn what fresh foods to buy or grow the most of, which ones to pull back on, and how much to preserve of each food to see you through a season. Then, when that particular fresh food is in season or on sale, you can begin your preservation process all over again.

Budget-Friendly Fresh Food for Preserving

We want the process of making food homemade and preserving it to be as affordable as possible. Today, there are many options for purchasing fresh food while staying within a reasonable budget. One of the best places to start, especially if you live in the suburbs or the city, is your local grocery store. In your store, an excellent place to begin shopping is the produce department before heading to the fresh meats, fish, and poultry areas.

When you are looking to buy fresh fruits and vegetables that you hope to preserve using one of the methods shared in this book, you always want to focus on what is in season. Seasonal produce, as well as locally grown produce, is going to be the freshest and the most affordable. There are some variables as to seasonality depending on where you live, so as you look through the lists below, you will find that certain fruits and vegetables span multiple seasons. Although not exhaustive, this list will give you some ideas on what to choose when you are ready to get started preserving fruits and vegetables.

SPRING AND SUMMER PRODUCE

- **Artichokes:** Old tales say that when artichokes make their debut in the garden, it is a signal that spring is on the way! Their peak season begins in March and lasts through May.

- **Asparagus:** Look for firm, bright spears in the spring.

- **Beets:** Although harvested in the fall and winter, you can also harvest them again in the early spring.

- **Berries:** A superb selection of berries will start appearing at the beginning of spring and will be available all summer long.

- **Broccoli:** Broccoli is planted in the spring for harvesting in the late spring/early summer.

- **Cabbage:** Look for varieties harvested in late summer. If temperatures are beginning to cool where you live, these varieties might be perfect for fermenting.

- **Carrots:** We can find carrots at the grocery store all year, but you might find them in abundance in the early spring at your farmer's market.

- **Cherries:** Cherries come into season generally in late spring for a short period through early summer. Make sure you pick cherries that have a firm texture and avoid any that are soft or have wrinkled skins.

- **Corn:** You'll find corn in season from May through September in most areas. This is the perfect time to stock up and start pressure canning sweet corn to last you through the year.

- **Cucumbers:** These are usually in most grocery stores all year long, but they are actually in season and at their peak starting in May and going through August. This is when you want to turn some of your cucumbers into pickles for the best texture.

- **Grapes:** Although you will find these in abundance in September and October, grapes come into season in August.

- **Herbs:** These can be quite plentiful in the spring and summer, and many home cooks will say they grow like weeds!

- **Melons:** You'll find a variety of melons in season usually beginning in May and lasting through to September.

- **Nectarines and peaches:** These fruits may begin to appear in the spring in certain regions, but they are at their peak in the summer. Make sure they are firm with only the slightest give when pressed.

- **Onions:** Late summer continuing into fall is the peak season for the onion family.

- **Peas:** All kinds of peas are in season in the spring and continue to be harvested through the summer.

- **Peppers:** You'll find sweet bell peppers at their peak in July and heading into the fall. Spicy peppers, such as jalapeños, will begin to come into season in June.

- **Radishes:** This hardy vegetable should be abundant in early spring at both your grocery store and the farmer's market.

- **Rhubarb:** Although the greens are not edible, the tart stalks of rhubarb make tasty additions to jams and pie fillings when mixed with fruit, especially strawberries.

- **Sweet potatoes:** These start their season in late August, but you'll probably find the best prices in the fall.

- **Tomatillos:** These are superb additions to homemade salsas and are in season in late summer into early fall.

- **Tomatoes:** All varieties are plentiful during the summer, but some will come into season as early as May. Depending on where you live, you might still see tomatoes in October. However, their season technically wraps up in September.

- **Zucchini:** Along with summer squash, these vegetables are available in large quantities at your grocery store or farmer's market. Or, if you grow them yourself, you'll find them taking over your kitchen garden!

FALL AND WINTER PRODUCE

- **Apples:** Apple harvesting begins in late summer and continues into early fall. Apples can be eaten as is, turned into home-canned pie filling, or dried for a quick snack.

- **Beets:** Yes, beets are in season in the fall, winter, and spring. They are a hardy crop that can withstand cold temperatures.

- **Cabbage:** Depending on the variety, you'll find cabbages in late summer, fall, and winter. I like to select nice firm heads of cabbage in the fall to turn into naturally fermented sauerkraut as the temperatures begin to cool down and provide the perfect fermentation temperature in my kitchen.

- **Cauliflower:** As with so many fruits and vegetables, you can find cauliflower in your grocery store almost all year round. However, depending on where you live, in-season cauliflower might start appearing at your farmer's market as early as June! Technically, peak season is from September through November.

- **Citrus fruits:** Various varieties begin to come into season in the fall and the winter while some are still available and considered in season in the spring.

- **Grapes:** The peak season for grapes starts in August but goes through October.

- **Onions:** Onions are another crossover crop that is still in season through the fall.

- **Pears:** This fall and winter fruit is often harvested before it is completely ripe, but it will soften over time. Pears can be purchased quite firm, making them the perfect candidates for water bath canning.

- **Peppers:** Both the sweet bell pepper varieties and their spicy cousins are harvested in the summer and into the fall until the first frost.

- **Pomegranates:** Although pomegranates begin to appear in season in October, they are usually in abundance come December.

- **Potatoes:** These are at their peak in the fall and also store very well.

- **Root vegetables:** We've already covered carrots and beets, but other root vegetables in season in the fall and winter include parsnips, rutabagas, and turnips. You may even find some in the spring after they have survived a cold winter. These spring-harvested root vegetables will have a sweeter flavor because their starches have been turned into sugars.

- **Sweet potatoes:** These can begin to make their in-season appearance in late August and will be in season through early November.

- **Tomatillos:** Even though the growing season has basically wrapped up, you should still be able to find tomatillos in early fall.

- **Winter squash:** There is always a huge variety of winter squash to choose from, beginning in the early fall and holding steady right through the winter months.

- **Zucchini:** You may be surprised to see zucchini listed since it and summer squash are prolific in the summer months. However, zucchini is often harvested right through to the fall in many climates.

What I have shared here applies to both grocery stores and farmer's markets. By regularly visiting your local farmer's market and building relationships with the farmers, you can save a significant amount of money compared to buying small quantities of food from various vendors. The key is to identify the vendors you like who offer the foods you want, and then buy in bulk. This not only fosters a long and happy relationship with local farmers but also helps you save money.

For instance, if you're interested in preserving apples or making apple pie filling, find farmers who sell the type and quality of apples you prefer. Inquire if they offer discounts for buying bushels of these apples. This can lead to significant savings compared to purchasing a bag of apples from a grocery store or farmer's market. Remember, the more you buy, the better the price the farmer can offer. And if you're open to buying uglies, chances are you can save even more!

Don't underestimate the potential of a small kitchen garden. Even a small windowsill garden with a few pots of herbs and green onions, which can be grown from grocery store cuttings, can be a great start. Herbs are particularly easy to grow, both indoors and out. Once you start regrowing green onions from their root scraps, you'll never need to buy them again. Add a few tins of cherry tomatoes to your windowsill, and you're on your way to developing your gardening skills.

If you are able to branch out to balcony gardening or patio gardening, vertical gardens have become quite popular. These tiered systems are affordable and allow you to grow your produce upward rather than outward. And in time, if you have room for a small kitchen garden, you'll want to learn all about square-foot gardening. Using the square-foot gardening method during the pandemic, I was able to grow 80 pounds of plum tomatoes in a small 4-foot by 4-foot raised bed! And when a small peach tree delivered a bountiful harvest, I had so many peaches I was giving them away in bushels to anyone who would take them! So never underestimate what a small kitchen garden can provide.

MEATS AND POULTRY

Once you've covered your fresh produce, it's time to move on to meats and poultry. There are a number of ways to find bargains even on these more costly foods. When you are just starting out, speak with the butchers at your local grocery store and find out if and when they mark down red meat and chicken. The markdowns can take place on various dates and times, but the butchers may be able to give you a heads up as you develop relationships with them and they recognize you as a regular shopper.

It's common to see markdowns on chicken and various cuts of beef once a week at my local grocery store. Even your high-end markets have started adopting these practices in an effort to cut down on waste. Generally, they'll reduce the price by 25 percent and sometimes by as much as 50 percent. The sell-by date is usually the same day or the next day on their marked-down food, so when I get home, I pop my bargains into my freezer to use in the future or use that same day by preserving the food in some way, such as pressure canning or creating a freezer meal.

You can also talk with the purveyors of meats and poultry at your local farmer's markets to learn more about what offerings they may have regarding bulk pricing for buying a case of chickens. You'll also want to inquire about which are their less expensive cuts of beef. Those tough cuts like chuck roasts become wonderfully tender when cubed and pressure canned!

If you are blessed to live near ranches that raise cattle, you can investigate buying a whole or part of a cow at a reduced price. Having a large amount of meat may initially seem overwhelming, but as your skills at pressure canning and drying become more proficient, you will find that you want to buy beef in bulk. But don't worry, ranchers will often sell as little as a quarter of a cow, where other people join in to buy the other three-quarters. You can get together with people you know to form a buying club, or the rancher may be able to match you up with other customers. No matter what way this works out, your price per pound of beef will be significantly lower than what you would pay for smaller quantities at your local grocery store or farmer's market.

Meal Planning Flexibility with Home-Preserved Foods

Once you have a well-stocked Four Corners Pantry, meal planning becomes very easy. Now, I use the term meal planning very loosely. I am not one to follow detailed meal plans requiring the purchase of many different ingredients, many of which you may only use a small portion of. I find that structured meal plans can often lead to waste.

For example, let's say you create a meal plan (or follow one online) and purchase all the ingredients you need to make a week's worth of meals. But then things change, and you're taken away from home or unable to make meals with what you bought. Or, imagine that it's six o'clock and you find yourself exhausted and not up to following a detailed recipe you've never made with ingredients you may have never cooked with before.

You might be able to relate to these scenarios. When I was first married, I found myself in these situations and more. By the week's end, I was literally dumping all my meal planning ingredients into a soup pot and calling it a day! But my mom came to the rescue and reminded me to keep a well-stocked pantry with home-preserved food that my family and I liked. She encouraged me to store foods I was familiar with cooking that wouldn't go to waste or spoil if plans changed. I had a new lease on life. Well, maybe more like a new lease in my kitchen, but it was life-changing!

For instance, being able to open any of your pressure-canned meals in a jar and simply warm them up on the stovetop takes only minutes, and dinner is ready. Your homemade beef stew will taste much better than anything you can buy in a can from your local grocery store. Freezer meals are also an easy way to have dinner on the table with little effort on your part. From freezer to oven to table and dinner is ready! However, meal planning with home-preserved foods goes well beyond these ideas.

When you have some time, you can use your single-ingredient home-preserved foods to create entire meals. These meals might use all home-preserved foods or be a mix of your home-preserved foods along with other ingredients you have stocked in your pantry that you purchased from the grocery store. Over time, you'll find that you're replacing many of the items you once purchased from the grocery store with your home-preserved foods. When this happens, you'll find yourself reaching into your pantry for foods you home canned, dried, fermented, froze, or pickled to easily make meals, including breakfast, lunch, dinner, and dessert!

But I don't want you to worry that you will be staring into your pantry with lots of home-preserved foods and wondering what to do with them—which can be a common concern among those new to home food preservation. You find yourself canning and dehydrating, freezing some foods and pickling others, but when it comes time to pull everything together to make a meal, you can feel a bit stumped.

Of course, there are those easy options I mentioned above—like having beef stew pressure canned in a jar and just pouring it into a pan. However, what about all those individual ingredients you stored in your pantry? How do you pull those together to get a meal on the table? I have an easy system that will make meal planning a breeze.

When you look at pictures of home-canned goods, you will often see similar items lined up with each other. All the peaches are together, all the green beans are together, so on and so forth. There is nothing wrong with this system, and it is certainly one way to organize your Working Pantry and Backup Pantry. When you want to grab a home-canned jar of green beans, you'll know right where they are. Plus, when you use the FIFO system and keep track of your inventory, you can easily see what you may be running low on or what you should be using up.

The same is true of your other home-preserved foods. You may have all the in-season fruit that you froze neatly lined up in your freezer. Or you may have placed all your fermented or pickled items together on the top shelf of your refrigerator. The only foods with multiple ingredients that might be easy to access and cook quickly are those that you home canned or froze as complete meals. But you might have just a few of those. Single ingredients are more likely to be stocked in all the areas of your Four Corners Pantry.

However, as you learn to create meals with home-preserved foods, a simple idea is to group meal ingredients together in your pantry. These meal ingredients can be all home-preserved foods or a combination of home-preserved and store-bought foods. This concept is often referred to as the meal-in-a-bag system. You can store these bag meals in your Working Pantry and use them whenever you want to create a quick meal, knowing that you have all of the ingredients, with an attached recipe, handy in one place. You can use this same concept for ingredients that need to be stored in the refrigerator and freezer.

When putting bag meals together, think about what you and your family and friends enjoy eating. Then build a bag meal around those ideas. It may be a 100 percent shelf-stable bag meal, one that can be tucked into your refrigerator or freezer or one that has ingredients stored in multiple places.

When creating bag meals, you can use simple brown bags from the grocery store or large plastic storage bags that you can see through. Any type of bag will work in the pantry, but in the refrigerator or freezer, you'll want to stick with plastic bags or plastic containers to corral all the ingredients together. The trick is to make sure what you put in the bag can be used to create an entire meal or, at the very least, a partial meal (more on that later). Then, once you've used the contents of the bag, refill it with the ingredients to make a future meal and put it back on the shelf in your Working Pantry or in a bin in your refrigerator or freezer.

On the outside of the bag, you'll want to attach a paper that tells you everything you need to know about what is in the bag, such as the bag's contents, how the ingredients can be used to make a meal, a recipe if it requires one, and any other important information. To make my bag system reusable, I usually put the attached paper in a transparent sheet protector (or a gallon-size plastic storage bag for the fridge or freezer) and clip it to the bag (or bin). I save all this information for future use. If I want to include the best-used-by date of the food in the bag, I usually attach a sticky note to the information since it only pertains to what is in the bag at that time. Then I discard the sticky note after using the bag's contents. (If you specify a best-used-by date for the bag, choose the date of the ingredient in the bag that has the earliest best-used-by date.)

A simple example of this type of bag meal is a bag filled with . . .

- Home-canned chicken
- Home-canned chopped tomatoes or store-bought canned chopped tomatoes
- Home-dried herbs, premeasured and packaged in small containers
- Rice, premeasured in the amount called for in the recipe

Having everything in the bag, premeasured and ready to go, makes life easy—especially when you are tired after a long day. All you need to do is open some bottles and cans—no measuring required! You can place all of these ingredients into a baking dish and pop the dish into the oven.

Remember that you never have to feel constrained by how you prepare a meal-in-a-bag. There is so much flexibility to this system, including making partial meals-in-a-bag. A partial bag meal may only contain some ingredients you need to make a meal. You might have various shelf-stable home-canned goods and some dried ingredients in a bag, but when you are ready to cook, you will add some ingredients from your refrigerator or freezer. Those perishable foods might include one ingredient or a group of ingredients kept together as another partial bag meal. Together, these ingredients become a complete meal.

The bottom line is that you want to make life easy for yourself and become comfortable using all of your home-preserved foods to create nutritious and delicious meals.

As you work your way through this book, you'll learn all the basic techniques you need to preserve a variety of foods and meals. And the recipes you'll learn, along with lots of tips and tricks for variations, will help you stock your Four Corners Pantry with endless food options for a variety of tasty recipes.

Chapter Two
ALL ABOUT HOME CANNING

ALL ABOUT HOME CANNING

Home canning is a popular way of preserving food for your pantry. When it comes to home food preservation, safety is of paramount importance. It's easy to adhere to safe practices to ensure your food will be preserved properly, stay fresh for an extended period of time, and be safe to consume. I'll show you how. So let's start with home canning!

There are a number of ways to preserve food through home canning, and the two most common are the boiling water method—often referred to as water bath canning—and pressure canning. We'll explore each of these types of canning, but I want to share a little bit about the history of preserving food through canning and how it all got started.

A NOTE ABOUT THE GUIDELINES FOLLOWED IN THIS BOOK

You can be assured that as we begin our home canning journey together, I will only share canning recipes with you that adhere to the guidelines put forth by the National Center for Home Food Preservation (NCHFP). The United States Department of Agriculture (USDA) founded the NCHFP to provide detailed methods for safe home food preservation. All the recipes I share with you throughout this book adhere to the NCHFP's safe practices for not only home canning but drying, fermenting, freezing, and pickling, too. All the water bath canning recipes and pressure canning recipes in the chapters that follow adhere to the guidelines put forth in the Complete Guide to Home Canning, Agriculture Information Bulletin No. 539, USDA, revised 2015.

A Little History about Home Canning

The concept of home canning was born from the idea of cooking food quickly at high temperatures, not preserving it. A French physicist and mathematician named Denis Papin created a vessel that today would be described as a pressure cooker, not a pressure canner. (Yes, there is a difference—more on that later.) Papin called his device a digester, and it made its debut in 1679.

Papin made the digester from heavy cast iron with a tight-fitting lid that locked in place. This invention had drawbacks, but Papin believed it could heat water under pressure to a temperature higher than if not under pressure. He thought this higher water temperature, along with the steam it created, would penetrate food quickly, reducing the food's cooking time. In 1679, scientists did not have an understanding about vitamins and minerals, but today, researchers believe that cooking food in this way preserves vitamin and mineral content better than if cooked by other methods.

The problem with the digester was that it did not initially have a pressure release valve. If it had existed, this valve would have been able to be opened to allow the pressure caused by the higher water temperature and steam to be controlled and released. If the pressure can't be controlled and released in a pressure cooker (or canner), it can become dangerous. And that is what happened with the digester. The early version was dangerous and would explode. But Papin eventually figured out how to fix the problem and added a pressure release valve to his digester. Even though modern-day pressure cookers and pressure canners are safe, the image of exploding cookers and canners often lives on! We can put an end to that image once and for all. Learning how to be a home canner is not only easy, it's also safe.

FROM COOKER TO CANNER

But how did we get from Denis Papin's understanding of pressure cooking to the development of pressure canning? We can thank a French chef for that leap. In 1809, Chef Nicolas François Appert debuted a method for preserving food in glass bottles or jars, which he developed by modifying Papin's pressure cooking concept. Although here in the United States today, we refer to preserving food in jars as canning, Appert and others in Europe referred to this method of food preservation as bottling or jarring—terms that are sometimes still used today.

As he tinkered with Papin's pressure cooking method, Appert created something more akin to what we know today as the boiling water method of canning—or what we commonly call water bath canning. Appert determined that if he put food in jars; sealed the jars with a cork, wax, and wire to protect the food from air; and then boiled the jars in very hot water for an extended period of time, he could preserve the food for what he believed would be an indefinite period.

So why did Appert, who as a chef would have prided himself on preparing fresh food to be enjoyed soon after cooking, want to develop a food preservation method? For that, we have to thank Napoleon! Feeding his soldiers who were far from home required the development of some form of food preservation. He needed a way to send food to his troops that could stay fresh even when shipped long distances. So, Napoleon put the task to his citizens as a contest in 1795, with prize money awarded to the winner. Chef Appert won the prize money in 1809 for his method of preserving food, and Napoleon's soldiers could be fed with jarred foods that were being preserved en masse, thanks to Appert's invention.

Today, we understand that there is a significant difference between pressure canning and water bath canning and how it relates to the safe preservation of food. These early attempts at experimenting with different ways of preserving food in bottles and jars by sealing out air and heating to high temperatures led to the invention of pressure canners and water bath canners. We developed two different types of canning equipment because different foods require different methods of canning. Appert did not understand this because germ theory had not yet become an accepted form of science. What he did understand is that if he boiled food in bottles and jars for an extended period of time, it appeared to become shelf stable and safe to be consumed at some later date. Although his process didn't involve pressure, which is the preferred method for canning low-acid foods, Appert's method was a step in the right direction.

FROM PASTEURIZATION TO APPERTIZATION

If we fast forward to the late 1850s, we meet Dr. Louis Pasteur who we often associate today with the word pasteurization—a common process of heating milk (or other foods) for a period of time to destroy what are believed to be harmful microorganisms. (As a raw milk drinker, I confess I am not a huge fan of pasteurizing milk today, but I understand the reasoning behind the need for this process in the 1850s.) The theory behind the science of pasteurization led us to the development of preserving food through modern methods of canning.

Dr. Pasteur discovered how three measurements (time, temperature, and acidic value) play a significant role in destroying harmful microorganisms—bad bacteria. Understanding this allowed him to develop a method for properly processing foods through pasteurization so the foods would be safe to consume. For home canners, the significant word here is process. We use the same word today when we are preserving food through home canning. We process food, either under pressure or in boiling water.

In the case of pasteurization, heating foods and liquids to a high temperature for an extended period of time and then allowing those foods to cool destroys germs that might otherwise cause food to spoil or cause food-borne illness if consumed. In the case of canning, heating food in jars to high temperatures kills microorganisms, then allowing the jars to cool creates a vacuum seal, preventing new microorganisms from getting into the jars. This system preserves the food in jars safely. As a nod to Appert, canning is sometimes called appertization, which is distinct from pasteurization.

A key measurement in Dr. Pasteur's discovery, as it applies to home canning today, is acidic value. The reason there are two methods of properly preserving food through canning comes down to the acidic value of the food being preserved. Low-acid foods need to be pressure canned, while high-acid foods can be water bath canned. To be safely canned and last for an extended period of time, low-acid foods need to be processed at higher temperatures which only a pressure canner can provide. High-acid foods can be processed at a lower temperature simply because of the food's acid content. This higher acid content, along with the boiling water processing, contributes to tamping down the development of harmful microorganisms that do not survive well in highly acidic environments.

Know Your Food: High-Acid Foods versus Low-Acid Foods

Before you can jump into either type of home canning, you need to know the acidic value of your food. Once you determine the acidic value of your ingredients or the acidic value of your complete recipe, you can then determine which type of canner you need to use: a water bath canner or a pressure canner.

To determine a food's acidic value, you need to use a scientific measurement known as pH (potential of hydrogen). The pH of food, as well as other substances, is measured using a scale from 0 to 14. A food that registers with a high number on this scale is considered to be a low-acid food, while a food that registers with a low number is considered to be a high-acid food. What is essential to know is that the dividing line for measuring acidity in foods—when it comes to home canning—is 4.6.

The good news is that all this work of determining pH has been done for you. There are countless references available online regarding the pH of food from the USDA/NCHF and state Agricultural Extension Services. Plus, all the recipes I share differentiate between high-acid foods and low-acid foods and indicate the proper canning method required.

Foods with a pH of 4.6 or lower are considered high-acid foods and can be water bath canned. A wide variety of fruits and fruit products, such as jams and jellies, as well as pickled products (like traditional pickles, pickled vegetables, and relishes), will have a pH of 4.6 or lower. Foods with a pH above 4.6 are classified as low-acid foods and must be pressure canned. These foods include vegetables, meats, and combination foods such as soup, stew, and chili.

It's important to differentiate between pickled vegetables canned in an acidic brine and plain vegetables canned in water. The first has a low pH (high acid), whereas the second has a high pH (low acid). So always remember that when you are home canning vegetables, if you choose the water bath canning method, you must use pickled vegetables.

HOW TO DECIDE WHICH CANNING METHOD TO USE BASED ON ACIDITY.

Low-acid foods have a high pH.
Foods with a pH of 4.7 or higher must be pressure canned.

High-acid foods have a low pH.
Foods with a pH of 4.6 or lower can be water bath canned.

Choosing the Right Canner

Once you determine the acidity level of the food you want to home can, you'll know which type of canner you'll need.

THE WATER BATH CANNER

High-acid foods must be processed in boiling water at a temperature of 212°F (100°C) to destroy harmful microorganisms. On the most basic level, this canning method involves packing jars with food, placing a lid and band on the jar, and then completely covering the jars with water in a large stockpot or water bath canner. Once the jars are submerged, you'll heat the water to boiling (212°F/100°C) and then keep the water boiling for a specified time as indicated in the recipe depending on the food in the jars, the size of the jars, and the altitude of the home canner's location.

Keep in mind that altitude affects home canning because water boils at lower temperatures at higher altitudes, which makes the boiling point at higher altitudes less effective at killing harmful microorganisms. To compensate for the change in boiling point, each home canning recipe will extend the boiling time for higher altitudes.

Choosing a water bath canner for home canning high-acid foods is easy. Today, you have a number of options, from something as simple as a large stockpot with a terrycloth towel or round metal cooling rack placed in the bottom of the pot, to an actual water bath canner with an internal rack made for the water bath process. We'll dive into all the equipment you'll need to water bath can successfully in the next chapter. But rest assured, you probably have some of what you will need already stowed in your kitchen cabinets. Not only is water bath canning easy, the entry point is also quite affordable!

THE PRESSURE CANNER

Low-acid foods must be processed at 240°F (115°C), and you can only achieve this temperature under pressure. To achieve this pressure, you need to use a specific type of equipment called a pressure canner. So when it comes to pressure canning low-acid foods, make sure you are using an actual pressure canner and not a pressure cooker. Here's why:

- Pressure cookers come in different sizes, but they usually resemble medium- to large-size saucepans with long handles and a steam release valve built into the lid or the handle. They are designed to cook food quickly, and typically hold up to 4 quarts of liquid.

- Pressure canners vary in size but are larger than pressure cookers. They are designed for pressure canning low-acid foods. They can hold from 4 to 14 quart-size jars or 7 to 24 half-pint jars. A pressure canner holds a minimum of 10 quarts of liquid.

- Because pressure cookers are smaller than pressure canners, the heat-up and cool-down times in a pressure cooker are significantly shorter than in a pressure canner. This difference may lead to jarred food that has been underprocessed in a pressure cooker. Food that has been underprocessed leaves an opportunity for dangerous botulism spores to survive.

- Most importantly, trying to use a pressure cooker as a pressure canner is unsafe because most pressure cookers do not have the proper mechanisms to measure the amount of pressure being applied to the jars. Even if a pressure cooker had the necessary mechanisms in place, the NCHFP and respected agricultural extension services found that pressure cooker mechanisms can frequently be inaccurate. You always need to know exactly what the pressure inside the canner is to ensure that the food in the jars is processed long enough and with the proper pressure to deactivate botulism spores.

ARE STEAM CANNING AND OVEN CANNING SAFE?

Steam canning is similar to water bath canning. The main difference is that steam canning uses less water than water bath canning. Steam canning requires specific equipment, including a shallow pan, a dome cover, and a wire rack that holds jars above the base of the shallow pan. You add a small amount of water to the shallow pan to produce steam that reaches 212°F (100°C) and circulates around the jars. This steam has the same sterilizing heat as boiling water, so the USDA/NCHFP approves of this canning method.

Oven canning is the process of putting sealed jars of food into a hot oven as a substitute for water bath canning or pressure canning. This form of canning is *not* considered to be safe by the USDA/NCHFP for the following reasons:

- The jars may explode.
- Oven heat is dry and slow, and the oven temperature is not the same as the temperature of the food in the jars.
- There are no research-tested and approved guidelines for canning food in the oven, so there is no way to know how long to keep the jars in the oven.
- You have no way of knowing if the food in the jar is reaching the temperature needed to destroy bad microorganisms and other bacteria that could cause serious illness if consumed.

To help you become successful with pressure
canning, we'll cover all the equipment you need,
including dial gauge and weighted gauge pressure
canners, in an upcoming chapter.

The Importance of Headspace, Altitude, and Processing Time

When it comes to home canning, whether water bath
canning or pressure canning, make sure to know
and understand three important terms: headspace,
altitude, and processing time. And technically, there
is a fourth term that you need to be aware of—canner
pressure—which is included in the processing time
information for tested home canning recipes. Each
recipe I share with you in the following chapters
will include all this information: headspace, altitude,
processing time, and, where appropriate, canner
pressure settings.

HEADSPACE

When you home can food, you will use clean jars
specifically designed for canning. You'll fit these jars
with canning lids and bands (sometimes referred to
as rings). Each time you use a jar to can food, you
need to use a new lid, but you can reuse the band.
Once you get the food into the jar, you need to check
the headspace before you put the lid on. You can
measure the headspace with a tool specifically
designed for this purpose or a food-safe ruler.

Headspace refers to the distance from the top
of the food in your jar to the rim of the jar.
The headspace is simply a small area of air
captured between the food and the lid of the jar.

As a general rule, most recipes will call for the
following headspace measurements:

- ¼ inch (6mm) for juices, jams, and jellies
- ½ inch (13mm) for fruits, tomatoes, and pickles
- 1 to 1½ inches (2.5cm to 3.8 cm) for meats and vegetables

Following these guidelines is essential, and I will
teach you how to measure for proper headspace in
the following chapter. Too much headspace results
in a lower vacuum effect because all the air may not
escape during the canning process. Plus, too much
headspace may create a weak jar seal. On the other
hand, too little headspace may force food to bubble
up under the lid during the canning process, causing
siphoning of the food which will not allow the lid to
seal securely.

Once you put the band on the jar and place the jar
into the canner, that air will escape from the jar
during the canning process. This scenario is
precisely what you want to happen. Different types
of food require different headspaces, but don't
worry—any home canning recipe that adheres to the
NCHFP home canning guidelines will include this
information. Different recipes call for different
headspaces because different foods have different
consistencies in terms of how much the food will boil
during the home canning process. You want to give
the food in your canning jar just enough room to boil
without bubbling up and out of the jar. If the food
were to bubble up and seep out under the lid on the
canning jar—siphoning—the lid would not be able to
seal properly because there would be food trapped
between the lid and the rim of the jar.

Once you've finished the canning process and
removed the jar from the hot canner, the change in
temperature causes the lid to create a vacuum seal.
With the air having seeped out of the jar underwater
during the canning process and then the change in
temperature outside of the canner creating a vacuum
seal, you now have food in a jar that is completely
protected from outside air. Being protected from
air keeps the food in the jar fresh and safe from
the development of harmful microorganisms
and bacteria.

ALTITUDE

When it comes to home canning, knowing your altitude (sometimes referred to as elevation) is a crucial piece of information to determine your correct home canning processing times. Knowing your altitude (the distance of your location above sea level) is important to home canners because water boils at lower temperatures at higher elevations. The lower water temperature makes it less effective at killing heat-resistant bacteria. So, as altitude increases and water boils at a lower temperature, the processing times and pressure (if pressure canning) need to be adjusted to destroy bacteria. To ensure safe home canning generally at altitudes above 1,000 feet you will need to adjust your processing times when water bath canning. For pressure canning, you will need to adjust your canner pressure.

As with pH values and many other important aspects of home canning, your altitude is easy to determine. You can find it by searching for your location online or calling your local agricultural extension service.

Once you know your altitude, you will be able to choose the correct processing time (as stated in every recipe that adheres to NCHFP home canning guidelines) for the particular food you are home canning. The general rule with water bath canning is that the higher your altitude, the longer the processing time. With pressure canning, your altitude may not affect the length of the processing time, but it will play a significant role in determining the proper pressure setting for your canner.

WATER BATH PROCESSING TIMES

Processing times for water bath canning take into consideration the size of the jar, such as pint or quart jars; the type of high-acid food in the jars; and your altitude.

Each recipe that adheres to NCHFP guidelines for water bath canning will state the proper processing time based on the specific high-acid food you are canning, the size of the jar you are using, and your altitude. There will be an incremental time increase that will correspond with a larger jar size and an increase in altitude. For example, for an altitude of 0–1,000 feet above sea level, the processing time for 6 pint jars of a high-acid food might be 10 minutes. If you increase the altitude to 1,000–3,000 feet above sea level, the processing time might be 15 minutes. And if you decide to can in quart jars, as opposed to pint jars, the processing time will generally also increase.

PRESSURE CANNING PROCESSING TIMES

Processing times for pressure canning, as with water bath canning, take into consideration the size of the jar you are using, such as pint or quart jars; the type of low-acid food in the jars; and your altitude. This is where altitude is especially important. As I shared earlier, your altitude will also determine what level of pressure you need for your canner.

For example, at an altitude of 0–1,000 feet above sea level, the processing time for 6 pint jars of a low-acid food might be 75 minutes with a canner pressure of 10 pounds, which is usually stated as 10 psi.

If you increase the altitude to 1,000–3,000 feet above sea level, the processing time will likely remain the same—75 minutes—but the canner pressure will need to be increased to 15 pounds (15 psi).

If you decide to can in quart jars, as opposed to pint jars, the processing time will generally increase—such as from 75 minutes to 90 minutes—but the canner pressure, based on altitude, will most likely stay the same.

> ·········· WHAT IS CANNER PRESSURE OR PSI? ··········
>
> Canner pressure is officially referred to as "pounds per square inch" or psi, which is simply a unit of measurement for pressure. Low-acid foods (a pH higher than 4.6) require a processing temperature higher than boiling water (212°F/100°C) to destroy harmful microorganisms. Low-acid foods must be processed at 240°F (115°C), which can be achieved only under pressure. But how much pressure? The general rule is that you need 10 pounds of pressure (10 psi) at sea level. And this amount of pressure will need to increase with an increase in altitude. Generally, you will find that most pressure canning recipes will call for a psi of 10 to 15. But don't be overwhelmed by this. How much pressure you need to set your canner for will always be clearly indicated in any pressure canning recipe that adheres to the NCHFP home canning guidelines.

Storing Home-Canned Food Safely

Once you have successfully home canned your food, you want to ensure that your food will stay at its maximum freshness. After the canning process is completed and your jars have cooled between 12 and 24 hours, check to make sure that the lids have sealed securely; remove the bands; and transfer your jars to a cool, dry, dark pantry or cupboard. Most importantly, remember not to stack one jar on top of another.

You want to remove the band because leaving it in place might create what is referred to as a false seal. If, for any reason, the lid fails and allows air to enter into the jar, the band may allow the lid to reseal. Unfortunately, you no longer have a vacuum seal if this resealing occurs. When you go to open the jar, you will most likely find that the food has spoiled. The reason we do not want to stack home-canned jars on top of each other is the same. If, for any

reason, a seal on a jar fails, the weight of another jar on top of it will most likely cause it to reseal. Again, this is not a vacuum seal. The jar has been compromised and the food will most likely spoil.

The manufacturer of the canning lids you use will recommend a best-used-by date for your home-canned goods. This date can range from one year up to two years from the date of canning, depending on the manufacturer. Does this mean that once you pass the best-used-by date you should throw out your home-canned food that has not yet been consumed? Most home canners will say "No!" But you always want to err on the side of caution. If opening a home-canned food that has gone past the best-used-by date on the lid, use your eyes and nose to determine if it still appears fresh. Chances are, if you have not gone far past the best-used-by date, the food will be safe to consume.

The Importance of Safe Home-Canning Practices

When it comes to safe home canning practices, you'll want to understand a number of important factors. First, always adhere to home canning recipes published from 1994 onward and adhere to the NCHFP home canning guidelines. Other sources for safe home canning recipes include those shared by agricultural extension services. These ag extensions, as they are often called, are usually associated with a large university and are located in all 50 US states. The home canning recipes they share adhere to the guidelines set by the NCHFP. Other countries around the world have similar organizations. As to recipes shared in home canning books, always make sure that they adhere to the NCHFP guidelines for home canning.

Why 1994 and beyond? You might wonder why you can't pull out your grandmother's old Ball Blue Book and start canning some food. The reason is that, as with so many things in life, improvements are made with the passage of time—even with home canning. We have come a long way from sealing jars with wax.

The main reason for making sure you are using modern home canning recipes is because recipes published before 1994 may not have adequate processing times or correct pressure requirements. Without this up-to-date information, your home-canned foods may be processed incorrectly and will likely spoil and be unsafe to eat.

Which Foods Should Not Be Canned?

It's important to note that certain foods, regardless of their pH, are not approved for home canning, whether using water bath canning or pressure canning. The general rule is that they are simply too thick or dense for heat to penetrate the food sufficiently during the home canning process. Or the time required to safely can the particular food would create a mushy product. The NCHFP and various state agricultural extension services generally recommend not to home can the following foods:

- Avocados
- Bananas or similar dense fruits*
- Refried beans
- Bread and cake
- Coconut milk
- Dairy products including milk and cheese (and do not add to soups for canning)
- Plain or pickled eggs
- Foods that are comprised mainly of fat, including butter, lard, oils, or mayonnaise
- Garlic (use only as a flavoring when preparing food; cloves should be removed before canning)
- Nuts (except green peanuts, which are technically a legume)

- Mashed potatoes
- Pumpkin or winter squash, purée or mash* (instead, can as cubes)
- Mashed vegetables*
- Vegetables, including broccoli, cauliflower (unless pickled), eggplant, summer squash, or zucchini (unless pickled or in small amounts in vegetable medleys)

Mashed or dense fruits and vegetables, including certain purées, should be dehydrated or frozen for preservation purposes, which we will discuss in detail in future chapters.

You should also not home can anything with a starch, such as cornstarch or modified cornstarch, flour, tapioca, or other starches, unless the recipe you are using has been formally tested by the NCHFP or an officially recognized state agricultural extension service and ensures that using this type of ingredient is safe. Along these lines, you do not want to include pasta, noodles, rice, barley, etc. in your home-canned products. The starch in these foods interferes with the heat transfer to the center of the jar. Instead, you will want to can foods such as spaghetti sauce or chicken broth on their own and then add the pasta, noodles, or rice when you heat the canned food and are ready to serve it.

Chapter Three
ALL ABOUT WATER BATH CANNING

GETTING STARTED WITH WATER BATH CANNING

Growing up, my mom and I often made homemade jams and jellies, pickled green beans, pie fillings, and more from fruits and vegetables we grew in our kitchen garden or purchased from a local farm stand. (Farm stands were a common sight in our area.) I have many wonderful memories of our summer outings, filled with shopping at local farm stands and touring our history-rich area. My mom and I would often bring a picnic lunch and visit an early American colonial site in the surrounding community of New York where we lived. Both of us especially enjoyed the colonial kitchens, where we could see the various equipment eighteenth-century home cooks used and learn about how they preserved food. It was always so much fun being with my mom, and I will treasure those memories always!

Upon arriving home, my mom and I would review our farm stand bounty and decide what to make first. In the late 1960s and early 1970s, how we home canned food was somewhat different from how we do it today. For example, we would simply ladle hot jam into repurposed jars, seal the jars with wax, and call it a day. Home canning has come a far way since then!

Over the years, my mom and I learned all about the art of water bath canning and would send my father with a list of supplies that we wanted him to pick up for us on workday trips into New York City. We started out with a large stockpot and eventually graduated to using an actual graniteware water bath canner that was perfect for my mom's gas stovetop. When my father brought home actual canning jars, lids, and bands, along with a Ball Blue Book, we were in business! To this day, I can still picture the shelves in my mom's Working Pantry and Backup Pantry chock-full of various home-canned foods glistening in their jars.

When it comes to making the most of the produce you find at your local grocery store, farm stand or farmer's market, or even what you may be growing in your own kitchen garden, you will love learning how to water bath can all of your precious produce. I'm here to show you how. I'm confident that after you have finished reading this chapter, you will be surprised at how easy water bath canning really is. However, if you feel a bit overwhelmed, don't worry. Just forge ahead and start with one of the simple water bath canning recipes that I share with you. I know from teaching water bath canning in my own kitchen, many home cooks have declared, "Wow! That is much easier than I thought!" And I am confident that you will have the same reaction, too.

If You Can Boil Water, You Can Water Bath Can!

Water bath canning is defined by the NCHFP as "a method of preserving high-acid foods using boiling water to create pressure that prevents harmful bacteria from growing on the food." Now, don't get confused by the phrase "to create pressure." Yes, the boiling water creates pressure to an extent, but not in the same way a pressure canner does. We'll advance to pressure canning in a future chapter, but for now, we'll focus on this way to preserve a wide variety of foods to make them shelf-stable. Beginning your home canning journey with the water bath method (also known as the boiling water method) is the easy way to get started. In simple terms, the water bath process involves packing your jars with food, covering them with boiling water, and processing (boiling) them for a set amount of time. That's it. If you can boil water, you can learn how to water bath can.

What Foods Can You Water Bath Can?

When using the water bath method for home food preservation, you have a wide variety of approved high-acid foods that you can choose from to home can. There are some exceptions to certain foods in these categories (as noted), but generally, foods that are safe to water bath can include:

- Applesauce
- Chutneys and conserves
- Jams, jellies, marmalades, preserves, and confitures
- Apple juice, grape juice, tomato juice, and tomato-vegetable juice blends
- Most fruit purées and fruit butters (with some exceptions)
- Most fruits, fruit syrups, and fruit pie fillings (with some exceptions)
- Pickles, pickled vegetables, and relishes with approved vegetables
- Savory salsas and fruit salsas with approved vegetables and/or fruits
- Whole tomatoes, tomato halves, and chopped tomatoes (with or without herbs)

The key to successful water bath canning is to make sure that the food you are canning allows the heat of the boiling water to completely penetrate through the jar. You want everything in the jar to reach the required temperature during the boiling process to ensure that any bad microorganisms are killed. That is why certain foods are not recommended for this form of food preservation (or for pressure canning).

For example, chutneys and conserves often contain nuts, but when home canning these foods, we have to leave out the nuts. Nuts are extremely dense, and the heat of the boiling water may not fully penetrate them. This may prevent the food in the middle of the jar from reaching the required temperature. Certain fruits, regardless of their form, simply can't be safely home canned. Examples of this are thick fruits such as bananas.

Essential Equipment for Water Bath Canning

For successful water bath canning, you need to make sure you have the correct equipment, tools, and supplies.

When it comes to the star of the show for water bath canning, the main piece of equipment you need is a vessel large enough to hold your canning jars. Your vessel can be as simple as a large stockpot or a kettle specifically made for water bath canning. Let's review all your options.

STOCKPOT

The general rule of thumb is that if you use a stockpot, you want to make sure it is at least a 10-quart stockpot with a lid. When choosing a stockpot to use, ensure that it does not extend more than 2 inches (5cm) beyond the burner when you center it over your stovetop burner.

If you start with a stockpot, make sure you have something you can put in the bottom of the pot for the jars to rest on. You do not want your jars to sit directly on the bottom of the pot. They need a bit of cushioning to keep the jars away from direct heat so they don't crack.

The easiest option to start with is an old-fashioned one. You can simply fold a terrycloth dish towel and place it on the bottom of your pot. Alternatively, a round metal cooling rack or canning bands tied together to make a rack will also work well.

WATER BATH CANNERS

As for actual water bath canners, there are basically three options:

Enameled water bath canner (A): This is the type of canner my mom had, and it's best for gas or electric stoves with coiled burners. Because these canners have a concave bottom, they are not recommended for use on glass-top stovetops because they may create a suction that will crack the glass.

Stainless steel water bath canner (B): This type of canner has a flat bottom and is perfect for using on glass-top stovetops.

Electric water bath canner (C): If your stovetop has limited burner space, this type of canner comes in very handy. It needs to be plugged into an electrical outlet and placed on a flat, heatproof surface such as a kitchen counter.

Essential Tools for Water Bath Canning

In addition to your choice of a water bath canner, you also need other costars, including glass canning jars, canning lids, and canning bands (sometimes called rings). A few tools are also essential when tackling water bath canning projects (as well as pressure canning ones). For some of the recommendations I share, can you jerry-rig a solution? Yes, but the equipment I recommend is relatively inexpensive and makes the job of home canning easier and neater.

GLASS CANNING JARS (1)

When choosing jars for canning, first make sure that the jars are approved for home canning. Approved canning jars are also known as Mason jars or Mason-type jars because this type of jar can withstand the high temperatures inside the canner better than other jars, such as recycled mayonnaise jars. If you try to use recycled jars for home canning, you might find that your jars do not seal properly because recycled jars often have a thinner rim than jars designed for canning. This thinner rim makes it harder for the rubber gasket on a canning lid to secure itself firmly to the rim. Using recycled jars often results in poor seals and worse—cracked jars.

The good news is you have a wide selection of approved canning jars to choose from. Plus, you can use canning jars that remain in good condition with no chips or cracks over and over again. Canning jars generally come in a variety of sizes, including 4 ounce, half pint (8 ounce), 12 ounce, pint (16 ounce), and quart (32 ounce). (You will also see larger canning jars, but at this time, most home canning recipes that adhere to NCHFP will call for using jars no larger than a quart.)

The opening, or mouth, of canning jars comes in two sizes: regular-mouth jars and wide-mouth jars. As you might have guessed, regular-mouth jars have a smaller diameter than wide-mouth jars. The inner diameter of a regular-mouth jar is approximately 2 ⅜ inches (6cm), and the outer diameter of the jar is approximately 2 ¾ inches (7cm). Regular-mouth jars are the original design for canning jars. They usually appear tapered at the top and wider at the bottom. Recipes for jellies, jams, and related fruit-type preserves will often call for these jars. Regular-mouth jars are also called for in recipes when canning pourable foods like chopped tomatoes or tomato sauce because their narrower opening minimizes spills when pouring out the contents.

Wide-mouth jars have an inner diameter of approximately 3 inches (7.6cm) and an outer diameter of approximately 3 ⅜ inches (8.5cm). Many home canners, including myself, will often choose wide-mouth jars when a recipe allows for that option because they are easier to fill when canning whole fruits, such as apricots, or pickled vegetables, such as string beans. A bonus to using wide-mouth jars is that they are easier to clean because you can get your hand into the jar with a dish rag.

When reviewing a water bath canning recipe, along with all the pertinent information on headspace, altitude, and processing times, you will also see the jar sizes recommended for proper processing. Do not deviate from these jar sizes. Some recipes may provide you with options such as pint jars or quart jars, but if so, the recipe will also include adjustments for the correct processing times for the different-sized jars.

> ······ WHERE DID MASON JARS GET THEIR NAME? ······
>
> Mason jars designed for canning were named after the American tinsmith John Landis Mason. He patented his jar design in 1858. The canning jar's mouth was designed with a thread on the outer perimeter of the rim so the home canner can screw a metal band onto the jar after placing a lid on the opening of the jar.

CANNING LIDS (2)

Canning lids are flat metal lids usually made of tin-plated steel (usually with a BPA-free coating) and come in two sizes: regular-mouth and wide-mouth. These lids are specifically made for fitting on top of canning jars. The underside of the circumference of the lids is coated with a rubber gasket. This allows the lid to create a tight seal with the rim of the jar during the canning process.

The top of the lid has a small, round, raised area in the center, which looks like a button and is often called such by home canners. It will be slightly raised before use and then slightly indented after going through the canning process. As you remove your canning jars from the water bath canner and place the jars on a cushioned surface, you may hear a sound often referred to as a ping by home canners. This sound is caused by the button moving from its raised position to its indented position because of the temperature difference between the canned contents and the surrounding environment.

Prior to using them in home canning, you should remove new canning lids from their packaging; wash them in warm, soapy water; rinse them well; and allow them to air dry. These clean lids should be placed on a clean surface, awaiting their jar rim placement. Never place these lids in boiling water to clean. Very hot temperatures may damage the rubber gasket and prevent the gasket from sealing tightly with the rim of the canning jar.

After you remove the lid from the jar when opening and using the home-canned food, you must discard and not reuse the lid. If all of the food in the jar is not used and will be transferred to the refrigerator, you can use the canning lid and a canning band on the jar to keep the food fresh in the refrigerator. But once you consume all the food, you must discard the lid. Alternatively, you can use a reusable plastic storage lid specifically made for use on canning jars that are opened and then refrigerated, in place of the canning lid and band.

CAN YOU USE REUSABLE LIDS FOR HOME CANNING?

Yes, there are specific canning lids made for reusing. They are made of plastic and come with a separate rubber gasket. You will place the rubber gasket on the cleaned rim of the jar, place the lid on the gasket-rimmed jar, and then secure a canning band in place. You can now put the jars into the canner. Once you consume the contents of the canned food, you can wash the lids and gaskets in warm, soapy water; rinse well; and allow them to air dry. Store them away until ready to use again. You will have to refer to the manufacturer's instructions for the reusable lids you use, but the general rule is, you can use the lids indefinitely, and the gaskets can be used up to 10 times and then discarded.

CANNING BANDS (3)

Canning bands are made of metal (usually tinplate or sometimes stainless steel) and look like a ring with grooves. These bands screw in place on top of a canning jar once the canning lid is put in place. These canning bands serve the purpose of keeping the lid in place during the boiling water process in the water bath canner.

There are a few important things you need to know about canning bands:

- You can reuse canning bands indefinitely as long as they are clean, rust-free, and in good working condition.

- When you are applying the band to the canning jar, you *do not* want to use brute force! You will simply tighten the band to what home canners refer to as fingertip-tight. You will tighten the band until you feel a slight resistance, then give it another small twist to secure. This second twist might amount to nothing more than ¼ inch (6mm) more.

- Once the jars have cooled after being removed from the canner and placed on a cushioned surface, you will remove the canning bands before storing your home-canned food. You should then wash, dry, and store the bands for later use.

·············· WHAT ABOUT WECK JARS? ··············

Weck jars are glass jars with separate rubber gaskets, glass lids, and stainless steel clips that secure the lid to the jar. These jars are used for home canning. The NCHFP does not recommend for or against using these types of jars for home canning. I prefer the canning lid and band system because the canning lid is designed for the home canner to have more ways of determining if the lid has sealed successfully or not.

FUNNEL (4)

Funnels come in a variety of sizes and are usually made from stainless steel or plastic. For home canning, you will need a funnel for your regular-mouth jars and one for your wide-mouth jars. Better yet, there are home canning funnels that are made to adjust to either size jar. If you choose a plastic funnel for home canning, make sure it is made to withstand the temperatures emanated by hot foods and liquids.

LADLE (5)

If you use a ladle specifically made for home canning, you will be happy you did. For years, I used a regular soup ladle until I discovered canning ladles that are specially designed with a small pour spout on both sides of the ladle. Whether you are right-handed, left-handed, pouring from the right, or pouring from the left, it's all easy and neat.

Plus, a canning ladle has a small hook on the lower underside of the handle. This small hook lets you attach the ladle to the side of the pot of hot food you are transferring into your canning jars. Once you have filled a jar, you can put the ladle back into the pot of hot food, making sure it's hooked onto the side of the pot, and then it's right there for you when you are ready to fill your next jar—not sunken down into your hot food and needing to be fished out!

DEBUBBLER AND HEADSPACE MEASURER (OR FOOD-SAFE RULER) (6)

Once you fill a jar with hot food, you need to move it around a bit to try and release any trapped air. A common canning tool used to do this is what is often nicknamed a debubbler. It's simply a long, narrow piece of plastic. (If you don't have one, a plastic knife can do the job, too.) If you don't want to use plastic and decide to debubble your food with a stainless steel knife, just tread gently. You don't want to accidentally crack your jar if the metal hits the glass.

I prefer a debubbler with notches on one end to measure headspace easily. These types of debubblers are commonly part of home canning tool kits sold at kitchen stores or online, but they can usually be purchased separately as well.

A simple debubbler with headspace measurement notches performs double duty. But if you find yourself happy using a plastic knife to debubble the food in your canning jars, you will want to keep a clean food-safe ruler handy for your home canning projects.

As a side note, a home canning dual-purpose funnel often displays headspace measurements. This makes it an exceptionally handy tool for the home canner.

MAGNETIC JAR LID LIFTER (7)

You can certainly use clean hands to pick up your canning lids. However, if you find you have a bit of food on your hands during the canning process, a magnetic jar lid lifter can save the day. Like the debubbler, this tool is commonly contained in home canning kits. A magnetic jar lid lifter is a long plastic stick with a magnet on the end. But the beauty of this tool is that you can pick up the stick, aim the magnet at the top of a clean canning lid to grab hold

of it and transfer the lid to the filled canning jar. Next, you simply angle the magnet tip sideways, and the stick will release from the lid while leaving the lid in place.

CUSHIONED MAT (8)

Once you have gathered these supplies, you will need a cushioned mat, such as a drying mat or a terrycloth dish towel. You can rest your jars on these once you remove them from your canner. You do not want to put your jars on a cool, hard surface, which might cause a drastic temperature change that would result in a cracked jar. Last but not least, you'll want to keep some clean rags or paper towels on hand. You'll dip these in white vinegar and clean the rim of your jars before placing the lids on the rim.

JAR LIFTER

A jar lifter is a home canning tool used to lift jars in and out of a canner. I prefer a spring-loaded jar lifter because it is easier to use with one hand. But whatever style jar lifter you use, this is a must-have. A jar lifter makes life very easy when you have to remove a jar from a canner filled with hot water that just a few minutes before was boiling water.

Essential Supplies for Water Bath Canning

When it comes to home canning, you will need various food-grade supplies or additives depending on the specific recipe. The following sections provide an overview of the most common ingredients used in water bath canning.

ACIDULANTS

If you have watched me on YouTube or read my first book, *The Modern Pioneer Cookbook*, you know I often use the term acidulate. It's a common term when discussing how to properly make bone broth, but it also pertains to water bath canning in the form of acidulants.

As we discussed earlier, the only foods that can be water bath canned are high-acid foods—foods with a pH of 4.6 or lower. However, certain foods may not meet this criteria or benchmark, but if you acidulate them, you can lower their pH, and they can now be water bath canned.

Examples of this are vegetables that, on their own, may have a pH much higher than 4.6, but once they are simmered in an acidulated brine, their pH is lowered. They can now be water bath canned in this brine. Green beans are probably one of the most popular vegetables to pickle in an acidulated brine and water bath can.

To lower the pH of a particular food to make it a candidate for water bath canning, you will need to use one of the following acidulants as specified in a particular recipe:

- **Citric acid:** This is a powder that was made from lemon juice.

- **Bottled lemon juice:** Many canning recipes call for the use of bottled lemon juice, as opposed to fresh-squeezed lemon juice, because the acidity of the bottled product is guaranteed. Fresh-squeezed lemon juice can vary from lemon to lemon. When it comes to water bath canning recipes, acidity is very important, so we always need to use products that can guarantee acidity.

- **Vinegar, white 5% or apple cider vinegar:** You do not need to worry about purchasing white vinegar with an acidity level higher than 5%, even though the higher versions may be labeled pickling vinegar. Most canning recipes call for the more standard white vinegar with a 5% acidity level. Some canning recipes may call for apple cider vinegar (ACV) when making a brine. If so, pasteurized ACV will do. Raw ACV is not necessary because you will be heating it, which will destroy any beneficial bacteria contained within.

- **Salt:** Canning salt, sometimes referred to as canning and pickling salt, is the recommended salt for home canning. It is just salt, finely milled so it dissolves quickly. Canning salt is specifically made to work with every canning recipe.

If you deviate from using canning salt, the important things to note when choosing salt for use in canning are the size of the grains of salt and any added ingredients.

The main difference between canning salt and table salt is that table salt contains anticaking agents and

has possibly been iodized (iodine has been added). These anticaking agents may cause a pickling brine used in home canning to be cloudy. However, if you are not able to find canning salt, table salt is safe to use for your home canning projects if it only contains anticaking agents. Table salt that has been iodized is generally not recommended for use in home canning (or other forms of food preservation) because it can cause discoloration and darkening of the food.

When buying kosher salt, remember that the grains may vary in size from one brand to the next. Some brands also contain anticaking ingredients. Always read the label on a box of kosher salt so you will be prepared if you use it for home canning and your brine is cloudy.

As with kosher salt, sea salt, whether fine ground or coarse ground, also has inconsistent grain size. Although sea salt does not generally contain anticaking agents, it often contains other minerals that can cause cloudiness or color discoloration when used in canning recipes. Sea salt is considered safe to use in home canning recipes. However, I generally recommend reserving it for fermentation recipes.

What is most important to know when using any salt other than canning salt is that other salts vary in weight. A ¼ teaspoon of canning salt weighs 1.6 grams. So you will have to weigh alternative salts to make sure you are using the correct amount of salt called for in the recipe. I generally prefer to use canning salt for my home canning projects so I can avoid the need for a scale.

COLOR PRESERVERS
Freshly cut fruit left out in the air will begin to brown or darken. To prevent this browning, you will need to soak the cut fruit in a mixture of water and a color preserver. Each canning recipe that calls for cut fruit will state how much color preserver you should use when soaking the fruit. You can choose from these options:

- **Citric acid:** As mentioned under acidulants, citric acid is simply a dried form of lemon juice. It can acidify food for home canning and also prevent browning.

- **Ascorbic acid:** This is a form of vitamin C that helps prevent food discoloration. It cannot be used as a substitute for citric acid when used as an acidulant; it can only be used as a color preserver. You can use crushed vitamin C tablets, which are sold under various brand names wherever canning supplies are sold. Six 500-milligram vitamin C tablets will equal approximately 1 teaspoon of ascorbic acid.

- **Texture enhancers:** Although pickling lime has been used for years to prepare cucumbers for home canning to maintain their crispness, I am not a fan because of the prep work involved. Luckily, you can add a little bit of food-grade calcium chloride to each jar of pickles to keep them crisp. This type of salt is sold under various brand names wherever canning supplies are sold. It will clearly indicate on the container that it is made to keep pickles crisp.

All of this said, recipes for canning pickles often state that if you start with fresh high-quality ingredients, such as Kirby cucumbers—specifically made for home canning—you should not need a texture enhancer. I have had mixed results with this. I like to add a bit of calcium chloride (approximately ¼ teaspoon) to my quart jars of pickles to ensure crispness.

THICKENING AGENTS

- **Pectin:** When making jams and jellies, you may frequently see the recipe call for pectin. Pectin occurs naturally in the cell walls of certain fruits, and you can use these natural pectins as thickening agents in home canning. When you heat the correct proportion of pectin, acid, sugar, and water and then allow the mixture to cool, a thickened gel forms. Tart apples, crab apples, and a few other fruits usually contain enough natural pectin to form a gel. Other fruits with less pectin or just a little pectin must be combined with fruits high in pectin or commercially packaged pectin to form a gel.

You can find packaged pectins with most canning supplies. Different types of packaged pectin are specifically manufactured to make full-sugar, low-sugar, and no-sugar jams and jellies (and freezer jams and jellies, too!). There are powdered pectins and liquid pectins, and they each are used in different ways. To obtain the best results with packaged pectin, always follow the instructions exactly as provided in the manufacturer's directions.

- **Starches:** Although most starches are not recommended for use in home canning recipes, there are some exceptions. Since the thickness of food during canning affects the amount of heat that can penetrate into the jars during processing, you want to follow the recipe exactly. Adding the wrong starch thickener or too much thickener may result in underprocessing. Use only the exact type of starch and the exact amount of starch specified and never modify canning recipes.

With water bath canning, the starch most commonly called for in recipes is modified food starch. It is sold under different names, but the packaging generally displays the word gel, and a quick look at the ingredient list on the packaging will make clear what it is. Modified food starch (or one of its brand names) will be recommended for use in small amounts when canning pie fillings. Modified food starch remains thin during processing, allowing heat to penetrate the jar, and thickens upon cooling. It also does not break down at high temperatures, which helps prevent a runny consistency in the final product.

CAN YOU USE PACKAGED GELATIN AS A THICKENING AGENT FOR HOME-CANNED FOOD?

Gelatin is an animal protein that forms a gel once it is refrigerated. Gelatin is not heat stable at the temperatures required for the successful canning of food. If you are familiar with my YouTube videos, have read the numerous bone broth blog posts on my website, or have a copy of my first book, *The Modern Pioneer Cookbook*, you know that I preach, preach, preach about not "breaking" the gelatin in bone broth. We work hard to maintain a very low simmer when making bone broth because we want all the rich gelatin that, when consumed, soothes our digestive system and adds strength to our skin, nails, and hair. But what happens if you use packaged gelatin when making a jam or a jelly that you plan to water bath can? You break that gelatin!

SWEETENERS

- **Granulated sugar:** When it comes to sweetening canned foods, granulated sugar (usually called sugar, table sugar, white sugar, or white cane sugar) works best. This is crystalized sugar, not what is commonly called powdered sugar or icing sugar. Powdered sugar is finely ground table sugar (sucrose), usually combined with a bit of cornstarch to prevent caking. Starch is best avoided in home canning recipes. In the case of powdered sugar, it may cause a brine used in canning to become cloudy.

  I know that using granulated sugar is often contrary to a lot of the recipes we make in our traditional foods kitchens, but substituting other sweeteners for granulated sugar changes the flavor of the final product. Plus, sweeteners other than granulated sugar may cause undesirable results during the canning process.

DO NOT USE DARK BROWN SUGAR AND UNREFINED WHOLE CANE SUGAR!

Using dark brown sugar or unrefined whole cane sugar may cause a strong flavor that overpowers the taste of the food and a considerable darkening of the final product. Also, the contents of the jar may burn during the processing in the canner.

- **Honey:** Some canning recipes allow you to substitute honey for table sugar. However, the flavor of home-canned foods sweetened with honey may be noticeably different than expected. If you decide to use honey in a home canning recipe, start with a small batch to determine if you like the flavor. And if you decide to use honey, do not use raw honey. It is unnecessary since the heating process will destroy the benefits associated with raw honey.

- **Maple syrup:** As with honey, some canning recipes will allow you to substitute table sugar with maple syrup. However, pure maple syrup has a strong flavor and can be too intense, especially when used to make jams, jellies, and other gelled fruit products. If you think you like

products at the grocery store that say they are made with maple syrup, such as a jam, keep in mind that the maple syrup is most likely cut with some type of corn syrup to lessen the intensity of the maple flavor. Just as with honey, using maple syrup in a home-canned recipe should be tried in a small batch.

- **Stevia:** Stevia is an herb with a sweet flavor but no calories. The NCHFP approves its use in home canning because it is heat stable. However, you should only use it for canning fruit and other foods where sugar is not critical to food safety or texture. Plus, some taste testers have found that stevia can create a bitter taste in home-canned foods.

HERBS, SPICES, AND PICKLING SPICE MIXES

Although home canning recipes tend to be quite precise and should be followed closely, you have a little leeway when it comes to herbs and spices. You can use fresh and dried herbs and spices either added directly to the jar or to a brine to be poured into a jar. Pickling spices are especially popular when making a brine. You can make your own homemade or buy a preprepared batch at most grocery stores.

CAN ARTIFICIAL SWEETENERS BE USED FOR WATER BATH CANNING?

Although I never recommend using artificial sweeteners, you should know which ones are safe for home canning if you decide to use them.

- Aspartame is not recommended as a sweetening ingredient in home-canned foods because it quickly dissipates into flavorless products during the canning process and storage.
- Saccharin is heat stable and can be used to make jellies and jams, but taste testers have noticed that it can leave behind a bitter aftertaste.
- Sucralose (sold under the brand name Splenda) is heat stable, so it can be used in home-canned foods. As with stevia, taste testers have noticed an aftertaste in the canned food.

Although alternative sweeteners and some artificial sweeteners will provide sweetness to home-canned foods, they will generally not assist in the gelling of jams, jellies, and other gelled products nor provide the firmness to canned fruits that table sugar does. In addition to sweetening home-canned foods, table sugar also serves as a preserving agent.

General Water Bath Canning Guidelines

Although water bath canning recipes in this book will detail the specifics for the particular food you will be water bath canning, these are the basic steps:

1 Prepare the jars by washing them in warm, soapy water and rinsing them well in hot water.

2 Place the clean, empty canning jars on a rack in your water bath canner (or prepared stockpot).

3 Fill each jar full of warm water.

4 Fill the canner about half full of warm water.

5 Bring the water in the canner to a boil and then turn down to a medium simmer.

6 Prepare the food to be water bath canned following a recipe that adheres to the NCHFP guidelines.

7 Using the jar lifter, remove one jar from the canner, empty the hot water from the jar back into the canner, and place the jar on a cushioned surface.

8 Working quickly, fill the jar with the prepared food using a funnel or ladle if appropriate. (Although the assembly line method [filling all the jars at the same time] is common practice when water bath canning, this method can be overwhelming for some beginners. As I explain here, it is acceptable to fill one jar at a time, seal it, keep it on the cushioned mat, and then remove your next jar from the water bath canner and continue the process. Most importantly, whichever method you use, you will want to work quickly so that each filled jar stays warm.)

9 Measure the headspace based on the recipe.

10 Insert a debubbler into the jar to remove air bubbles from the food.

11 Remeasure the headspace and add additional food to the jar if needed.

12 Use a clean rag or paper towel dipped in white vinegar and clean the rim of the jar.

13 Using clean hands or a magnetic lid lifter, place a clean lid on the jar.

14 Place a band around the rim of the jar and twist until fingertip-tight. (Repeat steps 7–14 with the remaining jars.)

15 Using the jar lifter, place all the filled jars back onto the rack in the canner.

16 Once the canner is full, check to make sure that all the jars are covered by at least 1 or 2 inches (2.5 or 5cm) of water. If not, add additional hot water to the canner.

17 Place the lid on the canner, turn the heat to high, and bring the water to a boil.

18 Once the water is boiling, set your timer according to the recipe. (If the water stops boiling at any time, return it to a boil and restart your timer.)

19 Once the processing time is completed, turn off the heat and carefully remove the lid of the canner. (Open the lid away from you so the steam does not hit your face.)

20 Leave the jars in the canner for 5 minutes. After 5 minutes, use the jar lifter to transfer the jars to a cushioned surface. Keep the jars upright, and do not turn them upside down.

21 Place the jars at least 2 inches (5cm) apart to allow for proper air circulation to cool. (If the bands are loose, do not retighten them.) You may hear a "ping" sound as the lids seal.

22 Allow the jars to cool for 12 to 24 hours. (Jars will take different times to cool depending on their size.) Once the jars are cool, remove the bands.

23 Check the lids of the jars to make sure they have sealed successfully. You can do this by checking to see if the button in the middle of the lid looks slightly concave and the lid does not flex up and down when pushed down. You can also use your fingertips to lift the jar by the rim, and if the lid stays firmly in place, the jar has sealed successfully.

24 If the jars have sealed, store the home-canned goods in a cool, dark, dry pantry. Do not stack the jars on top of each other.

STEP 7

STEP 8

STEP 9

STEP 10

STEP 12

STEP 13

STEP 14

STEP 15

If you have ever wondered why so many home canners always use the term fingertip-tight, it's because this technique serves a very important role in home canning. The canning band is screwed into place on top of the canning jar to gently—emphasis on gently—hold the canning lid in place during the canning process. It does not play a role in actually causing the lid to seal. And truth be told, you do not want it to!

During the canning process, the air allowed for the headspace must be able to escape from the jar. That is why the band should never be tight. If the band is tight, the air cannot escape. You want the lid to have a little give to allow that air to escape. You may even notice some bubbles coming from the lid of the jar when you first place it in your water bath canner.

Once the processing finishes and you remove the jar from the canner, you can be assured that you have food in the jar that has been sealed without air. Once cooled and you remove the band and check the lid for a tight vacuum seal, your home-canned food is now shelf-stable. And why do we want the air to be released underwater during the canning process and *not* be trapped in the jar? Because if the air is not allowed to escape, it can contribute to the spoilage of the canned food. When it comes to home canning, air is the enemy!

What's worse, if the air can't escape from the jar during the canning process, the buildup of pressure can cause the jar to explode and break, leaving glass shards strewn throughout the water in your canner. It's a mess to clean up. So always remember fingertip-tight when you screw the bands in place on your canning jars. And it's not hard to learn. Once you feel the resistance, you'll know you really don't need to turn the band that much more. Just a skosh.

Let's Get Started with Water Bath Canning

Now that you know the basics of water bath canning, let's start with the first simple recipe. I guarantee that it's foolproof! After you complete this recipe, you'll believe me when I say how easy water bath canning is. Afterward, you will be ready to move on to hone your skills with more simple water bath canning recipes, including jams, pickles, salsas, and lots more.

Home-Canned Frozen Peaches

When I bring friends into my kitchen and teach them how to water bath can, we start with frozen peaches. (Yes, frozen peaches!) These can be peaches you grew yourself and then blanched, peeled, pitted, sliced, and froze; or they can be frozen peaches you purchased from your local grocery store. And if you bought your frozen peaches in March—frozen food month in the United States—you may have even got them on sale!

You can store frozen peaches in your freezer, but freezer space can be valuable real estate. It makes much more sense to get those peaches canned and put on the shelves of your Working Pantry and Extended Pantry, where you have a lot more room.

It's also less work to begin home canning frozen peaches from your grocery store than starting from fresh peaches from your orchard or farmer's market. Manufacturers have already prepped the frozen peaches for you since they've blanched and peeled them, removed the pits, and sliced them before freezing.

So home canning frozen peaches from your grocery store couldn't be a more foolproof recipe—perfect for beginners. Best of all, during the cold winter months, you will be able to pop open a jar of home-canned peaches ready to be turned into a cobbler or other tasty dessert—or just eaten straight out of the jar for a taste of spring.

PREP TIME: **30 MINUTES**
COOK TIME: **10 MINUTES**
WATER BATH PROCESSING TIME: **20–35 MINUTES**
TOTAL TIME: **60–75 MINUTES**
YIELD: **APPROXIMATELY 9 PINTS**

EQUIPMENT

Water bath canner and supplies

Large saucepan sufficient to hold peaches and syrup

9 pint (16oz) wide-mouth canning jars

9 wide-mouth canning lids and bands

INGREDIENTS

6 ½ cups water

¾ cup granulated sugar

11 lb (5kg) frozen sliced yellow peaches, fully defrosted (see **Cook's Notes**)

Lemon juice (optional) (see **Cook's Notes**)

1   Steps 1–5: Follow steps 1–5 in the "General Water Bath Canning Guidelines" (p. 48).

2   Steps 6–11: These steps coordinate with steps 6–11 in the "General Water Bath Canning Guidelines" but are unique to this recipe.

6.   a. Prepare a very light syrup. Add the water and sugar to a large saucepan over high heat. Bring the mixture to a boil, stirring periodically until the sugar is completely dissolved.

b. Add the fully defrosted peaches to the syrup and return to a boil. Once the mixture returns to a boil, transfer the saucepan to a heatproof surface.

7. Using the jar lifter, remove one jar from the canner, empty the hot water from the jar back into the canner, and place the jar on a cushioned surface.

8. Place a wide-mouth funnel over the jar opening and ladle the peaches and syrup into the jar.

9. Measure the headspace, leaving ½ inch (1.25cm).

10. Insert a debubbler to remove any air bubbles from the jar.

11. Remeasure the headspace and add more hot syrup, if needed, to adjust the headspace to ½ inch (1.25cm).

3   Steps 12–24: Follow steps 12–24 in the "General Water Bath Canning Guidelines" (p. 48).

······················· COOK'S NOTES ·······················

What are the recommended processing times for pint jars of peaches, based on altitude?

- 0 to 1,000 feet: 20 minutes
- 1,001 to 3,000 feet: 25 minutes
- 3,001 to 6,000 feet: 30 minutes
- Above 6,000 feet: 35 minutes

How many cups of sliced peaches weigh 1 pound (454g)? The general rule is that approximately 3 cups of sliced peaches weigh 1 pound (454g).

Only home can yellow peaches! You can home can any variety of yellow peaches; however, you can never home can white-flesh peaches. Their proper acidity level can't be verified, and there are no tested recipes for home canning white-flesh peaches.

Do you always need to add lemon juice when water bath canning fruit? Yellow peaches are a naturally high-acid food (with a pH of 4.6 or lower), so you do not need to add standardized bottled lemon juice to each jar when they are home canned. However, if you like the flavor that lemon juice brings to home-canned fruit, you can add 1 tablespoon or less of bottled or fresh lemon juice to each pint jar.

What optional flavorings can you add? Once you learn the basics of home canning simple peaches, you can add additional flavorings when you are making the syrup. Options include cinnamon sticks, a vanilla bean, whole cloves or allspice berries, or a bit of ground ginger or freshly grated ginger.

What is the shelf life for Home-Canned Frozen Peaches? Home-canned peaches are shelf stable for 12 months or longer, depending on the canning lid manufacturer's recommendations. Once opened, your peaches will need to be refrigerated and will stay fresh for approximately 1 week. Do not refreeze peaches.

Wild Blueberry and Lemon Jam

When you cook fruit and a sweetener together, the phrase used to describe the state when the two have melded and turned into jam is "set up." If your jam does not set up, it's not the end of the world; you can always home can it and use it as syrup. But it can be disheartening to the new home cook making jam for the first time. That's where blueberries come to the rescue.

Although many home cooks start with strawberries when making homemade jam, blueberries are actually the better choice. Blueberries have more natural pectin than strawberries, so if you are new to making jam, blueberries are an ideal place to start. When using a powdered pectin, as called for in this recipe, you'll find that this jam will set up beautifully for you.

PREP TIME: **30 MINUTES**
COOK TIME: **15 MINUTES**
WATER BATH PROCESSING TIME: **5–15 MINUTES**
TOTAL TIME: **50–60 MINUTES**
YIELD: **APPROXIMATELY 6 HALF PINTS**

EQUIPMENT

Large (8-quart) high-sided stainless steel saucepan, large enameled high-sided Dutch oven, or Maslin jam pan

Potato masher (optional)

Long handled stainless steel or wooden spoon

Water bath canner and supplies

6 half-pint (8oz) regular-mouth canning jars

6 regular-mouth canning lids and bands

INGREDIENTS

5 cups ripe wild blueberries, washed (frozen wild blueberries can be substituted)

Juice and zest of 1 small lemon

¾ cup water

1 (1.75oz/49g) box regular powdered fruit pectin

5 ½ cups granulated sugar

1 **Steps 1–5:** Follow steps 1–5 in the "General Water Bath Canning Guidelines" (p. 48).

2 **Steps 6–11:** These steps coordinate with steps 6–11 in the "General Water Bath Canning Guidelines" but are unique to this recipe.

6.   a. Place a small plate in the freezer.

b. Add the blueberries to the saucepan. Crush the blueberries using the potato masher or a spoon.

c. Add the lemon juice, zest, water, and powdered pectin. Stir well and bring the mixture to a full, rolling boil over high heat. Stir continuously as it comes to a boil to prevent the mixture from sticking to the bottom of the pan.

d. Once the mixture is boiling, add the sugar and stir well. Bring the mixture back to a full rolling boil. Continue to maintain at a full rolling boil for 1 minute while stirring constantly.

e. After 1 minute, transfer the saucepan to a heatproof surface. Quickly skim off any foam that has risen to the top of the mixture.

f. Remove the plate from the freezer and place a teaspoon of the jam on the plate. Place the plate back into the freezer for 1 minute, then remove the plate from the freezer. After 1 more minute, run your index finger through the middle of the jam, dividing it in half. If the jam crinkles on top and stays separated, you've reached the correct gel stage. Your jam has set up. If not, return the saucepan to the stovetop, bring the mixture back to a rolling boil (stirring constantly) for 1 minute, and repeat the freezer test.

7. Using the jar lifter, remove one jar from the canner, empty the hot water from the jar back into the canner, and place the jar on a cushioned surface.

8. Place a wide-mouth funnel over the jar opening and ladle the hot jam into the jar.

9. Measure the headspace, leaving ¼ inch (0.65cm).

10. Insert a debubbler to remove any air bubbles from the jar.

11. Remeasure the headspace and add more jam, if needed, to adjust the headspace to ¼ inch (0.65cm).

3 **Steps 12–24:** Follow steps 12–24 in the "General Water Bath Canning Guidelines" (p. 48).

············· COOK'S NOTES ·············

What are the recommended processing times for half-pint jars of blueberry jam, based on altitude?

- · 0 to 1,000 feet: 5 minutes (If the jars have not been sterilized, process for 10 minutes.)
- · 1,001 to 6,000 feet: 10 minutes
- · Above 6,000 feet: 15 minutes

Do not take a shortcut! This recipe calls for bringing the blueberries, lemon juice, lemon zest, water, and powdered pectin to a boil before adding the sugar. Do not take a shortcut and add the sugar at the same time. Bringing the fruit to a boil before adding the sugar allows the cell walls of the blueberries to soften and release a greater amount of pectin. Once the pectin has been released, the sugar can do its job of absorbing liquid and allowing the pectin molecules to come together to create a strong gel.

Wild blueberries are best. In this recipe, I recommend wild blueberries for a reason. Did you know that the wild variety of this fruit is more nutritious than its commercially cultivated cousin? Researchers believe that wild blueberries are two times more nutritious than the cultivated variety, thanks to their higher concentration of antioxidants.

What is the shelf life for Wild Blueberry and Lemon Jam? Home-canned blueberry jam is shelf-stable for 12 months or longer, depending on the canning lid manufacturer's recommendations. Once opened, your jam will need to be refrigerated and will stay fresh for approximately 6 months. After 6 months, the jam may become crystalized.

Apple Jelly Three Ways

This recipe shows you how to make a classic apple jelly the traditional way without any added store-bought pectin. Once you know how to do this, the varieties of apple jelly you can make are endless, including two that I share here: mint apple jelly, perfect for serving with lamb, and spiced apple jelly, ideal for a charcuterie platter.

When making any jelly, you need to be able to strain the juice, which you will later turn into jelly. If, over time, you find that you like making jelly, you can purchase what is known as a jelly bag. But don't worry, a jelly bag is not required to make jelly. A simple colander or fine-mesh strainer lined with a flour-sack towel or cheesecloth works just fine.

Making this jelly will introduce you to the skill of making homemade juice. Once you learn this skill, you will be able to make other homemade juices and enjoy the juice as is—or turn it into jelly.

PREP TIME: **2 HOURS 30 MINUTES**
COOK TIME: **40 MINUTES**
WATER BATH PROCESSING TIME: **5–15 MINUTES**
TOTAL TIME: **3 HOURS 15 MINUTES TO 3 HOURS 25 MINUTES**
YIELD: **APPROXIMATELY 4 HALF PINTS**

EQUIPMENT

Large (8-quart) high-sided stainless steel saucepan, large enameled high-sided Dutch oven, or Maslin jam pan

Potato masher (optional)

Long-handled stainless steel or wooden spoon

Colander or fine-mesh strainer

Flour sack towel or cheesecloth (or a jelly bag)

Deep glass or stainless steel bowl

Water bath canner and supplies

4 half-pint (8oz) regular-mouth canning jars

4 regular-mouth canning lids and bands

INGREDIENTS

3 cups water

3 lb (1.35kg) Granny Smith apples or other tart apple variety (see **Cook's Notes**)

2 tbsp lemon juice, strained

3 cups granulated sugar

1 **Steps 1–5:** Follow steps 1–5 in the "General Water Bath Canning Guidelines" (p. 48).

2 **Steps 6–11:** These steps coordinate with steps 6–11 in the "General Water Bath Canning Guidelines" but are unique to this recipe.

6.   a. Place a small plate in the freezer. Add the water to the saucepan.

b. Wash the apples and remove the stem and blossom ends using a paring knife. (Do not peel or core the apples.) Cut the apples into small pieces, including the core, but remove the seeds. Add the apples to the saucepan, cover, and bring the apples to a boil over high heat, then reduce the heat to low and simmer the apples for about 30 minutes.

c. Every few minutes, remove the lid and stir the apples to make sure they are not sticking to the bottom of the saucepan. As the apples soften, mash them with a spoon or potato masher.

d. After approximately 30 minutes, the mashed apples should be very soft and resemble a chunky applesauce. At this point, transfer the saucepan to a heatproof surface.

e. Prepare a flour sack towel, cheesecloth, or jelly bag by dampening it with water and wringing it out. Line the colander (or fine-mesh strainer) with the damp flour sack towel and place it over a deep bowl. (If you are using a jelly bag, you will simply hang it over the bowl.)

f. Pour the apple mixture into the lined colander, fine-mesh strainer, or jelly bag and allow the apple juice to drip into the bowl for at least 2 hours or until the juice is no longer dripping into the bowl. (If you want clear jelly, do not squeeze the solids.)

g. As the apple mixture drains, clean the large saucepan and set it aside. Measure the apple juice that you have extracted. You will need 4 cups. If you do not have this much juice, pour some boiling water over the apple mixture in the lined colander (or fine-mesh strainer or into the jelly bag) and continue to let additional apple juice drip into the bowl. (You can discard the apple solids or run them through a food mill and use the apple purée to thicken soups and stews, add to smoothies, or stir into the saucepan when making homemade applesauce.)

h. Once you have 4 cups of apple juice, transfer the apple juice to the cleaned large saucepan placed on the stovetop. Add the lemon juice and sugar and bring this mixture to a boil on high heat, stirring constantly. Continue to keep the mixture at a full rolling boil that can't be stirred down. Continue to stir constantly for 1 minute. After 1 minute, transfer the saucepan to a heatproof surface. Immediately skim off any foam that has risen to the top.

i. Remove the plate from the freezer and place a teaspoon of the apple jelly on the plate. Place the plate back into the freezer for 1 minute. Remove the plate from the freezer and run your index finger through the middle of the jelly, dividing it in half. If the jelly crinkles on top and stays separated, it has reached the correct gel stage. If not, return the saucepan to the stovetop, bring the mixture back to a rolling boil (stirring constantly) for 1 minute, and repeat the freezer test.

7. Using the jar lifter, remove one jar from the canner, empty the hot water from the jar back into the canner, and place the jar on a cushioned surface.

8. Place a funnel over the jar opening and quickly ladle the hot jelly into the prepared jar.

9. Measure the headspace, leaving ¼ inch (0.65cm).

10. Insert a debubbler to remove any air bubbles from the jar.

11. Remeasure the headspace and add additional hot syrup, if needed, to adjust the headspace to ¼ inch (0.65cm).

3 **Steps 12–24:** Follow steps 12–24 in the "General Water Bath Canning Guidelines" (p. 48).

VARIATIONS

Mint Jelly: Once all the apples are added to the saucepan, add 1½ cups firmly packed fresh mint and continue with the recipe as is.

Spiced Apple Jelly: Once all the apples are added to the saucepan, add two 3-inch (7.5-cm) Ceylon cinnamon sticks broken into pieces, 1 teaspoon whole cloves, 1 teaspoon whole allspice berries, and ½ teaspoon red pepper flakes, and continue with the recipe as is.

COOK'S NOTES

What are the recommended processing times for half-pint jars of apple jelly, based on altitude?

- 0 to 1,000 feet: 5 minutes (If the jars have not been sterilized, process for 10 minutes)
- 1,001 to 6,000 feet: 10 minutes
- Above 6,000 feet: 15 minutes

How to measure apples: Three pounds (1.35kg) of Granny Smith apples will be approximately eight medium-size apples. When choosing apples to make this jelly, look for very firm apples even including some that are underripe. The less ripe the apples, the more tart they will be, which is a good indication that they will be high in pectin. The higher the pectin of the variety of apples you use, the better your apple jelly will gel.

Low and slow wins the game! When it comes to the stovetop heat, remember that low and slow wins the game. Do not rush this process. Simmering the apples at too high a temperature might begin to destroy the pectin, and you will not get a satisfactory gel. But also remember that if you do not extract the pectin sufficiently by heating it for the proper time, as stated in this recipe, you will also not get a good gel. So follow this recipe exactly, and you will be pleased with the end product.

What is the shelf life for Apple Jelly? Home-canned apple jelly is shelf-stable for 12 months or longer, depending on the canning lid manufacturer's recommendations. Once opened, your jelly will need to be refrigerated and will stay fresh for approximately 6 months. After 6 months, the jelly may become crystalized.

Sweet Tomato Basil Jelly

If you have an abundance of tomatoes from your kitchen garden or from a bargain at the farmer's market, reserve some to make this unique jelly. Tomato jelly has a pleasantly piquant taste profile, enhanced by the basil. Pull out a jar of this jelly in the middle of winter and use it as a spread on hamburgers in place of ketchup. You will be in for a treat that will fill your mouth with a burst of summer flavors!

PREP TIME: **2 HOURS 30 MINUTES**
COOK TIME: **40 MINUTES**
WATER BATH PROCESSING TIME: **5–15 MINUTES**
TOTAL TIME: **3 HOURS 15 MINUTES TO 3 HOURS 25 MINUTES**
YIELD: **APPROXIMATELY 7 QUARTER PINTS**

EQUIPMENT

Large (8-quart) high-sided stainless steel saucepan, large enameled high-sided Dutch oven, or Maslin jam pan

Long-handled stainless steel or wooden spoon

Potato masher (optional)

Colander or mesh strainer

Flour sack towel or cheesecloth (or a jelly bag)

Deep glass or stainless steel bowl

Whisk

Water bath canner and supplies

7 quarter-pint (4oz) regular mouth jars (also called jelly jars)

7 regular-mouth canning lids and bands

INGREDIENTS

8 cups sliced Italian plum tomatoes

½ cup water

1 cup fresh basil, coarsely chopped

¼ tsp red pepper flakes (optional) (this will create a sweet and spicy jelly)

Juice of 1 medium lemon

1 (1.75oz/49g) box regular powdered fruit pectin

3 ¼ cups granulated sugar

1 **Steps 1–5:** Follow steps 1–5 in the "General Water Bath Canning Guidelines" (p. 48).

2 **Steps 6–11:** These steps coordinate with steps 6–11 in the "General Water Bath Canning Guidelines" but are unique to this recipe.

6. a. Place a small plate in the freezer.

b. Place the large saucepan on the stovetop and add the tomatoes, water, basil, and red pepper flakes (if using). Bring to a boil over high heat, then reduce the heat to a medium simmer. Crush the tomatoes using the potato masher or spoon.

c. Continue simmering the tomato mixture for approximately 30 minutes or until the tomatoes are soft, stirring occasionally to prevent sticking.

d. Prepare a flour sack towel (or cheesecloth or jelly bag) by dampening it with water and ringing it out. Line the colander (or mesh strainer) with the damp flour sack towel and place it over a deep bowl. (If you are using a jelly bag, simply hang it over the bowl.)

e. Once the tomato mixture has cooled completely, pour the tomato mixture into the lined colander (or mesh strainer or jelly bag) and allow the tomato juice to drip into the bowl. If you want the tomato jelly to be as clear as possible, do not press the solids in the lined colander (or mesh strainer), and do not squeeze the jelly bag. Note that even with your best efforts, tomato jelly can sometimes be a bit cloudy. (See **Cook's Notes.**)

f. As the tomato mixture drains, clean the large saucepan and set aside.

g. Allow the mixture to drain until you have 1¾ cups of tomato juice. If you do not have this much juice, pour some cool water over the tomato mixture in the lined colander and continue to let additional tomato juice drip into the bowl.

h. Once you have 1¾ cups of tomato juice, place the cleaned saucepan on the stovetop and transfer the juice to the saucepan. Add the lemon juice and stir well to combine. Next, whisk in the powdered pectin until completely dissolved in the juice. Bring this mixture to a boil over high heat, stirring constantly.

i. Add the sugar all at once to the tomato juice mixture and return to a full rolling boil, stirring constantly. Keep the mixture at a full rolling boil that can't be stirred down. Continue to stir constantly for 1 minute.

j. After 1 minute, remove the saucepan from the stovetop and transfer it to a heatproof surface. Immediately skim off any foam that has risen to the top of the tomato jelly.

k. Remove the plate from the freezer and place a teaspoon of the tomato jelly on the plate. Place the plate back into the freezer for 1 minute. Remove the plate from the freezer after 1 minute and run your index finger through the middle of the jelly, dividing it in half. If the jelly crinkles on top and stays separated, it has reached the correct gel stage. If not, return the saucepan to the stovetop, bring the mixture back to a rolling boil (stirring constantly) for 1 minute, then repeat the freezer test.

7. Using the jar lifter, remove one jar from the canner, empty the hot water from the jar back into the canner, and place the jar on a cushioned surface.

8. Place a wide-mouth funnel over the jar opening, and ladle the hot jelly into the prepared jars.

9. Measure the headspace, leaving a ¼ inch (0.65cm).

10. Insert a debubbler to remove any air bubbles from the jar.

11. Remeasure the headspace and add more jelly, if needed, to adjust the headspace to ¼ inch (0.65cm).

3 **Steps 12–24:** Follow steps 12–24 in the "General Water Bath Canning Guidelines" (p. 48).

················ COOK'S NOTES ················

What are the recommended processing times for quarter-pint jars of tomato jelly, based on altitude?

· 0 to 1,000 feet: 5 minutes (If the jars have not been sterilized, process for 10 minutes.)
· 1,001 to 6,000 feet: 10 minutes
· Above 6,000 feet: 15 minutes

Why is the tomato jelly cloudy? If you have made the apple jelly, you may find that your tomato jelly is not as clear as your apple jelly (or as clear as some of the tomato jellies you see at your grocery store). This is normal, given the variations in the viscous nature of homemade tomato juice. Do not worry! Your sweet tomato basil jelly will be delicious.

What is the shelf life for home-canned tomato jelly? Home-canned tomato jelly is shelf stable for 12 months or longer, depending on the canning lid manufacturer's recommendations. Once opened, your jelly will need to be refrigerated and will stay fresh for approximately 6 months. After 6 months, the jelly may become crystallized.

Earl Grey Herbal Jelly

When it comes to tea, Earl Grey is my favorite. I crave its bergamot flavor. If you are unfamiliar with bergamot, it is a citrus fruit native to Italy. For me, nothing is better than a hot cup of Earl Grey tea alongside a crisp piece of toast slathered with homemade Earl Grey jelly! Best of all, this recipe will introduce you to making jelly with liquid pectin. It's very easy to use—dare I say, almost foolproof. And once you master this recipe, you can try it with any tea flavor you like!

PREP TIME: **10 MINUTES**
COOK TIME: **10 MINUTES**
WATER BATH PROCESSING TIME: **5–15 MINUTES**
TOTAL TIME: **25 MINUTES TO 35 MINUTES**
YIELD: **APPROXIMATELY 4 HALF PINTS**

EQUIPMENT

Large heatproof glass bowl

Large (8-quart) high-sided stainless steel saucepan, large enameled high-sided Dutch oven, or Maslin jam pan

Long-handled stainless steel or wooden spoon

Fine-mesh strainer

Water bath canner and supplies

4 half-pint (8oz) regular-mouth canning jars

4 regular-mouth canning lids and bands

INGREDIENTS

12 Earl Gray tea bags

1 tsp fresh lemon thyme leaves, removed from stems (see **Cook's Notes**)

1¾ cups water

3 cups granulated sugar

¼ cup unsweetened fruit juice (apple or white grape)

1 (3oz/90ml) package liquid pectin

1 **Steps 1–5:** Follow steps 1–5 in the "General Water Bath Canning Guidelines" (p. 48).

2 **Steps 6–11:** These steps coordinate with steps 6–11 in the "General Water Bath Canning Guidelines" but are unique to this recipe.

6. a. Place a small plate in the freezer.

b. Remove the paper tabs from the tea bags and place the bags and the thyme leaves into a large heatproof glass bowl.

c. Bring the water to a boil in a tea kettle, allow it to cool for 1 minute, and then pour the hot water over the tea bags and thyme leaves in the bowl. Steep for 5 minutes.

d. Remove the tea bags and strain the tea through a fine-mesh strainer placed over the saucepan. (The mesh strainer should catch all the thyme leaves.)

e. Add the sugar and fruit juice to the saucepan containing the brewed tea. Bring the mixture to a boil over high heat. Boil until the sugar is completely dissolved, stirring continuously, approximately 2 minutes, then add the liquid pectin to the saucepan and return the mixture to a boil. Boil for 1 minute, stirring continuously.

f. Transfer the saucepan to a heatproof surface. Immediately skim off any foam that has risen to the top.

g. Remove the plate from the freezer and place a teaspoon of the Earl Grey jelly on the plate. Place the plate back into the freezer for 1 minute, then remove the plate from the freezer. After 1 additional minute, run your index finger through the middle of the jelly, dividing it in half. If the jelly crinkles on top and stays separated, it has reached the correct gel stage. If not, return the saucepan to the stovetop, bring the mixture back to a rolling boil (stirring constantly) for 1 minute, then repeat the freezer test.

7. Using the jar lifter, remove one jar from the canner, empty the hot water from the jar back into the canner, and place the jar on a cushioned surface.

8. Place a wide-mouth funnel over the jar opening and quickly ladle the hot jelly into the jar.

9. Measure the headspace, leaving ¼ inch (0.65cm).

10. Insert a debubbler to remove any air bubbles from the jar.

11. Remeasure the headspace and add more jelly, if needed, to adjust the headspace to ¼ inch (0.65cm).

3 **Steps 12–24:** Follow steps 12–24 in the "General Water Bath Canning Guidelines" (p. 48).

"General Water Bath Canning Guidelines" (p. 48).

·········· COOK'S NOTES ··········

What are the recommended processing times for half-pint jars of Earl Grey jelly, based on altitude?

· 0 to 1,000 feet: 5 minutes (If the jars have not been sterilized, process for 10 minutes.)
· 1,001 to 6,000 feet: 10 minutes
· Above 6,000 feet: 15 minutes

Can you use other herbs in place of the lemon thyme?
You can replace the lemon thyme with other edible herbs, but I recommend you stick with those that have a lemon flavor, such as lemon verbena or lemon balm, because the lemon flavor complements the bergamot in the Earl Grey tea the best.

What is the shelf life for Earl Grey Herbal Jelly?
This jelly is shelf stable for 12 months or longer depending on the canning lid manufacturer's recommendations. Once opened, your jelly will need to be refrigerated and will stay fresh for approximately 6 months. After 6 months, the jelly may become crystallized.

Spiced Fresh Fig Preserves

Preserves are a type of jam where the fruit can be roughly chopped into bite-size pieces rather than smashed into small chunks or puréed as with a jam. And figs are perfect for this type of preparation. The best time to make fig jam is when figs are in season, so keep an eye out for fresh figs either in early or late summer and make sure to use some to make this jam. This recipe does not call for any added pectin, so this jam comes together easily and needs only a few ingredients.

Made from fresh figs, this jam is a treat compared to those made with dried figs. The tender nature of fresh figs creates a lighter jam with an easily spreadable consistency and mild flavor. You will want to have a good stock of this jam in your Extended Pantry so you can refresh the supply in your Working Pantry since you will frequently use this versatile jam in various recipes.

Fig jam is at home added to any charcuterie platter, stirred into sautés, or simply topped on buttered sourdough bread, but it's one of the best spreads for a variety of sandwiches. Replace cranberry sauce with fig jam on turkey sandwiches made with Thanksgiving leftovers, and your family and friends will ask for it again and again.

PREP TIME: **30 MINUTES**
COOK TIME: **15 MINUTES**
WATER BATH PROCESSING TIME: **5–15 MINUTES**
TOTAL TIME: **50 MINUTES TO 60 MINUTES**
YIELD: **APPROXIMATELY 10 HALF PINTS**

COOK'S NOTES

What are the recommended processing times for half-pint jars of fig preserves, based on altitude?

- 0 to 1,000 feet: 5 minutes (If the jars have not been sterilized, process for 10 minutes.)
- 1,001 to 6,000 feet: 10 minutes
- Above 6,000 feet: 15 minutes

Do not omit the bottled lemon juice from this recipe!
The pH of figs is not guaranteed to be 4.6 or lower. The lemon juice will guarantee that you will have a pH level that is safe for water bath canning. Plus, the lemon juice helps balance some of the sweetness contributed by the fresh figs and added sugar. It creates the perfect sweet-tart flavor.

EQUIPMENT

Large heatproof glass bowl

Large (8-quart) high-sided stainless steel saucepan, large enameled high-sided Dutch oven, or Maslin jam pan

Long-handled stainless steel or wooden spoon

Water bath canner and supplies

10 half-pint (8oz) regular-mouth canning jars

10 regular-mouth canning lids and bands

INGREDIENTS

45 fresh medium figs (about 5 lb/2.25 kg)

Boiling water sufficient to cover figs

¾ cup water

6 cups granulated sugar

1-inch (2.5-cm) piece fresh ginger, peeled and grated

1 (3- to 4-inch/7.5- to 10-cm) Ceylon cinnamon stick

¼ cup bottled lemon juice (see **Cook's Notes**)

---

1 **Steps 1–5:** Follow steps 1–5 in the "General Water Bath Canning Guidelines" (p. 48).

2 **Steps 6–11:** These steps coordinate with steps 6–11 in the "General Water Bath Canning Guidelines" but are unique to this recipe.

6. a. Place the figs in a large heatproof bowl and pour enough boiling water over the figs to cover them. Let the figs soak in the water for 10 minutes.

b. After 10 minutes, transfer the figs to a colander and drain. Rinse well with cool water. Remove the stems from the figs and chop them into bite-size pieces (approximately 1 inch/2.5 cm).

c. Place the chopped figs into the saucepan. Add the water and the sugar, along with the grated ginger and the cinnamon stick. Bring the mixture to a boil over high heat, stirring continuously until the sugar dissolves. Continue to boil, stirring continuously, until the mixture thickens. This may take a few minutes or more.

d. Once the preserves thicken, add the lemon juice and boil for 1 minute, stirring continuously.

e. Transfer the saucepan to a heatproof surface. Quickly skim off any foam that has risen to the top of the fig preserves and remove and discard the cinnamon stick.

7. Using the jar lifter, remove one jar from the canner, empty the hot water from the jar back into the canner, and place the jar on a cushioned surface.

8. Place a wide-mouth funnel over the jar opening and ladle the hot preserves into the jar.

9. Measure the headspace, leaving ¼ inch (0.65cm).

10. Insert a debubbler to remove any air bubbles from the jar.

11. Remeasure the headspace and add more preserves, if needed, to adjust the headspace to ¼ inch (0.65cm).

3 **Steps 12–24:** Follow steps 12–24 in the "General Water Bath Canning Guidelines" (p. 48).

COOK'S NOTES

Can you omit the ginger and cinnamon? If you want a simple, fresh fig jam that allows the flavor of the figs to shine through, yes, you can omit the ginger and cinnamon. But I highly recommend that you try the spiced version once, as it is the perfect accompaniment to jazz up a simple plate of cheese and crackers served to guests on a chilly fall day.

Why did we not do the freezer test for the fig preserves? You do not need to check the gel of a preserve, a confiture, a conserve, or a chutney. These all have a looser consistency than jams and jellies by their very nature, so they do not need to set up (gel) as tightly as jams and jellies. Also, these different types of confections usually contain larger pieces of fruit than jams and jellies, which would interfere with the freezer test. So don't worry, follow the recipe, and your preserves should have the correct texture—neither a firm gel nor a loose syrup. Instead, it will be somewhere in the middle and just right.

What is the shelf life for Spiced Fresh Fig Preserves? Home-canned fig jam is shelf stable for 12 months or longer, depending on the canning lid manufacturer's recommendations. Once opened, your fig jam will need to be refrigerated and will stay fresh for approximately 6 months. After 6 months, the jam may become crystallized.

Whole Fruit Three-Citrus Marmalade

I will confess I am a bit of a marmalade aficionado. I usually have quite a variety of marmalades on hand. I enjoy them all, but this three-citrus variety is my favorite. Plus, my no-waste heart loves the fact that we use the entire fruit in this recipe. If you have not had whole fruit marmalade, you are in for a treat. The softened citrus peel is suspended in the juicy fruit as opposed to just a simple gel. This makes for a toothsome marmalade that holds its gel very well and is perfect for slathering on toast or into a nut butter sandwich.

PREP TIME: **1 HOUR**
COOK TIME: **1 HOUR 30 MINUTES**
WATER BATH PROCESSING TIME: **5–15 MINUTES**
TOTAL TIME: **2 HOURS 35 MINUTES TO 2 HOURS 45 MINUTES**
YIELD: **APPROXIMATELY 8 HALF PINTS**

EQUIPMENT

Potato peeler

Sharp paring knife

Large (8-quart) high-sided stainless steel saucepan, large enameled high-sided Dutch oven, or Maslin jam pan

Small square of cheesecloth

Cotton kitchen twine

Slotted spoon

Heatproof liquid measuring cup

Long-handled stainless steel or wooden spoon

Water bath canner and supplies

8 half-pint (8oz) regular-mouth canning jars

8 regular-mouth canning lids and bands

INGREDIENTS

1 large grapefruit

2 large oranges

2 medium lemons

⅛ tsp baking soda

4 cups water

6 cups granulated sugar, divided

1 **Steps 1–5:** Follow steps 1–5 in the "General Water Bath Canning Guidelines" (p. 48).

2 **Steps 6–11:** These steps coordinate with steps 6–11 in the "General Water Bath Canning Guidelines" but are unique to this recipe.

6. a. Place a small plate in the freezer.

   b. Use a potato peeler or sharp paring knife to remove the zest from each piece of citrus fruit. (When removing the zest, make sure to include the white pith.) Chop the zest into small pieces (approximately ½ inch/1.25cm) and add to the saucepan.

   c. One piece of fruit at a time, cut each section (suprême) of fruit from between each membrane section. Set any seeds aside. Add each suprême of fruit to the saucepan with the zest. After you've removed all the suprêmes from the whole fruit, take the leftover membrane and squeeze it over the saucepan to release any remaining juice, then toss the membrane into the saucepan. Continue until all five whole fruits have had their suprêmes removed.

   d. Gather all the seeds, place them in the cheesecloth, and tie it closed with a piece of kitchen twine. Add this to the saucepan.

   e. Sprinkle the baking soda into the saucepan. (This will help break down the zest, make it softer during the cooking process, and assist the zest in releasing its pectin.)

   f. Add the water and bring the mixture to a boil over high heat, then turn the heat down to medium-low. Simmer the zest and fruit mixture for 30 minutes.

   g. Remove a piece of the zest from the pot using a slotted spoon. Allow it to cool and then press it between your fingers. If it is soft, you are ready to move on to the next step. If it is not soft, allow the mixture to simmer for a few more minutes.

   h. Once the zest is soft, transfer the mixture into an 8-cup heatproof liquid measuring cup. (If you do not have a large liquid measuring cup, measure this mixture, one cup at a time, using a standard 1-cup liquid measuring cup.) If you have 6 cups of the mixture, you are ready to proceed. If the mixture does not measure 6 cups, add water so you have a total of 6 cups of mixture. Now you are ready to proceed.

   i. Return the mixture to the saucepan and bring it to a boil. Slowly add 2 cups of the sugar to the boiling mixture and stir continuously with a long-handled spoon.

j. Once the first 2 cups of sugar have dissolved, add the next 2 cups and continue to stir. When the second 2 cups of sugar have dissolved, add the remaining 2 cups and continue to stir the mixture. Continue to boil the mixture until you cannot stir down the boil. This can take 30 minutes or more. (Be careful when doing this and consider wearing heatproof gloves for protection since the hot marmalade may splatter.)

k. If a significant amount of foam develops during boiling, begin skimming it off the top of the marmalade.

l. Once you can no longer stir down the boil, transfer the saucepan to a heatproof surface. Quickly skim off any additional foam that has risen to the top of the marmalade and remove all five membranes and the cheesecloth containing the seeds.

m. Remove the plate from the freezer and place a teaspoon of the marmalade on the plate. Place the plate back into the freezer for 1 minute, then remove the plate from the freezer. After 1 additional minute, run your index finger through the middle of the marmalade, dividing it in half. If the marmalade crinkles on top and stays separated, it has reached the correct gel stage. If not, return the saucepan to the stovetop, bring the mixture back to a rolling boil (stirring constantly) for 1 minute, then repeat the freezer test.

7. Use the jar lifter, remove one jar from the canner, empty the hot water from the jar back into the canner, and place the jar on a cushioned surface.

8. Place a wide-mouth funnel over the jar opening and ladle the hot marmalade into the prepared jars.

9. Measure the headspace, leaving ¼ inch (0.65cm).

10. Insert a debubbler to remove any air bubbles from the jar.

11. Remeasure the headspace and add more marmalade, if needed, to adjust the headspace to ¼ inch (0.65cm).

3 **Steps 12–24:** Follow steps 12–24 in the "General Water Bath Canning Guidelines" (p. 48).

COOK'S NOTES

What are the recommended processing times for half-pint jars of marmalade, based on altitude?

- 0 to 1,000 feet: 5 minutes (If the jars have not been sterilized, process for 10 minutes.)
- 1,001 to 6,000 feet: 10 minutes
- Above 6,000 feet: 15 minutes

What is the shelf life for Whole Fruit Three-Citrus Marmalade? Home-canned marmalade is shelf stable for 12 months or longer, depending on the canning lid manufacturer's recommendations. Once opened, your marmalade will need to be refrigerated and will stay fresh for approximately 6 months. After 6 months, the marmalade may become crystallized.

Chipotle Cherry Preserves

As I shared in an earlier recipe, preserves are basically a jam where the fruit can be rough chopped into bite-size pieces rather than smashed into small chunks or puréed. Cherry preserves are an excellent example where you can pit the fruit and chop each cherry in half. You don't have to worry about being perfect. Preserves are the rustic cousin of jams, so a rough chop is just fine. As to consistency, preserves are a bit looser than an American jam, so we will not need to do the freezer test.

Since a looser gel is acceptable when making preserves, we can replace the sugar normally called for in jam and use fruit juice as a sweetener instead. But when we sweeten a preserve with fruit juice, the juice needs to be in the concentrated form. These types of juices are usually sold in the freezer section of your local grocery store, but shelf-stable bottled juice concentrates may also be available. In addition to using a juice concentrate, this recipe will introduce you to how to use a particular type of pectin known as Pomona's Universal Pectin. This pectin has become more common and may be found at your local grocery store, specialty grocery store, or online. It's worth learning how to use this type of pectin, especially if you like the idea of making jams, jellies, and preserves sweetened with fruit juice instead of other types of sweeteners.

Best of all, we're going to take your standard cherry preserves and add a flavor booster that I love in pretty much anything I add it to—chipotles! If you've never tried chipotles, you're in for a treat. They are dried smoked jalapeños that take on a unique flavor that actually has a bit of sweetness. This bit of sweet combined with smoky heat is the perfect complement to create a preserve that is incredibly versatile. Your preserves make a great topping for toast when served with eggs that have been scrambled with sweet bell peppers and onions, but are equally welcome on a cracker topped with cotija, feta, or Parmigiano-Reggiano cheese.

PREP TIME: **45 MINUTES**
COOK TIME: **15 MINUTES**
WATER BATH PROCESSING TIME: **10–20 MINUTES**
TOTAL TIME: **1 HOUR 10 MINUTES TO 1 HOUR 20 MINUTES**
YIELD: **APPROXIMATELY 4 HALF PINTS**

EQUIPMENT

Medium-size heatproof glass bowl

Food processor or blender

Rubber spatula

Large (8-quart) high-sided stainless steel saucepan, large enameled high-sided Dutch oven, or Maslin jam pan

Small saucepan

Long-handled stainless steel or wooden spoon

Water bath canner and supplies

4 half-pint (8oz) regular-mouth jars

4 regular-mouth lids and bands

INGREDIENTS

2 chipotle peppers

Boiling water for soaking chipotles

¾ cup water, divided

½ tsp calcium powder (from a package of Pomona's Universal Pectin)

1 cup no-sugar-added juice concentrate (white grape or apple)

3 tsp Pomona's Universal Pectin powder (from a package of Pomona's Universal Pectin)

3 cups gently packed halved cherries, pitted (see **Cook's Notes**)

¼ cup lime juice (fresh or bottled)

⅛ tsp canning and pickling salt

1 **Steps 1–5:** Follow steps 1–5 in the "General Water Bath Canning Guidelines" (p. 48).

2 **Steps 6–11:** These steps coordinate with steps 6–11 in the "General Water Bath Canning Guidelines" but are unique to this recipe.

6. a. Thoroughly wash the chipotle peppers, then place them into a medium-size heatproof glass bowl and cover them with boiling water. Keep the chipotles submerged in the water by weighing them down with a small plate. Let them soak for 30 minutes then drain the chipotles and discard the soaking water. (It can be bitter.)

b. Remove and discard the stems from the chipotles. Finely chop the chipotles and add them to a blender or food processor with ¼ cup of water. Whirl the chipotles until they begin to turn into a paste.

c. Scrape down the sides of the blender or the food processor with a rubber spatula and add additional water if necessary to make a paste. Set aside.

d. Mix the calcium powder and ½ cup of water in a small jar. Place the lid on the jar securely and shake the mixture vigorously until the calcium powder is completely dissolved. Set aside.

e. Place the small saucepan on the stovetop, add the juice concentrate, and bring it to a boil over high heat.

f. Once the concentrate comes to a boil, transfer it to a blender. Add the pectin powder to the blender. Vent the lid of the blender and whirl the concentrate and powder together for 1 to 2 minutes or until the powder is completely dissolved. (This is your pectin concentrate.) Set aside.

g. Place the large saucepan on the stovetop and add the cherries, lime juice, and 4 teaspoons of the calcium water from the jar. Stir well. (Any unused calcium water can be refrigerated and used for a future jam-type product sweetened with fruit juice, stevia, honey, low sugar, or no sugar.) Add the chipotle paste and salt to the saucepan with the cherry mixture. Stir and bring the mixture to a full rolling boil over high heat. Once the mixture is boiling, add the pectin concentrate. Stir until the mixture returns to a full rolling boil, then transfer the saucepan to a heatproof surface.

7. Using the jar lifter, remove one jar from the canner, empty the hot water from the jar back into the canner, and place the jar on a cushioned surface.

8. Place a wide-mouth funnel over the jar opening and ladle the hot cherry preserves into the jar.

9. Measure the headspace, leaving ¼ inch (0.65cm).

10. Insert a debubbler to remove any air bubbles from the jar.

11. Remeasure the headspace and add more jam, if needed, to adjust the headspace to ¼ inch (0.65cm).

3 **Steps 12–24:** Follow steps 12–24 in the "General Water Bath Canning Guidelines" (p. 48).

.... COOK'S NOTES ....

What are the recommended processing times for half-pint jars of cherry preserves, based on altitude?

- · 0 to 1,000 feet: 10 minutes
- · 1,001 to 6,000 feet: 15 minutes
- · Above 6,000 feet: 20 minutes

What does "3 cups gently packed" mean? When measuring the cherries for this preserves recipe, you'll first remove the stems and the pit. Then, you will slice each cherry in half. Next, as you fill a measuring cup with the cherries, you will want to gently press the halved cherries into each cup measure. You don't need to press them down firmly because you do not want to crush them, but you want to leave as little space between the cherries as is reasonably possible while still keeping their shapes intact.

What is in a box of Pomona's Universal Pectin? If you are new to working with Pomona's Universal Pectin, you might be wondering exactly what comes in the box. Within the box there are two packages: one package contains a specific type of pectin for using with any type of sweetener, and the second package contains a powder which you will use to make the calcium water called for in this recipe.

What is the shelf life for Chipotle Cherry Preserves? Home-canned chipotle cherry preserves are shelf stable for 12 months or longer, depending on the canning lid manufacturer's recommendations. Once opened, your preserves will need to be refrigerated and will stay fresh for approximately 6 months. Unlike other confections, this preserve is unlikely to crystallize since it was sweetened with fruit juice instead of sugar.

French-Style Cranberry Confiture

Confiture is the French word for jam, but a French confiture differs from an American jam in a few ways. When I think of a confiture, I think of something fancy. The name alone sounds like this jam is something special. And it is! Confitures contain more fruit than common jams and are a very refined version of preserves. The fruit is often left whole, or sliced in the case of large fruit. There is no rough chopping allowed! Instead, the fruit is lovingly sliced into refined, even pieces. However, the best confitures are often made with small whole fruits, which are suspended in a syrup. (Using whole fruits is much easier than meticulously slicing larger fruits.) Since we are preparing this confiture with cranberries, which are naturally high in pectin, this recipe will be easy to make because we will not need to add any additional store-bought pectin.

A confiture is thinner in consistency than an American jam or preserves (so no freezer test is required), making it highly versatile. This particular confiture is a delightful novelty at any Thanksgiving table in place of traditional cranberry sauce. This cranberry confiture is almost like a gravy in consistency, making it the perfect piquant sauce for a thick slice of dark meat turkey.

Cranberry confiture is also delicious throughout the holiday season, spooned onto pancakes, waffles, or over ice cream. If you're feeling a bit French, add this confiture to homemade crêpes for a holiday breakfast treat! So be sure to snatch up a few packages of fresh cranberries on sale after Thanksgiving. You will want to make a few batches of this delightful confection throughout the Christmas season!

PREP TIME: **30 MINUTES**
COOK TIME: **15 MINUTES**
WATER BATH PROCESSING TIME: **15–25 MINUTES**
TOTAL TIME: **1 HOUR TO 1 HOUR 10 MINUTES**
YIELD: **4–5 HALF PINTS**

EQUIPMENT

Large (8-quart) high-sided stainless steel saucepan, large enameled high-sided Dutch oven, or Maslin jam pan

Long-handled stainless steel or wooden spoon

Water bath canner and supplies

5 half-pint (8oz) regular-mouth jars

5 regular-mouth lids and bands

INGREDIENTS

Zest and juice of 1 medium orange

2 cups water

2 cups granulated sugar

½ tsp ground ginger

½ tsp red pepper flakes (optional)

4 cups whole cranberries (fresh or frozen)

---

1 **Steps 1–5:** Follow steps 1–5 in the "General Water Bath Canning Guidelines" (p. 48).

2 **Steps 6–11:** These steps coordinate with steps 6–11 in the "General Water Bath Canning Guidelines" but are unique to this recipe.

6. a. Combine the orange juice, water, and sugar in a large saucepan over high heat. Bring to a boil, stirring continuously. (You will use the orange zest later.)

b. Once the mixture comes to a boil, add the ginger and red pepper flakes (if using) to the saucepan and stir well until completely distributed.

c. Add the cranberries to the saucepan, stir well to combine, and return to a boil. Reduce the heat to medium and simmer gently for 5 minutes, stirring occasionally to ensure that the confiture does not stick to the bottom of the saucepan and potentially burn. (Use a gentle hand when stirring to avoid crushing the cranberries.)

d. Add the orange zest and stir thoroughly but gently to completely distribute the zest through the confiture. Continue simmering gently for an additional 5 minutes, then transfer the saucepan to a heatproof surface.

7. Using the jar lifter, remove one jar from the canner, empty the hot water from the jar

back into the canner, and place the jar on a cushioned surface.

8. Place a wide-mouth funnel over the jar opening and ladle the hot cranberry confiture into the prepared jars.

9. Measure the headspace, leaving ¼ inch (0.65cm).

10. Insert a debubbler to remove any air bubbles from the jar.

11. Remeasure the headspace and add more confiture, if needed, to adjust the headspace to ¼ inch (0.65cm).

3 **Steps 12–24:** Follow steps 12–24 in the "General Water Bath Canning Guidelines" (p. 48).

(p. 48).

.... COOK'S NOTES ....

What are the recommended processing times for half-pint jars of cranberry confiture, based on altitude?

- · 0 to 1,000 feet: 15 minutes
- · 1,001 to 6,000 feet: 20 minutes
- · Above 6,000 feet: 25 minutes

What is the shelf life for French-Style Cranberry Confiture? Home-canned cranberry confiture is shelf stable for 12 months or longer, depending on the canning lid manufacturer's recommendations. Once opened, your confiture will need to be refrigerated and will stay fresh for approximately 6 months. After 6 months, the confiture may become crystallized.

Spring Peach Conserves

Terms like jam and jelly—and even preserves—are easy to understand, but when cookbooks start talking about conserves and chutneys, the difference between these foods can be confusing. The good news is that conserves and chutneys have a lot in common, and you don't need to become too concerned about clearly identifying them.

Conserves and chutneys can be smooth or chunky. They're both made with fresh and dried fruits, and sometimes nuts, herbs, spices, and even vegetables. The difference is that conserves lean on the sweet side and usually get a bit of tang from citrus, while chutneys, although still with a bit of sweetness, are on the more savory or spicy side, with vinegar adding a bit of tartness. But sometimes, these differences are tossed aside, and conserves and chutneys can become indistinguishable. So, as I mentioned earlier, there is no need to be a stickler; just enjoy the deliciousness of both in a variety of ways!

Conserves are delicious spread on toast, added to oatmeal or yogurt, included in a muffin or quick bread batter, drizzled across hot pancakes, or poured on top of a scoop of ice cream—and pretty much anything else you can think of! Conserves are one of those go-to confections that help the home cook in various ways.

Now let's make some peach conserves. I'll use fresh spring peaches grown here in the Texas Hill Country!

PREP TIME: **30 MINUTES**
COOK TIME: **45 MINUTES**
WATER BATH PROCESSING TIME: **5–15 MINUTES**
TOTAL TIME: **1 HOUR 20 MINUTES TO 1 HOUR 30 MINUTES**
YIELD: **APPROXIMATELY 6 HALF PINTS**

EQUIPMENT

Large glass bowl

Large (8-quart) high-sided stainless steel saucepan, large enameled high-sided Dutch oven, or Maslin jam pan

Sharp paring knife

Slotted spoon

Long-handled stainless steel or wooden spoon

Water bath canner and supplies

6 half-pint (8oz) regular-mouth canning jars

6 regular-mouth canning lids and bands

INGREDIENTS

14 medium peaches, any freestone yellow variety (see **Cook's Notes**)

3 medium oranges

1 medium lemon

3 ¼ cups granulated sugar

½ cup golden raisins

1 (5-inch/12.75-cm) sprig fresh peppermint

1   **Steps 1–5:** Follow steps 1–5 in the "General Water Bath Canning Guidelines" (p. 48).

2   **Steps 6–11:** These steps coordinate with steps 6–11 in the "General Water Bath Canning Guidelines" but are unique to this recipe.

6.   a. Fill a large glass bowl halfway with cold water and add a few ice cubes to the water. Set aside.

b. Fill a large saucepan halfway with water and bring it to a boil over high heat.

c. Using a sharp paring knife, score the blossom end of each peach.

d. Once the water in the saucepan comes to a boil, use the slotted spoon to lower the peaches, one at a time, into the boiling water. Blanch the peaches for 30 to 60 seconds or until you see the scored blossom end of the peach skin begin to split.

e. Once the peach skins have split, turn off the heat and transfer the saucepan to a heatproof surface. Use the slotted spoon to remove the peaches, one at a time, from the hot water into the cold water.

f. Empty the water from the saucepan and return it to the stovetop.

g. When you can comfortably handle the peaches, peel off the skins, slice the peaches in half around the pits, pull the peach halves apart, and remove the pits. Chop each peach half into bite-size pieces (about 1 inch/2.5cm). Set aside.

h. Do not peel the oranges or the lemon. Finely chop the oranges and the lemon, removing the seeds but making sure to collect all the juice.

i. Add the chopped peaches, the chopped citrus and juice, and all the remaining ingredients to the saucepan. Bring the mixture to a boil over high heat, stirring continuously, then reduce the heat to medium and simmer the mixture for approximately 15 minutes or until thickened. (Stir the mixture frequently as it thickens; otherwise, it might stick to the bottom of the pan and burn. This can happen quickly with this mixture, so keep a close eye on it.)

j. When the mixture has thickened, transfer the saucepan to a heatproof surface. Skim off any foam that has risen to the top of the conserves and remove the sprig of peppermint.

7. Using the jar lifter, remove one jar from the canner, empty the hot water from the jar back into the canner, and place the jar on a cushioned surface.

8. Place a wide-mouth funnel over the jar opening and ladle the hot peach conserves into the jar.

9. Measure the headspace, leaving ¼ inch (0.65cm).

10. Insert a debubbler to remove any air bubbles from the jar.

11. Remeasure the headspace and add more conserves, if needed, to adjust the headspace to ¼ inch (0.65cm).

3 **Steps 12–24:** Follow steps 12–24 in the "General Water Bath Canning Guidelines" (p. 48).

········· COOK'S NOTES ·········

What are the recommended processing times for half-pint jars of peach conserves, based on altitude?

- 0 to 1,000 feet: 5 minutes (If jars have not been sterilized, process for 10 minutes.)
- 1,001 to 6,000 feet: 10 minutes
- Above 6,000 feet: 15 minutes

What are freestone peaches? Freestone peaches are those with a pit that is easy to remove when the peach is cut in half. You want to choose this variety of peach when home canning peaches because it makes the job of removing the fruit from the pit very easy. With cling or clingstone peaches, the job is messy as you try to release the pit from the fruit. Plus, you lose some of the fruit in the process because it clings to the pit.

To include nuts or not to include nuts ... that is the question. When it comes to home canning, nuts should generally not be canned. However, some recipes, such as conserves and chutneys, will allow small amounts of nuts to be included. These recipes generally call for longer processing times to make sure that the heat of the boiling water can fully penetrate the nuts.

However, I tend to exclude nuts from the conserves and chutneys I plan to home can because the fats in nuts are fragile and can go rancid quickly. Since I will put these conserves on my pantry shelf, I like to ensure that my conserve or chutney will stay as fresh as possible for as long as possible. In the past, when I included nuts in these recipes and then opened one of my home-canned jars months later, I sometimes noticed an off-odor. Did the nuts go rancid? I can't say for sure, but after all that hard work, I don't want to chance it anymore, so I just leave the nuts out.

What is the shelf life for Spring Peach Conserves? Home-canned peach conserves are shelf stable for 12 months or longer, depending on the canning lid manufacturer's recommendations. Once opened, your conserves will need to be refrigerated and will stay fresh for approximately 6 months. After 6 months, the conserves may become crystallized.

Traditional Scottish Apple-Ginger Chutney

Traditional chutneys are perfect for serving alongside hearty meat dishes, which are generally served during colder months. The chutney adds a nice punch of flavor to each mouthful of meat and aids in digestion thanks to the vinegar and spices. This particular chutney is perfect for ginger lovers since it provides a double kick of the spice in its fresh and dried ground forms.

Generally, I recommend using table sugar (or, in some cases, fruit juice) when making condiments such as jams, jellies, preserves, confitures, and conserves. However, when making a chutney, using light brown sugar can create a rich depth of flavor that can only be achieved from the molasses in brown sugar. But only choose the light variety—dark brown sugar can be too overpowering, drowning out the flavor of the fruit and spices. Plus, dark brown sugar may take on a burnt flavor during the water bath canning process.

PREP TIME: **30 MINUTES**
COOK TIME: **1 HOUR**
WATER BATH PROCESSING TIME: **10–20 MINUTES**
TOTAL TIME: **1 HOUR 40 MINUTES TO 1 HOUR 50 MINUTES**
YIELD: **APPROXIMATELY 6 PINTS**

EQUIPMENT

Large (8-quart) high-sided stainless steel saucepan, large enameled high-sided Dutch oven, or Maslin jam pan

Long-handled wooden spoon

Water bath canner and supplies

6 pint (16oz) regular-mouth or wide-mouth canning jars

6 regular-mouth or wide-mouth canning lids and bands

INGREDIENTS

2 cups water

10 medium Granny Smith apples, or other tart apple variety (approximately 4 lb/1.75 kg)

4 cups packed light brown sugar

1 (2-inch/5-cm) piece fresh ginger, peeled and finely grated

2 tsp ground ginger

2 tsp canning and pickling salt

1 tsp ground allspice

1 tsp ground cloves

2 (3-inch/7.5-cm) Ceylon cinnamon sticks

1 cup golden raisins

4 cups 5%-acidity apple cider vinegar

---

1 **Steps 1–5:** Follow steps 1–5 in the "General Water Bath Canning Guidelines" (p. 48).

2 **Steps 6–11:** These steps coordinate with steps 6–11 in the "General Water Bath Canning Guidelines" but are unique to this recipe.

6. a. Add the water to the saucepan.

b. Wash the apples, then peel and core them. (Discard the seeds but save the peelings and core to use when making apple jelly.) Cut each apple into bite-size pieces (approximately 1 inch/2.5cm) and add the apples to the water in the saucepan.

c. Add all the remaining ingredients to the saucepan and slowly bring them to a boil over high heat, stirring continuously until all the brown sugar has dissolved. Reduce the heat to medium-low and simmer the chutney for approximately 45 minutes or until thickened, frequently stirring to ensure it does not stick to the bottom of the saucepan. (This will prevent the chutney from burning.)

d. Over the course of 45 minutes, periodically check the chutney. If possible, draw a wooden spoon across the bottom of the saucepan. If the chutney separates and the space that is left does not fill up with liquid, it is finished cooking. Otherwise, simply simmer until the mixture appears thickened and not watery.

e. Once the chutney has thickened to the proper consistency, transfer the saucepan to a heatproof surface. It is unlikely any foam will have accumulated on top of the chutney, but if it does, skim it off. Remove and discard the cinnamon sticks.

7. Using the jar lifter, remove one jar from the canner, empty the hot water from the jar back into the canner, and place the jar on a cushioned surface.

8. Place a wide-mouth funnel over the jar opening and ladle the hot chutney into the prepared jars.

9. Measure the headspace, leaving ½ inch (1.25cm).

10. Insert a debubbler to remove any air bubbles from the jar.

11. Remeasure the headspace and add more chutney, if needed, to adjust the headspace to ½ inch (1.25cm).

3 **Steps 12–24:** Follow steps 12–24 in the "General Water Bath Canning Guidelines" (p. 48).

Fruit Purée

When we think of puréed fruit, applesauce is often the first to come to mind. And purées are frequently referred to as sauce—hence the name applesauce as opposed to apple purée. But whatever you call them, you can purée a whole host of fruits and turn them into delicious alternatives to applesauce. Once you learn the basic process of making a fruit purée, you can experiment with mixing high-acid fruit purées together and adding a variety of spices to boost the flavor of any fruit purée.

Some fruits that make the best purées include apples (as in applesauce), assorted berries, kiwis, nectarines, yellow peaches, pears, and prunes.

PREP TIME: **30 MINUTES**
COOK TIME: **APPROXIMATELY 30 MINUTES (VARIES BASED ON FRUIT)**
WATER BATH PROCESSING TIME: **15–25 MINUTES**
TOTAL TIME: **1 HOUR 15 MINUTES TO 1 HOUR 25 MINUTES**
YIELD: **3–4 HALF PINTS**

EQUIPMENT

Large (8-quart) high-sided stainless steel saucepan, large enameled high-sided Dutch oven, or Maslin jam pan

Long-handled stainless steel or wooden spoon

Food mill or fine-mesh strainer

Large glass bowl

Water bath canner and supplies

4 half-pint (8oz) regular-mouth or wide-mouth canning jars

4 regular-mouth or wide-mouth canning lids and bands

INGREDIENTS

4 cups high-acid fruit (with a pH of 4.6 or lower)

1 cup water

Granulated sugar, to taste (optional)

1 **Steps 1–5:** Follow steps 1–5 in the "General Water Bath Canning Guidelines" (p. 48).

2 **Steps 6–11:** These steps coordinate with steps 6–11 in the "General Water Bath Canning Guidelines" but are unique to this recipe.

6. a. Prepare the fruit. (This will vary depending on the type of fruit you are using. Generally, larger fruits will need to be washed and peeled, and have their stems cores, seeds, and/or pits removed. Most berries are easy to purée because they require little more than a quick rinse under running water. Strawberries, however, will need their green stems removed.)

   b. Add the fruit and water to the saucepan and bring to a boil over high heat, stirring continuously. Immediately reduce the heat to low and simmer the fruit until soft, stirring frequently to prevent it from sticking to the bottom of the saucepan. (This will prevent the fruit from burning.)

   c. Once the fruit is soft, transfer the saucepan to a heatproof surface.

   d. Run the soft fruit through a food mill or fine-mesh strainer placed over a glass bowl. If you use a fine-mesh strainer, you will need to push the purée through the strainer with a spoon.

   e. Taste the purée. You can add sugar until you reach the desired sweetness, but this is completely optional. Set aside.

   f. Wash the saucepan and return it to the stovetop. Add the purée and stir continuously as you bring it to a boil over high heat. (If you added sugar, make sure it is completely dissolved.)

   g. Transfer the saucepan to a heatproof surface.

7. Using the jar lifter, remove one jar from the canner, empty the hot water from the jar back into the canner, and place the jar on a cushioned surface.

8. Place a wide-mouth funnel over the jar opening and ladle the hot fruit purée into the jar.

9. Measure the headspace, leaving ¼ inch (0.65cm).

10. Insert a debubbler to remove any air bubbles from the jar.

11. Remeasure the headspace and add additional fruit purée, if needed, to adjust the headspace to ¼ inch (0.65cm).

3 **Steps 12–24:** Follow steps 12–24 in the "General Water Bath Canning Guidelines" (p. 48).

············ COOK'S NOTES ············

What are the recommended processing times for half-pint jars of Fruit Purée, based on altitude?

- 0 to 1,000 feet: 15 minutes
- 1,001 to 6,000 feet: 20 minutes
- Above 6,000 feet: 25 minutes

Are there any fruits that should not be puréed for water bath canning? The NCHFP recommends that the following fruits not be turned into a fruit purée for water bath canning: bananas, dates, figs, Asian pears, tomatoes (yes, technically, these are fruits), cantaloupe (and other melons), papaya, persimmons, ripe mangoes, or coconut.

Can you purée more than 4 cups of fruit at one time? Yes, this recipe can easily be doubled or more. Just remember that for every additional 4 cups of fruit you add to the saucepan, you will need to add 1 cup of water.

What is the shelf life for Fruit Purée? Home-canned fruit purée is shelf stable for 12 months or longer, depending on the canning lid manufacturer's recommendations. Once opened, your fruit purée will need to be refrigerated and will stay fresh for approximately 6 months.

Cinnamon Apple Pie Filling

Spiced apple pie filling is a delightful addition to your Working Pantry and Extended Pantry. Having this delicious, shelf-stable filling on hand makes it incredibly convenient to whip up a homemade apple pie anytime you have a craving for pie or at holiday time when you are busy cooking other foods.

Home-canned apple pie filling saves time and ensures that you have a versatile dessert ingredient ready to go. You can use spiced apple pie filling to top ice cream, creating a delightful treat, or as a unique twist on shortcake, replacing strawberries with warmed spiced apples for a cozy fall dessert when temperatures start to dip. With its rich flavor and convenience, spiced apple pie filling is a must-have for any well-stocked pantry.

This recipe introduces you to using ascorbic acid (vitamin C) to prevent apples from browning, and the approved water bath canning thickener—modified food starch—otherwise known as clear jel or clear jell (usually followed by the words "cook type"). These two ingredients are generally available where canning supplies are sold and will help you make apple pie filling perfect for home canning.

As you read through the recipe, you will notice that you will be making 7 quarts of apple pie filling. This might seem like a lot, but it's best to make this in a large batch and get it onto your pantry shelf during apple season. Once the fall and winter seasons—and the various holidays that occur during that time—roll around, you will find that you quickly use 7 quarts of apple pie filling. Home-canned apple pie filling can be used as a quick dessert when unexpected guests stop by, for topping Saturday morning pancakes and waffles, and, of course, for making apple pies (for which you'll need 2 quarts for a 9-inch [23-cm] pie).

PREP TIME: **1 HOUR**
COOK TIME: **30 MINUTES**
WATER BATH PROCESSING TIME: **25–40 MINUTES**
TOTAL TIME: **1 HOUR 55 MINUTES TO 2 HOURS 10 MINUTES**
YIELD: **APPROXIMATELY 7 QUARTS**

EQUIPMENT

Very large glass bowl

Very large stainless steel bowl

Very large (10- to 12-quart) high-sided stainless steel or enameled saucepan, stockpot, or Dutch oven

Slotted spoon

Long-handled stainless steel or wooden spoon

Water bath canner and supplies

7 quart (32oz) regular-mouth or wide-mouth canning jars

7 regular-mouth or wide-mouth canning lids and bands

INGREDIENTS

1 tsp ascorbic acid powder or six 500mg vitamin C tablets, crushed

18 lb (8kg) Granny Smith apples (approximately 54 medium-size apples)

5 ½ cups granulated sugar

1 ½ cups clear jel cook type (modified food starch)

2–3 tsp ground cinnamon

½ tsp ground allspice (optional)

½ tsp ground cloves (optional)

2 ½ cups cold water

5 cups no-sugar-added apple juice

¾ cup bottled lemon juice

1 **Steps 1–5:** Follow steps 1–5 in the "General Water Bath Canning Guidelines" (p. 48).

2 **Steps 6–11:** These steps coordinate with steps 6–11 in the "General Water Bath Canning Guidelines" but are unique to this recipe.

6. a. Fill a very large glass bowl with a half-gallon of cold water. Add the ascorbic acid to the water and stir well until it is completely dissolved.

b. Wash the apples and then peel and core one apple at a time. (Discard the seeds but save the peel and cores to use when making apple jelly.) Cut the apple into ½-inch (1.25-cm) thick slices and place the slices into the water containing the ascorbic acid. (This prevents the apples from browning.) Allow all the apple slices to soak in the ascorbic acid water for 10 minutes.

c. While the apple slices are soaking, fill a very large saucepan with 1 gallon of water and bring to a boil over high heat.

d. While you are waiting for the water to come up to a boil, rinse a large stainless steel bowl with hot tap water, dry it, and place it on a cushioned surface such as a drying mat or thick terrycloth kitchen towel. Cover the stainless steel bowl with a second thick terrycloth kitchen towel.

e. Once the water is boiling, use a slotted spoon to remove 6 cups of apples from the ascorbic acid water and add them to the boiling water. Bring the water back to a boil and boil the apples for 1 minute.

f. Use the slotted spoon to remove the apples from the boiling water, transfer them to the stainless steel bowl, and re-cover the bowl.

g. Continue this process of boiling 6 cups of apples for 1 minute (after the water returns to a boil) and then transferring the apples to the stainless steel bowl until all the apples have been boiled.

h. Empty the water from the saucepan and place it back on the stovetop. Add the sugar, clear jel, spices, water, and apple juice. (If you omit the allspice and cloves, add 1 extra teaspoon of cinnamon.) Turn the heat to medium high and continually stir the mixture until it begins to bubble and thicken. At this point, add the lemon juice and boil for 1 minute, stirring continually. Then fold in the warm apple slices and stir to combine.

i. Transfer the saucepan to a heatproof surface.

7. Using the jar lifter, remove one jar from the canner, empty the hot water from the jar back into the canner, and place the jar on a cushioned surface.

8. Place a wide-mouth funnel over the jar opening and ladle the hot apple pie filling into the jar.

9. Measure the headspace, leaving 1 inch (2.5cm).

10. Insert a debubbler to remove any air bubbles from the jar.

11. Remeasure the headspace and add more apple pie filling, if needed, to adjust the headspace to 1 inch (2.5cm).

3 **Steps 12–24:** Follow steps 12–24 in the "General Water Bath Canning Guidelines" (p. 48).

············· **COOK'S NOTES** ·············

What are the recommended processing times for quart jars of apple pie filling, based on altitude?

- · 0 to 1,000 feet: 25 minutes
- · 1,001 to 3,000 feet: 30 minutes
- · 3,001 to 6,000 feet: 35 minutes
- · Above 6,000 feet: 40 minutes

What is the shelf life for Cinnamon Apple Pie Filling? Home-canned apple pie filling is shelf stable for 12 months or longer, depending on the canning lid manufacturer's recommendations. Once opened, your apple pie filling can be refrigerated but is best used within 2 weeks of opening.

Why do all the apple recipes in this chapter call for Granny Smith apples? I generally pick Granny Smith apples for all my home canning projects involving apples. They are perfect for making apple jelly thanks to the high amount of pectin they contain. I also like them for apple pie filling because they are tart, firm, and readily available, making them a perfect apple to withstand the heat of canning without becoming mushy. However, you can certainly experiment with other options—but I suggest you stick with firm apple varieties including Braeburn, Jonagold, and Pink Lady. The end product is usually better.

Estimating how many whole apples are needed for a recipe is not always easy. When it comes to home canning fresh fruit, whether in the form of jellies and jams or other confections—or apple pie filling—it's never easy to know exactly how much fruit you will need. Fresh fruit varies in size, and when it comes to apples, you can often feel a bit baffled as to whether you have small, medium, or large apples. A good rule of thumb is that a medium apple is approximately the size of a baseball. But that is just an approximation. Do your best, and if you wind up with more apple pie filling than you have canning jars, don't worry. Just store the extra amount in an airtight container in your fridge or freezer.

Always-Crisp Pickle Spears

Water bath canning pickle spears gives you the remarkable ability to create a shelf-stable, long-lasting supply of tangy, crunchy pickles that are ready to enjoy any time of the year. This method preserves the fresh taste and crisp texture of the cucumbers and enables you to control the ingredients, ensuring a delicious snack.

This recipe will introduce you to using calcium chloride, a product sold under the name "Pickle Crisp." You will only be using a tiny amount of calcium chloride when water bath canning these pickles, but you will be amazed at what a difference it will make compared to pickles you may have home canned in the past without this added ingredient. When you open a jar to enjoy, you will be delighted to find pickles that have a fabulous crunch and are not the least bit mushy.

PREP TIME: **30 MINUTES**
COOK TIME: **20 MINUTES**
WATER BATH PROCESSING TIME: **10–20 MINUTES**
TOTAL TIME: **1 HOUR TO 1 HOUR 10 MINUTES**
YIELD: **APPROXIMATELY 7 PINTS**

EQUIPMENT

Large (8-quart) high-sided stainless steel saucepan or large enameled high-sided Dutch oven

Long-handled stainless steel or wooden spoon

1 (5 × 5-inch/12.75 × 12.75-cm) piece of flour sack towel or cheesecloth

Food-safe kitchen twine

Water bath canner and supplies

7 pint (16oz) wide-mouth canning jars

7 wide-mouth canning lids and bands

INGREDIENTS

4 tbsp plus 1 tsp pickling spice, divided

8 cups water

6 cups 5%-acidity vinegar (white or apple cider)

¾ cup canning and pickling salt

¼ cup granulated sugar

8 lb (3.5kg) pickling cucumbers (see **Cook's Notes**)

⅞ tsp calcium chloride (Pickle Crisp), divided

1 **Steps 1–5:** Follow steps 1–5 in the "General Water Bath Canning Guidelines" (p. 48).

2 **Steps 6–11:** These steps coordinate with steps 6–11 in the "General Water Bath Canning Guidelines" but are unique to this recipe.

6. a. Take the square of flour sack towel or cheesecloth and lay it out on a flat surface. Place 2 tablespoons of the pickling spice on the cloth. Gather up the sides of the cloth to make a pouch and tie it closed with a piece of kitchen twine. (This is your pickling spice pouch.) Set aside.

   b. Add the water, vinegar, salt, sugar, and pickling spice pouch to a saucepan over high heat and bring to a boil, stirring continuously until the salt and sugar are dissolved. Reduce the heat to medium, place the lid on the saucepan, and simmer the mixture for 15 minutes, allowing the spices to infuse into the liquid. Transfer the saucepan to a heatproof surface and remove the pickling spice pouch. This liquid is the brine.

   c. While the mixture is simmering, wash the cucumbers and trim both ends. Cut each trimmed cucumber lengthwise into quarters to make 4 spears. Set aside.

7. Using the jar lifter, remove one jar from the canner, empty the hot water from the jar back into the canner, and place the jar on a cushioned surface.

8. Add 1 teaspoon of the pickling spice and ⅛ teaspoon of the calcium chloride to the jar. Tightly pack the jar with the pickle spears, leaving slightly more than a ½-inch (1.25-cm) headspace. Ladle the brine into the jar packed with the pickle spears.

9. Measure the headspace, leaving ½ inch (1.25cm).

10. Insert a debubbler to remove any air bubbles from the jar.

11. Remeasure the headspace and add more brine, if needed, to adjust the headspace to ½ inch (1.25cm).

3 Steps 12–24: Follow steps 12–24 in the "General Water Bath Canning Guidelines" (p. 48).

···· COOK'S NOTES ····

What are the recommended processing times for pint jars of pickle spears, based on altitude?

· 0 to 1,000 feet: 10 minutes
· 1,001 to 6,000 feet: 15 minutes
· Above 6,000 feet: 20 minutes

Why do you need to use pickling cucumbers for this recipe? The most common variety of pickling cucumbers are often sold under the name "Kirby." These cucumbers are quite firm and hold up beautifully to the hot temperatures required by the water bath canning process. If you can't find this variety, don't worry. "English" cucumbers, sometimes labeled "Hot House" cucumbers, can make a good substitute. The main difference is that English cucumbers are very long and will need to be cut into thirds before quartering lengthwise. Also, English cucumbers will be firm and tasty after canning; however, they will not be as crisp as when using Kirby cucumbers.

How many pickling cucumbers equal 8 pounds (3.5kg)? Depending on the length of the pickling cucumbers, which are generally 3 to 4 inches (7.5 to 10cm) each, 8 pounds (3.5kg) of cucumbers may be anywhere from 48 to 56 cucumbers. Err on the side of having too many cucumbers as opposed to too few, so have 56 cucumbers on hand. Start by cutting up 48 of them. As you pack the jars with the spears and find you are running short, just slice more cucumbers and forge ahead. Any that you don't need can be refrigerated.

What is the shelf life for Always-Crisp Pickle Spears? Home-canned pickle spears are shelf stable for 12 months or longer depending on the canning lid manufacturer's recommendations. Water bath-canned pickle spears are best left on your pantry shelf for a few weeks before opening. This will give the calcium chloride time to do its job and ensure that your pickles are crisp. Once opened, your pickle spears will need to be refrigerated and will stay fresh and crisp for approximately 3 months.

Simply Sweet Pickled Relish

This relish is a delightful blend of tangy and sweet, perfect for those who enjoy a lighter touch of sugar in their condiments. This homemade relish combines the crispness of pickling cucumbers with the sweetness of red bell peppers, creating a colorful and flavorful addition to any dish.

The subtle sweetness of this relish perfectly balances the tangy vinegar and the robust flavor of the pickling spices, making it an ideal topping for burgers, hot dogs, and sandwiches. But it's also perfect for adding into a homemade tartar sauce or tossing into a potato salad. With its refreshing taste and colorful appearance, thanks to the red bell peppers, Simply Sweet Pickled Relish provides a burst of flavor to pretty much anything you add it to. It's never overpowering or cloyingly sweet, it's just simply sweet!

PREP TIME: **30 MINUTES**
REFRIGERATION TIME: **12 HOURS**
COOK TIME: **15 MINUTES**
WATER BATH PROCESSING TIME: **15–25 MINUTES**
TOTAL TIME: **13 HOURS TO 13 HOURS 10 MINUTES**
YIELD: **APPROXIMATELY 7 PINTS**

EQUIPMENT

Sharp chef's knife or food processor

Large glass bowl

Colander

Large (8-quart) high-sided stainless steel saucepan or large enameled high-sided Dutch oven

Long-handled stainless steel or wooden spoon

Water bath canner and supplies

7 pint (16oz) regular-mouth or wide-mouth canning jars

7 regular-mouth or wide-mouth canning lids and bands

INGREDIENTS

8 lb (3.5kg) pickling cucumbers (48 to 56 cucumbers, 3 to 4 inches [7.5 to 10cm] in length)

Approximately 5 medium red bell peppers, seeded and finely chopped

½ cup canning and pickling salt

4 cups water

2 tsp ground turmeric

⅓ cup granulated sugar

4 cups apple cider vinegar

1 **Steps 1–5:** Follow steps 1–5 in the "General Water Bath Canning Guidelines" (p. 48).

2 **Steps 6–11:** These steps coordinate with steps 6–11 in the "General Water Bath Canning Guidelines" but are unique to this recipe.

6. a. Place one cucumber at a time on a secure cutting board. Using a chef's knife, quarter the cucumber lengthwise, then chop each quarter into 1-inch (2.5-cm) pieces.

b. Once you have chopped up a few cucumbers into 1-inch (2.5-cm) pieces, gather them together and begin rocking your knife back and forth over them until they are finely chopped. Transfer them to a large glass bowl. (Note: You can also use a food processor to make the job easier. Just be sure not to overdo it; you don't want to turn the cucumbers to mush.)

c. Add the chopped red bell peppers to the bowl with the cucumbers. Sprinkle the salt over the cucumbers and peppers. Add the water to the bowl. Cover the bowl and refrigerate it for at least 12 hours, or overnight.

d. Remove the cucumber-pepper mixture from the refrigerator and transfer it into a colander over the sink. Rinse the mixture with cool water for 1 minute and drain thoroughly.

e. To assist the draining process, use your hands to squeeze out any excess liquid from the mixture.

f. Add the drained cucumber mixture, turmeric, sugar, and vinegar to the saucepan. Bring the mixture to a boil over high heat, then reduce the heat to medium and simmer for approximately 10 minutes. As the mixture simmers, regularly stir it to ensure that it does not stick to the bottom of the saucepan. (This will prevent it from burning.)

g. When the mixture begins to thicken, transfer the saucepan to a heatproof surface.

7. Using the jar lifter, remove one jar from the canner, empty the hot water from the jar back into the canner, and place the jar on a cushioned surface.

8. Place a wide-mouth funnel over the jar opening and ladle the hot relish into the jar.

9. Measure the headspace, leaving ½ inch (1.25cm).

10. Insert a debubbler to remove any air bubbles from the jar.

11. Remeasure the headspace and add more relish, if needed, to adjust the headspace to ½ inch (1.25cm).

3 **Steps 12–24:** Follow steps 12–24 in the "General Water Bath Canning Guidelines" (p. 48).

> ·················· COOK'S NOTES ··················
>
> *What are the recommended processing times for pint jars of relish, based on altitude?*
>
> - 0 to 1,000 feet: 15 minutes
> - 1,001 to 6,000 feet: 20 minutes
> - Above 6,000 feet: 25 minutes
>
> *What is the shelf life for Simply Sweet Pickled Relish?* Home-canned relish is shelf stable for 12 months or longer, depending on the canning lid manufacturer's recommendations. Once opened, your relish will need to be refrigerated and will stay fresh for approximately 3 months.

Sweet and Tangy Green Beans

When you taste these green beans, you will find that they retain a delightful crispness and are preserved in a perfectly balanced vinegar-sugar brine. Green beans in just a water-vinegar brine, although delicious, can be overpowering for some palates. But with this recipe, the vinegar provides a refreshing zing while the sugar adds just the right touch of sweetness, creating a harmonious blend that enhances the natural taste of the green beans.

These green beans provide the perfect burst of flavor as a side dish, salad topping, or tasty snack straight from the jar. These are a versatile pantry staple and offer a taste of summer freshness all year round!

PREP TIME: **30 MINUTES**
COOK TIME: **15 MINUTES**
WATER BATH PROCESSING TIME: **5–15 MINUTES**
TOTAL TIME: **50 MINUTES TO 1 HOUR**
YIELD: **7–8 PINTS**

EQUIPMENT

Large (8-quart) high-sided stainless steel saucepan or large enameled high-sided Dutch oven

Long-handled stainless steel or wooden spoon

Water bath canner and supplies

8 pint (16oz) wide-mouth canning jars

8 wide-mouth canning lids and bands

INGREDIENTS

4 lb (1.75kg) fresh green beans

½ cup canning or pickling salt

2 cups granulated sugar

4 cups 5%-acidity apple cider vinegar

4 cups water

1 tsp red pepper flakes (optional)

8 fresh dill fronds (feathery leaflike part of the herb), divided (optional)

1 **Steps 1–5:** Follow steps 1–5 in the "General Water Bath Canning Guidelines" (p. 48).

2 **Steps 6–11:** These steps coordinate with steps 6–11 in the "General Water Bath Canning Guidelines" but are unique to this recipe.

6. a. Wash the green beans and remove any stems. Trim both ends of the green beans so that each green bean is approximately 4 inches (10cm) in length. (Do not discard the trimmed ends, save them for adding to a vegetable soup.)

b. Add the salt, sugar, vinegar, water, and red pepper flakes (if using) to the saucepan. Bring this mixture to a boil over high heat, then reduce the heat to medium and simmer until all the salt and sugar have dissolved. Stir the mixture occasionally to prevent the sugar from puddling on the bottom of the saucepan. Transfer the saucepan to a heatproof surface. (This is your brine.)

7. Using the jar lifter, remove one jar from the canner, empty the hot water from the jar back into the canner, and place the jar on a cushioned surface.

8. Place 1 dill frond (if using) into the jar. (Dill makes the perfect flavor complement to green beans.) Place the trimmed green beans upright in the jar. Pack the green beans tightly, leaving slightly more than a ½-inch (1.25-cm) headspace. If necessary, trim the green beans to ensure a proper fit in the jar. Ladle the hot brine into the jar packed with the green beans.

9. Measure the headspace, leaving ½ inch (1.25cm).

10. Insert a debubbler to remove any air bubbles from the jar.

11. Remeasure the headspace and add more hot brine, if needed, to adjust the headspace to ½ inch (1.25cm).

3 **Steps 12–24:** Follow steps 12–24 in the "General Water Bath Canning Guidelines" (p. 48).

COOK'S NOTES

What are the recommended processing times for pint jars of pickled* green beans, based on altitude?

- 0 to 1,000 feet: 5 minutes (If the jars have not been sterilized, process for 10 minutes.)
- 1,001 to 6,000 feet: 10 minutes
- Above 6,000 feet: 15 minutes

*Remember that only pickled green beans, such as these Sweet and Tangy Green Beans, can be water bath canned. Plain green beans must be pressure canned.

What is the shelf life for Sweet and Tangy Green Beans? Home-canned pickled green beans are shelf stable for 12 months or longer, depending on the canning lid manufacturer's recommendations. Once opened, your pickled green beans will need to be refrigerated and will stay fresh for approximately 3 months.

Easy Roasted Tomato Salsa

If this is your first time making salsa, you will love this recipe. Even if you are an old pro, you will still adore this recipe because you are in for a real treat when it comes to the time-saving tip I share for preparing the tomatoes.

Italian Roma or Campari tomatoes make a sweeter salsa. However, since they are smaller, that means there are more of them to crosshatch, blanch, and peel. But thanks to a little help from the oven, your workload will be cut in half. Be sure to check out the Cook's Notes for how to implement this easy technique.

PREP TIME: **30 MINUTES**
COOK TIME: **20 MINUTES**
WATER BATH PROCESSING TIME: **15–25 MINUTES**
TOTAL TIME: **1 HOUR 5 MINUTES TO 1 HOUR 15 MINUTES**
YIELD: **APPROXIMATELY 6 PINTS**

EQUIPMENT

Large (8-quart) high-sided stainless steel saucepan or large enameled high-sided Dutch oven

Long-handled stainless steel or wooden spoon

Water bath canner and supplies

6 pint (16oz) regular-mouth or wide-mouth canning jars

6 regular-mouth or wide-mouth canning lids and bands

INGREDIENTS

Approximately 28 Roma or Campari tomatoes, peeled, cored, and chopped (see **Cook's Notes**)

Approximately 5 medium green bell peppers, seeded and chopped

Approximately 5 medium yellow bell peppers, seeded and chopped

Approximately 4 medium red bell peppers, seeded and chopped

1 medium yellow onion, peeled and chopped

2 large green jalapeño peppers, seeded, membranes removed, and diced (see **Cook's Notes**)

1¼ cups 5%-acidity apple cider vinegar

¼ cup bottled lime juice

2 tbsp canning and pickling salt

1 tsp ground cumin

1 tsp ground coriander

1   **Steps 1–5:** Follow steps 1–5 in the "General Water Bath Canning Guidelines" (p. 48).

2   **Steps 6–11:** These steps coordinate with steps 6–11 in the "General Water Bath Canning Guidelines" but are unique to this recipe.

6.   a. Add all the ingredients to a large saucepan placed on the stovetop. Bring the tomato mixture to a boil over high heat, stirring continuously.

b. Once the mixture comes to a boil, reduce the heat to medium and simmer until the liquid begins to evaporate and the mixture thickens. The time it takes to thicken varies depending on how juicy the tomatoes are, but it generally takes approximately 20 minutes. Stir the mixture frequently to ensure it does not stick to the bottom of the saucepan. This will prevent it from burning.

c. Transfer the saucepan to a heatproof surface.

7. Using the jar lifter, remove one jar from the canner, empty the hot water from the jar back into the canner, and place the jar on a cushioned surface.

8. Place a wide-mouth funnel over the jar opening and ladle the hot salsa into the jar.

9. Measure the headspace, leaving ½ inch (1.25cm).

10. Insert a debubbler to remove any air bubbles from the jar.

11. Remeasure the headspace and add more salsa, if needed, to adjust the headspace to ½ inch (1.25cm).

3   **Steps 12–24:** Follow steps 12–24 in the "General Water Bath Canning Guidelines" (p. 48).

What are the recommended processing times for half-pint jars of salsa, based on altitude?

- 0 to 1,000 feet: 15 minutes
- 1,001 to 6,000 feet: 20 minutes
- Above 6,000 feet: 25 minutes

Here is an easy way to remove the skin from a tomato when making salsa.
Preheat the oven to 425°F (220°C). Line a baking sheet with parchment paper and then place the whole tomatoes on the baking sheet. Place the baking sheet on the middle rack of the oven and roast the tomatoes until the skins split and begin to char slightly. This process can take as little as 15 minutes or up to 30 minutes, depending on the size of the tomatoes.

Once the skins on the tomatoes have split, place the baking sheet on a heatproof surface. Once the tomatoes are cool enough to handle, use two fingers to pinch a piece of the tomato skin and slide the skin off the flesh of the tomato.

You now have tomatoes that are exactly like their blanched counterparts, and you can proceed with your recipe that calls for tomatoes that have had their skins removed.

How to make a spicy salsa.
In this recipe, I removed the seeds and the membrane from the jalapeños to create a mild salsa. If you want to make a spicy salsa, include the seeds and the membrane of the jalapeños when adding them to the saucepan.

What is the shelf life for Easy Roasted Tomato Salsa?
Home-canned salsa is shelf stable for 12 months or longer, depending on the canning lid manufacturer's recommendations. Once opened, your salsa will need to be refrigerated. Due to the significant amount of vinegar and lime juice in this salsa, it should remain fresh and at its peak flavor for 3 months.

Crushed Tomatoes with Herbs

When it comes to home-canned foods, there is nothing better than having crushed tomatoes tucked into your Working Pantry and Extended Pantry. This staple makes meal prep a breeze. Open a jar and toss it with pasta for a quick dinner or pour it on top of simmering boneless, skinless chicken breasts and allow it to liven up an otherwise bland dish. And if you are all out of picante, no problem. Whirl a jar of crushed tomatoes with a jalapeño or two in the blender and you have a picante that can almost pass for fresh made.

PREP TIME: **1 HOUR**
COOK TIME: **15 MINUTES**
WATER BATH PROCESSING TIME: **45–60 MINUTES**
TOTAL TIME: **2 HOURS TO 2 HOURS 15 MINUTES**
YIELD: **APPROXIMATELY 7 QUARTS**

EQUIPMENT

2 large glass bowls

Large (10- to 12-quart) high-sided stainless steel or enameled saucepan, stockpot, or Dutch oven

Sharp paring knife

Slotted spoon

Potato masher or long-handled wooden spoon

Water bath canner and supplies

7 quart (32oz) regular-mouth or wide-mouth canning jars

7 regular-mouth or wide-mouth canning lids and bands

INGREDIENTS

22 lb (10kg) Italian plum tomatoes (Roma or San Marzano varieties) (approximately 88 large plum tomatoes)

5 tbsp dried Italian herb blend

14 tbsp bottled lemon juice (do not use fresh lemon juice), divided

7 tsp granulated sugar (optional), divided

7 tsp canning and pickling salt (optional), divided

1 **Steps 1–5:** Follow steps 1–5 in the "General Water Bath Canning Guidelines" (p. 48).

2 **Steps 6–11:** These steps coordinate with steps 6–11 in the "General Water Bath Canning Guidelines" but are unique to this recipe.

6.   a. Fill the saucepan halfway with water. Bring the water to a boil over high heat, then reduce the heat to low. Put a lid on the saucepan to keep the water hot. Fill a large bowl halfway with water and add a dozen ice cubes to the water. (This is an ice water bath.) Set aside.

b. Wash the tomatoes, then score the blossom or stem end with a crosshatch. (I find it easier to remove the tomato skin if I crosshatch the stem ends.)

c. Remove the lid from the saucepan and return the water to a rolling boil. Working in batches of 4 to 6 tomatoes at a time, use a slotted spoon to lower the tomatoes into the boiling water for 30 to 60 seconds or until the skins split. (This process is called blanching.)

d. Once the tomato skins split, use the slotted spoon to remove the tomatoes, one at a time, from the saucepan and lower them into the ice water bath. Peel off the tomato skins and transfer the peeled tomatoes to a large, clean glass bowl. (Refresh the ice water periodically with more ice to keep the water very cold.) Repeat this process until all the tomatoes are peeled.

e. Slice the tomatoes in half, remove the cores, and trim off any discolorations or blemished areas. Roughly chop the tomatoes.

f. Empty the saucepan of any remaining water and return it to the stovetop. Add the tomatoes to the saucepan in batches. After adding each batch, crush the tomatoes using a potato masher or wooden spoon.

g. Add the dried Italian seasoning blend to the tomatoes. Stir well to combine.

h. Bring the tomatoes to a boil over high heat, stirring continuously. Boil the tomatoes for 5 minutes, then transfer the saucepan to a heatproof surface.

7. Using the jar lifter, remove one jar from the canner, empty the hot water from the jar back into the canner, and place the jar on a cushioned surface.

8. Add 2 tablespoons of bottled lemon juice to the jar. If using the salt and/or sugar, add 1 teaspoon of each to the jar and stir. Ladle the hot crushed tomatoes into the jar.

9. Measure the headspace, leaving ½ inch (1.25cm).

10. Insert a debubbler to remove any air bubbles from the jar.

11. Remeasure the headspace and add more tomatoes, if needed, to adjust the headspace to ½ inch (1.25cm).

3 **Steps 12–24:** Follow steps 12–24 in the "General Water Bath Canning Guidelines" (p. 48).

COOK'S NOTES

What are the recommended processing times for quart jars of crushed tomatoes, based on altitude?

- 0 to 1,000 feet: 45 minutes
- 1,001 to 3,000 feet: 50 minutes
- 3,001 to 6,000 feet: 55 minutes
- Above 6,000 feet: 60 minutes

The importance of acidification when home canning tomatoes. To ensure safe acidity levels in home-canned crushed tomatoes, remember to add the bottled lemon juice directly to each jar. Although not required, adding a bit of sugar to each jar, as specified in the recipe, can go a long way to balance the acidic taste of the tomatoes and the added lemon juice. If you prefer to use citric acid instead of bottled lemon juice, you can do so. You will need to add ½ teaspoon of citric acid to each quart jar.

Can you use vinegar in place of lemon juice? I do not recommend using vinegar in place of the lemon juice or citric acid. Although it is approved by the NCHFP as an acid for home canning, the vinegar can create an undesirable flavor when added to home-canned tomatoes. However, if you want to experiment with using vinegar as the acid for home-canned tomatoes, you will need 4 tablespoons of vinegar per quart jar to reach the proper acidity level. That is a lot of vinegar to add to tomatoes! So now you know why I don't recommend it.

What is the shelf life for Crushed Tomatoes with Herbs? Home-canned crushed tomatoes are shelf stable for 12 months or longer, depending on the canning lid manufacturer's recommendations. Once opened, your crushed tomatoes will need to be refrigerated and should be used within 7 days. Any unused crushed tomatoes can be stored in an airtight container and transferred to the freezer where they will remain fresh for 3 months.

Cowboy Candy

It will probably come as no surprise to you that this former New Yorker had never heard of cowboy candy until I moved to Texas. And I had no idea what I was missing! These candied jalapeños are so much more than an occasional treat. You will find yourself using this sweet and spicy condiment on—and in—everything where you want a boost of flavor.

There is a lot of wiggle room for variation in this recipe, so you can experiment with some added spices. (Some folks actually add cayenne pepper as if the jalapeños weren't spicy enough!) But I encourage you to make them according to the recipe the first time and then experiment with your second batch. I suspect you might love them this simple way and not want to change a thing!

Use these candied jalapeños as is, or to top sandwiches; blend into mayo for a spread, as a quick hors d'oeuvre to liven up cheese and crackers; add to sour cream to make a dip, top potatoes or pasta salads, toss in the pan with sautéed chicken breasts, and lots more. You will find that once you make these—and taste them—the possibilities for where to use them becomes endless!

PREP TIME: **30 MINUTES**
COOK TIME: **20 MINUTES**
WATER BATH PROCESSING TIME: **15–25 MINUTES**
TOTAL TIME: **1 HOUR 5 MINUTES TO 1 HOUR 15 MINUTES**
YIELD: **APPROXIMATELY 4 PINTS**

EQUIPMENT

Large (8-quart) high-sided stainless steel saucepan or large enameled high-sided Dutch oven

Long-handled stainless steel or wooden spoon

Water bath canner and supplies

4 pint (16oz) wide-mouth canning jars

4 wide-mouth canning lids and bands

INGREDIENTS

3 cups 5%-acidity apple cider vinegar

2 tsp canning and pickling salt

4 cups granulated sugar

4 lb (1.75 kg) green jalapeño peppers, sliced into ¼-inch (0.65-cm) rings (see **Cook's Notes**)

---

1 **Steps 1–5:** Follow steps 1–5 in the "General Water Bath Canning Guidelines" (p. 48).

2 **Steps 6–11:** These steps coordinate with steps 6–11 in the "General Water Bath Canning Guidelines" but are unique to this recipe.

6.   a. Add the vinegar, salt, and sugar to the saucepan and bring the mixture to a boil over high heat, stirring continuously until all the salt and sugar are completely dissolved. Reduce the heat to medium. (This is your syrup.)

    b. Carefully add all the jalapeños to the hot syrup in the saucepan and simmer for 15 minutes. (The jalapeños will become a dark green as they absorb the syrup.) Transfer the saucepan to a heatproof surface.

7. Using the jar lifter, remove one jar from the canner, empty the hot water from the jar back into the canner, and place the jar on a cushioned surface.

8. Place a wide-mouth funnel over the jar opening and ladle the hot jalapeños and syrup into the jar.

9. Measure the headspace, leaving ½ inch (1.25cm).

10. Insert a debubbler to remove any air bubbles from the jar.

11. Remeasure the headspace and add more syrup, if needed, to adjust the headspace to ½ inch (1.25cm).

3 **Steps 12–24:** Follow steps 12–24 in the "General Water Bath Canning Guidelines" (p. 48).

Spiced Pears in Apple Juice

These pears are a delightful treat that brings the warm flavors of autumn to your table. They are gently infused with aromatic spices and preserved in the natural sweetness of apple juice, creating a rich and flavorful combination.

This spiced delight is perfect for enjoying straight from the jar, served with a dollop of ice cream in the center of a halved pear, or used to make a special occasion dessert such as a pear galette. With their luscious texture and comforting taste, these spiced pears offer a touch of homemade elegance and a burst of seasonal flavor, ready to be enjoyed any time of the year.

PREP TIME: **30 MINUTES**
COOK TIME: **15 MINUTES**
WATER BATH PROCESSING TIME: **25–40 MINUTES**
TOTAL TIME: **1 HOUR 10 MINUTES TO 1 HOUR 25 MINUTES**
YIELD: **APPROXIMATELY 7 QUARTS**

EQUIPMENT

Very large glass bowl

Very large (10- to 12-quart) high-sided stainless steel or enameled saucepan, stockpot, or Dutch oven

Vegetable peeler or paring knife

Melon baller (optional)

Slotted spoon

Water bath canner and supplies

7 quart (32oz) wide-mouth canning jars

7 wide-mouth canning lids and bands

INGREDIENTS

Approximately 15 cups of apple juice, sufficient to cover the pears

35 medium ripe-but-firm Bartlett pears (approximately 17 ½ pounds [8kg])

7 whole star anise, divided

14 cracked cardamom pods, divided

3 ½ tsp allspice berries, divided

3 ½ tsp whole cloves, divided

14 (3- to 4-inch/7.5- to 10-cm) Ceylon cinnamon sticks

1 **Steps 1–5:** Follow steps 1–5 in the "General Water Bath Canning Guidelines" (p. 48).

2 **Steps 6–11:** These steps coordinate with steps 6–11 in the "General Water Bath Canning Guidelines" but are unique to this recipe.

6. a. Add the apple juice to the saucepan.

b. Using a potato peeler, peel each pear. Remove the stem, slice the pear in half lengthwise, and remove the core. (A melon baller can help with this job.) As you slice each pear in half, add it to the saucepan with the apple juice. Continue this process until all the peeled and halved pears are in the saucepan.

c. If the pears are not completely covered with apple juice, add more juice. Bring the juice and pears to a boil over high heat, then reduce the heat to medium and simmer the pears in the apple juice for 5 minutes. Transfer the saucepan to a heatproof surface.

7. Using the jar lifter, remove one jar from the canner, empty the hot water from the jar back into the canner, and place the jar on a cushioned surface.

8. Add 1 star anise, 2 cracked cardamom pods, ½ teaspoon allspice berries, and ½ teaspoon whole cloves to the bottom of the jar. Place a wide-mouth funnel over the jar opening and ladle the hot pears and juice into the jar, leaving slightly less than a ½-inch (1.25-cm) headspace. Gently slide two cinnamon sticks down into opposite sides of the jar, taking care not to bruise the pears.

9. Measure the headspace, leaving ½ inch (1.25cm).

10. Insert a debubbler to remove any air bubbles from the jar.

11. Remeasure the headspace and add more juice, if needed, to adjust the headspace to ½ inch (1.25cm).

3 **Steps 12–24:** Follow steps 12–24 in the "General Water Bath Canning Guidelines" (p. 48).

COOK'S NOTES

What are the recommended processing times for quart jars of pears, based on altitude?

- 0 to 1,000 feet: 25 minutes
- 1,001 to 3,000 feet: 30 minutes
- 3,001 to 6,000 feet: 35 minutes
- Above 6,000 feet: 40 minutes

Can pears be blanched like peaches to make the job of peeling easier? Yes, you can blanch pears in the same way you blanched the peaches in the peach conserves recipe. However, if you opt for this method, take care and use a very gentle hand. The process of blanching pears slightly differs from blanching peaches when it comes to removing the skin. You can peel off the peach skin, but in the case of blanched pears, the skin becomes quite soft and you have to rub it off the pear. This rubbing can create bruising and browning, which becomes even more accentuated when the pears are home canned.

What is the shelf life for Spiced Pears in Apple Juice? Home-canned spiced pears are shelf stable for 12 months or longer, depending on the canning lid manufacturer's recommendations. Once opened, your spiced pears will need to be refrigerated and will stay fresh for approximately 1 week.

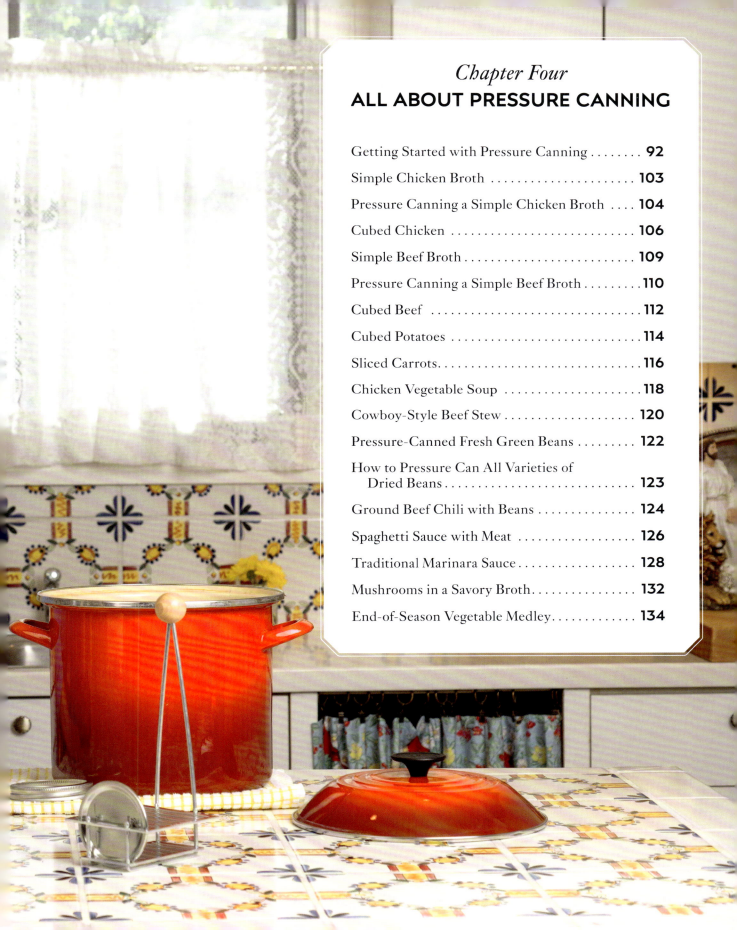

Chapter Four
ALL ABOUT PRESSURE CANNING

GETTING STARTED WITH PRESSURE CANNING

My memories of pressure canning are limited. My mom, along with many other moms in our community, primarily relied on water bath canning to preserve their high-acid foods. It was rare to meet someone in our neighborhood who had a pressure canner, so most home cooks preserved low-acid foods by drying or freezing.

Some of the moms had pressure cookers. Unfortunately, the distinction between pressure cookers and pressure canners was not clear, at least in my mom's social circle. One of her friends decided to try to use a pressure cooker as a pressure canner to less than stellar results. So it wasn't until I was much older that I was introduced to pressure canning. Yes, I was a little nervous when I first tried it. Those stories I shared with you in an earlier chapter about pressure cookers—and canners—exploding still swirled around in my head. But I told myself that most of those disasters dated back to earlier centuries! It's amazing how those stories can stick in your mind.

Nevertheless, I persevered, and I'm glad I did. Pressure canning is not difficult, and it's not scary. Just as you had success with your first foray into water bath canning and discovered how easy it was, I anticipate you will have the same reaction after you finish your first attempt at pressure canning food.

From Water Bath to Pressure Canning: Taking the Next Step

Pressure canning is a safe way to preserve low-acid foods like fish, meat, poultry, and vegetables, as well as different mixtures of low-acid foods. This process of home food preservation uses a piece of equipment called a pressure canner, which creates pressurized steam to raise the temperature of the contents inside the canner to 240°F (115°C) or higher. This high temperature kills bacteria (including botulism), yeasts, and molds that can otherwise spoil food. During the pressure canning process, pressure (physical force) seals the jars, making the food inside shelf stable.

The good news is that once you start your home canning journey with water bath canning, it's easy to take the next step and learn how to pressure can low-acid foods. For the most part, you have all the supplies you need from what you've already gathered for water bath canning. All you have to do now is decide what type of pressure canner you want.

Before we review what's available, let's discuss the elephant in the room. When it comes to home canning low-acid foods, often the first thing home cooks will hear or read is the word *botulism*. It's not to be taken lightly, but that is why we will always follow tested and approved pressure canning methods to ensure safety.

Botulism, or *Clostridium botulinum* (*C. botulinum* spores) by its full name, is the form of bacteria that is of the most concern in home canning, specifically when canning low-acid foods. Botulism spores are a toxin that causes severe food poisoning. Botulism spores proliferate on low-acid foods in the presence of moisture (liquid), in the absence of air, and at room temperature. As you can imagine, the conditions inside a jar of home-canned meat or vegetables are ripe for the development of botulism if proper pressure canning procedures are not followed. This is why we pressure can low-acid foods rather than water bath canning them. *Clostridium botulinum* spores may survive a boiling water bath, but they are destroyed when processed in a pressure canner where the temperature reaches 240°F (115°C) or higher. Plus, when you open a jar of pressure canned food, you will be heating it by bringing it up to a boil (if you follow recommended

USDA guidelines) to further ensure that the home-canned food is safe to eat. Now that we have that out of the way, let's move on to choosing the right pressure canner for you.

Types of Pressure Canners

When it comes to pressure canning, there are primarily two types of pressure canners: dial gauge canners and weighted gauge canners. Let's review each one.

DIAL GAUGE PRESSURE CANNER

As the name implies, a dial gauge pressure canner has a dial on the lid that is usually marked with one-pound increments. The dial moves as the pressure builds or decreases inside the canner. Once the processing pressure, as stated in a recipe, is reached within the canner, you set your timer, and the processing time begins.

This type of pressure canner has the advantage of adjusting the pressure by small increments, which prevents the use of more pressure than necessary. For example, according to most recipes, when pressure canning low-acid foods at an altitude of 1,000 feet or below, the pressure is brought to 11 pounds. You bring the pressure up by controlling the heat on your stovetop burner. If you are pressure canning at a higher altitude and the recipe calls for increased pressure, you will increase the heat on your stovetop burner until the dial gauge indicates the required pressure.

The drawback with a dial gauge canner is that you must closely monitor the dial gauge while processing food because you may need to adjust the burner heat up or down so the pressure stays at 11 pounds. If the pressure goes slightly above 11 pounds, just lower your heat. What is important is that if the pressure drops below 11 pounds you will need to bring the canner pressure back up to 11 pounds and start your timer all over again.

The good news is you don't need to worry about over pressurizing your canner. Certainly, you don't need 15 pounds of pressure to can low-acid foods if your altitude is 1,000 feet or below, but if the pressure gets that high, dial gauge canners also have a simple one-piece pressure regulator that usually sits on top of the vent pipe and serves as a safety device to prevent the development of pressure in excess of 15 pounds. The dial gauge pressure regulator for sealing off the open vent pipe may look like a weight, but do not confuse it with a weighted gauge (which you will learn more about later). This pressure regulator should not jiggle or rock like a weight on a weighted gauge canner. If the pressure regulator jiggles, it means excess pressure is being released from the canner. If this happens, check your dial gauge and adjust the heat of the stovetop burner to achieve the correct pressure.

A dial gauge pressure canner lid is made with a prelubricated rubber gasket (or similar material). This gasket creates a tight seal with the main vessel of the canner, allowing the steam to be contained in the pressure canner while building up pressure. On average, with normal use, you should replace a gasket every 2 to 3 years when you notice it's shrinking and becoming somewhat misshaped.

HAVE YOUR DIAL GAUGE RECALIBRATED REGULARLY

Pressure canner dial gauges can go out of calibration and should be tested for accuracy annually in the spring or before each canning season. Your local agricultural extension office may be able to help you with this. Alternatively, some pressure canner manufacturers will have you mail your dial gauge back to them, and they will recalibrate it and mail it back to you.

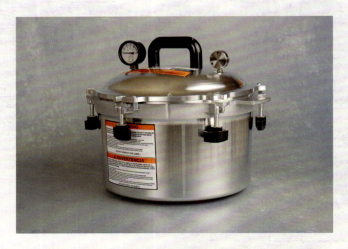

WEIGHTED GAUGE PRESSURE CANNER

The main difference between a dial gauge pressure canner and a weighted gauge pressure canner is that the weighted gauge canner has a small weight attached to the vent pipe on the canner lid. This weight "jiggles" to indicate the amount of pressure inside the canner. The weighted gauge is usually designed to indicate canner pressure at 5, 10, and 15 pounds. For pressure canning low-acid foods you will need 10 pounds of weight or 15 pounds of weight. (Five pounds of weight is needed to pressure can high-acid foods if you prefer to do this as opposed to simply water bath canning the food.)

Depending on the manufacturer of the weighted gauge pressure canner, the weights may look different in design, but they all serve the same purpose. Generally, there will be three weights, or one weight with three settings. If you are pressure canning at an altitude of 1,000 feet or lower, which calls for 10 pounds of pressure, you would use the 10-pound weight or set your single weight to 10 pounds. If you are pressure canning at a higher altitude, you would use the 15-pound weight or set your single weight to 15 pounds. It is not possible to make the incremental adjustments in pressure that you can make with a dial gauge pressure canner. But don't worry. Every recipe that adheres to the NCHFP will state the correct pressure needed when using a weighted gauge pressure canner as well as the more exact pressure requirements when using a dial gauge canner.

These weights fit on top of a vent pipe on the lid of the canner. Once they are placed on the lid, the canner can build up pressure. Before using the weights, you will want to thoroughly read the manufacturer's instructions that come with your weighted gauge pressure canner. Your pressure canner manual will state how many jiggles are required per minute and when to set your timer. Generally, you will find that the range of weight jiggles required to set your timer will vary from 1 to 4 jiggles per minute. (This can vary based on the heat source of the type of stovetop you are using.) Now all you need to do is make sure you hear the appropriate number of jiggles every minute.

A weighted gauge pressure canner has a steam gauge on the lid. This looks similar to the dial gauge on a dial gauge pressure canner. Sometimes your steam gauge will have a different reading than what your weighted gauge is indicating by its jiggling. Steam gauges are not always accurate, so focus on the jiggling of the canner weight. If the weight is jiggling every minute, this will indicate that the canner is maintaining the correct pressure.

The advantage of using a weighted gauge pressure canner is that you can hear the weight jiggling when it is at the correct pressure. This means that you do not need to be in close proximity monitoring a dial the entire time the food is processing. Another nice feature of a weighted gauge pressure canner is that the weights do not go out of calibration unless they are damaged in some way—which rarely happens. Therefore, weights do not require yearly recalibration.

General Pressure Canner Parts

As with dial gauge pressure canners, weighted gauge canners also have a rubber gasket on the lid, which creates a tight seal with the main vessel of the pressure canner once the lid is locked into place. However, one manufacturer of weighted gauge pressure canners does not use a rubber gasket. Instead, the lid and the main vessel have a tight metal-to-metal seal. The canner lid is held in place by six fasteners (wing nuts) that are screwed down tightly.

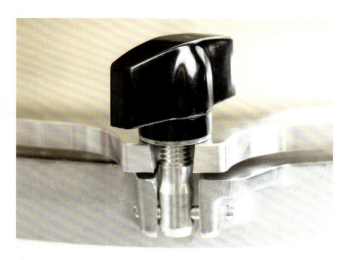

Cover Locking Device: The cover locking device locks the canner lid in place, preventing it from being opened when the unit is under pressure.

Vent Pipe: The vent pipe is a short, hollow pipe that sticks up above the canner lid. When the vent pipe is open, air and steam can escape from the canner. When the vent pipe is closed, it holds the steam inside.

Pressure Regulator: A pressure regulator is a safety device that prevents pressure from building up in the canner in excess of 15 pounds. Regulating pressure looks different on a dial gauge canner than on a weighted gauge canner (on the weighted gauge canner, the pressure regulator also serves as the weighted gauge), but both types of pressure canners have a form of this safety device.

Important Pressure Canner Information

Just as with water bath canners, pressure canners are large vessels that can accommodate canning jars. It's important to know that the USDA and the NCHFP do not endorse or recommend specific pressure canners (or water bath canners) for use. They use different types of canners when testing and approving canning recipes. When evaluating a modern-day pressure canner, I recommend that you stick with the more well-known and respected names in the world of pressure canning, such as Presto and All American. And I want to stress the term modern day, especially if you are new to pressure canning. It is in your best interest to start your pressure canning journey with a new pressure canner in perfect condition with complete instructions for its proper use.

Whatever brand of pressure canner you decide on, well-made, high-quality pressure canners have a number of features in common to ensure safe canning. These include a vent pipe (sometimes referred to as a steam vent or a petcock), a cover locking device (sometimes referred to as a cover locking bracket, lid lock, or locking bracket), and a pressure regulator (sometimes referred to as a counterweight or an overpressure plug).

A NOTE ON USING ALL AMERICAN PRESSURE CANNERS

Proper tightening of an All American pressure canner lid is crucial. When securing the lid to the base, simultaneously tighten two opposite wing nuts to ensure the lid is evenly attached. Tightening only one wing nut at a time can cause the lid to become unevenly secured, potentially leading to pressure loss and an unsuccessful canning experience.

Which Pressure Canner Is Right for You?

Now that you understand the difference between the two types of pressure canners available, let's look at some other things you might want to consider to determine which pressure canner is best for you.

Knowing the heating source on which you will be using your pressure canner is key to deciding which type to purchase. This will come down to investigating each canner's requirements. This information is generally provided on the websites of most canner manufacturers. Here are some factors to consider:

WILL YOU BE USING A GAS OR ELECTRIC STOVE?

You need to be aware of whether your stove's heating method cycles on and off as it reaches a certain temperature. This is unlikely with a gas stove but may be a problem with an electric stove. If this happens, the temperature inside the canner will fall, which could cause the food to be underprocessed and potentially unsafe. Check with the manufacturer of your stovetop to determine how the burner temperatures are maintained on your stovetop.

DO YOU HAVE A GLASS STOVETOP?

Some manufacturers of pressure canners recommend that you do not use certain models on a glass stovetop. In some cases, the weight of the canner has the potential to crack or damage a glass stovetop. If you have a glass stovetop, make sure that you choose a pressure canner model approved for it.

DO YOU HAVE AN INDUCTION BURNER?

If you have this type of burner, pressure canners have been developed with a stainless steel bottom that is suitable for an induction burner.

CAN YOU USE A PORTABLE BURNER?

Most pressure canner manufacturers caution against using portable burners because of the danger that the canner might tip over. However, if you decide to use a portable burner, ensure the portable burner can hold the weight of a fully loaded canner without tipping over. Tabletop units have been used successfully but stability is crucial.

What Size Canner Is Right for You?

Depending on the manufacturer, pressure canners come in a variety of sizes and heights. The taller canners allow for the placement of two layers of jars. The sizes of pressure canners range from approximately 10 quarts up to approximately 41 quarts. Consider how much pressure canning you think you will do and how many jars you may want to pressure can at one time. Keep in mind that the larger the canner, the heavier it will be to lift when full.

The smallest pressure canner available holds 7 pint jars or 4 quart jars. The largest pressure canner available holds 32 pint jars or 19 quart jars. In the larger canners, the jars are stacked—but not on top of each other. A two-rack system is provided with the larger canners. If you are new to pressure canning, starting with a small- or medium-size pressure canner can be a smart move. An average (and manageable) pressure canner can range in size from approximately 16 quarts to 23 quarts. A 16-quart pressure canner will hold 7 quart jars, while a 23-quart pressure canner can hold 20 pint jars or 7 quart jars.

> ····· CAN I USE AN ELECTRIC PRESSURE CANNER? ·····
>
> When shopping for a pressure canner, you might come across an electric pressure canner as opposed to one made for the stovetop. In many ways, this looks like the popular electric pressure cookers that have made a splash on the home cooking scene. You can place these electric pressure canners on a flat, heatproof surface, such as a kitchen counter, making these devices seem like a very easy way to pressure can. Unfortunately, the NCHFP has not used electric pressure canners when testing and approving pressure canning recipes. However, some manufacturers of these electric pressure canners state that they have tested their electric pressure canners according to USDA guidelines and they are safe for using to can low-acid foods. It's difficult to truly know for sure until there is more official testing. If you decide to experiment, I recommend you approach the process cautiously.

> CAN I USE MY ELECTRIC PRESSURE COOKER TO PRESSURE CAN FOOD IN JARS?
>
> If that were possible, it would certainly streamline your kitchen life and limit the amount of equipment you need. However, just like you can't pressure can in a stovetop pressure cooker, you can't pressure can in an electric pressure cooker (unless it is also designated as a pressure canner).

The Best Foods to Pressure Can

Earlier, we reviewed the basics of choosing food to pressure can—low-acid foods such as chicken, fish, meat, and vegetables. We also reviewed what foods you can't pressure can regardless of their pH. Now let's focus on some of the best foods to pressure can.

SEAFOOD AND POULTRY

- **Chicken:** For chicken (and also turkey and rabbit), remove excess fat and cut into reasonably sized pieces that fit comfortably into the canning jar size called for in the recipe. Bones may or may not be included. Chicken, turkey, and rabbit may be hot packed or raw packed.

- **Chicken or turkey broth:** Hot pack.

- **Fish:** Bluefish, mackerel, salmon, steelhead trout, trout, and other fatty fish (instructions generally require canning raw in pint jars; there are separate recommendations for tuna).

- **Fish (smoked):** Salmon, rockfish, sole, cod, and flounder. Canning smoked fish is considered a raw pack.

- **Clams:** Somewhat involved but can be hot packed.

- **Oysters:** Somewhat involved but can be hot packed.

- **Tuna:** Can be canned raw or cooked in half-pint or pint jars.

········ **CAN YOU PRESSURE CAN CRAB MEAT?** ········

The NCHFP recommends that you pressure can King crab meat or Dungeness crab meat; however, the process involves quite a few steps. Pressure-canned blue crab meat may develop a distinctly acidic flavor, so the NCHFP recommends that this type of crab meat only be frozen for the best quality. Personally, I would freeze all crab meat.

MEAT

- **Bear, beef, lamb, pork, veal, venison (strips, cubes, chunks):** Remove excess fat and large bones; hot or raw pack.

- **Bear, beef, lamb, pork, veal, venison (ground or chopped):** Hot pack.

- **Beef broth:** Hot pack.

VEGETABLES

- **Asparagus (spears or pieces):** Hot or raw pack.

- **Beans and peas (all varieties shelled, dried, properly prepared):** Hot pack.

- **Beans (fresh), green, Italian, snap, or wax (yellow):** Trim ends and leave whole or cut into 1-inch (2.5-cm) pieces; hot or raw pack.

- **Beets (whole, cubed, or sliced):** Hot pack.

- **Lima beans (fresh, shelled):** Hot or raw pack.

- **Carrots (peeled, sliced, or diced):** Hot or raw pack.

- **Corn (whole kernel, cut corn from cob):** Hot pack or raw pack.

- **Mixed vegetables (individually properly prepared):** Hot pack.

- **Mushrooms (whole or sliced):** Hot pack.

- **Okra (tender pods whole or cut into 1-inch/2.5-cm pieces):** Hot pack.

- **Onions, small (1-inch/2.5-cm diameter or less):** Raw pack.

- **Peas, green or English (fresh and shelled):** Hot or raw pack.

- **Peppers (hot or sweet, including chiles, jalapeño, and pimiento):** Small peppers may be left whole; large peppers may be quartered. Hot pack.

- **Potatoes (sweet; peeled, cubed, or whole):** Hot pack.

- **Potatoes (white; peeled, cubed, or whole):** Hot pack.

- **Pumpkins:** Peel, remove seeds, and cube; hot pack.

- **Spinach and other greens:** Remove tough stems; hot pack.

- **Tomatoes:** Skins removed and still require acidification as with water bath canning; hot pack.

- **Winter squash:** Peel, remove seeds, and cube; hot pack.

CAN YOU PRESSURE CAN SNOW PEAS OR SUGAR SNAP PEAS?

The NCHFP recommends freezing snow peas and sugar snap peas for the best quality. Pressure canning these vegetables can create a poor, mushy texture.

MIXED LOW-ACID FOODS

All the following foods are hot packed.

- Baked beans
- Chili with beans
- Soups and stews
- Succotash
- Spaghetti sauce, with or without meat

General Pressure Canning Guidelines

Although each pressure canning recipe in this book will detail the specifics for the particular food you will be pressure canning, these are the general guidelines:

1 Prepare the jars by washing them in warm, soapy water; then rinse them well in hot water.

2 Put the rack in the canner and then place the clean, empty canning jars on the rack in your pressure canner.

3 Fill each jar with warm water.

4 Add 2 to 3 inches (5 to 7.5cm) of water in the bottom of the pressure canner.

5 Bring the water in the canner up to a simmer.

6 Prepare the food to be pressure canned following a recipe that adheres to the NCHFP guidelines.

7 Using the jar lifter, remove one jar from the canner, empty the hot water from the jar back into the canner, and place the jar on a cushioned surface, such as a towel on the countertop.

8 Working quickly, fill the jar with the prepared food using a funnel or ladle if appropriate. (It's important to work quickly at this point so the jars remain hot as you fill them with the hot prepared foods. You may recall that there are two ways to pack food in jars: hot pack and raw pack. All the pressure canning recipes I share with you will be hot pack.)

9 Measure the headspace based on the recipe.

10 Insert a debubbler into the jar to remove air bubbles from the food.

11 Remeasure the headspace and add additional food to the jar if needed.

12 Use a clean rag or paper towel dipped in white vinegar to clean the rim of the jar.

13 Use clean hands or a magnetic lid lifter to place a clean lid on the jar.

14 Place a band around the rim of the jar and twist until fingertip-tight.

15 Using the jar lifter, place the filled jar on the rack at the bottom of the pressure canner. (Repeat steps 7–15 with the remaining jars.)

16 Once the canner is full, make sure the water is 2 to 3 inches high (or what the canner manufacturer recommends). If the water is too high, remove some.

17 Now that the canner is full and the water level has been checked and/or adjusted, fasten the pressure canner lid in place.

18 Heat the contents of the canner to boiling. This is done to exhaust steam from the canner for 10 minutes before adding the weight or closing the vent pipe (petcock).

19 After 10 minutes, add the weighted gauge or pressure regulator to the lid of the canner.

20 If using a weighted gauge pressure canner, set your timer once the weight begins jiggling.

STEP 7

STEP 8

STEP 9

STEP 10

STEP 12

STEP 13

STEP 14

STEP 15

21 If using a dial gauge pressure canner, allow the pressure to rise and then maintain the pressure at the level called for in the recipe by adjusting the burner heat. Once the correct pressure is reached, set your timer according to the recipe. If the pressure goes below the recommended pressure at any time during the processing, reset your timer to zero and restart the processing time.

22 Once the processing time is complete, turn off the heat. If you are canning on an electric stove and the canner can be lifted, you can carefully transfer it to a heatproof surface. Otherwise, it is best to leave the canner undisturbed on the stovetop as you allow the pressure canner to depressurize.

23 Allow the canner to cool naturally to 0 pounds pressure. Wait 5 minutes, then remove the weighted gauge or pressure regulator.

24 Wait 10 more minutes before removing the lid of the pressure canner. Then unfasten the lid and remove it very carefully, lifting the lid with the underside away from you so the steam coming out of the canner does not come toward you and potentially burn you.

25 Allow the jars to sit in the open canner for 5 minutes. This will reduce siphoning (loss of liquid from the jar).

26 After the 5 minutes have elapsed, use the jar lifter to transfer the jars to a cushioned surface. Keep the jars upright and do not turn them upside down.

27 Place the jars at least 2 inches (5cm) apart to allow for proper air circulation to cool.

28 If the bands are loose, do not retighten them.

29 Allow the jars to cool for 12 to 24 hours. (Jars will take different times to cool depending on their size.)

30 Once the jars are cool, remove the bands.

31 Check the lids of the jars to make sure they sealed successfully. You can do this by checking to see if the button in the middle of the lid looks slightly concave and if the lid does not flex up and down when pushed down. You can also use your fingertips to lift the jar by the rim, and if the lid stays firmly in place, the jar has sealed successfully.

32 If the jars have sealed, you can store the home-canned goods in a cool, dark, dry pantry. (Do not stack the jars on top of each other.)

············· **WHAT IS SIPHONING?** ·············

Siphoning in home canning occurs when some of the liquid in your jars gets lost during and sometimes after the processing step. You might notice the liquid level is lower right after you take the jars out of the canner, or the lower level might become apparent after the jars have cooled. This is because your jars experienced some type of stress either during the canning process or when being removed from the canner.

When the liquid, and in some cases a small amount of fat, has siphoned out of the jar, the seal of the lid may be compromised. This means that your home-canned jar of food is not safe to keep on your pantry shelf and should be refrigerated. However, you can avoid the siphoning problem by strictly following the headspace guidelines in a recipe and leaving the jars in the canner according to the recipe before removing them with a jar lifter to a cushioned surface to cool.

Even with the best practices, sometimes siphoning happens. Don't be discouraged. Just consume the food right away or, as mentioned above, refrigerate it. If you refrigerate the food, be sure to consume it within a few days.

The Importance of Following Manufacturer's Directions

As we begin our pressure canning recipes, please review the following information from the National Center for Home Food Preservation (Preserving Food: Using Pressure Canners Fact Sheet FDNS-E-37-3, Revised January 2024 National Center for Home Food Preservation):

"Today's pressure canner may have a dial gauge for indicating the pressure or a weighted gauge, for indicating and regulating the pressure. Weighted gauges are usually designed to 'jiggle' several times a minute or to keep rocking gently when they are maintaining the correct pressure. Read your manufacturer's directions to know how a particular weighted gauge should rock or jiggle to indicate that the proper pressure is reached and then maintained during processing.

Dial gauge canners will usually have a counterweight or pressure regulator for sealing off the open vent pipe to pressurize the canner. This weight should not be confused with a weighted gauge and will not jiggle or rock as described for a weighted gauge canner. Pressure readings on a dial gauge canner are only registered on the dial and only the dial should be used as an indication of the pressure in the canner."

In the pressure canning recipes that follow, I will use the terms weighted gauge or pressure regulator when explaining the step in which you will be sealing the canner to pressurize it.

How to Properly Reheat Home Pressured Canned Foods

I'm sharing this guidance with you from the start so it will always be at the forefront of your mind when you serve foods you previously home canned under pressure. When you take a jar of any of these pressure-canned foods off your pantry shelf, you must reheat it by bringing it to a boil, then reducing the heat to medium and continuing to simmer it until the food is completely heated through before consuming it.

If you ever notice mold, unusual discoloration, or a foul odor when opening a jar of home-canned food, don't take any chances. Discard it immediately—do not consume it! While these instances of contamination are rare, they can happen.

Let's Get Started with Pressure Canning

If you are new to home canning, pressure canning might sound a bit complicated, maybe even a bit overwhelming. Once you work your way through the first foolproof pressure canning recipe I share in this book, you will have the basics of pressure canning under your belt and realize that it is not a difficult skill to learn. Afterward, you'll be ready to move on to the remaining simple recipes I share and taste the rewards of the pressure canning skill you've gained.

Simple Chicken Broth

Understanding how to home can meat- and poultry-based broths is the best place to start learning how to pressure can. The canning process is simple for broths since all you are dealing with is a liquid, but the end product is anything but simple. Having a good supply of homemade broth on your pantry shelf saves you considerable money and provides you with a base for making a variety of foods, from soups and stews to gravies and sauces.

The key to high-quality home-canned broth starts with learning how to make a flavorful broth, which is different from stock or bone broth. I don't recommend home canning stock or bone broth since both are quite gelatinous, with bone broth being the most gelatinous. As traditional home cooks, we take great care in making stock and bone broth to ensure we do not overheat the liquid when preparing them, but instead work to protect the gelatin they contain.

If we pressure can stock or bone broth, we will expose the liquid to a high temperature for an extended period of time, which risks "breaking" the gelatin. This means the gelatin becomes damaged and loses some of its excellent gut-soothing properties. So rather than losing the gelatin in our stock and bone broth, pressure canning broth is the better option. Broth is flavorful, nutritious, and rich in protein, but it is not as gelatinous as stock and bone broth, which makes it the perfect liquid for pressure canning.

PREP TIME: **30 MINUTES**
COOK TIME: **APPROXIMATELY 1 HOUR 30 MINUTES**
TOTAL TIME: **APPROXIMATELY 2 HOURS**
YIELD: **APPROXIMATELY 2 QUARTS**

EQUIPMENT

Large (10- to 12-quart) stainless steel or enameled stockpot

Long-handled stainless steel or wooden spoon

Food-safe kitchen twine

Slotted spoon

Fine-mesh strainer or colander

Flour sack towel or cheesecloth

Large, deep glass bowl

INGREDIENTS

1 (4–5 lb / 1.75–2.25 kg) whole chicken, cut into pieces and skin left on (remove the giblets and save them for another recipe)

Cold water sufficient to cover chicken parts

1 cup white vermouth (see **Cook's Notes**)

1 medium yellow onion, unpeeled and quartered

1 large carrot, unpeeled and rough chopped

1 celery rib, rough chopped

1 tsp whole black peppercorns

1 bay leaf

6 sprigs fresh Italian flat-leaf parsley

3 sprigs fresh thyme or ½ tsp dried thyme

1 Add the chicken pieces to a large stockpot. Fill the stockpot with just enough cold water to cover the chicken pieces. (Do not add too much water.)

2 Bring the water to a boil over high heat, then immediately reduce the heat to low. Skim off any foam that rises to the top. Add the white vermouth, onion, carrot, celery, black peppercorns, and bay leaf to the stockpot.

3 Using food-safe kitchen twine, tie the parsley and thyme sprigs together to make a bouquet garni. Add to the stockpot.

4 Bring the mixture back to a boil, stir well, and put the lid on the stockpot. Reduce the heat to low and simmer for 1½ hours or until the chicken is cooked through.

5 Once the chicken is cooked through, transfer the stockpot to a heatproof surface. Using a slotted spoon, remove the chicken pieces, vegetables, bay leaf, and the bouquet garni from the broth. (The chicken and vegetables can be eaten as is or saved for another recipe.)

6 Place a fine-mesh strainer or colander lined with a damp flour sack towel or cheesecloth over a large, deep bowl and pour the broth through it.

7 Either use a fat separator to de-fat the chicken broth or chill the broth. Once chilled, the fat will rise to the top, solidify, and then be easily removed. (Do not discard this fat! Save it for use in other recipes where you need a fat to sauté poultry or potatoes.) You now have a de-fatted, richly flavored chicken broth that can be pressure canned.

.... COOK'S NOTES ....

What nonalcoholic option can you use in place of white vermouth when making chicken broth? If you would prefer not to use alcohol when making chicken broth, you can substitute ¼ cup of apple cider vinegar or 2 tablespoons lemon juice. We want to acidify the broth in the making because the acid will leach out important nutrients from the chicken bones, creating a richly flavored broth that will also aid in digestion and assist in the assimilation of nutrients by our body.

Pressure Canning a Simple Chicken Broth

Pressure canning chicken broth ensures you have a rich, flavorful base ready for soups, stews, and other dishes at any time. This method preserves the deep, savory flavors and nutrients of homemade chicken broth, making it a convenient and healthy pantry staple.

PREP TIME: **30 MINUTES**
COOK TIME: **5 MINUTES**
PRESSURE CANNING PROCESSING TIME: **25 MINUTES**
TOTAL TIME: **1 HOUR**
YIELD: **APPROXIMATELY 2 QUARTS**

EQUIPMENT

Medium (6- to 8-quart) saucepan
Ladle
Wide-mouth funnel
Pressure canner and supplies
2 quart (32oz) regular-mouth or wide-mouth canning jars
2 regular-mouth or wide-mouth canning lids and bands

INGREDIENTS

2 quarts homemade de-fatted chicken broth
2 tsp canning and pickling salt, divided (optional)

1 **Steps 1–5:** Follow steps 1–5 in the "General Pressure Canning Guidelines" (p. 98).

2 **Steps 6–11:** These steps coordinate with steps 6–11 in the "General Pressure Canning Guidelines" but are unique to this recipe.

6. Pour the chicken broth into a medium saucepan over high heat. Bring the broth just to a boil, then transfer the saucepan to a heatproof surface.

7. Using the jar lifter, remove one jar from the canner, empty the hot water from the jar back into the canner, and place the jar on a cushioned surface.

8. Place a funnel over the opening of a prepared jar and use a ladle to fill the jar with the hot chicken broth. Add 1 teaspoon of salt, if desired.

9. Measure the headspace, leaving 1 inch (2.5cm).

10. Use a debubbler to remove any air bubbles from the jar.

11. Remeasure the headspace and add more hot chicken broth, if needed, to adjust the headspace to 1 inch (2.5cm).

3 **Steps 12–32:** Follow steps 12–32 in the "General Pressure Canning Guidelines" (p. 98).

························ COOK'S NOTES ························

What are the recommended processing times in a dial-gauge pressure canner for quart jars of chicken broth, based on altitude?

- 0 to 2,000 feet: 25 minutes, 11 psi
- 2,001 to 4,000 feet: 25 minutes, 12 psi
- 4,001 to 6,000 feet: 25 minutes, 13 psi
- 6,001 to 8,000 feet: 25 minutes, 14 psi

What are the recommended processing times in a weighted-gauge pressure canner for quart jars of chicken broth, based on altitude?

- 0 to 1,000 feet: 25 minutes, 10 psi
- Above 1,000 feet: 25 minutes, 15 psi

Why do you need to remove the canner lid soon after the processing is complete and then remove the jars from the canner within 5 minutes once the canner lid is removed?
Once the pressure canning processing is complete, including the depressurizing step, it's important not to delay the cool-down process. Leaving jars inside a closed or open canner slows the cooling significantly. If thermophilic bacteria (bacteria that thrive in relatively hot temperatures) are present, they can survive and grow, leading to spoilage, which results in an undesirable flavor and smell and can compromise the safety of your food.

What is the shelf life for Simple Chicken Broth?
Home-canned chicken broth is shelf stable for 12 months or longer, depending on the canning lid manufacturer's recommendations. Once opened, chicken broth must be refrigerated and will stay fresh for 3–4 days. If frozen, it will remain at peak freshness for 2–3 months.

Cubed Chicken

Hot packing cubed chicken allows you to preserve tender, juicy pieces that are perfect for quick meals. By pressure canning, you ensure that the chicken remains flavorful and safe for long-term storage and ready to be added to soups, casseroles, and salads. For extra nutrition, use chicken broth in place of water as the canning liquid.

PREP TIME: **30 MINUTES**
COOK TIME: **20 MINUTES**
PRESSURE CANNING PROCESSING TIME: **90 MINUTES**
TOTAL TIME: **2 HOURS 20 MINUTES**
YIELD: **APPROXIMATELY 2 QUARTS**

EQUIPMENT

Medium (6- to 8-quart) stainless steel saucepan or enameled Dutch oven

Tongs

Wooden spoon

Wide-mouth funnel

Slotted spoon

Ladle

Pressure canner and supplies

2 quart (32oz) regular-mouth or wide-mouth canning jars

2 regular-mouth or wide-mouth canning lids and bands

INGREDIENTS

1 (4–5 lb / 1.75–2.25kg) whole chicken (remove the giblets and save them for another recipe)

1 tbsp chicken fat (schmaltz) or other fat suitable for browning chicken

2 tsp canning and pickling salt, divided (optional)

Water or chicken broth (homemade or store-bought)

1 **Steps 1–5:** Follow steps 1–5 in the "General Pressure Canning Guidelines" (p. 98).

2 **Steps 6–11:** These steps coordinate with steps 6–11 in the "General Pressure Canning Guidelines" but are unique to this recipe.

6. a. On a clean work surface, use a sharp knife to cut up the chicken. Remove the chicken skin and then remove the chicken meat from the bones. (Save the skin and the bones for making bone broth.)

   b. Once all the chicken meat is removed from the bones, cut the meat into 1-inch (2.5-cm) pieces and set it aside.

   c. Melt the chicken fat in the saucepan over medium heat.

   d. Once the fat has melted, use the tongs to transfer the cubed chicken to the saucepan (working in batches, if necessary, so the chicken is not crowded in the pan).

   e. Brown the cubed chicken on all sides but only allow it to cook two-thirds of the way, about 10 minutes per batch. (This may take two batches to complete.) Drain off any fat from the saucepan.

   f. With the cubed chicken in the saucepan, add sufficient water (or chicken broth) to cover the chicken. Bring the water (or chicken broth) to a boil. Use a wooden spoon to scrape up any brown bits from the bottom of the saucepan. Stir well, then transfer the saucepan to a heatproof surface. (The water with the deglazed bits is your canning broth.)

7. Using the jar lifter, remove one jar from the canner, empty the hot water from the jar back into the canner, and place the jar on a cushioned surface.

8. Place a funnel over the opening of a prepared jar. Use a slotted spoon to remove some of the cubed chicken from the saucepan and transfer the chicken to the jar, leaving a 1¼-inch (3-cm) headspace. Add 1 teaspoon of salt to the jar, if desired. Using a ladle, fill the jar with the hot canning broth from the saucepan.

9. Measure the headspace, leaving 1¼ inch (3cm).

10. Use a debubbler to remove any air bubbles from the jar.

11. Remeasure the headspace and add more hot broth, if needed, to adjust the headspace to 1¼ inch (3cm).

3 **Steps 12–32:** Follow steps 12–32 in the "General Pressure Canning Guidelines" (p. 98).

COOK'S NOTES

What are the recommended processing times in a dial-gauge pressure canner for quart jars of cubed chicken, based on altitude?

- 0 to 2,000 feet: 90 minutes, 11 psi
- 2,001 to 4,000 feet: 90 minutes, 12 psi
- 4,001 to 6,000 feet: 90 minutes, 13 psi
- 6,001 to 8,000 feet: 90 minutes, 14 psi

What are the recommended processing times in a weighted-gauge pressure canner for quart jars of cubed chicken, based on altitude?

- 0 to 1,000 feet: 90 minutes, 10 psi
- Above 1,000 feet: 90 minutes, 15 psi

What is the shelf life for Hot-Packed Cubed Chicken?
Home-canned cubed chicken is shelf stable for 12 months or longer, depending on the canning lid manufacturer's recommendations. Once opened, cubed chicken must be refrigerated and will stay fresh for 3–4 days. If frozen, it will stay at peak freshness for 3 months.

Simple Beef Broth

Making homemade beef broth offers a wealth of benefits, including rich, deep flavors that far surpass store-bought versions. Often considered an elixir in traditional cultures, this broth contains protein, vitamins, and minerals that support digestion and immune function. By simmering beef with vegetables and herbs, you create a homemade broth that is delicious and free from artificial additives and preservatives.

Best of all, this form of beef broth is a by-product of making a delicious beef-based meal to feed a crowd. In the past, you may have discarded the water in which you simmered your roast—but never again! Now you know what a valuable commodity this liquid gold is in a traditional foods kitchen.

PREP TIME: **30 MINUTES**
COOK TIME: **APPROXIMATELY 4 HOURS**
TOTAL TIME: **APPROXIMATELY 4 HOURS 30 MINUTES**
YIELD: **APPROXIMATELY 2 QUARTS**

EQUIPMENT

Large (10- to 12-quart) stainless steel or enameled stockpot

Long-handled wooden spoon

Kitchen twine

Slotted spoon

Fine-mesh strainer or colander

Flour sack towel or cheesecloth

Large, deep glass bowl

INGREDIENTS

4 lb (1.75kg) beef shanks (bone-in chuck roast or 7-bone roast) (see **Cook's Notes**)

1 cup red vermouth or other fortified wine, such as Port, Marsala, or Madeira

Cold water sufficient to cover beef

1 medium yellow onion, unpeeled and quartered

1 large carrot, unpeeled and rough chopped

1 celery rib, rough chopped

1 tsp whole black peppercorns

1 bay leaf

2 sprigs fresh rosemary or ½ tsp dried rosemary

3 sprigs fresh thyme or ½ tsp dried thyme

1 Heat a large stockpot over medium heat for a few minutes.

2 Once you feel heat radiating from the bottom of the stockpot, add the beef. Allow it to brown a bit on all sides, moving it around with a wooden spoon. (You may have to do this in two batches if you are using shanks.) This should only take a few minutes. You are not looking for a dark sear, just some gentle browning which will add color and flavor to the final product.

3 Once the beef has browned, add the red vermouth (or other fortified wine) to the stockpot. Use a long-handled wooden spoon to help deglaze the bottom of the stockpot, loosening any brown bits that may have accumulated. If you prefer to omit alcohol, substitute ¼ cup apple cider vinegar or 2 tablespoons lemon juice.

4 Fill the stockpot with just enough cold water to cover the beef. Do not add too much water.

5 Bring the water to a boil over high heat, then immediately turn the heat down to low. Skim off any foam that rises to the top. Add the onion, carrot, celery, black peppercorns, and bay leaf to the stockpot.

6 Using food-safe kitchen twine, tie the rosemary and thyme sprigs together to make a bouquet garni. Add to the stockpot.

7 Bring the mixture back to a boil, stir well, put the lid on the stockpot, and reduce the heat to low. Simmer for 4 hours or until the beef is cooked through, falling-off-the-bone tender, and easy to shred.

8 Once the beef is cooked through, transfer the stockpot to a heatproof surface. Using a slotted spoon, remove the beef, vegetables, bay leaf, and bouquet garni from the broth.

9 The beef and vegetables can be eaten as is or saved for another recipe. (If you used shanks to make this broth, be sure to remove the marrow from the bones. Beef marrow is a nutrient-dense food and can be eaten as is or spread on toast points. If you do not plan to eat it immediately, you will want to refrigerate it.)

10 Place a mesh strainer or colander lined with a damp flour sack towel or cheesecloth over a large, deep bowl and pour the broth through it.

11 Either use a fat separator to de-fat the beef broth or chill the broth. Once chilled, the fat will rise to the top, solidify, and then be easily removed. (Do not discard this fat! Save it for use in other recipes where you need a fat with a high smoke point suitable for frying.) You now have a richly flavored, de-fatted beef broth that can be pressure canned.

COOK'S NOTES

What is a 7-bone roast? By today's standards, a 7-bone roast might be considered an old-fashioned cut of beef, but if you are lucky enough to find one at the farmer's market or from a local rancher, be sure to pick it up. (It may also be referred to as a center-cut pot roast or 7-bone steak.) This particular cut is from the chuck section of the cow (steer or heifer), so it is in the family of chuck roasts. But when so many chuck roasts today are sold boneless, searching for a 7-bone roast can provide the bone that will add a bit more richness and nutrients to your broth. This cut of beef includes a crosscut of the shoulder blade bone that is shaped like the number 7, which gives this roast its name.

But all of this might beg the question as to why we want to make broth with a bone if we are not looking to make a gelatinous broth to pressure can. Even though we are making a broth, as opposed to a stock or a bone broth, having a small amount of bone in relation to the amount of meat is crucial to traditional methods of preparing cooked meats and their broth. When meat is cooked on the bone, as has been done for centuries by traditional cultures, the meat and the broth are infused with nutrients from the bone as well as the connective tissues. This infusion makes the meat easier to digest and the broth more soothing to our digestive system, allowing us to better absorb the nutrients from our meals.

Pressure Canning a Simple Beef Broth

Pressure canning beef broth captures the hearty, robust flavors of homemade broth, making it an essential pantry item to be used as a base for soups, stews, gravies, and sauces—or simply as a sipping broth. This method locks in the nutrients and deep, savory taste, providing a convenient pantry staple you can use throughout the year.

PREP TIME: **30 MINUTES**
COOK TIME: **5 MINUTES**
PRESSURE CANNING PROCESSING TIME: **25 MINUTES**
TOTAL TIME: **1 HOUR**
YIELD: **APPROXIMATELY 2 QUARTS**

EQUIPMENT

Medium (6- to 8-quart) saucepan

Wide-mouth funnel

Ladle

Pressure canner and supplies

2 quart (32oz) regular-mouth or wide-mouth canning jars

2 regular-mouth or wide-mouth canning lids and bands

INGREDIENTS

2 quarts homemade de-fatted beef broth

2 tsp canning and pickling salt, divided (optional)

---

1 **Steps 1–5:** Follow steps 1–5 in the "General Pressure Canning Guidelines" (p. 98).

2 **Steps 6–11:** These steps coordinate with steps 6–11 in the "General Pressure Canning Guidelines" but are unique to this recipe.

6. Pour the beef broth into a medium saucepan over high heat. Bring the broth just to a boil, then transfer the saucepan to a heatproof surface.

7. Using the jar lifter, remove one jar from the canner, empty the hot water from the jar back into the canner, and place the jar on a cushioned surface.

8. Place a funnel over one of the prepared canning jars. Use a ladle to fill the jar with the hot beef broth. Add 1 teaspoon of salt to the jar, if desired.

9. Measure the headspace, leaving 1 inch (2.5cm).

10. Use a debubbler to remove any air bubbles from the jar.

11. Remeasure the headspace and add more hot beef broth, if needed, to adjust the headspace to 1 inch (2.5cm).

3 **Steps 12–32:** Follow steps 12–32 in the "General Pressure Canning Guidelines" (p. 98).

······················· COOK'S NOTES ·······················

What are the recommended processing times in a dial-gauge pressure canner for quart jars of beef broth, based on altitude?

- 0 to 2,000 feet: 25 minutes, 11 psi
- 2,001 to 4,000 feet: 25 minutes, 12 psi
- 4,001 to 6,000 feet: 25 minutes, 13 psi
- 6,001 to 8,000 feet: 25 minutes, 14 psi

What are the recommended processing times in a weighted-gauge pressure canner for quart jars of beef broth, based on altitude?

- 0 to 1,000 feet: 25 minutes, 10 psi
- Above 1,000 feet: 25 minutes, 15 psi

What is the shelf life for Simple Beef Broth? Home-canned beef broth is shelf stable for 12 months or longer, depending on the canning lid manufacturer's recommendations. Once opened, beef broth must be refrigerated and will stay fresh for 3–4 days. If frozen, it will stay at peak freshness for 2–3 months.

Cubed Beef

Hot packing cubed beef ensures that you have tender, flavorful meat ready for any meal. Pressure canning preserves the beef in a combination of water and its own juices, keeping it deliciously moist and convenient for stews, stir-fries, and more. However, you can also use beef broth as the liquid in which you can the cubed beef. This creates the most nutritious option. To get you started, this recipe calls for making only 1 quart of cubed beef, but you can increase the amount. If you add more cubed beef, you will most likely not need to add any additional fat, but you will need 1 teaspoon of salt per additional quart jar if you are using salt.

PREP TIME: **30 MINUTES**
COOK TIME: **5 MINUTES**
PRESSURE CANNING PROCESSING TIME: **90 MINUTES**
TOTAL TIME: **2 HOURS 5 MINUTES**
YIELD: **APPROXIMATELY 1 QUART**

EQUIPMENT

Medium (6- to 8-quart) stainless steel saucepan or enameled Dutch oven

Tongs

Wooden spoon

Wide-mouth funnel

Slotted spoon

Ladle

Pressure canner and supplies

1 quart (32oz) regular-mouth or wide-mouth canning jar

1 regular-mouth or wide-mouth canning lid and band

INGREDIENTS

2 lb (1kg) boneless rump roast (top round or bottom round), chuck roast, or similar cut

1 tbsp tallow or other fat suitable for browning beef

1 tsp canning and pickling salt (optional)

Water or beef broth (homemade or store-bought)

1 **Steps 1–5:** Follow steps 1–5 in the "General Pressure Canning Guidelines" (p. 98).

2 **Steps 6–11:** These steps coordinate with steps 6–11 in the "General Pressure Canning Guidelines" but are unique to this recipe.

6. a. Cut the beef into 1-inch (2.5-cm) cubes, removing as much visible exterior fat as possible. Set aside.

b. Melt the tallow in the saucepan over medium heat. Once the tallow has melted, use tongs to transfer the beef cubes to the saucepan, working in batches if necessary, so the beef is not crowded. Brown the beef on all sides but keep it rare—do not fully cook the beef—about 5 minutes per batch. (Most likely this can be accomplished in one batch.) Drain off any fat from the saucepan.

c. With the cubed beef still in the saucepan, add sufficient water or beef broth to deglaze the saucepan, then bring the water or beef broth to a boil over high heat. Use a wooden spoon to scrape up any brown bits from the bottom of the saucepan. Stir well, then transfer the saucepan to a heatproof surface. (The water with the deglazed bits is your canning broth.)

7. Using the jar lifter, remove one jar from the canner, empty the hot water from the jar back into the canner, and place the jar on a cushioned surface.

8. Place a funnel over the opening of the jar. Use a slotted spoon to remove the cubed beef from the saucepan and transfer it to the jar, leaving a 1-inch (2.5-cm) headspace. Add 1 teaspoon of salt to the jar, if desired. Using a ladle, fill the jar with the hot canning broth from the saucepan.

9. Measure the headspace, leaving 1 inch (2.5cm).

10. Use a debubbler to remove any air bubbles from the jar.

11. Remeasure the headspace and add more hot broth, if needed, to adjust the headspace to 1 inch (2.5cm).

Note: If you have enough beef to fill a second quart jar, repeat this process until a second jar is filled and placed into the canner. If you have just a small amount of beef left over, but it is not enough to fill a second jar, finish cooking the beef and then refrigerate it.

3 **Steps 12–32:** Follow steps 12–32 in the "General Pressure Canning Guidelines" (p. 98).

COOK'S NOTES

What are the recommended processing times in a dial-gauge pressure canner for a quart jar of cubed beef, based on altitude?

- 0 to 2,000 feet: 90 minutes, 11 psi
- 2,001 to 4,000 feet: 90 minutes, 12 psi
- 4,001 to 6,000 feet: 90 minutes, 13 psi
- 6,001 to 8,000 feet: 90 minutes, 14 psi

What are the recommended processing times in a weighted-gauge pressure canner for a quart jar of cubed beef, based on altitude?

- 0 to 1,000 feet: 90 minutes, 10 psi
- Above 1,000 feet: 90 minutes, 15 psi

What is the shelf life of Hot-Packed Cubed Beef?
Home-canned cubed beef is shelf stable for 12 months or longer, depending on the canning lid manufacturer's recommendations. Once opened, cubed beef must be refrigerated and will stay fresh for 3–4 days. If frozen, it will stay at peak freshness for 3 months.

Cubed Potatoes

Hot-packed cubed potatoes are a versatile addition to your pantry. Pressure canning these potatoes ensures they remain firm and flavorful, ready to be added to soups, stews, or corned beef hash; or simply sautéed with olive oil, garlic, and flat-leaf Italian parsley for a quick side dish.

For this recipe, you have the option of pressure canning in pints or quarts to have some flexibility as to which size will work best for the various recipes where you might use these cubed potatoes.

PREP TIME: **1 HOUR**
COOK TIME: **2 MINUTES**
PRESSURE CANNING PROCESSING TIME: **35 TO 40 MINUTES**
TOTAL TIME: **1 HOUR 37 MINUTES TO 1 HOUR 42 MINUTES**
YIELD: **APPROXIMATELY 7 QUARTS OR 9 PINTS**

EQUIPMENT

Very large glass bowl

Medium (6- to 8-quart) saucepan

Colander

Large (10- to 12-quart) stainless steel or enameled stockpot

Slotted spoon

Wide-mouth funnel

Ladle

Pressure canner and supplies

7 quart (32oz) or 9 pint (16oz) regular-mouth or wide-mouth canning jars

7 or 9 regular-mouth or wide-mouth canning lids and bands

INGREDIENTS

1 tsp ascorbic acid powder (or six 500mg vitamin C tablets, crushed)

20 lb (9kg) waxy potatoes for quarts (approximately 40 medium potatoes) or 13 lb (6kg) waxy potatoes for pints (approximately 26 medium potatoes), washed

7 tsp canning and pickling salt for quart jars or 3 ½ tsp for pint jars, divided (optional)

1 **Steps 1–5:** Follow steps 1–5 in the "General Pressure Canning Guidelines" (p. 98).

2 **Steps 6–11:** These steps coordinate with steps 6–11 in the "General Pressure Canning Guidelines" but are unique to this recipe.

6.   a. Fill a very large glass bowl with a half gallon of cold water. Add the ascorbic acid to the water and stir well until it is completely dissolved.

b. Working one at a time, peel a potato, rinse it under cold water, then dice the potato into ½-inch (1.25-cm) cubes. Place the potato cubes in the water containing the ascorbic acid. (This will prevent the potato cubes from darkening.) Continue in this way until you have processed all the potatoes. Set aside.

c. Fill the medium saucepan three-quarters full of water. Bring the water to a boil over high heat. The potatoes do not go into this saucepan. You will use this clean, fresh water later to fill the prepared jars.

d. Meanwhile, fill the large stockpot half full with water. Bring the water to a boil over high heat.

e. Drain the potato cubes from the ascorbic acid water in a colander placed in the sink.

f. Using a slotted spoon, carefully transfer the drained potatoes to the boiling water in the stockpot. Return the empty colander to the sink. Boil the potatoes for 2 minutes, then drain the potatoes into the colander that has been placed in the sink. Bring the colander over to the work surface near the canner.

7. Using the jar lifter, remove one jar from the canner, empty the hot water from the jar back into the canner, and place the jar on a cushioned surface.

8. Place a funnel over the opening of a prepared jar and use a slotted spoon to remove some of the hot cubed potatoes from the colander and transfer them to the jar, leaving a 1-inch (2.5-cm) headspace. Add 1 teaspoon of salt per prepared quart jar or ½ teaspoon of salt per prepared pint jar, if desired. Using a ladle, fill the jar with the clean boiling water from the saucepan. (The water in which you boiled the potato cubes should have been drained down the sink. You do not want to use the water you cooked the potato cubes in, because this water contains too much starch.)

9. Measure the headspace, leaving 1 inch (2.5cm).

10. Use a debubbler to remove any air bubbles from the jar.

11. Remeasure the headspace and add more clean hot water, if needed, to adjust the headspace to 1 inch (2.5cm).

3 **Steps 12–32:** Follow steps 12–32 in the "General Pressure Canning Guidelines" (p. 98).

········· COOK'S NOTES ·········

What are the recommended processing times in a dial-gauge pressure canner for pint jars of cubed potatoes, based on altitude?

- 0 to 2,000 feet: 35 minutes, 11 psi
- 2,001 to 4,000 feet: 35 minutes, 12 psi
- 4,001 to 6,000 feet: 35 minutes, 13 psi
- 6,001 to 8,000 feet: 35 minutes, 14 psi

What are the recommended processing times in a dial-gauge pressure canner for quart jars of cubed potatoes, based on altitude?

- 0 to 2,000 feet: 40 minutes, 11 psi
- 2,001 to 4,000 feet: 40 minutes, 12 psi
- 4,001 to 6,000 feet: 40 minutes, 13 psi
- 6,001 to 8,000 feet: 40 minutes, 14 psi

What are the recommended processing times in a weighted-gauge pressure canner for pint jars of cubed potatoes, based on altitude?

- 0 to 1,000 feet: 35 minutes, 10 psi
- Above 1,000 feet: 35 minutes, 15 psi

What are the recommended processing times in a weighted-gauge pressure canner for quart jars of cubed potatoes, based on altitude?

- 0 to 1,000 feet: 40 minutes, 10 psi
- Above 1,000 feet: 40 minutes, 15 psi

Don't throw out your potato peels! If you keep a sourdough starter, be sure to save your potato peels. Cover them with water and simmer them on the stovetop for a few minutes. Drain this "potato water" into a heatproof vessel. Once cool, use it to feed your sourdough starter in place of water. Your starter will thrive on the starchy potato water!

In addition to the water you make with the potato skins, you can also save the water you boiled the potatoes in rather than draining it down the sink. Your sourdough starter will love this potato water as well. But if you decide to save this water, make sure that you do not get confused and accidentally add it to your prepared canning jars.

What is the shelf life for Hot-Packed Cubed Potatoes? Home-canned cubed potatoes are shelf stable for 12 months or longer, depending on the canning lid manufacturer's recommendations. Once opened, cubed potatoes must be refrigerated and will stay fresh for 3–4 days. If frozen, cubed potatoes are best used within 3 months.

Sliced Carrots

Pressure canning sliced carrots is an excellent way to preserve their vibrant color, sweet flavor, and nutritional value, making them a pantry staple. By pressure canning, you ensure these low-acid vegetables are safely preserved and ready to use in a variety of dishes. Having a stock of home-canned sliced carrots means you can quickly add a nutritious side dish or ingredient to your meals without the need for refrigerator or freezer space. Plus, they retain their texture and taste, making them a delightful addition to your pantry.

PREP TIME: **30 MINUTES**
COOK TIME: **15 MINUTES**
PRESSURE CANNING PROCESSING TIME: **25 MINUTES**
TOTAL TIME: **1 HOUR 10 MINUTES**
YIELD: **APPROXIMATELY 9 PINTS**

EQUIPMENT

Large (10- to 12-quart) stainless steel or enameled stockpot

Crinkle cutter (optional)

Slotted spoon

Wide-mouth funnel

Ladle

Pressure canner and supplies

9 pint (16oz) wide-mouth canning jars

9 wide-mouth canning lids and bands

INGREDIENTS

About 11 lb (5kg) slim carrots with a diameter no larger than 1¼ inches (3cm) (approximately 100 medium-length, slim carrots)

4 ½ tsp canning and pickling salt, divided (optional)

1 **Steps 1–5:** Follow steps 1–5 in the "General Pressure Canning Guidelines" (p. 98).

2 **Steps 6–11:** These steps coordinate with steps 6–11 in the "General Pressure Canning Guidelines" but are unique to this recipe.

6.   a. Wash the carrots and then use a sharp knife to first remove the tip and the stem. (Save these scraps for making bone broth.) Peel the carrots and then rewash them.

b. Slice the carrots into round coins about ½ inch (1.25cm) thick. (If desired, a crinkle cutter can be used instead of a sharp knife for this process.)

c. Fill a large stockpot half full with water and bring to a boil over high heat.

d. With the water boiling, carefully add the sliced carrots to the stockpot. Return the water to a rolling boil, then reduce the heat to medium and simmer the carrots for 5 minutes.

e. After 5 minutes, transfer the stockpot to a heatproof surface.

7. Using the jar lifter, remove one jar from the canner, empty the hot water from the jar back into the canner, and place the jar on a cushioned surface.

8. Place a funnel over the opening of a prepared jar. Use a slotted spoon to remove some of the carrots from the stockpot and transfer them to the prepared jar, leaving a 1-inch (2.5-cm) headspace. Using a ladle, fill the prepared jar with the hot water from the stockpot.

9. Measure the headspace, leaving 1 inch (2.5cm).

10. Use a debubbler to remove any air bubbles from the jar.

11. Remeasure the headspace and add more hot water, if needed, to adjust the headspace to 1 inch (2.5cm).

3 **Steps 12–32:** Follow steps 12–32 in the "General Pressure Canning Guidelines" (p. 98).

COOK'S NOTES

What are the recommended processing times in a dial-gauge pressure canner for pint jars of sliced carrots, based on altitude?

- 0 to 2,000 feet: 25 minutes, 11 psi
- 2,001 to 4,000 feet: 25 minutes, 12 psi
- 4,001 to 6,000 feet: 25 minutes, 13 psi
- 6,001 to 8,000 feet: 25 minutes, 14 psi

What are the recommended processing times in a weighted-gauge pressure canner for pint jars of sliced carrots, based on altitude?

- 0 to 1,000 feet: 25 minutes, 10 psi
- Above 1,000 feet: 25 minutes, 15 psi

What is the shelf life for Sliced Carrots? Home-canned sliced carrots are shelf stable for 12 months or longer, depending on the canning lid manufacturer's recommendations. Once opened, the sliced carrots must be refrigerated and will stay fresh for 3–4 days. Home-canned carrots do not freeze well. Their texture can become quite mushy once defrosted. If you have an abundance of carrots and prefer not to pressure can them, it is better to blanch them, then freeze them. Their texture will hold up much better.

Chicken Vegetable Soup

Pressure canning Chicken Vegetable Soup allows you to have a hearty, homemade meal ready at a moment's notice. This method preserves the flavors and nutritional benefits of the chicken broth, chicken meat, and vegetables, making it a convenient and delicious option for busy days.

After you warm your home-canned soup on the stovetop, you can add cooked noodles or rice to make it a heartier soup if you wish. You can go even further to make your warmed soup a complete meal by adding some crusty sourdough bread on the side for the perfect dipping companion. A small salad with a simple olive oil and apple cider vinaigrette provides additional nutrition by rounding out the meal with some uncooked salad greens to aid digestion.

PREP TIME: **30 MINUTES**
COOK TIME: **45 MINUTES**
PRESSURE CANNING PROCESSING TIME: **75 MINUTES**
TOTAL TIME: **2 HOURS 30 MINUTES**
YIELD: **APPROXIMATELY 4 QUARTS**

EQUIPMENT

Large (10- to 12-quart) stockpot

Tongs

Slotted spoon

Wide-mouth funnel

Ladle

Pressure canner and supplies

4 quart (32oz) regular-mouth or wide-mouth canning jars

4 regular-mouth or wide-mouth canning lids and bands

INGREDIENTS

2 medium ears of fresh corn, husks removed

3 medium carrots, peeled and cut into ½-inch (1.25-cm) cubes

1 cup fresh green beans, cut into ½-inch (1.25-cm) pieces

1 medium yellow onion, chopped into ½-inch (1.25-cm) pieces

1 lb (450g) cooked chicken, shredded to ½ inch (1.25 cm) or less in width

½ tsp freshly ground black pepper

¼ tsp red pepper flakes (optional)

Approximately 12 cups chicken broth (homemade or store-bought)

Canning and pickling salt, to taste

1 Steps 1–5: Follow steps 1–5 in the "General Pressure Canning Guidelines" (p. 98).

2 Steps 6–11: These steps coordinate with steps 6–11 in the "General Pressure Canning Guidelines" but are unique to this recipe.

6.   a. Fill a stockpot half full with water. Bring the water to a rolling boil.

b. Using the tongs, lower the two ears of corn into the boiling water and blanch for 3 minutes.

c. Remove the corn from the water and remove the corn kernels from each cob. (Important! See **Cook's Notes** for the proper procedure for removing the kernels.) Set aside.

d. Empty the water from the stockpot, return the stockpot to the stovetop, and add the carrots, corn, green beans, onions, chicken, and black pepper. Add the red pepper flakes (if using).

e. Add all the chicken broth to the stockpot and bring the mixture to a rolling boil. Reduce the heat slightly and gently boil the soup for 30 minutes. Do not add anything else to the soup. (See **Cook's Notes**.)

f. Taste the soup and add salt, if desired. Transfer the stockpot to a heatproof surface.

7. Using the jar lifter, remove one jar from the canner, empty the hot water from the jar back into the canner, and place the jar on a cushioned surface.

8. Place a funnel over the opening of a prepared jar. Use a slotted spoon to remove some of the solids from the stockpot and transfer them to the jar, only filling the jar halfway. Using a ladle, fill the prepared jar with the hot broth from the stockpot.

9. Measure the headspace, leaving 1 inch (2.5cm).

10. Use a debubbler to remove any air bubbles from the jar.

11. Remeasure the headspace and add more hot broth, if needed, to adjust the headspace to 1 inch (2.5cm).

3 Steps 12–32: Follow steps 12–32 in the "General Pressure Canning Guidelines" (p. 98).

············· COOK'S NOTES ·············

What are the recommended processing times in a dial-gauge pressure canner for quart jars of soup, based on altitude?

- 0 to 2,000 feet: 75 minutes, 11 psi
- 2,001 to 4,000 feet: 75 minutes, 12 psi
- 4,001 to 6,000 feet: 75 minutes, 13 psi
- 6,001 to 8,000 feet: 75 minutes, 14 psi

What are the recommended processing times in a weighted-gauge pressure canner for quart jars of soup, based on altitude?

- 0 to 1,000 feet: 75 minutes, 10 psi
- Above 1,000 feet: 75 minutes, 15 psi

Important! How to properly remove corn kernels from the cob to prepare for pressure canning. When removing corn kernels from a corn cob, you will want to cut the corn from the cob at about three-fourths the depth of the kernels. Do not scrape the cob. You want to avoid collecting any additional and unnecessary starch.

Can you add noodles to this soup before pressure canning it? Do not add noodles, pasta, rice, flour, cream, milk, or other thickening agents to home-canned soups before pressure canning them. These ingredients are not approved for pressure canning. If you want to add any of these ingredients to your soup, you must add them when reheating the home-canned soup.

What is the shelf life for Chicken Vegetable Soup? Home-canned soup is shelf stable for 12 months or longer, depending on the canning lid manufacturer's recommendations. Once opened, the soup must be refrigerated and will stay fresh for 3–4 days. If frozen, it will stay at peak freshness for 3 months.

Cowboy-Style Beef Stew

Pressure canning Cowboy-Style Beef Stew means you can enjoy a robust, flavorful meal anytime. This hearty stew, filled with tender beef, vegetables, and savory spices, is preserved to perfection, ensuring a quick and satisfying dinner is always within reach.

PREP TIME: **1 HOUR**
COOK TIME: **30 MINUTES**
PRESSURE CANNING PROCESSING TIME: **90 MINUTES**
TOTAL TIME: **3 HOURS**
YIELD: **APPROXIMATELY 7 QUARTS**

EQUIPMENT

4-quart (or larger) saucepan

Large (10- to 12-quart) stockpot

Tongs

Wide-mouth funnel

Ladle

Pressure canner and supplies

7 quart (32oz) regular-mouth or wide-mouth canning jars

7 regular-mouth or wide-mouth canning lids and bands

INGREDIENTS

Boiling water or beef broth (homemade or store-bought), sufficient to cover all ingredients in stockpot

1 (4–5 lb / 1.75–2.25 kg) beef chuck roast or rump roast

1 tbsp tallow

15 medium waxy potatoes, peeled and cubed in ½-inch (1.25-cm) pieces

16 medium carrots, peeled and cubed in ½-inch (1.25-cm) pieces

2–3 medium yellow onions, chopped

3 green chiles, chopped (Anaheim or Hatch)

3 cups cooked pinto beans

1 tsp ancho chili powder

½ tsp coarsely ground black pepper

Canning and pickling salt, to taste

1 **Steps 1–5:** Follow steps 1–5 in the "General Pressure Canning Guidelines" (p. 98).

2 **Steps 6–11:** These steps coordinate with steps 6–11 in the "General Pressure Canning Guidelines" but are unique to this recipe.

6.   a. Prepare the water, beef broth, or a combination of the two by bringing it to a boil in a saucepan large enough to hold at least 4 quarts.

b. Cut the beef into 1-inch (2.5-cm) cubes, removing as much visible exterior fat as possible. Set aside.

c. Melt the tallow in a stockpot over medium heat.

d. Once the tallow has melted, use tongs to transfer the beef cubes to the stockpot, working in batches if necessary, so the beef is not crowded. Brown the beef on all sides, approximately 5 minutes per batch.

e. Transfer the browned beef to a plate and drain any residual fat from the stockpot.

f. Return the beef to the stockpot and add the potatoes, carrots, onions, green chiles, beans, chili powder, and black pepper.

g. Add enough boiling water, boiling beef broth, or a combination of the two to the stockpot to cover all the ingredients. Stir well and bring to a boil. Reduce the heat to medium and simmer for 5 minutes. Taste the stew and season with salt, if desired. Turn off the heat and transfer the stockpot to a heatproof surface.

7. Using the jar lifter, remove one jar from the canner, empty the hot water from the jar back into the canner, and place the jar on a cushioned surface.

8. Place a funnel over the opening of a prepared jar and use a ladle to add the hot beef stew to the jar.

9. Measure the headspace, leaving 1 inch (2.5cm).

10. Use a debubbler to remove any air bubbles from the jar.

11. Remeasure the headspace and add more beef stew, if needed, to adjust the headspace to 1 inch (2.5cm). Do not thicken the stew. (See **Cook's Notes**.)

3 **Steps 12–32:** Follow steps 12–32 in the "General Pressure Canning Guidelines" (p. 98).

······················ COOK'S NOTES ······················

What are the recommended processing times in a dial-gauge pressure canner for quart jars of beef stew, based on altitude?

- 0 to 2,000 feet: 90 minutes, 11 psi
- 2,001 to 4,000 feet: 90 minutes, 12 psi
- 4,001 to 6,000 feet: 90 minutes, 13 psi
- 6,001 to 8,000 feet: 90 minutes, 14 psi

What are the recommended processing times in a weighted-gauge pressure canner for quart jars of beef stew, based on altitude?

- 0 to 1,000 feet: 90 minutes, 10 psi
- Above 1,000 feet: 90 minutes, 15 psi

The beef stew is very watery. Can you thicken it before pressure canning it? No. This beef stew will appear watery, but *do not* thicken it. Thickening agents will interfere with successful canning. When you are ready to consume the contents of the jar, you can thicken the stew while you are warming it.

You can thicken one quart jar of this beef stew by adding a beurre manié (kneaded butter). This paste is made of equal parts soft butter and flour and is used to thicken soups and sauces—and in this case, pressure-canned stew. Knead 1 tablespoon butter with 1 tablespoon all-purpose flour and add it to the stew as you warm it on the stovetop. Mix well, bring the stew to a boil, then turn down to a simmer, and the stew should thicken nicely.

What is the shelf life for Cowboy-Style Beef Stew? Home-canned beef stew is shelf stable for 12 months or longer, depending on the canning lid manufacturer's recommendations. Once opened, the beef stew must be refrigerated and will stay fresh for 3–4 days. If frozen, it will stay at peak freshness for 3 months.

Pressure-Canned Fresh Green Beans

Green beans are sometimes called string beans, but most green beans today are stringless, making them easy to prepare for pressure canning. You can use this method for pressure canning fresh green beans, French haricots verts, Italian flat green beans (sometimes called Romano green beans), and yellow wax beans.

PREP TIME: **30 MINUTES**
COOK TIME: **15 MINUTES**
PRESSURE CANNING PROCESSING TIME: **20 MINUTES**
TOTAL TIME: **1 HOUR 5 MINUTES**
YIELD: **APPROXIMATELY 9 PINTS**

EQUIPMENT

Large (10- to 12-quart) stainless steel or enameled stockpot

Wide-mouth funnel

Slotted spoon

Ladle

Pressure canner and supplies

9 pint (16oz) wide-mouth canning jars

9 wide-mouth canning lids and bands

INGREDIENTS

9 lb (4kg) fresh green beans

4 ½ tsp canning and pickling salt, divided (optional)

1 **Steps 1–5:** Follow steps 1–5 in the "General Pressure Canning Guidelines" (p. 98).

2 **Steps 6–11:** These steps coordinate with steps 6–11 in the "General Pressure Canning Guidelines" but are unique to this recipe.

6. a. Wash the beans and trim the ends. Leave them whole or cut them into pieces ranging in size from 1 to 2 inches (2.5 to 5cm).

b. Fill a stockpot with water and bring it to a boil over high heat.

c. Carefully add the beans to the boiling water and boil for 5 minutes.

d. Transfer the stockpot to a heatproof surface.

7. Using the jar lifter, remove one jar from the canner, empty the hot water from the jar back into the canner, and place the jar on a cushioned surface.

8. Place a funnel over the opening of a prepared jar. Use a slotted spoon to remove some of the beans from the stockpot and transfer them to the jar, leaving a 1-inch (2.5-cm) headspace. Add a ½ teaspoon salt to the jar, if desired. Using a ladle, fill the jar with the hot cooking liquid from the stockpot.

9. Measure the headspace, leaving 1 inch (2.5cm).

10. Use a debubbler to remove any air bubbles from the jar.

11. Remeasure the headspace and add more hot cooking water, if needed, to adjust the headspace to 1 inch (2.5cm).

3 **Steps 12–32:** Follow steps 12–32 in the "General Pressure Canning Guidelines" (p. 98).

········· COOK'S NOTES ·········

What are the recommended processing times in a dial-gauge pressure canner for pint jars of green beans, based on altitude?

- 0 to 2,000 feet: 20 minutes, 11 psi
- 2,001 to 4,000 feet: 20 minutes, 12 psi
- 4,001 to 6,000 feet: 20 minutes, 13 psi
- 6,001 to 8,000 feet: 20 minutes, 14 psi

What are the recommended processing times in a weighted-gauge pressure canner for pint jars of green beans, based on altitude?

- 0 to 1,000 feet: 20 minutes, 10 psi
- Above 1,000 feet: 20 minutes, 15 psi

What is the storage time for Fresh Green Beans?
Home-canned green beans are shelf stable for 12 months or longer, depending on the canning lid manufacturer's recommendations. Once opened, the green beans must be refrigerated and will stay fresh for 3–4 days. Home-canned green beans, like most cooked green beans, do not freeze well. Their texture can become quite mushy and unappetizing once defrosted.

How to Pressure Can All Varieties of Dried Beans

Examples of dried beans include garbanzo, navy, and pinto beans, but this method of pressure canning will work for all varieties of beans. Make sure that you are canning relatively fresh dried beans. Old beans are not good candidates for pressure canning.

PREP TIME: **12 HOURS TO 18 HOURS**
COOK TIME: **30 MINUTES**
PRESSURE CANNING PROCESSING TIME: **75 MINUTES**
TOTAL TIME: **13 HOURS 45 MINUTES TO 19 HOURS 45 MINUTES**
YIELD: **APPROXIMATELY 9 PINTS**

EQUIPMENT

Colander

Large (10- to 12-quart) stockpot

Slotted spoon

Wide-mouth funnel

Ladle

Pressure canner and supplies

9 pint (16oz) wide-mouth canning jars

9 wide-mouth canning lids and bands

INGREDIENTS

3 ¼ lb (1.5kg) dried beans (any variety)

4 ½ tsp canning and pickling salt, divided (optional)

1   Rinse the beans well in a colander and pick out any stones or discolored beans.

2   Place the beans in a large stockpot and cover them with cool water by at least 2 inches (5cm). If any beans float to the top, remove and discard them. You can soak the beans for anywhere from 12 to 18 hours, based on the package directions and your schedule.

3   **Steps 1–5:** Follow steps 1–5 in the "General Pressure Canning Guidelines" (p. 98).

4   **Steps 6–11:** These steps coordinate with steps 6–11 in the "General Pressure Canning Guidelines" but are unique to this recipe.

6.   a. After the soaking time is completed, drain the water from the beans and re-cover the beans with fresh water. Bring the beans to a rolling boil over high heat.

b. When the beans come to a full boil, skim off any foam that rises to the top of the water. Boil the beans, uncovered, for 30 minutes.

c. Transfer the stockpot to a heatproof surface.

7. Using the jar lifter, remove one jar from the canner, empty the hot water from the jar back into the canner, and place the jar on a cushioned surface.

8. Place a funnel over the opening of a prepared jar and use a slotted spoon to remove some of the hot beans from the stockpot and transfer them to the jar, leaving a 1-inch (2.5-cm) headspace. Add ½ teaspoon of salt to the jar, if desired. Using a ladle, fill the prepared jar with the cooking water from the stockpot.

9. Measure the headspace, leaving 1 inch (2.5cm).

10. Use a debubbler to remove any air bubbles from the jar.

11. Remeasure the headspace and add more hot cooking water, if needed, to adjust the headspace to 1 inch (2.5cm).

5   **Steps 12–32:** Follow steps 12–32 in the "General Pressure Canning Guidelines" (p. 98).

COOK'S NOTES

What are the recommended processing times in a dial-gauge pressure canner for pint jars of beans, based on altitude?

- 0 to 2,000 feet: 75 minutes, 11 psi
- 2,001 to 4,000 feet: 75 minutes, 12 psi
- 4,001 to 6,000 feet: 75 minutes, 13 psi
- 6,001 to 8,000 feet: 75 minutes, 14 psi

What are the recommended processing times in a weighted-gauge pressure canner for pint jars of beans, based on altitude?

- 0 to 1,000 feet: 75 minutes, 10 psi
- Above 1,000 feet: 75 minutes, 15 psi

What is the shelf life for Home-Canned Dried Beans?
Home-canned beans are shelf stable for 12 months or longer, depending on the canning lid manufacturer's recommendations.

Ground Beef Chili with Beans

Pressure canning Ground Beef Chili with Beans captures the hearty flavors of homemade chili, making it a perfect pantry addition. This method ensures your chili is ready to serve on busy nights, offering a delicious and comforting meal with minimal effort. Just pop open a jar and heat through—dinner is served! If you want to get fancy, top your chili with grated cheese, sliced avocado, and a dollop of sour cream.

PREP TIME: **30 MINUTES**
COOK TIME: **30 MINUTES**
PRESSURE CANNING PROCESSING TIME: **75 MINUTES**
TOTAL TIME: **2 HOURS 15 MINUTES**
YIELD: **APPROXIMATELY 9 PINTS**

EQUIPMENT

Large (10- to 12-quart) stockpot

Wide-mouth funnel

Ladle

Pressure canner and supplies

9 pint (16oz) wide-mouth canning jars

9 wide-mouth canning lids and bands

INGREDIENTS

3 lb (1.35kg) lean ground beef

1 medium yellow onion, chopped

6 green chiles, seeded and chopped (Anaheim or Hatch)

1 tsp freshly ground black pepper

1 tbsp ground coriander

1 tbsp ground cumin

1 tbsp chili powder of your choice (see **Cook's Notes**)

6 cups cooked dark red kidney beans (from dried or canned)

2 quarts crushed tomatoes (see **Cook's Notes**)

Canning and pickling salt, to taste (optional)

9 tbsp bottled lime juice, divided, or 2 ¼ tsp citric acid, divided (see **Cook's Notes**)

9 tsp sugar, divided (optional)

1 **Steps 1–5:** Follow steps 1–5 in the "General Pressure Canning Guidelines" (p. 98).

2 **Steps 6–11:** These steps coordinate with steps 6–11 in the "General Pressure Canning Guidelines" but are unique to this recipe.

6. a. Add the ground beef, onion, and green chiles to a large stockpot over medium heat. Sauté until the ground beef is browned and the onions and chiles have softened. Drain off any fat that has accumulated in the stockpot.

b. Add the black pepper, coriander, cumin, and chili powder to the stockpot with the ground beef mixture. Stir well so the spices coat the mixture, then add the cooked kidney beans and tomatoes. Stir well to combine.

c. Bring the mixture to a boil over high heat, stirring periodically to prevent it from sticking to the bottom of the stockpot or burning. Once the mixture comes to a boil, reduce the heat to medium and simmer for 5 minutes. Taste the chili and season with salt, if desired. Transfer the stockpot to a heatproof surface. (Do not thicken this chili before pressure canning it.)

7. Using the jar lifter, remove one jar from the canner, empty the hot water from the jar back into the canner, and place the jar on a cushioned surface.

8. Place a funnel over the opening of a prepared jar and use a ladle to add the chili to the jar, slightly shy of a 1-inch (2.5-cm) headspace. Add 1 tablespoon lime juice or a ¼ teaspoon citric acid to the jar. Add 1 teaspoon sugar to the jar, if desired.

9. Measure the headspace, leaving 1 inch (2.5cm).

10. Use a debubbler to remove any air bubbles from the jar.

11. Remeasure the headspace and add more chili, if needed, to adjust the headspace to 1 inch (2.5cm).

3 **Steps 12–32:** Follow steps 12–32 in the "General Pressure Canning Guidelines" (p. 98).

What are the recommended processing times in a dial-gauge pressure canner for pint jars of ground beef chili with beans, based on altitude?

- 0 to 2,000 feet: 75 minutes, 11 psi
- 2,001 to 4,000 feet: 75 minutes, 12 psi
- 4,001 to 6,000 feet: 75 minutes, 13 psi
- 6,001 to 8,000 feet: 75 minutes, 14 psi

What are the recommended processing times in a weighted-gauge pressure canner for pint jars of ground beef chili with beans, based on altitude?

- 0 to 1,000 feet: 75 minutes, 10 psi
- Above 1,000 feet: 75 minutes, 15 psi

Which chili powder is best to add when making chili with ground beef and beans? There are quite a few possibilities for adding chili powder to any recipe. In this case, you can use basic chili powder, which is labeled as such and sold at most grocery stores. Other options I like are ancho chili powder or chipotle chili powder for a smoky flavor. One tablespoon of chili powder in this recipe makes a mildly spicy chili. If you like a lot of heat, you can add more chili powder, but taste it as you go, using a clean spoon each time. Too much chili powder will make your chili unpalatable!

Are you required to add the bottled lime juice to this chili recipe? The NCHFP does not require bottled lemon juice (lime juice or citric acid) to be added to pressure-canned chili with crushed tomatoes. However, the lime juice in this recipe adds a nice flavor and helps cut some of the heaviness of the meat and beans.

What can you use in this recipe if you do not have 2 quarts of crushed tomatoes on hand? Store-bought crushed tomatoes are generally sold in 28-ounce (794g) cans. Although not an exact substitution, you can use two 28-ounce (794g) cans of crushed tomatoes in this recipe, but add an additional 1 cup of water to the stockpot along with the canned crushed tomatoes.

What is the shelf life for Ground Beef Chili with Beans? Home-canned Ground Beef Chili with Beans is shelf stable for 12 months or longer, depending on the canning lid manufacturer's recommendations. Once opened, the chili must be refrigerated and will stay fresh for 3–4 days. If frozen, it will stay at peak freshness for 3 months.

Spaghetti Sauce with Meat

Having homemade Spaghetti Sauce with Meat tucked into your pantry makes it easy to throw together a spaghetti dinner in minutes. This sauce is also budget friendly since it uses only a modest amount of ground beef. But it's certainly not lacking in flavor thanks to the Italian plum tomatoes used as the base, along with a sprinkling of Italian seasoning. You'll have the perfect, yet simple, sauce ready and waiting on your pantry shelf. Plus, it's a fantastic way to take advantage of seasonal ingredients, ensuring you have a taste of summer's bounty from your kitchen garden—or the farmer's market—all year round.

PREP TIME: **1 HOUR**
COOK TIME: **1–2 HOURS**
PRESSURE CANNING PROCESSING TIME: **70 MINUTES**
TOTAL TIME: **3 HOURS 10 MINUTES TO 4 HOURS 10 MINUTES**
YIELD: **APPROXIMATELY 5 QUARTS**

EQUIPMENT

Large (10- to 12-quart) stainless steel or enameled stockpot

Long-handled wooden spoon

Slotted spoon

2 large glass bowls

Large stainless steel or enameled skillet

Immersion blender or blender

Wide-mouth funnel

Ladle

Pressure canner and supplies

5 quart (32oz) regular-mouth or wide-mouth canning jars

5 regular-mouth or wide-mouth canning lids and bands

INGREDIENTS

30 lb (13.5kg) Italian plum tomatoes, Roma or San Marzano varieties (approximately 120 large Italian plum tomatoes)

2 ½ lb (1.15kg) lean ground beef (see **Cook's Notes**)

5 cloves garlic, minced

1 medium yellow onion, chopped into ½-inch (1.25-cm) pieces

1 large green bell pepper, chopped into ½-inch (1.25-cm) pieces

2 medium carrots, peeled and chopped into ½-inch (1.25-cm) pieces

¼ cup fresh flat-leaf Italian parsley, minced

1 tbsp dried Italian seasoning (optionally, you can use ½ tbsp dried oregano and ½ tbsp dried basil)

1 tsp freshly ground black pepper

1 tsp red pepper flakes (optional)

Canning and pickling salt, to taste

5 tsp granulated sugar, divided (optional)

1 **Steps 1–5:** Follow steps 1–5 in the "General Pressure Canning Guidelines" (p. 98).

2 **Steps 6–11:** These steps coordinate with steps 6–11 in the "General Pressure Canning Guidelines" but are unique to this recipe.

6.   a. Fill a large bowl half full with ice and water. Set aside. (This is your water bath.)

b. Fill the stockpot half full with water. Put the lid on the stockpot. Slowly bring the water to a rolling boil as you prepare the tomatoes. This will be your blanching water.

c. Wash the tomatoes and score the blossom or stem ends with a crosshatch. (I find it easier to remove the tomato skin if I crosshatch the stem end.)

d. Remove the lid from the stockpot and check to make sure the water is at a full rolling boil. Working in batches of 4 to 6 tomatoes at a time, use a slotted spoon to lower the tomatoes into the boiling water for 30 to 60 seconds or until the skins split. This process is called blanching.

e. Once the tomato skins split, use a slotted spoon to remove the tomatoes one at a time from the stockpot and lower them into the bowl containing the ice water bath. (Refresh the ice water periodically with more ice to keep the water very cold.) Peel the skins off each tomato and transfer the peeled tomatoes to a large, clean glass bowl. Repeat this process until all the tomatoes have had their skins removed.

f. Slice the skinless tomatoes in half, remove the cores, trim off any discolorations or blemished areas, and then slice each tomato half in half again. Set aside.

g. Empty the blanching water from the stockpot and place the stockpot back on the stovetop. Add all the tomatoes to the stockpot and bring them to a boil over high heat. Stir continuously to keep the tomatoes from sticking to the bottom of the stockpot or burning. Once the tomatoes come to a boil, reduce the heat to medium, cover the stockpot with a lid, and allow the tomatoes to simmer.

h. Periodically remove the lid and stir the tomatoes with a wooden spoon to make sure they are not sticking to the bottom of the stockpot. If they are, reduce the heat to low, re-cover the stockpot, and continue simmering.

i. As the tomatoes simmer, use a large skillet to sauté the ground beef until brown. Add the garlic, onions, peppers, and carrots to the skillet and continue to sauté until the vegetables are tender.

j. Remove the lid from the stockpot and turn off the heat. Carefully use an immersion blender to purée the tomatoes. Alternatively, working in batches, transfer the tomatoes to a blender and purée. Return the tomatoes to the stockpot.

k. Once the tomatoes are puréed to a smooth texture, add the contents of the skillet to the stockpot. Add the parsley, Italian seasoning, black pepper, and red pepper flakes (if using). Stir well to combine.

l. Bring the mixture in the stockpot to a boil over high heat, then reduce the heat to medium and simmer the mixture uncovered. Stir the mixture periodically to prevent it from sticking to the bottom of the stockpot. Taste the mixture and add salt, if desired. Stir well to distribute the salt.

m. Reduce the sauce by half.

n. When the proper consistency of the sauce is reached, transfer the stockpot to a heatproof surface.

7. Using the jar lifter, remove one jar from the canner, empty the hot water from the jar back into the canner, and place the jar on a cushioned surface.

8. Place a funnel over the opening of a prepared jar and use a ladle to add the hot spaghetti sauce to the jar, leaving a 1-inch (2.5-cm) headspace. Add 1 teaspoon sugar to the jar, if desired.

9. Measure the headspace, leaving 1 inch (2.5cm).

10. Use a debubbler to remove any air bubbles from the jar.

11. Remeasure the headspace and add more sauce, if needed, to adjust the headspace to 1 inch (2.5cm).

3 **Steps 12–32:** Follow steps 12–32 in the "General Pressure Canning Guidelines" (p. 98).

···················· COOK'S NOTES ····················

What are the recommended processing times in a dial-gauge pressure canner for quart jars of spaghetti sauce with meat, based on altitude?

- 0 to 2,000 feet: 70 minutes, 11 psi
- 2,001 to 4,000 feet: 70 minutes, 12 psi
- 4,001 to 6,000 feet: 70 minutes, 13 psi
- 6,001 to 8,000 feet: 70 minutes, 14 psi

What are the recommended processing times in a weighted-gauge pressure canner for quart jars of spaghetti sauce with meat, based on altitude:

- 0 to 1,000 feet: 70 minutes, 10 psi
- Above 1,000 feet: 70 minutes, 15 psi

Can you use other meats in place of the ground beef in this recipe? Yes, you can use ground turkey, or if you are a hunter or have access to wild game, you can use ground venison in this recipe. Although ground pork is approved for pressure canning as part of a meat-based spaghetti sauce, you need to make sure that you brown the ground pork very well to release as much fat as possible and then drain off the fat before proceeding with the recipe. Too much fat in a canning jar can seriously impede the lid from making a tight, clean seal if the fat is siphoned out of the jar during the canning process.

A note about changes in texture of ground beef in pressure canned spaghetti sauce: If you think the amount of ground beef called for in this recipe seems small, you're right. But there is a good reason for this. When ground beef is pressure canned, it can sometimes change in texture and be chewy. This change can be considered, by some, to be less than desirable. However, this change is less noticeable when you add a modest amount of ground beef to the tomato sauce.

What is the shelf life for Spaghetti Sauce with Meat? Home-canned Spaghetti Sauce with Meat is shelf stable for 12 months or longer, depending on the canning lid manufacturer's recommendations. Once opened, the spaghetti sauce must be refrigerated and will stay fresh for 3–4 days. If frozen, it will stay at peak freshness for 3 months. After 3 months it may develop freezer burn and its flavor will begin to degrade.

Traditional Marinara Sauce

Pressure canning Traditional Marinara Sauce ensures you have a rich, savory sauce ready to enhance your favorite Italian dishes. This method preserves the fresh, robust flavors of tomatoes, garlic, and basil, making it a convenient and delicious pantry staple.

You might have encountered many variations on how to make marinara, but the basic recipe is actually a very simple sauce made from passata, or more accurately, passata di pomodoro. This Italian phrase translates to tomato purée in English.

Passata is simply fresh tomatoes, generally Italian plum "paste" varieties such as Roma or San Marzano, that have been chopped up, usually salted to pull out some of the liquid, and then run through a food mill to create a simple, perfectly smooth tomato purée. When commercially prepared and sold at the grocery store, passata is usually available in two varieties: plain or with a basil leaf added to it. It doesn't have any additional flavorings, making it useful in any recipe calling for tomato purée.

You can use passata to make marinara sauce. So, in essence, it is the building block for creating a traditional marinara with an unadulterated tomato flavor. Your marinara can be as simple as simmering the passata along with a bit of olive oil and garlic. You can also add basil to a basic marinara if the passata does not contain it. Some home cooks will add a bit of onion, some oregano (dried or fresh), black pepper, a bit of red wine, and maybe a few red pepper flakes for spice, but none of this is required. The marinara is then cooked down a bit to allow for some evaporation so it can thicken slightly and become a deep, rich red.

Traditionally, the bottom line is that a marinara should be smooth. Today, many home cooks make marinara chunky, but that makes it less versatile. You can use a traditional smooth marinara as a pasta sauce, a topping sauce, or a dipping sauce.

PREP TIME: **4–5 HOURS–IF WORKING ALONE (HELPFUL FRIENDS MAKE THE JOB GO QUICKER!)**
COOK TIME: **30 MINUTES TO 1 HOUR**
PRESSURE CANNING PROCESSING TIME: **25 MINUTES**
TOTAL TIME: **4 HOURS 55 MINUTES TO 6 HOURS 25 MINUTES**
YIELD: **APPROXIMATELY 7 QUARTS**

STEP 1: MAKE THE PASSATA DI POMODORO

Before we make the traditional marinara, we will make the passata. The first thing I want to say about this process is that we are going old school here, and it is a labor of love. But it can be a fun activity when friends pitch in to help. Plus, you can send them home with some homemade, home-canned marinara as a reward!

For the most part, making passata is easy; it's just time-consuming. However, I highly recommend that you use a food mill. This kitchen tool is relatively inexpensive and will come in handy for making a host of other homemade foods, including applesauce. (You don't need to peel, core, or deseed the apples!)

If you do not have a food mill, you will first need to blanch the tomatoes to remove the skins, then slice them in half, remove the core and seeds, and purée them. The tomatoes are best puréed with an immersion blender. You can also use a regular blender; however, investing in a food mill will save you considerable time and create a better final product.

If you have an old-fashioned potato ricer tucked in the back of your kitchen cabinet, you can use the ricer in place of a food mill. The only drawback is that you will have to work in smaller batches than you would with a food mill. As a last resort, you can use a fine-mesh strainer to push the tomatoes through, leaving the skins and seeds behind. But this last technique takes a good amount of elbow grease!

The other supplies you will need to make a traditional passata include a few large plastic tubs (approximately the size of a large rectangular laundry basket), a few rectangular perforated plastic laundry baskets (preferably the stronger type that have the thick plastic handles on each side), and some type of cloth to strain the tomatoes. You will want to use something thicker than cheesecloth. In a pinch, a flour sack towel will work, but you will need to work in batches, which drags out this process. An old, clean, cotton king-size pillowcase is an option. But for the best way to do this, you can do what my Italian relatives have done for generations and use an old clean bed sheet. Yes, a bed sheet! They grew a lot of tomatoes and made a boatload of passata!

EQUIPMENT

Large glass or stainless steel bowl

Food mill fitted with fine blade

3–4 large plastic rectangular laundry baskets (approximately 26 × 18 inch/66 × 46cm)

3–4 large clean cotton cloths, pillowcases, or bed sheets

3–4 large plastic rectangular tubs (approximately the 60-quart size)

INGREDIENTS

Approximately 50 lb (23kg) large Italian plum tomatoes, Roma or San Marzano varieties (see **Cook's Notes**)

Canning and pickling salt

1 The easiest way to start this process is to place a plastic perforated laundry basket into a large plastic tub and line the basket with a cotton sheet. Otherwise, use an old pillowcase with the open end facing up in which you can place the tomatoes. The laundry basket should be slightly larger than the plastic tub so that when you lower it into the tub, it is slightly elevated.

2 Wash a tomato, cut out and discard the top (the stem end), and cut out any discolored bits. Next, cut the tomato in half and remove the watery pulp, seeds, and core. (Don't discard these. Save them for making Tomato Powder [p. 160].) Place the tomato onto the sheet or into the pillowcase.

3 Continue this process until you have about 2 pounds (1kg) of tomatoes on the sheet. Sprinkle the tomatoes with approximately 1 tablespoon salt, then place another 2-pound layer of tomatoes on top of the salted tomatoes. Sprinkle this second layer with 1 tablespoon salt. Continue this process until the sheet-covered laundry basket is full of tomatoes.

4 Prepare a second tub with a sheet-lined laundry basket and continue to layer with tomatoes and salt.

5 Continue preparing tubs and sheet-lined laundry baskets until all the tomatoes have been layered and salted.

6 Once all the tomatoes have been layered and salted, allow the tomatoes to drain for 2 to 3 hours to draw out as much moisture as possible.

7 After the allotted time, bundle up and twist each individual sheet or pillowcase and do your best to wring out any remaining tomato liquid. (See **Cook's Notes**.)

8 Working in batches, run the tomatoes through a food mill fitted with the fine blade and placed over a large bowl. (If the passata still appears chunky after running it through the food mill, run it through a second time.)

9 When all the tomatoes have been run through the food mill, taste the passata and add additional salt, if desired. (Do not discard what remains in the food mill. This can be dehydrated into Tomato Powder [p. 160].) You now have homemade passata ready to turn into marinara sauce.

> ···················· COOK'S NOTES ····················
>
> ***Do you really need approximately 50 pounds of tomatoes for this recipe?*** 50 pounds of tomatoes equals approximately 200 or so large Italian plum tomatoes. That's a lot! (This is a rough estimate, but you will find that 4 large Italian plum tomatoes will weigh approximately 1 pound. If you have small or medium Italian plum tomatoes, you will need more per pound.) But we're canning here, and when it comes to canning tomatoes, we don't want to be shy because after you turn them into passata and then turn the passata into marinara, you will probably only have about 7 quarts of marinara!
>
> This recipe is perfect if you grow Italian plum tomatoes in your kitchen garden. A few years ago, I grew about 80 pounds (36kg) of a combination of cherry tomatoes and Italian Roma tomatoes in three 4 × 4-feet (1.25 × 1.25m) raised beds! You may also be able to buy a case or more of tomatoes from your local farmer's market. But I don't want you to be overwhelmed. You can use fewer tomatoes to make a smaller amount of marinara. Just keep in mind you will be pressure canning less than 7 quarts.
>
> ***What should you do with all the tomato liquid from the drained and salted tomatoes?*** Do not discard this liquid! You can refrigerate it and use it within a few days or freeze it and use it within 6 months. It's ideal for adding to soups and stews and even as a base for homemade salad dressing. Just be sure to taste it before using it and then make any necessary adjustments to the salt in your recipe .
>
> ***What if you don't want to make marinara. Can you simply pressure can the passata?*** Yes, you can pressure can the passata. The only difference will be that you will need to heat your passata on the stovetop by bringing it to a boil, reducing the heat to medium, and simmering it for 5 minutes. Stir continuously to prevent sticking. Remember that you will need to add lemon juice or citric acid to your passata, as you do with the marinara. You may also add the sugar, if desired, to counterbalance the lemon juice. Plus, you will need more canning jars since you will not be reducing the passata to make the marinara sauce. Once the prepared jars are filled with the passata, follow the same guidelines for pressure canning marinara.

What if you want to skip making passata? Can you still make marinara? Definitely! Today, there are so many variations for making marinara. If you simply want to blanch, peel, and deseed your tomatoes, and then purée them with an immersion blender (or regular blender), you are all set. In a stockpot, sauté a bit of garlic in a tablespoon of extra virgin olive oil, add in your puréed tomatoes, and add a bit of fresh chopped basil. Bring the marinara to a boil, then reduce the heat to medium, and simmer the sauce for 30 minutes to 1 hour until it reaches the consistency you like. Remember that you will need to add lemon juice or citric acid to your marinara if you decide to pressure can it. You may also add the sugar, if desired, to counterbalance the lemon juice. Proceed with the marinara pressure canning instructions to make your sauce shelf stable.

STEP 2: MAKE THE TRADITIONAL MARINARA SAUCE

There are many ways to make marinara sauce today. This is a basic marinara that is easy to adjust for pressure canning.

EQUIPMENT

Large (10- to 12-quart) stainless steel or enameled stockpot

Long-handled stainless steel or wooden spoon

INGREDIENTS

1 tbsp olive oil

5 cloves garlic, minced

Passata from the previous recipe

¼ cup fresh basil leaves, chopped

1   Heat the olive oil in the stockpot on medium. Once the olive oil is warmed and shimmers, add the garlic and sauté until fragrant and softened but not browned. This should just take a few minutes.

2   Add the passata to the stockpot and stir well to incorporate all the garlic throughout the passata. Simmer the passata for 30 minutes or up to 1 hour until the marinara sauce is the consistency you like.

3   Once the proper consistency is reached, add the chopped basil and stir well to incorporate. Simmer for 1 minute more.

4   Transfer the stockpot to a heatproof surface and proceed with the pressure canning instructions.

STEP 3: PRESSURE CAN THE MARINARA SAUCE

Some "watery" or looser tomato preparations can be water bath canned, but a marinara sauce must be pressure canned to ensure that it will be thoroughly heated through to the center of the jar during the canning process.

Although this is a traditional marinara, we need to make certain acidification adjustments to keep it safe for pressure canning. But don't worry! I'm confident you'll find it delicious once you pop open a jar, heat it up on the stovetop, and enjoy it as a pasta sauce, a topping for sautéed chicken breasts or chicken parmigiana, or as a dipping sauce for pretty much anything—including fried mozzarella sticks!

EQUIPMENT

Wide-mouth funnel

Ladle

Pressure canner and supplies

7 quart (32oz) regular-mouth or wide-mouth canning jars

7 regular-mouth or wide-mouth canning lids and bands

INGREDIENTS

Marinara sauce from the previous recipe

7 tsp canning and pickling salt, divided (optional)

14 tbsp bottled lemon juice, divided, or 3½ tsp citric acid, divided

7 tsp sugar, divided (optional)

1   **Steps 1–5:** Follow steps 1–5 in the "General Pressure Canning Guidelines" (p. 98).

2   **Steps 6–11:** These steps coordinate with steps 6–11 in the "General Pressure Canning Guidelines" but are unique to this recipe.

6. If cooled, reheat the marinara sauce in the stockpot on the stovetop, bringing it to a boil, then transfer the stockpot to a heatproof surface.

7. Using the jar lifter, remove one jar from the canner, empty the hot water from the jar back into the canner, and place the jar on a cushioned surface.

8. Place a funnel over the opening of a prepared jar and use a ladle to add the hot marinara sauce to the jar, a bit shy of a 1-inch (2.5-cm) headspace. Add 1 teaspoon salt to the jar, if desired. Add 2 tablespoons lemon juice or ½ teaspoon citric acid to the jar. Add 1 teaspoon sugar to the jar, if desired.

9. Measure the headspace, leaving 1 inch (2.5cm).

10. Use a debubbler to remove any air bubbles from the jar.

11. Remeasure the headspace and add more of the hot marinara sauce, if needed, to adjust the headspace to 1 inch (2.5cm).

3 Steps 12–32: Follow steps 12–32 in the "General Pressure Canning Guidelines" (p. 98).

········· COOK'S NOTES ·········

What are the recommended processing times in a dial-gauge pressure canner for quart jars of marinara sauce, based on altitude?

- 0 to 2,000 feet: 25 minutes, 11 psi
- 2,001 to 4,000 feet: 25 minutes, 12 psi
- 4,001 to 6,000 feet: 25 minutes, 13 psi
- 6,001 to 8,000 feet: 25 minutes, 14 psi

What are the recommended processing times in a weighted-gauge pressure canner for quart jars of marinara sauce, based on altitude?

- 0 to 1,000 feet: 25 minutes, 10 psi
- Above 1,000 feet: 25 minutes, 15 psi

What is the shelf life for Traditional Marinara Sauce? Home-canned marinara sauce is shelf stable for 12 months or longer, depending on the canning lid manufacturer's recommendations. Once opened, the marinara must be refrigerated and will stay fresh for 3–4 days. If frozen, it will stay usable for 6 months but will be at its peak freshness if used within the first 3 months.

Mushrooms in a Savory Broth

Pressure canning mushrooms in a savory broth, either chicken broth or beef broth, locks in their earthy flavors and tender texture. This method ensures that you have ready-to-use mushrooms that add richness to soups, stews, and sauces in place of meat.

PREP TIME: **30 MINUTES**
COOK TIME: **15 MINUTES**
PRESSURE CANNING PROCESSING TIME: **45 MINUTES**
TOTAL TIME: **1 HOUR 30 MINUTES**
YIELD: **APPROXIMATELY 9 HALF PINTS**

EQUIPMENT

Large (10- to 12-quart) stainless steel or enameled stockpot

Colander

Medium (6- to 8-quart) saucepan

Wide-mouth funnel

Ladle

Pressure canner and supplies

9 half-pint (8oz) regular-mouth or wide-mouth canning jars

9 regular-mouth or wide-mouth canning lids and bands

INGREDIENTS

7 ½ lb (3.5kg) small whole white button mushrooms (see **Cook's Notes**)

1 ½ tsp canning and pickling salt, divided (optional)

Rounded ½ tsp ascorbic acid powder (vitamin C powder)

4 cups chicken broth or beef broth, homemade or store-bought

---

1 **Steps 1–5:** Follow steps 1–5 in the "General Pressure Canning Guidelines" (p. 98).

2 **Steps 6–11:** These steps coordinate with steps 6–11 in the "General Pressure Canning Guidelines" but are unique to this recipe.

6. a. Fill a clean sink (or large plastic or enameled dish pan) halfway full with cold water.

b. Trim the stems and discolored parts from the mushrooms, then cut each mushroom in half. As you trim the mushrooms, toss them into the cold water and allow them to soak. The dirt from the mushrooms should sink to the bottom.

c. After all the mushrooms are sliced in half and added to the cold water, gently move them around with your hands to release the last of any dirt that might be clinging to them.

d. Lift the mushrooms gently out of the sink, transfer them in batches to a colander, and rinse them with clean water.

e. Fill a stockpot halfway full with water. Bring the water to a boil over high heat.

f. With the water boiling, carefully add the mushrooms to the stockpot. Return the water to a rolling boil over high heat and boil for 5 minutes.

g. While the mushrooms are boiling, warm the chicken broth or beef broth in a medium saucepan. Bring the broth to a boil over high heat, place a lid on the saucepan, reduce the heat medium, and allow the broth to simmer. (You want to put a lid on the saucepan because you do not want the broth to evaporate.)

h. After 5 minutes, drain the mushrooms into a colander placed in the sink. (If desired, place the colander over a bowl and save the cooking liquid for use in other recipes.) If all the boiled mushrooms do not fit in the colander, do this in batches, periodically transferring the mushrooms to a clean glass bowl.

i. Transfer the bowl of mushrooms to a work surface near the canner.

7. Using the jar lifter, remove one jar from the canner, empty the hot water from the jar back into the canner, and place the jar on a cushioned surface.

8. Place a funnel over the opening of a prepared jar. Use a ladle to remove some of the hot mushrooms from the colander or bowl and transfer them to the jar, leaving a 1-inch (2.5-cm) headspace. Add ¼ teaspoon of salt to the jar, if desired. Add approximately $\frac{1}{16}$ teaspoon of

ascorbic acid to the jar. (This will help retain the mushrooms' appetizing color.) If you do not have ascorbic acid, you can add 1 crushed 250-milligram vitamin C tablet to the jar. Using a ladle, fill the jar with the hot canning broth from the saucepan.

9. Measure the headspace, leaving 1 inch (2.5cm).

10. Use a debubbler to remove any air bubbles from the jar.

11. Remeasure the headspace and add more hot broth, if needed, to adjust the headspace to 1 inch (2.5cm).

3 **Steps 12–32:** Follow steps 12–32 in the "General Pressure Canning Guidelines" (p. 98).

····· COOK'S NOTES ·····

What are the recommended processing times in a dial-gauge pressure canner for half-pint jars of mushrooms, based on altitude?

- 0 to 2,000 feet: 45 minutes, 11 psi
- 2,001 to 4,000 feet: 45 minutes, 12 psi
- 4,001 to 6,000 feet: 45 minutes, 13 psi
- 6,001 to 8,000 feet: 45 minutes, 14 psi

What are the recommended processing times in a weighted-gauge pressure canner for half-pint jars of mushrooms, based on altitude?

- 0 to 1,000 feet: 45 minutes, 10 psi
- Above 1,000 feet: 45 minutes, 15 psi

Can you pressure can wild mushrooms? No, wild mushrooms are not safe for home canning.

What is the shelf life for Mushrooms in Savory Broth? Home-canned mushrooms are shelf stable for 12 months or longer, depending on the canning lid manufacturer's recommendations. Once opened, mushrooms must be refrigerated and will stay fresh for 3–4 days. There are many different opinions as to how long cooked mushrooms can be stored in the freezer; however, they generally stay at peak freshness for approximately 1 month when frozen.

End-of-Season Vegetable Medley

Pressure canning an End-of-Season Vegetable Medley allows you to capture the bounty of your garden in a jar. This method preserves the flavors and nutritional benefits of a variety of vegetables, making it easy to enjoy a taste of summer year-round.

As you review the ingredients for this recipe, keep in mind that you can adjust the suggested proportions or substitute your favorite vegetables. However, when creating a vegetable medley, the NCHFP recommends avoiding the use of leafy greens, dried beans (if they have not been cooked first), creamed corn, winter squash, sweet potatoes, broccoli, cauliflower, or cabbage in a vegetable medley .

PREP TIME: **30 MINUTES**
COOK TIME: **30 MINUTES**
PRESSURE CANNING PROCESSING TIME: **90 MINUTES**
TOTAL TIME: **2 HOURS 30 MINUTES**
YIELD: **APPROXIMATELY 7 QUARTS**

EQUIPMENT

Large (10- to 12-quart) stainless steel or enameled stockpot

Wide-mouth funnel

Slotted spoon

Ladle

Pressure canner and supplies

7 quart (32oz) regular-mouth or wide-mouth canning jars

7 regular-mouth or wide-mouth canning lids and bands

INGREDIENTS

6 medium ears of fresh corn, husks removed

12 medium carrots, peeled and cut into ½-inch (1.25-cm) cubes

8 cups fresh green beans cut into ½-inch (1.25-cm) pieces

2 medium zucchini, cut into ½-inch (1.25-cm) cubes

7 tsp canning and pickling salt (optional)

1 **Steps 1–5:** Follow steps 1–5 in the "General Pressure Canning Guidelines" (p. 98).

2 **Steps 6–11:** These steps coordinate with steps 6–11 in the "General Pressure Canning Guidelines" but are unique to this recipe.

6. a. Fill a stockpot halfway with water. Bring the water to a rolling boil and use tongs to lower the ears of corn into the boiling water, blanching for 3 minutes.

    b. Remove the corn from the water and remove the corn kernels from each cob. (Important! See **Cook's Notes** for proper procedure for removing the kernels.) Set aside.

    c. Empty the water from the stockpot, return the stockpot to the stovetop, and fill it halfway with water. Bring the water to a boil.

    d. With the water boiling, carefully add all the vegetables, including the corn, to the stockpot. Return the water to a rolling boil over high heat, then reduce the heat to medium and simmer the vegetables for 5 minutes. The vegetables should be tender but still crisp.

    e. Transfer the stockpot to a heatproof surface.

7. Using the jar lifter, remove one jar from the canner, empty the hot water from the jar back into the canner, and place the jar on a cushioned surface.

8. Place a funnel over the opening of a prepared jar. Using a ladle, fill the prepared jar from the stockpot with the hot pieces of vegetables and water, leaving a 1-inch (2.5-cm) headspace. Add 1 teaspoon of the salt to the jar, if desired.

9. Measure the headspace, leaving 1 inch (2.5cm).

10. Use a debubbler to remove any air bubbles from the jar.

11. Remeasure the headspace and add more hot water from the stockpot, if needed, to adjust the headspace to 1 inch (2.5cm).

3 **Steps 12–32:** Follow steps 12–32 in the "General Pressure Canning Guidelines" (p. 98).

COOK'S NOTES

What are the recommended processing times in a dial-gauge pressure canner for quart jars of mixed vegetables, based on altitude?

- 0 to 2,000 feet: 90 minutes, 11 psi
- 2,001 to 4,000 feet: 90 minutes, 12 psi
- 4,001 to 6,000 feet: 90 minutes, 13 psi
- 6,001 to 8,000 feet: 90 minutes, 14 psi

What are the recommended processing times in a weighted-gauge pressure canner for quart jars of mixed vegetables, based on altitude?

- 0 to 1,000 feet: 90 minutes, 10 psi
- Above 1,000 feet: 90 minutes, 15 psi

Important! How to properly remove corn kernels from the cob to prepare for pressure canning. When removing corn kernels from a corn cob, you will want to cut the corn from the cob at about three-fourths the depth of the kernels. Do not scrape the cob. You want to avoid collecting any additional and unnecessary starch.

What is the shelf life for End-of-Season Vegetable Medley? Home-canned mixed vegetables are shelf stable for 12 months or longer, depending on the canning lid manufacturer's recommendations. Once opened, mixed vegetables must be refrigerated and will stay fresh for 3–4 days. Home-canned mixed vegetables do not freeze well; their texture can become quite mushy and unappetizing once defrosted.

I thought the NCHFP said not to pressure can zucchini? That is correct. Zucchini should not be pressure canned by itself. However, it can be included in a mixed vegetable medley as in this recipe.

Chapter Five
ALL ABOUT DRYING AND DEHYDRATING

GETTING STARTED WITH DRYING AND DEHYDRATING

For the most part, all the home food preservation skills I learned were taught to me by my sweet mom, Gloria. She was the consummate homemaker who loved taking care of her family and running a home that was truly a haven from the noisy outside world. One of my mom's favorite pastimes—when she was able to catch a minute or two to herself—was reading about the kitchen life of homemakers who came before her from the seventeenth and eighteenth centuries. She was fascinated by the foods they were able to prepare even, in some cases, under the most primitive of conditions.

I shared earlier that my mom and I often spent our summers together touring early American landmarks in the area of New York where I grew up. Our favorites were the old homes from the colonial days. And you can guess what our favorite room was in those houses: If you guessed the kitchen, you'd be right! My mom and I would study all the different types of furniture, china, and utensils used by those early American home cooks. We also took in every bit of quaint scenery those kitchens offered, including the drying herbs tied in bunches and hanging upside down from the low rafters.

Whatever else she grew in her garden, my mom made sure there would be a large area reserved for herbs. She believed in the power of herbs not only for their culinary purposes, but for their medicinal purposes as well. Many of the dishes she whipped up in our cozy kitchen included basil, oregano, and thyme. And, of course, she couldn't resist tying up a variety of herbs, from chamomile to lavender to mint, and hanging them from her kitchen ceiling beams. We had a complete assortment. Once dried, she would crush some and store

them in jars in her Working Pantry. Others were tucked away in her Healing Pantry, ready to be turned into teas for soothing a cold or cough, or steeped in olive oil which would later be turned into a healing salve. I often joke about this, but for as refined and sophisticated as my mom was, underneath her pearl necklace and matching earrings, she had the heart of an all-natural crunchy granola mama!

But my mom's food drying adventures didn't stop at herbs. She dried a whole host of foods—including fruits and vegetables—all without an electric dehydrator. Sometimes she took advantage of the sun and hot weather, while other times she relied on her oven on its lowest setting. Certainly, in time, if you want to add an electric dehydrator to your kitchen, you can. But you can get started with drying food just fine without it.

Food Drying: One of the Oldest and Easiest Preservation Methods

Did you know that drying food is one of the oldest methods of preserving food for later use? Today, it is a safe and convenient alternative to home canning for stocking your pantry with shelf-stable food that does not require refrigeration. It can also free up some of your freezer space. Drying food is probably the simplest way to preserve food. It also has one of the easiest learning curves of all the various food preservation methods.

I will walk you through the various options for drying or dehydrating food, but keep in mind that not every method is suitable for every type of food. Certain foods lend themselves best to one option or another. However, here is a general list of foods that can be dried either through air drying, sun drying, oven drying, or using an electric dehydrator.

Foods Suitable for Drying or Dehydrating

There are numerous options when it comes to drying or dehydrating foods. You may be surprised that you can even use this method of food preservation to transform some canned or frozen fruits and vegetables. This clever trick can free up space in your Working Pantry, freezer, and Backup Pantry. Plus, canned or frozen foods can speed up the process because you can skip some of the pretreatment steps normally required for fresh fruits and vegetables.

- Aromatics including herbs, garlic, and onions
- Small fruits such as berries
- Larger sliced fruits such as apples, bananas, pears, etc.
- Assorted canned fruits
- Assorted frozen fruits
- Fruit purées for making jams and fruit leather
- Meat, poultry, and nonoily fish for making jerky
- Seeds including pumpkin and sunflower
- Sourdough starter
- Assorted fresh small vegetables such as corn and peas
- Assorted sliced, diced, or cubed fresh vegetables
- Assorted canned vegetables
- Assorted frozen vegetables
- Vegetable bouillon (a mixture of puréed vegetables and salt)

Simple Air Drying

One of the easiest ways to dry most herbs is through simple air drying. You can take a bunch of herbs, tie them up, and hang them upside down in your home in a well-ventilated area out of direct sunlight. It's that easy. But there are a few steps to take to ensure that your herbs dry properly. Yes, they can look very charming hanging from the rafters, but the best way to air dry hanging herbs is to tie them with a rubber band and place them in a brown paper bag that you punch with holes. The rubber band will shrink as the stems dry and hold all the herbs in place, and the brown paper bag will keep the herbs dust-free and protect the essential oils in the herbs from sunlight. Additionally, the punched holes will allow for good air circulation.

It is also important where you hang your herbs. Make sure they are in an area with low humidity and good air circulation. Avoid places near a stove or sink or an area that may receive rising hot steam from a dishwasher.

Different herbs take different times to dry. Those herbs that have less moisture will do well with this drying method. These include herbs like lavender, oregano, rosemary, and thyme.

Herbs that contain more moisture should be tied in very small bunches to facilitate fast drying. Alternatively, you can lay out the more watery herbs on a stainless steel rack set over a baking sheet and allow them to air dry at room temperature (or in a low oven—more on oven drying later).

Sun Drying

Of all the ways to dry food, air drying and sun drying are the oldest methods. Sun drying lends itself beautifully to certain fruits because of their high sugar and acid content. You just need to ensure the conditions outside are suitable for safely and successfully drying fruit. One of the most popular sun-dried fruits you are familiar with—and which you can find at your local grocery store—are sun-dried raisins. Grapes are perfect for sun drying when the conditions are right.

To dry fruit outside, it's best if your weather can maintain a temperature of 85°F (29°C) or higher and a humidity level below 60%. For best results, you need hot, dry, breezy weather. For fruits that lend themselves to being dried outside, it can take a number of days to complete the process, so always check your weather. If rain is in the forecast, hold off on your outside drying projects.

You will also need to cover the food that is drying outside at night. Or you can transfer the food inside. You want to avoid the condensation (moisture) that can develop from the cool night air that may rehydrate the drying food. Plus, you want to protect your food from nocturnal animals who might enjoy a snack!

As an alternative to making your own sun-drying device, there are reasonably priced mesh sun-drying devices that resemble a tier of hanging baskets—just baskets covered in mesh. With a quick search online, you should be able to find one that will fit your space and your budget.

WHAT ABOUT SOLAR DRYING?

There are a few premade solar dehydrators available. However, they can be difficult to find, and they may be expensive. Solar dehydrators are often homemade contraptions that capture the heat of the sun in a box. This box contains a solar-powered fan to provide good air circulation, with a chimney-looking device on top of the box that allows moisture to escape. If you enjoy home projects, this is certainly worth exploring. There are numerous resources online and in books about off-grid living to show you how to make solar dehydrators. As a final note, just remember not to confuse this with a solar oven. Those ovens are not made for drying or dehydrating food.

EQUIPMENT NEEDED FOR SUN DRYING

My father-in-law, Tom, was a talented woodworker. He made me a set of screens stretched between wood racks that were perfect for sun drying food during our extremely hot, dry, and sunny central Texas summers. If you can create something like this, it can work very well for drying food outside. Just make sure that the screening you use is food safe, such as stainless steel screening.

You will want to make a set of screens—one to place the food on and one to place on top of the first screen to protect the food from birds, insects, squirrels, and other small daytime animals looking for a snack. Some small insects may get through the screens, but you will address this possibility at the end of the drying process. You can place these racks in an area that reflects the heat, such as a concrete patio, or put a piece of aluminum foil under each rack, which will reflect the heat. Alternatively, if making two screens is not possible, you can cover one screen with sheer cheesecloth and tuck it under the frame of the screen.

If you make your drying racks a size slightly smaller than large storage containers, you can flip the containers upside down to cover your food at night. Just be sure to put a weight on the container so an animal can't knock it aside. Alternatively, homemade drying racks are easy to move inside to protect them during the night. All you have to do is transfer them back outside to their sunny spot in the morning.

Once you have successfully sun dried your foods, you will need to ensure that they are free of pests. Inspect the food and remove any visible insects. Next you will want to ensure that you kill any less visible insects or their eggs that may be on the food. To do this, you have two options:

· **The Freezer Method:** Put all your sun-dried food in a sealed freezer-proof bag placed in the freezer set at 0°F (−18°C) for 48 hours. This should kill insects and their eggs.

· **The Oven Method:** Spread the sun-dried food on a baking sheet in a single layer and bake in the oven at 160°F (70°C) for 30 minutes. If your oven can't be set to 160°F (70°C), use the freezer method.

Drying Food in an Oven

Drying food in an oven is certainly possible, but as
with all the different ways to dry food, oven drying
lends itself best to certain foods. Drying food in
an oven was easier with older ovens that had
temperature controls that could be set as low as
150°F (65°C). Today, most ovens can't be set lower
than 170°F (75°C), and some can only be set as low
as 200°F (95°C). If an oven is too hot, it can cook
the food instead of drying it.

Depending on your recipe, an oven that is first
warmed but then turned off and heated only by the
pilot light or the electric light may provide you
the level of warmth you need to dry certain foods.
An ovenproof thermometer can be a great asset in
helping you know the internal temperature of your
oven under these conditions and allowing you to dry
certain foods. During very warm months, I am able
to dry some of my sourdough starter by spreading it
in a thin layer on some parchment paper right on my
kitchen counter. However, during colder or damp
months, I find using a warm oven with nothing more
than the electric light turned on to be the perfect
drying environment. Using this method can take trial
and error, but it is doable.

Some modern ovens may have a bread-proofing
option with a lower temperature setting, usually
around 100°F (40°C). You can use this setting
to dry foods that would require this temperature
if dried in an electric dehydrator. Check your oven
manual to determine if you have a bread-proofing
option. Then check whether this setting also turns
on an oven fan (as in a convection oven option).
If so, this combination can closely mimic an
electric dehydrator.

In my first book, *The Modern Pioneer Cookbook*,
I shared recipes for drying apples and sliced
citrus fruits in the oven. This process can work
exceptionally well for ovens whose temperature can't
be set lower than 170°F (75°C). Thinly sliced citrus
and thinly sliced apples can be dried in an oven at
temperatures from 170°F to 200°F (75°C to 95°C)
without fear of cooking the fruit. Just make sure that
you use baking sheets that fit onto your oven racks
while still allowing for air to move around all four
sides. Placing food on wire racks that are then placed
onto your baking sheets can also help with good air
circulation. As the fruit is drying, periodically open
the oven door and rotate the baking sheets. This
practice will help with ventilation and uniform
drying. You do not have to prop the oven door
open—which I prefer not to do and is something you
should never do with children in the house.

The one major drawback of using your oven to dry
food is that it is not designed for large-scale drying.
In the case of drying thinly sliced fruit, the job may
take up to 8 hours, while other foods may take days
to dry correctly. That means your oven is out of
commission to cook other foods. So you should only
occasionally reserve an oven to dry food. Also,
although ovens with a convection option have a fan,
most ovens do not. Without a fan, you can't put more
than two racks of food into an oven because you have
to allow for good airflow.

Drying Food in an Electric Dehydrator

If you enjoy drying foods, it might be time to invest in an electric dehydrator. These devices come in different sizes and are priced to meet pretty much anyone's budget. You may even be clever enough to spy one at a thrift shop after the holidays when they are often resold at bargain basement prices. (Dehydrators can be a common Christmas present, but not everyone realizes their value!)

Electric dehydrators, often called food dehydrators, are small- to medium-size kitchen appliances that dry foods indoors. They can sit on a counter as long as an electrical plug is nearby. These appliances may look like cylinders or cubes. Both have multiple mesh trays contained within (and some allow adding additional trays), along with a fan and vents for air circulation. Most food dehydrators also have a temperature setting that will enable you to adjust the heat requirement based on the recipe for the food you are dehydrating. This temperature setting usually ranges from 85°F to 160°F (30°C to 70°C).

Different food dehydrators offer various features, but one to look for is a model with a timer. You can set the timer according to the instructions in the dehydrator recipe you are following. If the food is finished dehydrating in the middle of the night, the timer will turn off the dehydrator and prevent the food from overdrying and possibly scorching.

A second feature to look for when shopping for a dehydrator is accessories for drying very small foods or making fruit leather. For box-style dehydrators, these add-ons usually come in the form of silicone sheets that fit on top of the mesh sheets. In cylinder-style dehydrators, these usually take the form of a large donut shape made of plastic. Either option will work well, but as an alternative, you can also use parchment paper cut to size.

Although you can certainly dry some foods in other ways, especially when you are first getting started with this type of food preservation, dehydrating food with an electric dehydrator is as close to foolproof as it gets. And if you like to make jerky, I highly recommend it. Whenever we are working with raw meat and poultry, there are risks of creating an environment ripe for foodborne illness. But with proper pretreatments (more about that below) followed by an approved method for drying raw meats and poultry in a dehydrator, you can be assured that your jerky will be safe to consume.

WHAT IS THE APPROVED METHOD FOR DRYING RAW MEATS AND POULTRY IN A DEHYDRATOR?

Due to outbreaks of food poisoning from home-dried jerky, scientists at Colorado State University, the University of Georgia, and the University of Wisconsin conducted significant research to determine when home-dehydrated jerky can be considered "done." They found that dehydrated jerky is only safe to eat when it is heated sufficiently to destroy any pathogens present, and dry enough to be shelf stable (can be stored at room temperature and will not support microbial growth). Heating sufficiently can involve precooking the raw meat, post-cooking the jerky, or, interestingly enough, presoaking the raw meat in vinegar (vinegar can cook raw food due to its acidity) prior to going into the dehydrator. I cover this in detail in the following section on pretreating foods before drying and dehydrating.

As for other foods, an electric dehydrator will save you money on your electric bill over oven drying. Plus, having this type of appliance frees up your oven for other jobs.

Pretreating Food Prior to Drying or Dehydrating

Once you decide on your method of drying or dehydrating food, you will want to take a few steps to ensure a successful outcome.

Pretreating Fruit

If you are concerned about fruit darkening, you can pretreat it. This isn't a concern when drying citrus, nor, in my experience, when drying apples—it's not uncommon to see these darken when dried, especially if they have been dusted with cinnamon to make them a special treat. However, you can pretreat apples and other fruits whose color you prefer to preserve, such as when making banana chips or dried, peeled apricots.

There are many ways to prevent darkening, but some of those ways involve using sulfites or other chemicals I prefer to avoid in my traditional foods kitchen. It is important to note that if you or anyone to whom you may be serving your home-dried food is susceptible to asthma attacks, avoid using sulfites, which can aggravate that condition.

A simple way to pretreat fruit before drying it is by using an acidulated mixture of ascorbic acid (vitamin C) and water. If you are using the powdered form of ascorbic acid, you only need to dissolve 1 teaspoon of the powder into 2 cups of water in a bowl. (If you are crushing 500mg vitamin C tablets, you will need 6 tablets.) You can use this solution to soak two batches of cut fruit. If you need to use this solution more than twice, add an additional teaspoon of the ascorbic acid powder to the water.

Place the cut fruit into the ascorbic acid solution and allow it to soak for a minimum of 3 minutes or up to 5 minutes. Soft fruits, such as banana slices, do best with the shorter soak, while firmer fruits, such as apples and pears, can hold up well with the longer soak. Once the soak time has elapsed, remove the fruit from the solution and drain well, but do not rinse. Place the fruit on the drying screens, wire racks on a baking sheet, or on the electric dehydrator racks and proceed with drying.

ALTERNATIVES TO USING PURE ASCORBIC ACID

There are several alternatives to pretreating fruit. If you use one of these methods, the same rules apply. You can use them for two soaks, but then they will need to be refreshed.

Ascorbic Acid Mixtures: You may come across various ascorbic acid mixtures sold under different brand names where home canning supplies are sold. These will work as a fruit drying pretreatment, but they are likely to be more costly than pure ascorbic acid and tend not to work as well.

Acidic Fruit Juice: You can also use any acidic fruit juice, such as citrus juices. However, you will need to use the juice at full strength, not mixed with water. Plus, you will want to consider that the fruit juice used will add its unique flavor to whatever fruit you are pretreating.

Honey Dip: A honey dip is a lovely way to pretreat fruit prior to drying that adds a touch of sweetness. Although the name for this type of pretreat uses the word honey, it is a bit misleading. For this pretreat to work well and prevent fruit from darkening during the drying process, you need to use sugar in addition to the honey. And unfortunately, the sugar that works best is regular granulated sugar. Although I would love to be able to use whole sweeteners for this purpose, they tend to be dark in color, which defeats the purpose of trying to maintain the original color of the fruit. The good news is that the amount of sugar contained on each piece of fruit after being drained from the honey dip is relatively minimal.

To make a honey dip pretreat, mix together ½ cup sugar with 1½ cups boiling water. Mix well so the sugar dissolves. Allow the mixture to cool to lukewarm (like bath water), then add ½ cup honey and mix well until the honey completely dissolves. Once this dip cools completely, soak the cut fruit in it for 3 to 5 minutes. Once the soaking time is finished, drain the fruit and place it on wire racks on a baking sheet or on dehydrator trays and proceed with drying. (With a honey dip, you will want to avoid sun drying.) You can use this honey dip multiple times without needing to refresh it.

BLANCHING

What I have shared previously are the best ways to retain the color and texture of fruits prior to drying. A final method for retaining the color of fruit prior to drying or dehydrating is steam blanching. You blanch the fruit in a double boiler or in a colander set over a pot of boiling water before drying or dehydrating. However, I find that this can significantly change the texture of the final product, and I do not recommend it. Blanching, whether with steam or in water, is better used for vegetables.

Pretreating Vegetables

To prepare fresh vegetables for drying or dehydrating, follow these steps:

1 Wash the vegetables in cool water to remove any dirt.

2 Discard any vegetables that are decayed, mushy, or have blemishes, such as brown or black spots.

3 Depending on the type of vegetable you are planning on drying or dehydrating, you will want to remove any cores, stems, or fibrous parts such as tough stems.

4 Prepare the vegetables as called for in the recipe: for example, cutting them into pieces. If you will be cutting the vegetables, make sure all your pieces are the same size. This will allow them to dry evenly.

5 Once the vegetables are properly prepared, some will need to be blanched. For others, blanching is optional. Blanching inhibits the enzymes contained in fresh vegetables, which in turn preserves the color and flavor of the vegetables. The recipe you are following will state whether steam blanching or water blanching is the best option.

WATER BLANCHING

Fill a medium pot ⅔ full of water, cover it, and bring to a rolling boil. Once boiling, remove the lid, place a cup or two of the vegetables in a wire basket, fine-mesh strainer, or colander, and submerge them in the water. Do not try to blanch too many vegetables at one time. Crowding will cause the water to take longer to return to a boil and may then overblanch the vegetables and begin to cook them. Blanch the vegetables according to the time specified in the recipe directions. Begin timing the blanching process when the water returns to boiling.

STEAM BLANCHING

You will follow the steps from water blanching; the only difference is that you will not submerge the vegetables in the water but instead let them rest above the water in a wire basket, fine-mesh strainer, or colander and blanch according to the recipe directions.

After water blanching or steam blanching the vegetables, dip them briefly in cold water until you can handle the vegetables comfortably. Drain the cold water and transfer the vegetables to whatever drying or dehydrating option you are using.

Pretreating Meats and Poultry

Pretreating raw meat and poultry before dehydrating helps prevent foodborne illness. There are three ways to pretreat this type of food.

BOILING BRINE OR MARINADE

Once you have prepared raw meat or poultry according to the recipe directions, you will need to heat thin slices by dipping them in a brine or marinade (called for in the recipe) that has been brought to a boil in a saucepan. Leave the meat or poultry in the boiling liquid until the meat reaches a temperature of 160°F (71°C) or the poultry reaches 165°F (74°C) . (Use a meat thermometer to verify the correct temperature.) These temperatures will destroy any pathogens present.

BAKING

Preheat your oven to 325°F (165°C). Dip thin strips of raw meat or poultry in a brine or marinade according to the recipe used. Then, spread them onto a baking sheet so they are not touching or overlapping. Bake until they reach an internal temperature of 160°F (71°C) for meat and 165°F (74°C) for poultry. This method is as effective at killing pathogens as the boiling method. As with the boiling method, be sure to use a meat thermometer to verify the correct temperatures have been reached.

VINEGAR SOAK

To use this method, soak thin slices of meat or poultry in 5% full-strength vinegar for 10 minutes. You can then proceed to marinate the meat or poultry according to the recipe and transfer it to the dehydrator. The acid of the vinegar, combined with the heat of the dehydrator, destroys any pathogens that may be present in the meat or poultry. (Note that this method is *not* approved for game meat.)

Post-Treating Meats and Poultry

Alternatively, there is a post-treating method that I prefer to use to ensure that homemade jerky is free of pathogens and safe to consume. To post-treat jerky, preheat your oven to 275°F (135°C). Once the oven reaches this temperature, heat the meat or poultry jerky on a baking sheet for 10 minutes. Remove the jerky from the oven and let it cool to room temperature. It will then be safe to consume.

Storing Dried and Dehydrated Foods

Dried foods of any type are susceptible to becoming infested with insects as well as reabsorbing moisture, which is why it is essential to store dried and dehydrated foods properly. You'll want to pack your food in clean containers that are resistant to insects. Some options include:

- Clean, dry canning jars with tight-fitting lids
- Glass containers with tight-fitting lids
- Vacuum jar packaging
- Vacuum bag packaging that is then stored in an insect-proof container

Once the food is packed, it is best stored in a cool, dark, dry pantry. Your Working Pantry or Backup Pantry are the perfect places for this.

Dried and dehydrated foods do best when stored in small amounts that can be consumed immediately when opened or used all at once in a recipe.

Otherwise, every time you open a jar, container, or bag, you expose the food to the moisture in the air.

Estimating the shelf life of these types of foods can be difficult. The general rule is that dried or dehydrated foods will last anywhere from 4 months to 1 year. But the main question is, do these foods go bad after those times? Chances are the answer is no. Foods that contain about 20% moisture—your more pliable dried foods, including jerky and some fruits—are best eaten within 6 months to 1 year for best quality. Over time, they might degrade somewhat and become a bit drier, to the point of becoming tough. On the other hand, which is even less desirable, they may take on some extra moisture and become susceptible to mold. If that happens, you need to discard the food.

Food that has been dried to a crisp—most likely having approximately a 10% moisture content—has a shelf life that can be considerably longer than 1 year. However, you want to check on this type of food regularly to ensure that it does not take on any moisture, which could cause spoilage. And keep in mind that the longer the food is stored, even under ideal conditions, the more it may degrade in color and nutrition.

CAN YOU USE SILICA GEL PACKETS OR OXYGEN ABSORBERS WHEN STORING DRIED OR DEHYDRATED FOODS?

Yes, you can add food-safe silica gel packets to your stored dried or dehydrated food. They will remove any excess moisture, making them ideal for this type of use, especially if you think you may be periodically opening and resealing the jar, container, or bag. Just make sure you use the correct size packet for the amount of food you are storing. The manufacturer of the silica gel packets will provide this information.

On the other hand, when it comes to oxygen absorbers, you need to be very careful. Only certain foods can be stored using oxygen absorbers. Botulism poisoning can occur if insufficiently dried food is stored in packaging that reduces oxygen. When storing foods in airtight containers with oxygen absorbers, products must be very dry—containing 10% moisture or less. When it comes to home drying and dehydrating, it can be difficult to know for sure exactly how dry the food is. I would err on the side of caution and use a food-safe silica gel packet instead of an oxygen absorber when storing dried or dehydrated foods.

Reconstituting (Rehydrating) Dried or Dehydrated Foods

Generally, you can eat meat jerky and dried or dehydrated fruits as is. If you want, you can reconstitute dried or dehydrated fruits. However, dried or dehydrated vegetables will definitely need to be reconstituted (sometimes referred to as rehydrated). Once you reconstitute your vegetables, you can use them in the same way you would use fresh vegetables.

To reconstitute dried or dehydrated fruits or vegetables, all you need to do is add water and soak them until the desired volume is restored. Using warm water will speed up this process. Generally, reconstituting should take less than 2 hours for most foods, so you will want to check your food regularly. Be careful not to over-rehydrate your food, which will create a mess of mush! If, for some reason, you find that it is taking longer than 2 hours to reconstitute your food, transfer it to the refrigerator. This will serve two purposes: It will allow the food to rehydrate slowly but effectively without becoming mushy, and the refrigeration will prevent the development of any foodborne pathogens during the rehydration process.

General Guidelines for Successfully Drying or Dehydrating Food

When it comes to successfully drying or dehydrating food, here are a few pointers to keep in mind:

- Place food in a single layer.
- Allow space between each piece of food for good air circulation.
- Dry meat jerky until pliable but with no sign of moisture remaining. Additional precautions are necessary when making jerky at home, which will be expanded upon in the Sweet-and-Spicy Beef Jerky recipe (p. 166).
- Dry most fruits until they are pliable but no longer sticky. (Because most fruits contain more acid—a natural preservative—than vegetables, they do not need to be dried to a crisp state. They generally contain 20%

moisture instead of the 10% moisture of foods dried to a crisp state.)

- When drying fruits into "chips," dry until they are crisp (also referred to as being brittle) and can easily be snapped into pieces).
- Dry berries until crisp or with a feeling similar to a small stone.
- Dry vegetables until crisp or, in the case of certain vegetables like corn kernels, until they feel like small stones.
- If you are sun-drying food, remember to take the extra step of freezing or oven warming to kill any insects and their eggs.
- Allow all dried or dehydrated food to cool completely before storing.
- For foods dried to a pliable state: Once cool, immediately pack food loosely into plastic bags or containers and then seal them to prevent air—which brings moisture—from getting into the bag or container and rehydrating the food. Shake the bag or container daily to redistribute the food. This is the conditioning phase. *Do not* skip this phase. It is necessary to ensure that your dried or dehydrated food will remain mold-free. Keep an eye on the food in the loose packaging for 7 to 10 days. If any condensation (moisture) forms in the packaging, immediately remove the food from the packaging and redry all the food. (Foods dried to a crisp/brittle state do not need conditioning.)

Once the food is completely dry, you can store it in an airtight container in a cool, dark, dry pantry.

Let's Get Started with Drying and Dehydrating Food

Now that you understand the different ways that food can be dried or dehydrated, let's get started with a very simple recipe for drying herbs and turning them into a flavorful salt that will liven up savory dishes. Once you see how easy it is to dry herbs, you'll be ready to tackle a whole host of drying projects to fill your pantry to the brim with a bounty of tasty shelf-stable foods.

Salt-Dried Herbs

Even with our hot Texas Hill Country summers, I always have an abundance of herbs growing in my kitchen garden. I have found that drying herbs in salt is a delightful way to preserve the fresh flavors of my garden all year round. Best of all, you will find that this is probably the easiest way to make an herb salt. You can use this versatile condiment in a variety of ways to enhance and customize everything from a dip for crudités to roasted vegetables to grilled meats. Best of all, it's an outstanding way to use up an abundance of herbs with nothing going to waste. Whether you're a seasoned cook or just starting your traditional foods journey, this recipe will add a burst of summer flavor to your recipes!

PREP TIME: **10 MINUTES**
DRYING TIME: **10–12 HOURS**
TOTAL TIME: **10–12 HOURS 10 MINUTES**
YIELD: **APPROXIMATELY 2 CUPS**

EQUIPMENT

Food processor or blender
(see **Cook's Notes**)

Electric dehydrator
(optional)

Baking sheet

Parchment paper

INGREDIENTS

2 packed cups fresh herbs
(see **Cook's Notes**),
divided

1 cup fine-ground sea salt
(use 1¼ cups if using
coarse-ground salt), divided

1 tsp lemon zest (optional)

½ tsp red pepper flakes
(optional)

1 garlic clove, peeled and
chopped (optional)

1 Using a food processor (or blender), add half of the herbs and half of the salt. Pulse for 30 seconds. Stop and scrape down the sides. Pulse again for 30 seconds. (See **Cook's Notes**.)

2 If using additional aromatics like the lemon zest, red pepper flakes, or chopped garlic (as shared in the **Cook's Notes**), add them now along with the remaining herbs and salt. Pulse for 1 minute, stopping after 30 seconds to scrape down the sides of the bowl. If the herbs do not appear finely minced and well incorporated with the salt, continue pulsing and scraping down the sides until the proper consistency is reached. The salt should take on a green hue.

3 Transfer the herb salt to a parchment paper-lined baking sheet. Allow it to dry in an oven with only the pilot light or electric light turned on but the oven turned off. Toss periodically and reposition the baking sheet to ensure even drying. This will take about 10–12 hours.

4 Alternatively, you can air dry the herb salt, tossing periodically to ensure even drying. This may take a few days to dry.

5 If using a dehydrator (and not adding garlic), dry at 110°F (45°C) for 10–12 hours, checking at 4 hours and tossing periodically to ensure even drying. If garlic is included, dry at 125°F (50°C) for 10–12 hours, checking at 4 hours. I recommend moving your dehydrator outside when you are drying an herb salt that contains garlic. The strong smell will permeate your home!

6 Once dried, store your herb salt in a jar or crock at room temperature. It's shelf stable and will stay fresh for at least 1 year.

COOK'S NOTES

Can you use a blender instead of a food processor? This process works best in a food processor, but you can use a blender. You may have to stop and start more frequently and scrape down the sides.

What are the best herbs to use in this recipe? You can use any fresh herb, but some have stronger flavors than others. Soft, leafy herbs such as flat-leaf Italian parsley, chives, dill, and tarragon are perfect to start with. If you decide to try the more woody-stemmed herbs, such as rosemary or thyme, that tend to have a stronger flavor, start with small amounts and then adjust to your taste.

What are the best additions to add to these herb salts? Try experimenting with a host of other additions, including grated garlic, onion, ginger, or any type of citrus zest other than lemon (such as lime, orange, or grapefruit). For one of the best lamb seasonings, blend salt with fresh mint and flat-leaf parsley. If you run out of mint jelly, this salt is the next best thing! Cooked greens, including creamed spinach, often call for adding a bit of grated nutmeg. Why not try making an herb salt with flat-leaf Italian parsley and nutmeg? Your guests will be asking what your secret ingredient is.

Blanched Oven-Dried Vibrant Herbs

If you want to preserve the vibrant colors and flavors of your garden herbs, blanching and oven drying is the way to go. This simple yet effective technique locks in that fresh-picked goodness, giving you beautifully colored and flavorful dried herbs unlike anything you can buy at the grocery store. And they are a sight to behold—all lined up in glass jars tucked into your pantry.

What I love most about this method is how it brings out the best in every herb, from chives and parsley to oregano and thyme. Blanching helps maintain their bright green hues, while gentle oven drying preserves their essential oils, ensuring they stay fragrant and full of flavor. Whether you're sprinkling them into soups, stirring them into sauces, or using them to season homemade breads, these vibrant herbs will add a touch of garden-fresh goodness to your cooking all year long. Preserving herbs in this way also makes them a superb addition to your Healing Pantry—ready for use when you need a soothing herb tea or a base for a variety of home remedies.

PREP TIME: **15 MINUTES**
COOK TIME/DRY TIME: **1–2 HOURS**
TOTAL TIME: **1 HOURS 15 MINUTES TO 2 HOURS 15 MINUTES**
YIELD: **VARIES**

EQUIPMENT

Clean towel or salad spinner

Medium (6- to 8-quart) saucepan

Large bowl

Baking sheet

Parchment paper

Spice grinder or blender (optional)

Airtight container

INGREDIENTS

3 large bunches of fresh herbs (basil, parsley, thyme, oregano, etc.)

Ice water

1 Wash the fresh herbs thoroughly and pat them dry with a clean towel or whirl them in a salad spinner.

2 Fill a medium saucepan half full with water and bring to a boil over high heat.

3 Fill a large bowl with ice water.

4 Drop the herbs into the boiling water for about 10 to 15 seconds, then quickly transfer them to the ice water bath to stop the cooking process. (This blanching step helps retain their vibrant color.)

5 Gently pat the herbs dry with a clean towel or use a salad spinner to remove excess moisture.

6 Preheat the oven to 170°F (75°C) or the lowest setting. Line a baking sheet with parchment paper and spread the blanched herbs in a single layer.

7 Dry the herbs in the oven for about 1 to 2 hours, checking them occasionally. They should be dry and crisp but not brown or burnt.

8 Once fully dried, let the herbs cool completely. Then use clean hands to run along the stems of the herbs to remove the leafy parts. (Save the stems for making bone broth.)

9 Crumble the herbs with your hands or whirl them in a spice grinder or blender to mince.

10 Store the dried herbs in an airtight container in a cool, dark pantry. These herbs will stay fresh and vibrant for 6 months.

Dried Red Chili–Infused Olive Oil

When most of our vegetable harvest has dried up in the blazing summer sun here in Central Texas, our chili peppers forge on bravely. Nothing seems to stop them! So, with an abundance of chilies in my kitchen garden, there is nothing I love more than making a spicy chili oil. Once you make this oil, you will find that adding a touch of spice to your dishes has never been easier or tastier than with this homemade dried red chili–infused olive oil. This oil brings just the right touch of heat and complexity to everything from roasted vegetables to grilled meats or chicken. Whether you're new to infusing oils or a seasoned pro, this recipe will become a staple in your refrigerator!

PREP TIME: **10 MINUTES**
COOK TIME: **5–10 MINUTES**
TOTAL TIME: **15–20 MINUTES**
YIELD: **APPROXIMATELY 1 CUP**

EQUIPMENT

Medium (6- to 8-quart) saucepan

Liquid measuring cup or pitcher

Fine-mesh strainer

Narrow-mouth funnel

Glass bottle with tight-fitting screw-on cap or swing top

INGREDIENTS

8 dried red chilies, any variety (see **Cook's Notes**)

1 cup extra-virgin olive oil

1 Add the olive oil to the saucepan and heat it to 180°F (82°C).

2 Add the dried chilies to the heated olive oil and allow to simmer for at least 5 minutes but no longer than 10 minutes. The longer the simmer, the stronger the flavor of the oil will be.

3 While the chili oil simmers, place a fine-mesh strainer over a liquid measuring cup or pitcher.

4 Once the chili oil has finished simmering, strain the hot oil through the fine-mesh strainer.

5 Use a narrow-mouth funnel to pour the oil into a glass bottle. Seal the bottle tightly and store it in the refrigerator. The red chili oil will stay fresh for 2 to 3 weeks. The oil will solidify when refrigerated. Simply allow the oil to return to room temperature for 15 minutes before using, then immediately return it to the refrigerator.

······················· COOK'S NOTES ·······················

Use dried chilies only! Always use dried chilies to avoid the risk of spoilage that can be caused by chilies that still contain some moisture. You can buy dried chilies at your local grocery store or dry some chilies yourself. When it comes to drying chilies, I often let them dry right on the vine in my kitchen garden. I then pick them and let them dry out a bit more by laying them flat in a single layer in a shallow basket covered with a bit of mesh. I keep them out of direct sunlight, but on our 100°F (40°C) days, they dry quickly!

If you decide to dry your chilies in a dehydrator, pierce them with the tip of a sharp knife, lay them out on the mesh dehydrator trays, and set the temperature to 125°F (50°C). Depending on their size, it can take up to 24 hours to dry chilies. Start checking them around 8 hours. You want them to dry to the point where they are quite brittle and exude no moisture.

You can also do this in the oven on a wire rack placed on a baking sheet. Set the oven to the lowest setting and check on the chilies occasionally until they are completely dry.

A favorite weekend supper: One of my favorite ways to use this oil is to cut up a chicken and then place the cut pieces on a baking sheet, skin side down. I drizzle the underside of the chicken generously with this oil and add a sprinkling of salt and pepper. I then put the chicken under the broiler until golden, flip over the chicken pieces, drizzle on more chili oil, and broil it for a few more minutes or until the skin is crispy and the chicken is cooked through. This chicken served with steak fries was one of our favorite (and Mom's easiest!) Saturday night movie night suppers!

Oven-Dried Candied Tomatoes

Although there is no sugar in this recipe, these tomatoes taste delightfully sweet once dried, hence my use of the word candied. These oven-dried tomatoes are a traditional foods kitchen staple because you can use them in a variety of ways: added to salads, sliced thin and added to sautéed chicken or fish dishes, or simply as a snack. But best of all, they are perfect for making the homemade Spicy Texas-Style Ketchup (p. 172) and the Tangy BBQ Sauce (p. 170) that I share with you in this chapter.

Slow-drying tomatoes in the oven transforms them into a treat that's far superior to the leathery sun-dried tomatoes commonly found in packages at most grocery stores. But you have to do it the right way. Here is the secret to drying these tomatoes in a way that preserves their sweetness, intense flavor, and plumpness.

PREP TIME: **10 MINUTES**
COOK TIME: **2 HOURS**
DRYING TIME: **4–6 HOURS**
TOTAL TIME: **6–8 HOURS 10 MINUTES**
YIELD: **APPROXIMATELY 18 PIECES**

EQUIPMENT

Baking sheet

Parchment paper

Wire rack

Sharp paring knife

Cutting board

Quart (32oz) glass jar with tight-fitting lid

INGREDIENTS

9 Italian plum tomatoes

¼ cup extra-virgin olive oil, plus more for storing tomatoes

1 tbsp coarse-ground sea salt (optional)

Dried oregano (optional)

1 Preheat the oven to 300°F (150°C).

2 Line a baking sheet with parchment paper and then place a wire rack onto the baking sheet.

3 Slice the tomatoes in half lengthwise with a sharp paring knife on a cutting board and then cut a small V-shape on either side of the stem to remove it. Scrape out the core, pulp, and seeds. (Do not discard this mixture. Save it to make tomato powder.)

4 Place the sliced tomatoes, cut sides up, on the wire rack, making sure they do not touch.

5 Drizzle olive oil over the tomatoes, then sprinkle each tomato half with a bit of sea salt (if using) and dried oregano (if using). (You can use fine-ground sea salt, but the coarse ground provides a unique and delightful taste and texture to the tomatoes.)

6 Roast the tomatoes for approximately 2 hours or until they become quite soft and slightly caramelized. Because every oven is different, keep an eye on them during the last 30 minutes to prevent them from burning.

7 Turn the oven temperature down to its lowest setting and leave the tomatoes in the oven for 3 to 5 hours or until they are shriveled around the edges but still plump.

8 When the tomatoes reach the proper texture, remove the baking sheet to a heatproof surface. Allow the tomatoes to cool.

9 Once the tomatoes have cooled, layer them into the quart glass jar and fill the jar with olive oil. Cap the jar tightly and store it in the refrigerator. The oil will solidify, but when you remove the tomatoes from the oil to use in a recipe, the oil clinging to the tomatoes will quickly liquefy.

10 These tomatoes will stay fresh in the refrigerator for 6 months.

> .... COOK'S NOTES ....
>
> ***What if you would prefer really dried tomatoes?*** Yes, you can dry tomatoes until they have a more leathery appearance. Do not use any olive oil or seasoning on the tomato halves; simply place them in the oven on its lowest setting or into a dehydrator set at 125°F (50°C). This may take anywhere from 10 to 16 hours for the tomato halves to become completely dried and shriveled. I would recommend that these dried tomatoes be stored in the refrigerator as opposed to on a pantry shelf.

The Easy Way to Dehydrate Vegetables

Dehydrating vegetables the easy way means starting with frozen vegetables. All the peeling and chopping has been done for you, so there is very little hands-on work on your part. Dehydrating frozen veggies also frees up valuable real estate in your freezer by allowing you to transform your store-bought frozen veggies and place them in other parts of your Four Corners Pantry. This simple method provides you with a convenient, ready supply of ingredients tucked on your pantry shelves for soups, stews, casseroles, and side dishes.

PREP TIME: **5 MINUTES**
DRYING TIME: **8–12 HOURS**
TOTAL TIME: **8–12 HOURS 5 MINUTES**
YIELD: **VARIES**

EQUIPMENT

Colander or fine-mesh
  strainer
Electric food dehydrator
Quart (32oz) jars with lids
  (for conditioning)
Airtight containers or jars

INGREDIENTS

1 (12oz/340g) bag of frozen
vegetables (I recommend
carrots, corn, green beans,
lima beans, and peas)

1 Empty the bag of frozen vegetables into a colander or fine-mesh strainer.

2 Rinse the vegetables under warm water for a few minutes to defrost them. Shake the colander to help drain any excess water.

3 Transfer the vegetables to a mesh dehydrator tray. Use your hands to evenly spread the vegetables across the tray. Continue this process until all the dehydrator trays are filled with vegetables.

4 Set the temperature to 125°F (50°C) and dehydrate the vegetables for 8 to 12 hours or until completely dry and hard to the touch. The dehydrated vegetables will feel like pebbles. Periodically check on the vegetables and move them around for even drying. (If you are drying different vegetables on different trays but all at the same time, start checking the vegetables at the 8-hour mark since some vegetables will require less drying time than others.)

5 To ensure the dehydrated vegetables are fully dehydrated and safe to store, put them into the quart jars, filling them about ⅔ full. Shake the jars a couple of times per day for 1 week. (This process is often referred to as conditioning.) If any condensation appears, the vegetables are not sufficiently dried and need to go back into the dehydrator for a few more hours.

6 Once the vegetables are completely dehydrated, store them in airtight containers or jars with airtight lids in a cool, dark, and dry pantry. If you live in an exceptionally damp or humid climate, you should add a food-safe silica gel pack to the storage container or jar with the dehydrated vegetables. Generally, dehydrated vegetables will be at their peak for 1 year. (See **Cook's Notes**.)

.... COOK'S NOTES ....

Rehydrating Dehydrated Vegetables:

- **Boiling Water Method:** Place the dehydrated vegetables in a heatproof bowl and cover them with boiling water so the water is 2 inches (5cm) above the vegetables. Allow the vegetables to rehydrate for at least 30 minutes. After rehydrating the vegetables, drain the water.
- **Direct Addition to Soups or Stews:** Dehydrated vegetables can be added directly to a soup or stew if there is sufficient liquid and extended cooking time.
- **Simmering Method:** If you want to serve the dehydrated vegetables on their own as a side dish, place them in a saucepan and cover them with water. Bring the water to a boil over high heat, then turn it down to a low simmer, and place the lid on the saucepan. Allow the vegetables to rehydrate and cook for approximately 20 minutes or until completely rehydrated and tender.

How long do dehydrated vegetables stay fresh? There are different opinions on how long dehydrated vegetables will actually stay fresh. Although most authorities agree that they will stay fresh for 1 year, a lot depends on how you store them and what type of climate you live in. Properly stored, dehydrated vegetables will fare very well in dry climates. In more humid climates, you will want to be exceptionally judicious about storing your dehydrated vegetables in airtight containers and using food-safe silica gel packs.

Oven-Dried Hardtack

Hardtack, also known as Ship's Biscuits, is a historical staple that has stood the test of time. This simple, portable, long-lasting food dates back to the eighteenth century and provided lifesaving calories to sailors and soldiers. Today, due to its indefinite shelf life. It's perfect for the Emergency Pantry or Survival Pantry section of your Extended Pantry.

You might be surprised how hard this biscuit is once it is dried, but it's that hardness that gives it such a long shelf life. Just make sure that when you store this in your Extended Pantry, you also include a hammer. You'll need it to crack the biscuits into pieces so you can add them to a bowl of hot soup or tea. Once submerged, the broken pieces will take on the liquid and soften beautifully.

PREP TIME: **15 MINUTES**
BAKE TIME: **1 HOUR 30 MINUTES**
COOLING TIME: **8 HOURS**
TOTAL TIME: **9 HOURS 45 MINUTES**
YIELD: **9 BISCUITS**

EQUIPMENT

Baking sheet

Parchment paper

Large mixing bowl

Rolling pin

Pizza cutter or sharp knife

Fork, chopstick, or clean nail

INGREDIENTS

3 cups all-purpose flour or bread flour (see **Cook's Notes**)

2 tsp fine-ground sea salt

1 cup water

1 Preheat the oven to 350°F (180°C). Line a baking sheet with parchment paper.

2 Add the flour and sea salt to a large bowl and mix well. Make a well in the center, pour in the water, and mix until a dough forms.

3 Transfer the dough to a flat surface and knead for about 1 minute or until smooth. (Dust the dough with flour if it sticks to the surface.)

4 Roll out the dough to ½ inch (1.25cm) thick.

5 Use a pizza cutter or knife to cut the dough into 9 squares or use a biscuit cutter to create round shapes. If you use a biscuit cutter, reroll the scraps and cut out additional rounds.

6 Place the dough onto the prepared baking sheet and use a fork, chopstick, or nail to make indentations in each biscuit.

7 Bake on the middle rack for 30 minutes. Transfer the baking sheet to a heatproof surface. Allow the biscuits to cool completely. (You can leave the oven on or turn it off. If you turn it off, you will need to preheat it again after the biscuits have cooled.)

8 Return the cooled biscuits to the oven at 350°F (180°C) and allow them to bake for 1 hour. After 1 hour, turn off the oven and let the biscuits cool inside the oven. This can take up to 8 hours.

9 Once the oven and the biscuits have completely cooled, store the biscuits in an airtight container or jar. They have an indefinite shelf life.

COOK'S NOTES

What is the difference between all-purpose flour and bread flour? Both flours have had all the bran and germ removed. The difference is that bread flour, as the name implies, is best used for making bread because it is slightly higher in protein. A higher-protein flour will provide a better structure than all-purpose flour, which in turn will create a higher-quality bread dough. All-purpose flour is also known as plain flour or white flour, and bread flour is also known as strong flour.

Can you use whole-grain flour to make hardtack? Yes, but their shelf life will only last for 6 months. After that time, the flour used to make the whole-grain hardtack will begin to go rancid.

Tropical Fruit Leather

When my son, Ben, was a little boy, he loved fruit leather. When we were out and about shopping at our local grocery store and he spied some in a plastic package, his eyes would light up. Although pricey, it was an occasional impulse-buy treat! So you don't bust your grocery budget, you can make fruit leather at home for a fraction of what you would pay at the store. Even better, you control the ingredients, including how much sweetener you want to add. And making it in a dehydrator ensures you retain the fresh fruits' essential nutrients and flavors.

PREP TIME: **20 MINUTES**
DRYING TIME: **6 HOURS**
TOTAL TIME: **6 HOURS 20 MINUTES**
YIELD: **APPROXIMATELY 16 STRIPS**

EQUIPMENT

Sharp knife

Food processor or blender

Electric food dehydrator

Parchment paper or silicone mats

Spatula or offset spatula (icing spatula)

Airtight container

INGREDIENTS

1 large fresh pineapple

1 cup shredded unsweetened coconut

Zest and juice of 1 medium lime

2 tbsp raw honey plus more to taste (optional)

1 Use a sharp knife to remove the outer rind of the pineapple. Remove the core, then chop the pineapple into small pieces. You should have approximately 4 cups of pineapple.

2 In a blender or food processor, combine the pineapple, shredded coconut, and lime zest and juice. Blend until completely puréed. Taste the purée and determine if you want to add the honey. If so, start with 2 tablespoons. After adding the honey, blend well until it is completely incorporated in the purée. Continue adding more honey, 1 teaspoon at a time, until you reach the desired sweetness. Always purée well to completely incorporate any additional honey.

3 Divide the puréed pineapple mixture evenly onto lined dehydrator trays and spread it out using a spatula. (An offset spatula works best.) If you don't have the silicone mats, you can cut parchment paper to fit your trays. Try to spread the fruit mixture approximately ⅛ inch (3mm) thick, leaving it slightly thicker around the edges. (This will prevent the edges from overdrying.)

4 Set the temperature to 135°F (55°C) and dehydrate the pureed pineapple mixture for approximately 6 hours. At 3 hours, rotate the dehydrator trays to encourage even drying.

5 At 6 hours, check the fruit mixture. The fruit leather is done when it is no longer sticky and has a leathery texture. If this texture has not yet been achieved, continue to dehydrate, but keep a close eye on it. If overdried, fruit leather will become brittle and crack. (See **Cook's Notes**.)

6 Once the fruit leather reaches the proper consistency, let it cool to room temperature, then carefully peel it off the parchment paper or silicone mats and cut it into long strips of even width.

7 Roll the fruit leather strips and then wrap them individually in parchment paper. Store the fruit leather in an airtight container at room temperature for several weeks or refrigerate it for several months.

COOK'S NOTES

What other fruits can you use to make tropical fruit leather? In place of the pineapple, experiment with fruits like mango, papaya, or banana for different flavor combinations. Just keep in mind that you will need a total of 4 cups of chopped fruit to make this recipe. And of course you can use any local fruits available to you in your area to make a basic fruit leather.

What can you do if you overdry the fruit leather and it becomes brittle? Not to worry. All you have to do is soak a flour sack towel (or paper towel) in water, wring it out well, and then place the towel over the fruit leather and leave it overnight. Your fruit leather should rehydrate by the next day.

Simple Dehydrator Strawberry-Lemon Jam

Welcome to a delightful twist on classic strawberry jam! This jam bursts with the sweet and tangy flavors of fresh strawberries and zesty lemons and is a breeze to make. Using your dehydrator, you'll capture all the natural goodness of these fruits, resulting in a jam that's packed with concentrated flavor and nutrients.

This jam is perfect for spreading on toast, dolloping on yogurt, or even adding a spoonful to your favorite baked goods. The dehydration process intensifies the flavors, giving you a rich, fruity jam that tastes like summer in a jar. Plus, it's an ideal way to preserve those abundant strawberry harvests if you are blessed to be able to grow this luscious berry in your kitchen garden or get an incredible deal on a couple of flats at your local farmer's market.

PREP TIME: **15 MINUTES**
DRYING TIME: **5 HOURS**
TOTAL TIME: **5 HOURS 15 MINUTES**
YIELD: **APPROXIMATELY 3 QUARTER PINTS**

EQUIPMENT

Blender or food processor

3 quarter-pint (4oz) regular mouth jars with lids (also called jelly jars)

Electric food dehydrator

INGREDIENTS

1 lb (454g) fresh strawberries

Juice of 1 large lemon

½ cup raw honey, or more to taste (see **Cook's Notes**)

1   Wash the strawberries thoroughly and remove the stems. Quarter each strawberry for even blending.

2   In a blender or food processor, combine the strawberries, lemon juice, and honey. Pulse a few times until you have a mixture with small chunks. (No large chunks should remain.) Taste the mixture, add more honey if desired, and mix with a spoon to distribute the honey.

3   Distribute the strawberry mixture evenly between the jars.

4   Remove some of the trays from your dehydrator to make headspace, and place the jars on one of the dehydrator trays.

5   Set the dehydrator to 110°F (45°C) for 5 hours. Stir the mixture in each jar at 2 hours and again at 4 hours. This stirring will help with even drying. Each time you stir the mixture, check the consistency. When the jam has reached a consistency you like, it's done. (Although 5 hours is usually sufficient, the drying process can sometimes take a bit longer.)

6   Let the jam cool to room temperature, then put the lids on the jars and refrigerate.

7   This jam will last approximately 6 months in the refrigerator.

······················· COOK'S NOTES ·······················

Do you have to use honey in this recipe? Because of the unique way dehydrator jams are made, you can choose from different liquid ingredients for your sweetener. The dehydrator helps evaporate some of the liquid in sweeteners like honey while not compromising the quality of the end product. (I find that honey works perfectly with strawberries.) However, you could also try other liquid sweeteners, including maple or coconut syrup. I would not recommend using date syrup, because the flavor will overpower the strawberries. Dry sweeteners are best avoided for this type of jam since we are not cooking it. Without the cooking time required to give granulated sweeteners time to dissolve, you might end up with a grainy jam.

Traditional Pemmican

Pemmican, in its most basic form, is a mixture of dried meat and tallow. The meat is traditionally American bison, and the tallow is rendered suet—otherwise known as the fat that surrounds the kidneys of a bison or cow. Foraged berries were often added for a bit of tang or sweetness. Pemmican is a nutritious powerhouse packed with protein and nutrient-dense fats, which makes it the ultimate survival food!

It's believed that the Cree people originally developed pemmican as a food for survival and travel. Its popularity spread and it was enjoyed by other Indigenous groups and explorers throughout North America. What I like about pemmican is that it offers a taste of a traditional food while providing long-lasting energy for our modern-day adventures, including hiking and camping. It is also the perfect food to have on hand for emergency preparedness.

PREP TIME FOR MEAT: **1 HOUR 30 MINUTES**
DRYING TIME: **8–12 HOURS**
PREP TIME FOR PEMMICAN: **30 MINUTES**
COOLING TIME: **2–4 HOURS**
TOTAL TIME: **12–18 HOURS**
YIELD: **VARIES BASED ON SHAPE**

EQUIPMENT

Wire racks

Baking sheets

Blender or food processor

Large mixing bowl

Small saucepan

Parchment paper

Rolling pin

Airtight container

INGREDIENTS

1 lb (454g) lean beef or bison roast

1 cup small unsweetened dried berries such as cranberries (p. 164), blueberries, etc.

1 tsp fine-ground sea salt (optional)

1 cup tallow rendered from beef or bison suet (no substitutions allowed)

¼ cup raw honey (optional)

········· COOK'S NOTES ·········

Can you use your dehydrator to dry the sliced beef or bison? This is a touchy subject. Some people will say yes. However, since the meat has not been marinated, I recommend drying it in an oven at 170°F (75°C) to avoid foodborne illness.

1 Partially freeze the beef or bison for about 1 hour. This will make slicing much easier. After 1 hour, slice the beef or bison against the grain into ¼-inch- (5-mm-) thick strips, trimming off as much visible fat as possible.

2 Preheat the oven to 170°F (75°C).

3 Place wire racks onto baking sheets, then place the sliced meat on the racks. Dry the meat in the oven for at least 8 hours and up to 12 hours, periodically rotating the baking sheets to ensure even drying, until the meat is very dry and brittle.

4 Once the meat is dried, pulverize it into a coarse powder using a blender or food processor. Set aside.

5 Pulverize the dried berries into a powder using a blender or food processor.

6 In a large mixing bowl, combine the ground meat and ground berries. Add the salt, if desired. Mix well and set aside.

7 Add the tallow to a small saucepan and melt over low heat. (Make sure you use real tallow rendered from suet and not plain beef fat, which is not hard enough at room temperature.)

8 Slowly drizzle the melted tallow into the bowl with the meat and berry mixture. Mix until completely combined. Add the honey, if desired. Mix well.

9 Place the mixture on a piece of parchment paper and roll it into a rectangle ½ inch (1.25cm) to 1 inch (2.5cm) thick. Cut into bars approximately 1 to 2 inches (2.5 to 5cm) by 3 to 4 inches (7.5 to 10cm).

10 Allow the pemmican to cool completely at room temperature or in the refrigerator. (Tallow is very hard at room temperature, so these pemmican bars should be firm when they have cooled.)

11 Place the cooled pemmican in an airtight container with parchment paper between the bars. Store in a cool, dark pantry. Some say that pemmican made just from dried meat and tallow is a "forever food." I'm not sure about that, so I would recommend that homemade pemmican be consumed within 1 year of being made.

Tomato Powder

Whenever you are preparing a dish that involves blanching and peeling away the skin of the tomatoes, do not throw out those tomato skins! Or if you are passing tomatoes through a food mill, be sure to save the tomato pomace. You can use both to make tomato powder. And don't worry if you are collecting only a few tomato skins at a time. Just throw them into your freezer in an airtight container. When you have enough for this recipe, it's time to make tomato powder!

Making tomato powder is a terrific way to create an intense tomato flavor that can enhance soups, stews, and even sauces. Best of all, a tablespoon in a cup of hot water makes an instant tomato soup—perfect when you are craving a cup to go along with a grilled cheese sandwich. The process is simple and rewarding whether you dry the skins in an oven or a dehydrator. Tomato powder is a staple in a no-waste kitchen and an excellent addition to your Working Pantry. If you cook with a lot of tomatoes, as I do, you might have an ongoing supply of ingredients to make an abundance of tomato powder for your Extended Pantry!

PREP TIME: **15 MINUTES**
DRYING TIME: **3–8 HOURS 15 MINUTES**
TOTAL TIME: **3–8 HOURS 30 MINUTES**
YIELD: **VARIES**

EQUIPMENT

Electric food dehydrator or oven

Baking sheets (if using an oven)

Parchment paper or silicone mats

Spatula or offset spatula (icing spatula)

Spice grinder, blender, food processor, or mortar and pestle

Glass jar with tight-fitting lid

INGREDIENTS

The skins, pomace, or both from tomatoes (you can use any tomato skins, but those from Italian plum tomatoes are preferred because they tend to create the best flavor)

DEHYDRATING TOMATO SKINS IN A DEHYDRATOR:

1 Place the tomato skins in a single layer on lined dehydrator trays. If you don't have the silicone mats, you can cut parchment paper to fit your trays. If you are using tomato pomace, spread it as thinly as possible with a spatula (an offset spatula works best) on the lined dehydrator trays.

2 Set the temperature to 135°F (55°C) and dry for about 6 hours. Check after 3 hours, move the skins around, and make sure none are sticking to the lined trays.

3 Make sure the tomato skins are completely dry. (You should be able to snap them as if they were a potato chip.) If, after 6 hours, the skin still feels tacky, continue to dehydrate. Pomace can take up to 8 hours to dehydrate and should also be dried to a crisp.

DRYING TOMATO SKINS IN THE OVEN:

1 Place the tomato skins in a single layer on parchment paper–lined baking sheets. If you are using tomato pomace, spread it as thinly as possible with a spatula (an offset spatula works best) on the lined baking sheets.

2 Place the baking sheets into the oven and set the oven to its lowest setting, ideally under 200°F (95°C).

3 Periodically move the tomato skins around and rotate the baking sheets.

4 Drying time will vary wildly from 3 to 6 hours depending on how low you can set your oven temperature and whether you are drying the skins or the pomace. Watch closely to avoid cooking or burning the skins or pomace.

MAKING TOMATO POWDER:

1 Preheat the oven to 350°F (180°C).

2 Once fully dried, grind the skins into a fine powder using a spice grinder, blender, food processor, or mortar and pestle.

3 To ensure the tomato powder is completely dry, spread it out on a parchment paper–lined baking sheet. Turn off the oven and place it in the preheated oven for 15 minutes.

4 Transfer the baking sheet to a heatproof surface and let cool completely. Store the tomato powder in a glass jar with a tight-fitting lid in a cool, dark pantry. If you live in a humid climate, you can include a food-safe silica gel pack with the tomato powder. This tomato powder will retain its flavor for about 6 months.

························· COOK'S NOTES ·························

Is there a quick way to make tomato powder if you don't want to collect tomato skins or pomace? You bet! If you have canned tomatoes, it's easy to make tomato powder quickly. You can choose from canned crushed tomatoes, diced tomatoes, tomato halves, or whole tomatoes. All you have to do is empty a can of tomatoes into a blender, purée them, and then spread the purée on a dehydrator rack lined with parchment paper. Dehydrate the tomato purée until crisp as described previously, then break it into pieces and grind it into a powder in a spice grinder or blender.

As you can see, this process is a little different than using tomato skins, but the taste is even more intense than the powder made from the skins. Plus, tomato powder made from canned tomatoes takes up a lot less space on your pantry shelf than the original bulky cans of tomatoes. You can use this form of tomato powder in the same way you would use your canned tomatoes. Just add some water, garlic, and Italian seasoning, and you will have some of the easiest tomato sauce you have ever made!

Apple Peel Powder

Apple peel powder is an amazing way to capture the health benefits of apple peels in a concentrated form. Packed with fiber, antioxidants, and essential vitamins, apple peel powder is a nutritious addition to your pantry. The high pectin content helps with digestion and can even support the growth of beneficial gut bacteria like *Akkermansia muciniphila*.

By making apple peel powder, you are working toward creating a no-waste kitchen and making a wholesome ingredient that enhances your meals. You can sprinkle this versatile powder on oatmeal, mix it into smoothies, or use it in baking to add a nutritional boost.

PREP TIME: **15 MINUTES**
DRYING TIME: **4-10 HOURS 15 MINUTES**
TOTAL TIME: **4-10 HOURS 30 MINUTES**
YIELD: **VARIES**

EQUIPMENT

Electric food dehydrator
  or oven
Baking sheets (if using
  an oven)
Parchment paper or
  silicone mats
Spice grinder, blender, or
  food processor
Glass jar with tight-fitting lid

INGREDIENTS

Apple peels, preferably from organic apples, any variety (see **Cook's Notes**)

DEHYDRATING APPLE PEELS IN A DEHYDRATOR:

1   Place the apple peels in a single layer on lined dehydrator trays. If you don't have the silicone mats, you can cut parchment paper to fit your trays.

2   Set the temperature to 135°F (55°C), and dry for about 6 hours. Check at 3 hours, move the peels around and make sure none are sticking to the lined trays.

3   Check again at 6 hours, move the apple peels around and make sure none are sticking to the lined trays.

4   At 8 hours, most of the apple peels should be dehydrated to a crisp and easily snapped in half. Make sure the skins are completely dry. If, after 8 hours, the skins still feel tacky, continue to dehydrate. (If there is a good amount of apple flesh left on the peel, the dehydrating process may take up to 10 hours.)

DRYING APPLE PEELS IN A DEHYDRATOR:

1   Place the apple peels in a single layer on parchment paper–lined baking sheets.

2   Place the baking sheets in the oven and set the oven to its lowest setting, ideally under 200°F (95°C).

3   Periodically move the apple peels around and rotate the baking sheets. Continue drying until the skins are dried to a crisp and can easily be snapped in half. (The drying time will vary wildly from 4 to 7 hours depending on how low you can set your oven temperature and how much apple flesh remains on the apple peel. Watch closely to avoid cooking or burning the apple peels.)

MAKING APPLE PEEL POWDER:

1   Preheat the oven to 350°F (180°C).

2   Once fully dried, grind the apple peels into a fine powder using a spice grinder, blender, or food processor. (Although you can use a mortar and pestle to make tomato powder, it does not work as well for making apple peel powder.)

3 To ensure the apple peel powder is completely dry, spread it out on a parchment paper–lined baking sheet. Turn off the oven and place it in the preheated oven for 15 minutes.

4 Set aside to cool. Once cooled, store the apple peel powder in a glass jar with a tight-fitting lid in a cool, dark pantry. If you live in a humid climate, you can include a food-safe silica gel pack with the apple peel powder. This apple peel powder will retain its flavor for about 6 months.

·········· COOK'S NOTES ··········

Do you really need to use apple peels from organic apples? Normally, I am not a stickler for insisting that everyone buy organic produce. Sometimes the budget simply doesn't allow it, and we don't want to stop eating fruits and vegetables because we can't afford organic! But apples are a crop in which pesticides are used heavily, so when it comes to turning apple peels into apple peel powder, organic apples are best. Yes, we can wash the apples and do our best to remove some residue, but it's not perfect. By dehydrating the peels, we would concentrate all those pesticides, and that's not a smart idea for our health.

Unsweetened Dehydrated Cranberries

Drying unsweetened cranberries is one of the best ways to preserve these tart and nutritious berries. Although it may make them a bit too tangy to eat as a snack, drying cranberries without any added sweetener makes them highly versatile for adding to a variety of recipes. They can add a burst of tangy flavor to baked goods and trail mix, both of which will most likely be sweetened to compensate for the unsweetened cranberries. But one of the best ways to use unsweetened dried cranberries is when making Traditional Pemmican (p. 159), the ultimate survival food! And since dried cranberries can last up to a year or longer when stored properly, they make the perfect Extended Pantry staple.

PREP TIME: **30 MINUTES**
DRYING TIME: **8–14 HOURS**
TOTAL TIME: **8–14 HOURS 30 MINUTES**
YIELD: **2–2 ¼ CUPS**

EQUIPMENT

Colander

Sharp paring knife

Food processor (optional)

Electric food dehydrator or oven

Baking sheet, if using an oven

Parchment paper or silicone mats

Quart (32oz) jar with lid (for conditioning)

Airtight container

INGREDIENTS

1 (12oz/340g) bag fresh cranberries (approximately 3 cups)

PREP:

1   Rinse the cranberries under cold water in a colander, removing any debris. Discard any soft or mushy cranberries. Pat them dry with a clean, lint-free kitchen towel to remove excess moisture.

2   Using a sharp paring knife, slice each cranberry in half lengthwise from the stem. This approach helps the cranberries dehydrate more efficiently than if they are left whole or cut crosswise, which exposes less flesh of the berry. (Alternatively, lay the cranberries out on a clean, lint-free kitchen towel; use a second clean, lint-free towel to cover them; and then lay a heavy skillet on top of the cranberries and firmly press down on them until they split. You can also pulse the cranberries in a food processor to create a rough chop. But don't overdo this—you do not want to mince them!)

DEHYDRATING INSTRUCTIONS (DEHYDRATOR):

1   Place the cranberries in a single layer on lined dehydrator trays. If you don't have silicone mats, you can cut parchment paper to fit your trays.

2   Set the dehydrator to 125°F (50°C) and dehydrate the cranberries for 14 hours. (How long they will take to dehydrate will depend on their cut size.)

3   After 8 hours, check the cranberries and gently move them around on their trays to help with even drying. Between 10 and 12 hours, check the cranberries once again. They may be fully dry at this point and will feel like little pebbles but can be smashed into a powder. If not, keep the cranberries in the dehydrator and continue to let them dry.

DRYING INSTRUCTIONS (OVEN):

1   Preheat the oven to its lowest setting. Place a baking sheet of cranberries in the oven and let them dry for 8 to 12 hours. After 8 hours, check on the cranberries and gently move them around on the baking sheet to help with even drying.

2   After 10 hours, check on the cranberries once again. They may be fully dry and will feel like little pebbles but can be smashed into a powder. If not, keep the cranberries in the oven and continue to let them dry. (See **Cook's Notes**.)

CONDITIONING AND STORING:

1   To ensure the cranberries are fully dehydrated and safe to store, put them into a quart glass jar. Shake the jar a couple of times per day for 1 week. (This is often referred to as conditioning.) If any condensation appears, the cranberries are not sufficiently dried, and they need to go back into the dehydrator for a few more hours.

2   After conditioning, store the dehydrated cranberries in an airtight container in a cool, dry, dark pantry. You can add a silica gel pack to the container to help ensure that the cranberries stay fully dehydrated. This addition can be especially helpful for those who live in humid climates. The dried cranberries will stay fresh for up to 1 year.

Sweet-and-Spicy Beef Jerky

Whenever we are on a road trip in Texas, we always make it a point to stop at a Buc-ee's. I am not kidding when I tell you that any Buc-ee's is an actual tourist attraction to visitors from out of state and from around the world who travel to Texas. Yes, it may be a gas station (with probably more than 100 pumps!), but the Walmart-size convenience store is the true showstopper. You can find pretty much anything under the sun at Buc-ee's. (And yes, the logo is a big sun with a smiling beaver in the middle.) You can find barbecue, sweets, every imaginable snack food, books, clothes, home decor, and more at Buc-ee's. But for our son, Ben, one of the highlights is the impressively long counter of every type of jerky you can imagine!

Now, you may not be able to choose from Buc-ee's extensive selection of jerky, but you can come close by making your own homemade Sweet-and-Spicy Beef Jerky. It's a delightful treat that perfectly balances sweetness with a kick of black pepper and red pepper flakes. This flavorful snack is also an excellent way to preserve beef for

longer periods. By making your own beef jerky, you can control the ingredients and adjust the heat to your liking, ensuring a personalized snack that is satisfying and nutritious. So, enjoy making this jerky, and feel free to tweak the recipe to suit your taste!

PREP TIME: **1 HOUR 15 MINUTES**
MARINATING TIME: **24 HOURS**
DRYING TIME: **6–8 HOURS 15 MINUTES**
TOTAL TIME: **1 DAY 7–9 HOURS 30 MINUTES**
YIELD: **APPROXIMATELY 1 POUND (454G)**

EQUIPMENT

Large mixing bowl

Airtight container

Electric food dehydrator or oven

Baking sheet and wire rack

INGREDIENTS

2 lb (907g) boneless beef top round or eye of round roast (see **Cook's Notes**)

1 cup Worcestershire sauce

½ cup soy sauce

½ cup unrefined whole cane sugar, maple sugar, or coconut sugar

⅓ cup honey or maple syrup (see **Cook's Notes**)

1 tsp garlic powder

1 tsp onion powder

1 tsp freshly ground black pepper

1 tsp red pepper flakes (adjust to taste) (see **Cook's Notes**)

1 cup fresh-squeezed orange juice (approximately 3 medium oranges)

1   It's best to partially freeze the beef for about 1 hour. This will make slicing much easier. Slice the beef against the grain into ¼-inch- (5-mm-) thick strips, trimming off as much visible fat as possible. Set aside.

2   In a large mixing bowl, combine all the remaining ingredients. Stir well to ensure the sugar is fully dissolved.

3   Place the beef and marinade into an airtight container or a large ziplock bag. (A thicker freezer-proof bag works best.) Refrigerate for 24 hours, occasionally turning to ensure even marination.

4   Remove the beef strips from the marinade and pat them very dry with lint-free cotton kitchen towels or paper towels. This step is crucial to remove excess marinade and ensure proper dehydration.

5   Arrange the beef strips in a single layer on the mesh dehydrator trays or on a wire rack placed over a baking sheet if using an oven. Make sure there is space between the strips for air circulation.

6   Set the dehydrator to 160°F (70°C) or the oven to its lowest setting. Dehydrate for 6-8 hours, checking the jerky periodically and occasionally rotating the dehydrator trays (or the baking sheet) for even drying.

7   The jerky is dry once it is somewhat stiff but slightly pliable and can be bent. The jerky should show no signs of moisture or uncooked meat.

8   Once the jerky has reached the proper doneness, if it was dried in a dehydrator, it will need to be transferred, in a single layer, to a wire rack placed over a baking sheet and placed in the oven. If the jerky was dried in the oven, it can remain in the oven for the next step.

9   Set the oven temperature to 275°F (135°C). Once the oven has reached temperature, bake the jerky for 15 minutes. Once finished baking, transfer the baking sheet to a heatproof surface. Allow the jerky to cool completely.

10 Once cooled, store in an airtight container in a cool, dark pantry for 2 weeks. For a longer shelf life, up to 2 months, refrigerate the jerky.

·· COOK'S NOTES ··

What is a beef top round or eye of round roast? These lean, inexpensive beef cuts come from a cow's rump and hind legs, where the muscles are located for movement, so the beef is leaner and less tender from this part of the animal. You may also see these cuts of meat labeled as London broil. It's the perfect type of meat for making jerky because it is so lean.

How can you adjust the spice? For a milder jerky, reduce the amount of red pepper flakes in the marinade. For extra heat, add more red pepper flakes to the marinade.

Do you need raw honey for this recipe? No. Since we will be dehydrating this meat at 160°F (70°C), raw honey is not required because the heat would damage the beneficial profile that raw honey contains.

Chipotles (Smoked and Dried Jalapeños)

One of the lovely dates my sweet husband, Ted, took me on was visiting the Lady Bird Johnson Wildflower Center in Austin, Texas. The highlight of the visit was when he took me to the little café on the grounds. I ordered a salad with a creamy pink dressing. At first glance, I thought it was something like a Thousand Island dressing, but when I took my first bite, my mouth was filled with a delicious flavor that I had never experienced before. It was chipotles!

Chipotle peppers are dried, smoked jalapeños that add a smoky, spicy flavor to various foods—including the Chipotle Cherry Preserves (p. 64) found in the chapter on water bath canning—that enhances a variety of recipes.

Chipotle peppers are a staple in many Mexican dishes and are typically made from red jalapeños, though ripe green jalapeños can also be used. The traditional method involves smoking the peppers for an extended period to dry them while infusing them with smoke. However, we're going to take a little shortcut that is easier for the home cook. We will bake our chipotles in the oven with one special but simple ingredient. No fancy smoker or wood chips needed!

PREP TIME: **15 MINUTES**
COOK TIME: **4–6 HOURS**
TOTAL TIME: **4–6 HOURS 15 MINUTES**
YIELD: **10–12 CHIPOTLE PEPPERS**

EQUIPMENT

Small knife
Medium bowl
Baking sheet
Parchment paper
Wire rack
Airtight container

INGREDIENTS

10-12 fresh jalapeño peppers, preferably red (see **Cook's Notes**)

1 tsp extra-virgin olive oil

1 tsp fine-ground smoked sea salt

1 Preheat the oven to 200°F (95°C). (This low temperature will ensure the peppers dry out slowly, preserving their smoky flavor.)

2 Wash and dry the jalapeño peppers. Using a small knife, make a small slit down one side of each pepper to allow moisture to escape during the drying process.

3 Place the peppers in a bowl. Drizzle the olive oil over them and then sprinkle with smoked sea salt. Toss the peppers to ensure they are evenly coated. The olive oil will help the smoked salt stick to the peppers as they dry.

4 Line a baking sheet with parchment paper. Place a wire rack on top of the parchment paper and arrange the seasoned peppers on the wire rack, ensuring they are not touching each other.

5 Bake the peppers for 4 to 6 hours or until they are completely dried out and have a smoky aroma. The peppers should be wrinkled and darkened but not burnt.

6 Transfer the baking sheet to a heatproof surface. Allow the peppers to cool completely.

7 Once cooled, store the chipotle peppers in an airtight container in a cool, dark pantry. They will stay at their peak freshness for 1 year, but they are often still quite potent after 2 to 3 years.

COOK'S NOTES

What can you do to lessen the chipotles' intensity? If you prefer a milder chipotle pepper, remove the seeds before baking.

What can you do with the smoked chipotles? You can chop up these homemade chipotle peppers and add them to soups, stews, salsas, and marinades. You can also grind them into a powder to add to salad dressings, mayonnaise, and dips for a smoky, spicy kick. Powdered chipotles are also a unique addition to any homemade spice blend.

Tangy BBQ Sauce

This BBQ sauce is a delightful blend of sweet, tangy, and smoky flavors that elevates any dish it touches. Better than store-bought, this homemade version is free of preservatives, allowing the natural ingredients to shine. Whether slathering it on ribs or grilled chicken legs (our favorite!), or using it as a dipping sauce, this BBQ sauce will surely become a staple in your traditional foods kitchen. Best of all, this BBQ sauce comes together quickly without needing a lot of additional spices because you will start with Spicy Texas-Style Ketchup (p. 172) which is made with Oven-Dried Candied Tomatoes (p. 152).

PREP TIME: **10 MINUTES**
COOK TIME: **20 MINUTES**
TOTAL TIME: **30 MINUTES**
YIELD: **APPROXIMATELY 2 CUPS**

EQUIPMENT

Small (2- to 4-quart) saucepan
Whisk
Glass bottle with a tight-fitting cap

INGREDIENTS

2 cups Spicy Texas-Style Ketchup (p. 172)
¼ cup apple juice or apple cider
¼ cup apple cider vinegar
¼ cup honey or maple syrup
2 tbsp yellow mustard
2 tbsp Worcestershire sauce
Fine-ground sea salt, to taste
Freshly ground black pepper, to taste
½ tsp cayenne pepper (optional)

1. Combine the ketchup, apple juice, vinegar, honey, mustard, and Worcestershire sauce in a small saucepan and bring the mixture to a gentle boil over medium-high heat, whisking continuously. Once boiling, immediately turn the heat down to medium-low and simmer for 15 to 20 minutes, whisking occasionally. The mixture should thicken slightly and begin to darken in color.

2. Once thickened, remove the saucepan from the heat. Taste the BBQ sauce and season to taste with salt and pepper. For a bit more of a spicy taste, add the cayenne pepper.

3. Let the BBQ sauce cool completely, then transfer it to a glass bottle with a tight-fitting lid and store it in the refrigerator. This homemade BBQ sauce will stay fresh for about 1 month.

Dehydrated Pineapple (Fresh or Canned)

Dehydrating pineapple is a splendid way to enjoy its tropical sweetness year-round. Whether you start with fresh or canned pineapple, the process is straightforward and rewarding. Fresh pineapple provides the best flavor and texture, but canned options are convenient and work quite well. My favorite way to dehydrate pineapple is in rings. They make the perfect handheld grab-and-go snacks and can also stand in for fresh pineapple when making a pineapple upside-down cake.

PREP TIME: **15 MINUTES**
DRYING TIME: **8–18 HOURS**
TOTAL TIME: **8–18 HOURS 15 MINUTES**
YIELD: **VARIES**

EQUIPMENT

Food dehydrator or oven

Baking sheet

Wire rack

Parchment paper

Airtight container

INGREDIENTS

1 large fresh pineapple or 1 (20oz/565g) can of pineapple rings

PREPARING THE PINEAPPLE:

1 **If using fresh pineapple:** Remove the crown and bottom of the pineapple, then cut off the rind. (If you have a tool for removing the core of the pineapple, go ahead and use it.) Slice the pineapple into rings about ¼ to ½ inch (0.65 to 1.25cm) thick. If you did not remove the core of the pineapple, use a sharp paring knife to cut it out of each individual slice.

2 **If using canned pineapple rings:** Drain the canned pineapple and rinse it. (Save the juice you drain. You can drink this juice or use it in place of water in recipes. It even makes the ideal base for marinades for tenderizing meats.)

DEHYDRATING THE PINEAPPLE:

1 **Dehydrator method:** Place the pineapple slices on mesh dehydrator trays, ensuring they don't overlap. Set the dehydrator to 135°F (55°C). Depending on the thickness of the pineapple rings, the drying time will vary from 10 to 18 hours. You will know they are dry when the pineapple rings look leathery but are pliable. Be sure to check the rings at 8 hours and rotate the trays for even drying.

2 **Oven method:** Preheat the oven to the lowest temperature (usually around 170°F [75°C]). Line a baking sheet with parchment paper (this will make for easy clean-up) and then place a wire rack on the baking sheet. Arrange the pineapple rings on the wire rack and dry them for 8 to 16 hours, depending on the thickness of the pineapple rings. Check the rings at 6 hours and rotate the baking sheet at least once for even drying.

COOLING, CONDITIONING, AND STORING THE DRIED PINEAPPLE:

1 Allow the dried pineapple to cool completely before storing.

2 Loosely pack the dried pineapple in an airtight container for 7 to 10 days, shaking the container daily to prevent sticking and checking for moisture. If moisture appears, return to the dehydrator or oven and dry for an additional hour. This additional hour should be sufficient to dry the pineapple completely, but repeat step 2 if necessary before storing the pineapple.

3 Store the dried pineapple rings in a cool, dark pantry in an airtight container using parchment paper to divide the layers. If the pineapple rings are thoroughly dried and stored properly, they can stay fresh for up to 1 year.

> .... COOK'S NOTES ....
>
> ***Can you rehydrate the pineapple rings?*** Definitely! If your recipe calls for fresh pineapple, simply soak the dried pineapple in room-temperature water for 20 to 30 minutes and proceed with your recipe.

Spicy Texas-Style Ketchup

Spicy Texas-Style Ketchup is a bold and flavorful condiment that combines the sweetness of traditional ketchup with a spicy kick. It's commonly found at a popular burger chain throughout Texas. Whether dipping fries, topping a burger, or adding a kick to your homemade barbecue sauce, this ketchup will surely impress. Plus, by making it yourself, you can adjust the level of heat and sweetness to suit your taste, ensuring every bite is just right.

What makes this ketchup truly special is the rich depth of flavor that comes from using Oven-Dried Candied Tomatoes (p. 152). Slow-drying the tomatoes in the oven concentrates their natural sweetness, while a touch of caramelization enhances their savory, umami goodness. This gives the ketchup an irresistibly bold, well-rounded flavor that you just can't get from store-bought versions. Plus, because these tomatoes are already packed with intense flavor, you need less added sugar—making this ketchup a wholesome, homemade twist on a Texas favorite!

PREP TIME: **10 MINUTES**
COOK TIME: **10–15 MINUTES**
TOTAL TIME: **20–25 MINUTES**
YIELD: **APPROXIMATELY 2 CUPS**

EQUIPMENT

Food processor or blender
Small (2- to 4-quart) saucepan
Whisk
Glass bottle with a tight-fitting cap

INGREDIENTS

1 ½ cups Oven-Dried Candied Tomatoes (p. 152)
½ cup apple cider vinegar
¼ cup unrefined whole cane sugar, maple sugar, or coconut sugar
2 tbsp Worcestershire sauce
1 tsp chili powder (see **Cook's Notes**)
1 tsp ground coriander
1 tsp ground cumin
1 tsp garlic powder
1 tsp onion powder
1 tsp smoked paprika
1 tsp fine-ground sea salt
¼ tsp freshly ground black pepper
½–1 cup apple juice or apple cider
1–2 tbsp raw honey (optional)
Cayenne pepper (optional)

1. Add the Oven-Dried Candied Tomatoes and vinegar to a food processor or blender. Process until completely smooth in texture.

2. Add the sugar, Worcestershire sauce, chili powder, coriander, cumin, garlic powder, onion powder, smoked paprika, sea salt, and black pepper. Process again until completely incorporated.

3. Transfer the tomato mixture to a small saucepan. Begin adding the apple juice or cider to thin the mixture if it appears overly thick. Then bring the mixture to a boil over high heat, whisking continuously. Once boiling, immediately turn the heat down to medium-low and simmer for approximately 10 minutes, whisking occasionally.

4. After 10 minutes, add more apple juice or cider if needed to reach the proper ketchup consistency. Whisk well and continue to warm through.

5. Once the mixture has warmed through and reached the proper consistency, remove the saucepan from the heat.

6. Allow the mixture to cool slightly, then taste. If you want more sweetness, add the honey, 1 tablespoon at a time, and whisk well to incorporate. Taste and add more honey if needed. If you want a spicier kick, add the cayenne pepper, ¼ teaspoon at a time until you reach the heat you like.

7. Let the ketchup cool completely, then transfer it to a glass bottle with a tight-fitting cap and store it in the refrigerator. This homemade ketchup will stay fresh for about 1 month.

> ············· COOK'S NOTES ·············
>
> *What is a good chili powder to use in this recipe?* You can use the basic chili powder sold at most grocery stores, but if you like the smoky flavor of chipotles, grind up some of your homemade chipotle peppers and use that powder for your chili powder in this recipe. For something a bit milder, use ancho chili powder. It is usually available in green (labeled poblano) and red varieties and is quite tasty!

Dehydrated Fresh Figs

If you are blessed to have a fig tree, receive a windfall from a neighbor, or even get an exceptional buy on a case of fresh figs from the farmer's market, this is the recipe for you! And if you like the famous Fig Newtons, these dehydrated figs will provide the base for making those scrumptious cookie cakes at home.

Dehydrating figs is a simple yet rewarding process that allows you to preserve this delicious fruit for year-round enjoyment. This method involves slowly removing the moisture using a dehydrator while retaining the figs' natural sweetness and chewy texture. Here's a tip: make sure you start with thoroughly ripe but unblemished figs. Through dehydration, you can concentrate the flavor of the fresh figs, making them a sweet pantry staple for any fig lover!

PREP TIME: **10 MINUTES**
DRYING TIME: **14–18 HOURS**
TOTAL TIME: **14–18 HOURS 10 MINUTES**
YIELD: **1 ½ CUPS**

EQUIPMENT	INGREDIENTS
Electric food dehydrator	1 lb (454g) fresh figs
Airtight container	
Parchment paper	

1 Wash and dry the figs. Remove the stems and slice each fig lengthwise into 4 slices.

2 Lay the fig slices flat in a single layer on mesh dehydrator trays.

3 Set the dehydrator to 125°F (50°C) and allow the fig slices to dry for 14 to 18 hours. Check the fig slices at 7 hours and rotate the trays for even drying.

4 The figs are dehydrated when they are leathery in appearance but pliable. For fig slices, this should take about 14 hours, but if they have not reached this consistency, continue to dehydrate them, checking every hour for up to 4 more hours. Once fully dehydrated, allow the figs to cool completely.

5 To ensure the fig slices are fully dehydrated and safe to store, put them into a glass jar, filling it about ⅔ full. Shake the jar a couple of times per day for 1 week. This process is often referred to as conditioning. If any condensation appears, the sliced figs are not sufficiently dried and will need to go back into the dehydrator for a few more hours.

6 Once conditioned, store the dried fig slices in an airtight container with parchment paper between the layers to prevent sticking. They can last 6 to 12 months if stored properly and placed in a cool, dark pantry. Beyond 12 months, the natural sugars present in figs may begin to crystallize and take on a white appearance as though dusted in powdered sugar. This is not a bad thing, just something to be aware of so you do not mistake it for mold. The crystallization actually intensifies the flavor of the figs.

Crystallized Ginger

Crystallized ginger is a delightful treat that combines the spicy zing of ginger with the sweet crunch of sugar. You can enjoy this versatile confection on its own, add it to baked goods, or use it as a garnish for desserts. Making crystallized ginger at home allows you to control the sweetness and ensure a fresh, potent flavor. I always have crystalized ginger in the Healing Pantry section of my Extended Pantry because of its numerous health benefits, including aiding digestion and reducing nausea.

PREP TIME: **30 MINUTES**
COOK TIME: **1 HOUR**
COOLING TIME: **2 HOURS**
DRYING TIME: **4–6 HOURS**
TOTAL TIME: **7 HOURS–9 HOURS 30 MINUTES**
YIELD: **SLIGHTLY LESS THAN 1 POUND (454G)**

EQUIPMENT

Medium (6- to 8-quart) saucepan

Candy thermometer

Colander

Large bowl

Baking sheet

Wire rack

Parchment paper or silicone mats

Food dehydrator or oven

Airtight container

INGREDIENTS

1 lb (454g) fresh ginger, peeled and sliced

Water to cover

5 cups granulated sugar, divided

1 Place the sliced ginger in a medium saucepan and cover with water. Bring the mixture to a boil over high heat, then immediately turn the heat down to medium-low and simmer for 30 minutes.

2 Place a colander over a bowl and drain the ginger, reserving the ginger water for this recipe.

3 Return the peeled and sliced ginger to the saucepan and add 4 cups of the ginger water and 4 cups of the sugar. (If you have extra ginger water, save it for use in other recipes.) (See **Cook's Notes**.)

4 Bring the mixture to a boil over high heat, then turn the heat down to medium and simmer uncovered for 35 to 40 minutes or until the temperature reaches 225°F (105°C) on a candy thermometer. (Keep an eye on this: the sugar and

water will create a syrup, and you do not want the syrup to scorch or evaporate.)

5 Place a colander over a bowl and drain the ginger, reserving the syrup for another use. Remove the ginger slices from the colander and spread them on a wire rack over a parchment paper–lined baking sheet. Let them cool for 2 hours.

6 Once cool, toss the ginger slices in the remaining 1 cup of sugar until fully coated.

DRYING INSTRUCTIONS (OVEN):

1 Preheat the oven to its lowest setting, preferably 170°F (75°C).

2 Place the sugared ginger slices on a baking sheet lined with parchment paper.

3 Dry in the oven for 4 to 6 hours or until dry to the touch but still tender and chewy.

4 After drying in the oven, allow it to cool completely, then store in an airtight container in a cool, dark pantry. Crystalized ginger has a very long shelf life since the sugar acts as a preservative. The ginger will be at its peak freshness within the first 2 years of being crystallized.

DRYING INSTRUCTIONS (DEHYDRATOR):

1 Place the sugared ginger slices onto a lined dehydrator tray. If you don't have the silicone mats, you can cut parchment paper to fit your trays. Set the temperature at 150°F (65°C).

2 Dehydrate for 3 to 5 hours, checking periodically for doneness. As with the oven method, the sugared ginger should be dry to the touch but still tender and chewy.

3 After drying in the oven or dehydrator, allow it to cool completely, then store in an airtight container in a cool, dark pantry. Crystalized ginger has a very long shelf life since the sugar acts as a preservative. The ginger will be at its peak freshness within the first 2 years of being crystallized.

········· COOK'S NOTES ·········

What should you do with the sugar syrup that drained into the bowl? This syrup is now a delightfully flavored citrus simple syrup. It can be used to flavor hot or cold beverages, mixed with fresh fruit, or drizzled over ice cream. It is best stored in an airtight container in the refrigerator and will stay at peak freshness for at least 3 months.

Candied Citrus Curls

Candied citrus curls are a visually appealing way to prepare citrus peels. They make a charming addition to your culinary creations, especially as an elegant garnish for topping special-occasion cakes and cupcakes. These delicate curls are made by simmering strips of citrus peel in a sugar solution until they become soft and then baking them to achieve the perfect curls. They add a burst of tangy sweetness wherever used, including as a festive treat at Christmastime.

PREP TIME: **30 MINUTES**
COOK TIME: **1 HOUR 45 MINUTES**
TOTAL TIME: **2 HOURS 15 MINUTES**
YIELD: **APPROXIMATELY 50 ½-INCH-WIDE (13MM-WIDE) CURLS**

EQUIPMENT

Medium (6- to 8-quart) saucepan
Colander or fine-mesh strainer
2 large bowls
Baking sheet
Parchment paper
Wire cooling rack
Airtight container

INGREDIENTS

2 medium lemons
2 medium limes
1 medium navel orange
Water to cover, plus an additional 2 cups water
3 cups granulated sugar, divided

1 Rinse the citrus, then slice off the top and bottom of each fruit and score the peel into quarters.

2 Remove the peels from the fruit and slice the peels into strips about ½ inch (13mm).

3 Place the strips into a medium saucepan and add water to cover. Bring the water and peel mixture to a boil over high heat. Once boiling, turn the heat down to low and simmer for 3 minutes.

4 Drain using a colander or fine-mesh strainer placed in the sink. (Do not save the hot water.) This process will remove the bitter flavor present in the peels.

5 Fill the medium saucepan with 2 cups water and then add 2 cups sugar. Dissolve the sugar over low heat, stirring regularly until no sugar crystals remain.

6 Add the strips to the saucepan and bring the mixture to a boil over high heat, stirring continuously, then immediately reduce the heat to low, stirring the peels for a few more minutes. Cover and simmer for 30 minutes.

7 Remove the lid and continue simmering on low. Keep an eye on the peels and stir occasionally to prevent sticking. Simmer the peels until they become translucent, which may take another 5 to 15 minutes.

8 Once the peels appear translucent, remove the saucepan from the heat. Place a colander or fine-mesh strainer over a large bowl and drain the peels. (Do not discard the syrup that will drain into the bowl.) (See **Cook's Notes**.)

9 Preheat the oven to 175°F (80°C). Line a baking sheet with parchment paper.

10 Put the remaining 1 cup sugar into a second bowl. Once you can comfortably handle the peels, toss them in the sugar until they are very well coated.

11 One at a time curl the sugar-coated peel strips into rounds and place them on the lined baking sheet. Make sure they do not touch each other.

12 Place the baking sheet on the middle rack of the oven and bake for 1 hour.

13 Transfer the baking sheet to a heatproof surface. Allow the curls to cool on the baking sheet for a few minutes, then transfer them to a wire cooling rack.

14 When the curls have cooled completely, transfer them to an airtight container, but do not pile them on top of each other. Make one layer of curls, place a piece of parchment paper over the first layer, then add the second layer of curls, and continue to place them in the container with parchment paper between each layer.

15 Candied citrus curls are best stored in a cool, dark pantry. They will stay at peak freshness for at least 2 months.

Chapter Six
ALL ABOUT FERMENTATION

GETTING STARTED WITH FERMENTATION

Growing up, I ate a variety of fermented foods. My mom always had a selection of vegetables in jars bubbling away, including my dad's favorite: sauerkraut. We also enjoyed milk cultured into homemade yogurt, and my mom's kitchen counter always had a crock of sourdough starter ready to be used to make a loaf of sourdough bread at a moment's notice. All I knew at the time was that these foods were delicious. Little did I know that they were rich in gut-loving good bacteria—probiotics—that kept my entire body healthy. And this is why traditional cultures survived robustly on fermented foods for millennia!

Once I realized just how good fermented foods were for me, I wanted to make sure that I fed them to my own family just like my mom had fed them to us. I started out making the same fermented foods she had prepared. Then, with the rise in popularity of fermented foods that started in the early part of this century, I was introduced to a whole new selection of foods, including kefir and kombucha, that I added to my repertoire. It was fun experimenting and making a wide variety of fermented foods and beverages that my family and I still enjoy to this day.

Thousands of years ago, traditional cultures probably weren't aware of how good fermented foods were for the digestive system. What they did know was that fermenting foods was a way to preserve them. Long before refrigeration was available, these cultures fermented foods to extend their food's life past what it would have been if these foods were left in their original fresh form. Even today, many traditional foods cooks will ferment a variety of foods that will live on their kitchen counter for weeks or possibly months when stored in a cool, dry, dark pantry. Thanks to refrigeration, fermented foods, specifically beverages, fruits, and vegetables, can be preserved for 6 months—and maybe longer—on the top shelf or in the door of our refrigerators.

Fermentation: An Ancient Art of Food Preservation

When it comes to foods and beverages, you might be wondering what exactly fermentation is and what its role is in food preservation. Fermentation is a process that takes raw ingredients combined with microorganisms like yeasts and bacteria (and sometimes even molds) and transforms them into foods that are not only preserved, but whose vitamins and minerals are magnified into a nutritional powerhouse! Best of all, when foods are fermented, they develop a completely different flavor profile that has a slight tanginess (and sometimes even a bit of effervescence) that is especially pleasing for fulfilling the sour taste that many a palate craves.

If you are new to preserving foods through fermentation, remember that you always want to start the process with the freshest food possible. This is not the time to clear your refrigerator of food looking a bit past its prime. For ferments, the fresher, the better is the rule. The fresher your ingredients are to begin with, the better the end product will be.

You can ferment a wide variety of foods, including beans, beverages, breads, dairy, fish, fruits, meats, nuts and seeds, and vegetables. Traditional cultures have been preparing and consuming fermented foods, including fermented vegetables and condiments such as kimchi, sauerkraut, and miso; beverages, such as tibicos (water kefir) and tepache; a variety of breads made by souring grains; cultured dairy as well as cheese curds injected with mold spores to create Roquefort and Gorgonzola; and lots more. This is why fermented foods are the perfect complement to the Four Corners Pantry of any traditional foods kitchen.

Types of Fermentation

The term *fermentation* is a broad one. Yes, it includes what we may immediately think of, such as cultured vegetables like sauerkraut and fermented drinks like the popular kombucha. But also under the umbrella of fermentation are foods that are fermented under the term *cultured*, including yogurt and kefir, as well as foods that are soured, such as sourdough bread. We can create all of these foods through one form or another of fermentation.

ANAEROBIC FERMENTATION

The process of fermentation is often conducted in the absence of air, as when making fermented vegetables. This anaerobic fermentation is a form of lacto-fermentation, which is a type of fermentation that uses lactic acid–producing beneficial bacteria (good bacteria) called Lactobacillus. These bacteria are naturally occurring on fresh produce, in milk, in flour, and in the air. These good bacteria are basically everywhere, including inside our own digestive systems.

AEROBIC FERMENTATION

Certain forms of lacto-fermentation can benefit from a bit of fresh air. When air is involved in the fermentation processes, it is referred to as aerobic—with air. For example, when exposed to air, a sourdough starter will go through a two-step process of aerobic fermentation. The first phase is the alcoholic fermentation caused by yeasts in the air, which causes the starter to take on an aroma of beer or alcohol. Next, acetic bacteria, which are also in the air, will create an acetic fermentation in the starter. This acetic fermentation can give a sourdough starter the smell of vinegar. If you like a really sour starter, which will create a very tangy loaf of sourdough bread, then be sure to give your starter a bit of air from time to time.

The Importance of Temperature

Trying to understand all the natural processes in the different fermentation forms can be overwhelming. As home cooks, all we need to focus on is the successful outcome of our ferment. I have often shared when teaching fermentation to others that ferments can be persnickety! The secret to success is finding that sweet spot in your kitchen or other area of your home where your ferments will thrive. And by sweet spot, I mean the proper temperature range for the ferment you are making.

Generally speaking, the process of lacto-fermentation will thrive the best and keep bad bacteria at bay when kept at temperatures between 60°F and 80°F (16°C and 27°C), with the ideal temperature range being between 68°F and 72°F (20°C and 22°C). I always try to err on the cooler side, around 68°F (20°C). As you get closer to 80°F (27°C), the entire process might speed up too quickly. Bad bacteria prefer warmer temperatures, which can allow them to get a firm foothold on the ferment before the good bacteria in the ferment are strong enough to fend them off. When the balance tips in bad bacteria's favor, mold and spoilage will develop, and you'll have to discard the food.

When the ferment moves along more slowly at cooler temperatures, the good bacteria are given time to create an inhospitable environment for the bad bacteria. Once the lacto-fermentation process goes into high gear, the ferment becomes more acidic, and bad bacteria do not like to take up residence in this acidic environment!

When it comes to temperature, ferments do not like fluctuations. So, once you discover the sweet spot in your home where your ferments start to thrive, make sure your ferments will never be the victim of direct sunlight at any point during the day in that spot. Sunlight will change the temperature in the jar and may cause your ferment to fail.

The Role of pH

Remember when we discussed the pH of high-acid foods in the previous sections on home canning? Well, pH also plays an important role in fermentation. Although not a major concern when making a sourdough starter or cultured dairy, pH is a significant player when making certain fermented foods—especially fermented vegetables—to ensure the ferment's success. It's easy to determine the pH of a vegetable ferment by using pH strips. These strips are very affordable, available from various manufacturers, and can be found at most pharmacies and online.

Using a pH strip to test your vegetable ferment can give you peace of mind that it is safe to eat. When you use these strips, you remove a bit of liquid from your ferment with a clean spoon and place the strip directly into the liquid. What you are looking for is that your ferment registers a pH of 4.6 or lower. At this pH, your vegetable is a high-acid food that has created an environment inhospitable to bad bacteria.

Over time, as you become a more experienced fermenter, you will begin to recognize a satisfactory ferment versus an unsatisfactory one easily. At this point, you may no longer need to rely on pH strips, but they can be reassuring as you are starting out.

...... **WHAT CAUSES THE BUBBLES IN FERMENTS?** ......

You may have noticed that a well-made loaf of sourdough bread has many air holes in the crumb, that homemade cultured dairy has a touch of effervescence when it hits your tongue, or that the vegetable ferment on your counter has bubbles that float from the bottom of the jar to the top. Whenever any of this occurs, it's a good sign. So, what causes all these holes, effervescence, and bubbling?

Carbon dioxide, or CO_2, is a byproduct of successful fermentation. All the yeasts and good bacteria are gobbling up the naturally occurring sugars in the food being fermented. As they consume these natural sugars and proliferate, they create gas, or CO_2. You can see this gas as the holes in sourdough bread, the effervescence in fermented beverages and cultured dairy, and all those bubbles accumulating in the jars of fermented vegetables on your kitchen counter.

Tools of the Fermentation Trade

The best thing about making fermented foods is that the entry point is easy and affordable. If you have already begun your home-canning journey, you most likely have some of the supplies you'll need to start making the fermented foods I share with you in this chapter, which will focus on beverages, condiments, fruits, and vegetables.

Yes, there are professional tools of the trade for making fermented foods that you can find at any kitchen store or online, and they can make some of

your steps easier. However, you can always start with the simple, old-fashioned ways of making these probiotic-rich provisions successfully and safely right in your kitchen. To get started with making the fermented food recipes that follow, you will need the following items:

For anaerobic fermentation:

- Wide-mouth glass jars with tight-fitting lids, assorted sizes
- Four-ounce canning jars (often called jelly jars)
- pH strips

For aerobic fermentation:

- Glass jars, assorted sizes
- Clean cloth, paper towels, or paper coffee filters

And that's it.

In my first book, *The Modern Pioneer Cookbook*, I shared how easy it is to make homemade yogurt with nothing more than two bowls—no electric yogurt maker in sight. I like to rely on simple kitchen tools to get the job done when I can. Since I already have to make room for my canners and dehydrator, I try to limit getting fancy with other forms of food preservation when I can rely on what I already have on hand. This is the case when it comes to making beverage, condiment, and vegetable ferments, which comprise most of the following recipes.

My favorite jar sizes for most fermentation projects are . . .

- Four-ounce canning jars (often called jelly jars)
- Wide-mouth pint jars
- Quart jars
- Half-gallon jars with tight-fitting lids

You can use jelly jars instead of the common glass weights sold for fermentation projects. You can certainly use those glass weights, but I recommend that you first try my jelly jar system with fermentation recipes that call for weights. These recipes are usually for vegetable ferments in which the veggies need to be weighted down under a salted brine in order for them to ferment successfully.

I'll share more details in the recipes that call for a jelly jar, but the beauty of using a jelly jar as a weight is that these jars (or any small jar you have on hand) are easy to find locally; you don't need to order them online. Second, when used as a weight on top of fermenting food in a jar, these jelly jars are easy to remove when the fermentation process is complete. Jelly jars are also excellent at catching liquid as the CO_2 from the fermentation process causes liquid to bubble up to the top of the jar. The jelly jar is placed right side up on top of the ferment and will often fill with this liquid before it bubbles up and out underneath the lid of the jar.

For some, this old-fashioned way of making ferments can have a drawback. When your jar begins to build up CO_2, you will have to loosen the jar lid to allow the gas to escape and then quickly retighten the lid. This technique is referred to as burping the jar. You may have to burp your jar once or twice per day. Yes, various jar-top devices will release the gas without you getting involved in the process. I have tried them all, and I still think my old-fashioned way works the best and creates the best ferment. Is it a bit more work to have to loosen the jar lid? Yes, but it's a good reminder that helps you check on your ferment on a regular basis to see how it's doing, which is something I have always enjoyed as a traditional foods home cook. Watching my burping baby ferment progress in the right direction gives such a sense of fulfillment!

How Long Does It Take to Make Fermented Foods?

Since there is a wide variety of fermented foods, the time it takes to make them will vary. For most of the recipes shared here, the prep time is relatively short, but the fermentation time will range from a few days to no more than 14 days.

WHICH SALT AND WATER ARE BEST TO USE WHEN MAKING FERMENTED FOODS?

The key to a successful ferment often comes down to the salt and water used. Make sure to always use salt that is just salt. My preferred salt is sea salt, but pickling and canning salt works great, too. Just make sure whatever salt you use does not contain any other ingredients, such as anticaking agents. These interfere with the fermentation process and may result in a failed final product. Iodized salt is also not recommended for fermenting vegetables because the iodine contained in the salt may inhibit the beneficial bacteria needed for the fermentation process. The added iodine in salt may also cause an unfavorable change in the taste of the ferment as well as the possibility for some discoloration when fermenting light-colored vegetables that will appear unappetizing.

As for water, try to use as pure a water as you can find. Bottled spring water is my usual choice. If your only option is tap water, fill a pitcher with the water and allow some of the chlorine to evaporate overnight. Chlorine, like anticaking agents, can interfere with the fermentation process.

The more pure and simple the salt and water you use, the better your chances of a successful ferment.

The Role of Tannins in Certain Ferments

Tannins are naturally occurring compounds commonly found in tea, grape leaves, bay leaves, and other plants. When used in fermenting certain foods, they help the food stay crisp. Tannins can be especially important when fermenting cucumbers into pickles. I discovered that a black tea bag, caffeinated or decaffeinated, placed in the bottom of a quart jar works best at keeping pickles quite crisp as they go through the fermentation process. Plus, I have not found that the tea adds any noticeable flavor. The tea adds a mild color to the brine, but it is not significant and in no way unappealing or unappetizing in appearance.

CAN YOU USE HONEY TO SWEETEN A FERMENT?

When it comes to sweetening a ferment, honey is often misunderstood. Since honey contains antibacterial properties, will it interfere with the fermentation process? The answer is no. Although honey can kill bacteria—both good and bad—it does this through suffocation. Once honey is diluted in a fermentation brine, its bacteria-killing properties are deactivated. This makes honey a great sweetening alternative to sugar.

How Long Fermented Foods Stay Fresh

Different fermented foods have different shelf lives; however, for the food recipes shared here, most will stay fresh for 6 months when refrigerated, with many being at their peak within the first 2 to 3 months. As to beverages, if you don't store them in swing-top bottles specifically made to hold fermented beverages, they will lose their "fizz" after a few days. I prefer to enjoy fermented beverages within the first few days of being made, since swing-top bottles can sometimes be unpredictable and explode. Although this is not common when proper bottles are used, I still prefer to avoid them. Keep in mind that many fermented beverages are equally tasty even after they have lost their fizz.

Storing Ferments

As you make ferments according to the recipes shared here, you will want to store them in your refrigerator once they have finished the fermentation process. Ferments generally like to be stored at temperatures that hover around 40°F (4°C). Most refrigerators run a bit cooler than this, which will be fine. However, the top shelf and the door of most refrigerators tend to hover around 40°F (4°C). If you have a root cellar that maintains a cool temperature close to this range, you can experiment with keeping your fermented foods there, but only storing those made in a salty brine.

Most ferments, once refrigerated, will begin to mellow a bit as the flavors meld. I recommend that once placed on the top shelf or in the door of your refrigerator, see if you can hold off eating your ferments for about a week or two. Certain ferments are so tasty right away that waiting to eat them doesn't always work out. That's actually a good sign! However, for some saltier ferments, giving the brine a week or two to continue to permeate the food to a greater extent will improve the flavor.

Note that when you store fermented foods with a salty brine, you may notice cloudiness developing over time. This is completely normal and is part of the fermentation process. You will just want to keep an eye out for mold or a foul odor. If either of these develop, discard the ferment.

General Guidelines for Making Fermented Beverages, Condiments, Fruits, and Vegetables

As I shared earlier, ferments can be persnickety! When you first learn how to ferment foods, there is a bit of a learning curve, but not one that is insurmountable. Usually, there is a short period of trial and error, but often around the time you are working on your third ferment, you will start to master this craft.

Here are my general guidelines:

· Always begin a fermentation project with a clean work surface, tools, jars (or other vessels being used)—and, most of all, clean hands.

· Follow the recipe exactly.

· For recipes that will turn out best if the fermented food remains crisp, consider adding a black tea bag to the bottom of a quart jar before adding any additional ingredients.

· For recipes that call for a brine, always remember to add the salt to each jar individually, then add the water.

· Find the sweet spot in your home where the temperature is just right for your ferment.

· Keep all ferments out of direct sunlight.

· Once the CO_2 begins to build up, remember to burp your jar daily.

· Check the recipe to see when it recommends tasting your ferment or using a pH strip to check its acidity level.

· Once the ferment has reached the proper taste or acidity level, refrigerate the ferment on the top shelf or in the door of your refrigerator.

· If you made the ferment using a salty brine, wait 1 or 2 weeks before eating. Other ferments are generally ready to consume immediately but are often tastiest once chilled.

· Enjoy all ferments within 6 months.

Making Whey for Ferments

Cultured whey is used in some of the recipes in this book as a booster for starting the fermentation process. Cultured whey is easy to make at home. All you need to do is line a fine-mesh strainer with a flour sack towel or cheesecloth and place it over the bowl. Add a 32-ounce container of plain yogurt that has been cultured with various strains of good bacteria (this is what's in most plain yogurt brands) to the fine-mesh strainer and let it drain for eight hours or longer. (You can leave this on the kitchen counter or put it in the refrigerator.) The liquid that drips down into the bowl is your whey. The strained yogurt will look like a soft cheese and is perfect for spreading on crackers or using as a base for dips.

Let's Get Started with Fermentation

Now that you understand the basics of fermentation, we'll forge ahead and start this journey by making a few simple, probiotic-rich fermented beverages that are perfect for maintaining, or improving, our digestive health. Plus, fermented beverages are a wonderful alternative to store-bought sodas. Once you master making these beverages, you'll see how easy fermentation is and be ready to advance to an assortment of fermented foods to fill your refrigerator.

Fermented Lemonade

Welcome to a refreshing twist on a beloved classic! Fermented Lemonade is not your ordinary summer drink. Instead, it is lightly sweet with a bit of tang and is brimming with probiotics that support your gut health. This easy-to-make beverage is perfect for hot days when you need a cool, nourishing sip. Plus, it's a fantastic, healthier alternative to store-bought lemonades that are little more than sugar and water.

PREP TIME: **15 MINUTES**
FERMENTATION TIME: **3–7 DAYS**
TOTAL TIME: **3–7 DAYS 15 MINUTES**
YIELD: **1 GALLON (128OZ)**

EQUIPMENT

Gallon (128oz) glass jar with screw-on lid

Wooden spoon

pH strips

Fine-mesh strainer

Narrow-mouth funnel

Bottles with airtight, screw-on caps

INGREDIENTS

8 cups chlorine-free water

1 cup fresh-squeezed lemon juice (approximately 5 medium lemons)

1 cup raw honey

¼ tsp fine-ground sea salt

¼ cup cultured whey (see "Making Whey for Ferments" on page 185)

1 medium lemon, thinly sliced

1 Combine the water, lemon juice, honey, and salt in the gallon glass jar. Stir well with a wooden spoon until the honey and salt are completely dissolved.

2 Add the whey to the lemonade mixture and stir well to combine. (This step enhances the probiotic content of the lemonade and will aid in the fermentation process.)

3 Add the thinly sliced lemons to the jar, stirring gently to incorporate them into the mixture. Place the lid on the jar and tighten.

4 Place the jar in a shallow bowl (to catch any seepage) in an area away from direct sunlight for 3 days. For best results, you should maintain the temperature between 68°F and 72°F (20°C and 22°C). During this time, the lemonade will begin to ferment and develop effervescence, which appears as bubbles floating to the top of the jar. This carbon dioxide gas is a normal by-product of the fermentation process. Each day during the fermentation process, unscrew the lid and release the gas, stir the lemonade with a wooden spoon, then screw the lid back on the jar. (**Note:** This fermented lemonade can withstand warmer temperatures up to 80°F (27°C); however, keep a close eye on it because the fermentation process might speed up and reach the proper acidity sooner.)

5 After 3 days, use a pH strip to check the level of acidity. You want to reach a pH of 4.6 or lower. Once this pH is reached, taste the lemonade. If it is to your liking, you can strain it and bottle it. If not, let it ferment for up to a total of 7 days.

6 Once the lemonade has fermented to your liking, strain the mixture through a fine-mesh strainer into a bowl or pitcher to remove the lemon slices.

7 Using a funnel, transfer the fermented lemonade into bottles with screw-on caps. Leave at least a 2-inch (5-cm) headspace in each bottle to allow for any additional fermentation. (**Note:** Initially, the fermented lemonade may have some effervescence to it. However, refrigerating the bottled lemonade and allowing it to chill thoroughly before serving will slow down the fermentation process so the lemonade will lose some of the effervescence.)

8 Homemade fermented lemonade will stay fresh in the refrigerator for up to 2 weeks.

Fermented Strawberry Soda

If you have ever made homemade ginger ale, you will love this variation on a classic. Homemade fermented strawberry soda is a delightful, probiotic-rich drink that refreshes and supports gut health. You'll make this effervescent beverage using a ginger bug, which acts as a natural starter culture. The process is simple and yields a lightly sweet and tangy soda that's perfect for summer days. This homemade soda is an excellent alternative to store-bought versions, offering a refreshing and healthy drink for the whole family.

PREP TIME: **15 MINUTES**
FERMENTATION TIME: **2–4 DAYS**
TOTAL TIME: **2–4 DAYS 15 MINUTES**
YIELD: **4 SERVINGS**

EQUIPMENT

Blender or food processor

Colander or fine-mesh strainer

Flour sack towel or cheesecloth

Large bowl

Half-gallon (64oz) jar with screw-on lid (you need sufficient space for stirring with no mess)

Narrow-mouth funnel

4 glass bottles (approximately 8 ounces each) with screw-on caps

INGREDIENTS

6 cups fresh strawberries, washed, stems removed, and sliced

⅓ cup granulated sugar

Juice of 1 medium lemon

¼ cup Ginger Bug (see **Cook's Notes**)

Chlorine-free water

1. Purée the strawberries with the sugar and lemon juice in a blender or food processor.

2. Line a colander or fine-mesh strainer with a flour sack towel or cheesecloth, place it over a large bowl, and strain the mixture.

3. Add the Ginger Bug to the liquid in the bowl and add enough water to make 4 cups of liquid.

4. Pour the liquid into the jar. Place the lid on the jar and tighten.

5. Place the jar in an area away from direct sunlight. For best results, you should maintain the temperature between 68°F and 72°F (20°C and 22°C). On the floor of a cool, dark pantry is a good option, but the fermentation happens quickly, so a bit cooler or warmer will still work. The fermentation time may vary by 1 day, one way or the other.

6. Within 24 hours, you should see bubbles begin to form in the jar and float to the top. This is carbon dioxide, a normal by-product of the fermentation process. Loosen the lid of the jar, allow the gas to escape, then retighten the lid.

7. Since pH strips do not work well with highly colored ferments, use your eyes and nose to determine success. By the second day, this soda should look somewhat effervescent and have a pleasant strawberry aroma. Unfortunately, if you see any mold or the soda has a foul odor, it will need to be discarded.

8. If the soda looks to be progressing along nicely, taste it.

9. If you like the taste of the soda, you can begin decanting it as early as the second day, but you can allow it to ferment for up to 4 days. It will become more effervescent and less sweet the longer it ferments. Use a funnel to decant the soda into glass bottles with screw-on caps. Leave a 2-inch (5-cm) headspace in each bottle to allow for any additional fermentation. Refrigerate.

10. The fermented strawberry soda will stay fresh for up to 4 weeks in the refrigerator but will lose carbonation over time. To retain a greater level of carbonation, you will need to decant the soda in swing-top air-tight bottles specifically made for carbonated beverages. But I generally don't recommend this. Swing-top bottles are at risk of exploding, so great caution should be taken when choosing to use them.

····················· COOK'S NOTES ·····················

How to make a Ginger Bug: Making a Ginger Bug is an easy way to create a fermentation starter for probiotic-rich homemade sodas. This recipe only takes a few minutes of daily preparation over 5 days. The result is a bubbly, gut-friendly beverage starter.

PREP TIME: **15 MINUTES**
FERMENTATION TIME: **5 DAYS**
TOTAL TIME: **5 DAYS 15 MINUTES**
YIELD: **APPROXIMATELY 1½ CUPS**

EQUIPMENT
Quart (32oz) glass jar with screw on lid

INGREDIENTS
10 tbsp freshly grated peeled ginger, divided
5 tbsp granulated sugar, divided
10 tbsp filtered, chlorine-free water, divided

1. Add 2 tablespoons grated ginger, 1 tablespoon sugar, and 2 tablespoons water to the jar. Stir well. Place the lid on the jar and tighten. Place the jar in a warm area away from direct sunlight for 24 hours.

2. Repeat Step 1 each day for the next 4 days.

3. After 5 days, your Ginger Bug is ready to use.

4. You can store any remaining Ginger Bug in the jar at room temperature, but it must be fed every day, as stated in Step 1. Only plan on doing this if you make a lot of fermented soda. Otherwise, simply refrigerate your Ginger Bug until you are ready to make a new batch of fermented soda. (Refrigeration slows down the fermentation process and puts your Ginger Bug to "sleep.") You will need to wake up your Ginger Bug with a few daily feedings until it is bubbly again, so plan ahead.

Traditional Fruit and Herbal Cordial (Nonalcoholic)

A Traditional Fruit and Herbal Cordial is a delightful, nonalcoholic concentrate that captures the essence of fruits and herbs in a sweet, syrupy form that you can turn into a refreshing beverage. A classic drink made with a fruit-based cordial is perfect for adding a touch of nostalgia to any gathering, especially for guests who prefer not to drink alcoholic beverages. The process of making a cordial is simple and versatile, allowing you to use just a handful of ingredients including various fruits and herbs to create your own unique flavor combinations. The possibilities are endless, and the result is always a charming historical beverage that everyone will love.

PREP TIME: **5 MINUTES**
COOK TIME: **30 MINUTES**
STEEPING TIME: **1 HOUR**
FERMENTATION TIME: **24 HOURS**
TOTAL TIME: **25 HOURS 35 MINUTES**
YIELD: **APPROXIMATELY 1 ½ QUARTS (48OZ)**

EQUIPMENT

Medium (6- to 8-quart) stainless steel saucepan or enamelled Dutch oven

Colander or fine-mesh strainer

Flour sack towel or cheesecloth

Large bowl

Narrow-mouth funnel

Large glass bottle with screw-on cap that can hold approximately 1 ½ quarts (48oz) of liquid

INGREDIENTS

5 cups mixed berries (e.g., strawberries, raspberries, blackberries)

Small handful of fresh herbs (basil, mint, or lemon balm all work well) (optional)

5 cups chlorine-free water

2 cups granulated sugar

Zest and juice of 5 medium lemons

1   Rinse the berries thoroughly. If using herbs, rinse them as well and set aside.

2   Add the berries, water, sugar, and lemon zest to a medium saucepan. Bring to a boil over high heat, then immediately reduce the heat to medium and simmer for approximately 20 minutes, stirring occasionally until the berries are soft and the sugar has dissolved.

3   Add the herbs in the last 5 minutes of simmering.

4   Turn off the heat but leave the saucepan on the burner. Allow the fruit and herbs to steep in the sugar water for 1 hour. After 1 hour, the mixture should have cooled completely. Remove the herbs and discard them.

5   Place a colander or fine-mesh strainer lined with a flour sack towel or cheesecloth over a large bowl. Pour the mixture through the lined colander or mesh strainer into the bowl. Allow the liquid from the mixture to drip into the bowl. When the drip slows, gather up the flour sack towel or cheesecloth into a ball and squeeze out as much liquid as you can. (Do not discard the pulp! Transfer it to ice cube trays and freeze. Use frozen cubes to add to smoothies or as fancy ice cubes for sparkling water.)

6   Pour the lemon juice into the bowl with the berry liquid and stir well to combine.

7   Using a funnel, pour the berry cordial into a clean glass bottle with a screw-on cap, leaving a 2-inch (5-cm) headspace.

8   Leave the bottle at room temperature for 24 hours. (Given the short time at room temperature, the exact temperature is not crucial.)

9   After 24 hours, remove the cap from the bottle and release any built-up gas from the vessel, then retighten the cap and transfer the bottle to the refrigerator. The cordial will stay at peak freshness for 3 months. After that, it may begin to crystallize.

10   To prepare a beverage using the cordial, shake the bottle well, then add 1 ounce of the cordial to 8 ounces of still or sparkling water. The amount of cordial can be increased to taste.

COOK'S NOTES

Did you know ... there are several definitions for the word cordial, one of which is the nonalcoholic fruit drink concentrate that we made here. The other refers to an alcohol-based distilled spirit that is often used to add a sweet flavor to cocktails. Plus, a cordial can also refer to chocolate that has a liquid filling or center.

Nonalcoholic fruit and herbal cordials were an old-fashioned natural remedy that was taken orally by the teaspoonful. The sweet flavor helped the believed-to-be curative powers of the fruit and herbs go down a bit easier to soothe a cough, a cold, or other minor respiratory ailments, as well as the general aches and pains from hard physical labor that were common years ago when over-the-counter medications were not available.

Hibiscus-Ginger Fermented Iced Tea

Hibiscus-Ginger Fermented Iced Tea is a refreshing, tangy beverage that combines the tartness of hibiscus with the warm spice of ginger. This tea quenches your thirst and offers a host of health benefits due to its rich probiotic content that supports gut health. Serve this tea chilled over ice on hot summer days and you'll have a refreshing, healthful treat that everyone will love.

This recipe will introduce you to aerobic fermentation (with air) as opposed to anaerobic fermentation (without air), where we put a tight lid on a jar. We will expose the tea to air where it will incorporate yeasts and good bacteria that are all around us, not just those that are present on the hibiscus flowers. This form of fermentation lets the beverage take on a pleasant tang, different from the more pickled flavor common with anaerobic fermentation. Instead, this aerobic fermentation will have a mild flavor as though a hint of lemon or apple cider vinegar had been added. It's the perfect complement to the added sweetener.

PREP TIME: **20 MINUTES**
FERMENTATION TIME: **3–5 DAYS**
TOTAL TIME: **3–5 DAYS 20 MINUTES**
YIELD: **APPROXIMATELY 1 QUART (32OZ)**

EQUIPMENT

Half-gallon (64oz) heatproof jar (you need sufficient space for stirring with no mess)

Paper coffee filter, cheesecloth, or breathable cloth

Rubber band or string

Long-handled wooden spoon

Colander or fine-mesh strainer

Flour sack towel or cheesecloth

Large bowl

Narrow-mouth funnel

Large bottle with screw-on cap that can hold approximately 1 quart (32oz)

INGREDIENTS

¼ cup unrefined whole cane sugar, coconut sugar, or maple sugar

4 cups hot chlorine-free water

¼ cup cultured whey (see "Making Whey for Ferments" on page 185) (see **Cook's Notes**)

2 cups tightly packed dried hibiscus flowers

¼ cup freshly grated peeled ginger

1 Combine the sugar and water in the jar. Stir until the sugar is fully dissolved. Let it cool to room temperature. Once the sugar water has cooled completely, add the whey and stir well.

2 Add the dried hibiscus flowers and grated ginger to the jar. Stir well.

3 Cover the jar with a paper coffee filter, a small piece of cheesecloth, or other breathable cloth. Secure with a rubber band or string tied around the neck of the jar.

4 Place the jar in an area away from direct sunlight. (This is not a fussy ferment. A wide range of room temperatures is fine. If your room is cool, such as 65°F [18°C], the tea will take longer to ferment. If your room is warm, such as 80°F [27°C], the tea will ferment very quickly.)

5 Remove the paper or fabric and stir the mixture vigorously twice daily, starting on the second day, for up to 5 days to oxygenate the mixture and help prevent the growth of unwanted bacteria. Re-cover the jar with the paper or fabric.

6 After 3 days, the mixture should smell very yeasty and be effervescent. This is a sign that the good bacteria are thriving. If your room is warm, the tea may be ready. If your room is cool, the tea will most likely require the full 5 days of fermentation to reach the proper taste. This tea will be a deep reddish-brown color, making it difficult to use pH strips to check the acidity level. However, if you do not see any mold forming on top of the beverage and there is no foul smell, but the tea has a yeasty smell and is bubbly, it is progressing in the right direction. Taste the tea. Once it reaches the desired level of sweetness and tanginess, it's ready to strain. If you want it a bit more tangy, allow the tea to ferment for 1 to 2 days more for a total of no more than 5 days.

7 Line a colander or fine-mesh strainer with a flour sack towel or cheesecloth and place it over a large bowl. Strain the tea to remove the solids.

8 Use a funnel to decant the tea into a large glass bottle with a screw-on cap. Leave a 2-inch (5-cm) headspace to allow for any additional minor fermentation. Refrigerated, this tea will stay fresh for up to 3 months.

·············· COOK'S NOTES ··············

*Are there any other types of starter cultures other than
cultured whey that you can use to make this tea?*
Definitely! If you make water kefir, you can use ½ cup
of the water kefir in place of the cultured whey.

Rejuvelac

Rejuvelac is a refreshing, slightly tangy fermented drink made from sprouted grains using the aerobic fermentation method. It's rich in probiotics, enzymes, and vitamins, making it an excellent addition to any diet for promoting strong gut health. This simple and budget-friendly beverage requires minimal ingredients and effort, making it an ideal choice for those new to fermentation. You can enjoy the wonderful benefits of this homemade probiotic tonic any time of year, but it is the perfect drink to start your new year after a month or more of indulging in lots of sweet treats over the holidays that can often unbalance our gut health. Rejuvelac will have your digestive system back to normal in no time.

PREP TIME: **5 MINUTES**
SPROUTING TIME: **3–5 DAYS**
FERMENTATION TIME: **3–7 DAYS**
TOTAL TIME: **6–12 DAYS 5 MINUTES**
YIELD: **APPROXIMATELY 1 QUART (32OZ)**

EQUIPMENT

Large bowl

Flour sack towel or cheesecloth

Colander or fine-mesh strainer

Half-gallon (64oz) jar (you need sufficient space for stirring with no mess)

Paper coffee filter, cheesecloth, or other breathable cloth

Rubber band or string (see **Cook's Notes**)

Narrow-mouth funnel

pH strips

Large bottle with screw-on cap that can hold approximately 1 quart (32oz)

INGREDIENTS

2 cups whole wheat berries (or other whole grains in the wheat family, including einkorn, emmer, or spelt)

Cool tap water

6 cups chlorine-free water, plus more if needed

SPROUT THE WHEAT BERRIES:

1   Place the wheat berries in a large bowl and completely cover them with tap water. (Don't worry if some of the wheat berries float to the top.) Stir for a few minutes to help saturate the wheat berries, then cover the bowl with the flour sack towel or cheesecloth and allow the wheat berries to soak for 12 hours at room temperature.

2   After 12 hours, drain the wheat berries into a colander in the sink. Place the colander over a large bowl. Using clean hands, spread the wheat berries along the bottom and up the sides of the colander to create a single layer.

3   Cover the colander with a flour sack towel or cheesecloth and leave it at room temperature for another 12 hours.

4   Every 12 hours, remove the cloth covering the wheat berries and rinse the wheat berries in cool tap water in the colander over the sink. If the wheat berries have overlapped during rinsing, use clean hands to spread them back along the bottom and up the sides of the colander to create a single layer. Then, place the colander back over the bowl and cover the wheat berries with the cloth.

5   Continue to rinse the wheat berries every 12 hours until they develop small sprouts. This process can take from 3 to 5 days, depending on your room temperature. (If after 5 days the wheat berries have not sprouted, they may never sprout. Turn them into a porridge.)

MAKE THE REJUVELAC:

1   Add the sprouted grains to the jar and fill it with the chlorine-free water until completely covered. Stir well. Cover the jar with a paper coffee filter, a small piece of cheesecloth, or other breathable cloth. Secure the paper or cloth with a rubber band or string tied around the neck of the jar.

2   Place the jar in an area away from direct sunlight. This ferment is not fussy. A wide range of room temperatures is fine. If your room is cool, such as 65°F (18°C), the Rejuvelac will take longer to ferment; if your room is warm, such as 80°F (27°C), the Rejuvelac will ferment very quickly.

3 Remove the paper or fabric and stir the mixture vigorously twice daily for 3 days to oxygenate it and help prevent the growth of unwanted bacteria, then, re-cover with the paper or fabric. The liquid in the jar will begin to become bubbly, and with each passing day, it will also appear a bit cloudier than the day before. This is a sign that the fermentation is successful.

4 On the third day, use your pH strips to check the acidity level of the Rejuvelac. If it is 4.6 or below, it is ready to be tasted. If you like the taste, it is ready to be strained. If the pH has not reached 4.6 or below or you do not like the flavor, stir the mixture well, re-cover, and allow it to ferment for up to 5 days, checking it with the pH strips each day. Generally, Rejuvelac does not need to be fermented past 5 days because the taste may become highly acidic. However, if at 5 days you find that you want to increase the acidic taste, you can let it ferment for 1 or 2 more days.

5 Line a colander or fine-mesh strainer with a flour sack towel or cheesecloth and place it over a large bowl. Strain to remove the sprouted grains. (Do not discard the sprouted grains! Use them to make a second batch of milder Rejuvelac. After the second batch is finished, use the sprouted grains to make porridge as you would oatmeal. The porridge will have a slightly tangy but pleasant flavor, which you can sweeten with honey or maple syrup.)

6 Use a funnel to decant the Rejuvelac into a large glass bottle with a screw-on cap. Leave a 2-inch (5-cm) headspace to allow for any additional minor fermentation.

7 Refrigerate the bottle of Rejuvelac. It will stay fresh, refrigerated, for 1 or 2 weeks. However, if you see mold developing on the top of the Rejuvelac or it takes on a foul odor, discard it immediately.

8 The Rejuvelac should have a pleasant yeasty aroma and a fresh and slightly tangy taste. Drink 2 ounces of Rejuvelac before each meal to improve your digestion.

.... COOK'S NOTES ....

Can you use a canning band in place of the rubber band or string? Definitely! Canning bands work great for securing paper coffee filters, a piece of flour sack towel, or cheesecloth to a jar.

Fermented Fresh Berries

Fermenting berries with cultured whey is a delightful and healthy way to preserve fresh berries while adding probiotics to your diet. This simple fermentation process not only enhances the natural flavors of the berries but also provides a significant boost to gut health with its beneficial bacteria. The result is an effervescent, tangy, slightly sweet treat that can be enjoyed on its own or added to various dishes, including as a topping for pancakes, waffles, ice cream, or yogurt.

This recipe lets you preserve an overabundance of summer berries that might otherwise go soft if not consumed quickly. Blackberries, blueberries, raspberries, and strawberries are all perfect candidates for this form of preservation.

Fermenting with cultured whey is a traditional method that has been used for centuries to preserve and enhance the nutritional value of foods. The beneficial bacteria in this type of whey helps kick-start the fermentation process, resulting in a probiotic-rich fermented fruit that supports gut health. Try this simple and rewarding process, and you'll never have to discard overripe fruit again!

PREP TIME: **10 MINUTES**
FERMENTATION TIME: **4 DAYS**
TOTAL TIME: **4 DAYS 10 MINUTES**
YIELD: **APPROXIMATELY 1 PINT**

EQUIPMENT
Pint (16oz) jar with
  screw-on lid

INGREDIENTS
1½ cups fresh berries

2 tbsp cultured whey
  (see "Making Whey for
  Ferments" on page 185)

2 tbsp raw honey

¼ tsp fine-ground sea salt

3 tbsp chlorine-free water,
  plus more to cover the
  berries

1. Rinse the berries thoroughly and remove any stems or leaves. Cut larger berries like strawberries into halves or quarters. Place the washed berries in a pint jar, leaving about a 1-inch (2.5-cm) headspace.

2. In a bowl, combine the whey, honey, salt, and 3 tablespoons water. Stir until the salt and the honey are fully dissolved. This is your brine.

3. Pour the brine over the berries. Add more water, if necessary, to keep the berries completely submerged under the brine. Place the lid on the jar and tighten.

4. Place the jar in a shallow bowl (to catch any seepage) in an area out of direct sunlight. For best results, you should maintain the temperature between 68°F and 72°F (20°C and 22°C). If it is too warm, bad bacteria can proliferate before the good bacteria can get a foothold. Also, if it is too warm, the fermentation might advance too quickly, creating something alcoholic or vinegary. Maintaining this temperature spread can be difficult when fermenting berries in the summer when they are in season. Heat rises, so keep your ferment on the floor in a cool, dark pantry if possible.

5. Fruit begins to ferment very quickly. Within 24 hours, you should see bubbles begin to form in the jar and float up the sides to the top. This is carbon dioxide, a normal by-product of the fermentation process. Loosen the lid of the jar and allow the gas to escape, then retighten the lid. Once the lid is tightened, gently turn the jar upside down a few times, then return the jar to the shallow bowl and continue to allow the berries to ferment.

6. After 2 days, transfer the jar to the refrigerator, placing it in the door or on the top shelf. Allow the fruit to continue to ferment for 2 more days.

7. After a total of 4 days (2 days at room temperature and 2 days in the refrigerator), the fruit is ready to enjoy.

8. Stored in the refrigerator, the fermented berries will stay at peak freshness for up to 1 month.

Traditional Fermented Fruit Shrub

A Traditional Fermented Fruit Shrub is a sweet and sour beverage concentrate that combines fresh fruit, sweetener, and vinegar to create a refreshing drink with a probiotic punch. Fermenting fruit has been around for millennia, but the idea of creating a shrub is believed to have originated in the eighteenth century as a way to preserve fruits and create a flavorful drink as well. Perfect for making homemade sodas and mocktails, this shrub is a versatile addition to your beverage repertoire.

PREP TIME: **15 MINUTES**
FERMENTATION TIME: **3–5 DAYS**
TOTAL TIME: **3–5 DAYS 15 MINUTES**
YIELD: **APPROXIMATELY 1 ½ PINTS (24OZ)**

EQUIPMENT

Quart (32oz) jar

Wooden spoon

Paper coffee filter, small piece of cheesecloth, or other breathable cloth

Rubber band or string

pH strips (optional)

Colander or fine-mesh strainer

Flour sack towel or cheesecloth

Large bowl

Narrow-mouth funnel

Bottle with a screw-on cap that can hold a minimum of 1 pint (16oz) of liquid, allowing for a 2-inch (5-cm) headspace

INGREDIENTS

1 cup fresh fruit (e.g., berries, peaches, plums)

1 cup raw apple cider vinegar

1 cup raw honey

1 Wash and prepare the fruit. Berries can be left as is, except strawberries, which should be quartered, and all stone fruits should be pitted and cut into bite-size pieces. Place the fruit in the quart jar.

2 Pour the vinegar and honey over the fruit. Mix well with a wooden spoon.

3 Cover the jar with a paper coffee filter, a small piece of cheesecloth, or other breathable cloth. Secure the paper or cloth with a rubber band or string tied around the neck of the jar.

4 Place the jar in an area away from direct sunlight. For best results, you should maintain the temperature between 68°F and 72°F (20°C and 22°C). If it is too warm, bad bacteria can proliferate before the good bacteria can get a foothold, and the fermentation might advance too quickly, creating something alcoholic or vinegary. Maintaining this temperature spread can be difficult when fermenting berries in the summer when they are in season, so keep your ferment on the floor in a cool, dark pantry, if possible.

5 Remove the paper or fabric and stir the mixture vigorously twice daily for 3 days to oxygenate it and help prevent the growth of unwanted bacteria, then re-cover the jar with the paper or fabric.

6 After 3 days, the mixture should smell very yeasty and be effervescent. This is a sign that the good bacteria are thriving. If so, move on to the next step. If not, continue the fermentation for up to a total of 5 days, then move on to the next step.

7 Depending on what type of fruit you've used, the mixture may or may not be able to be tested with a pH strip due to the color. If the shrub is light in color, you can check the pH to see if it is 4.6 or below. If you are not able to use a pH strip but do not see any mold forming on top of the shrub, there is no foul smell, and the mixture has a yeasty smell and is bubbly, it is progressing in the right direction.

8 Line a colander or fine-mesh strainer with a flour sack towel or cheesecloth and place it over a large bowl. Strain to remove the solids. The liquid in the bowl is your shrub. (Do not discard the solids! You can store them in ice cube trays to add a tangy flavor to smoothies or use as fancy ice cubes added to sparkling water.)

9 Use a funnel to decant the shrub into a glass bottle with a screw-on cap. Leave a 2-inch (5-cm) headspace in the bottle to allow for any additional minor fermentation. Refrigerate the bottle of shrub. It will stay fresh, refrigerated, for up to 1 year. (The sugar and vinegar are strong preservatives.)

10 To use the shrub to make a simple homemade soda or mocktail, mix ¼ cup of the shrub with still or sparkling water and stir well.

Pineapple-Cinnamon Tepache

Pineapple-Cinnamon Tepache is a traditional Mexican fermented drink that combines the refreshing taste of pineapple with a spicy kick of cinnamon. This delicious probiotic-rich beverage supports a healthy digestive system.

But you are in for a surprise with this particular recipe for tepache. I added a secret ingredient that most likely would otherwise find its way to the discard pile: the pineapple core! The core of the pineapple is rich in bromelain, which has anti-inflammatory properties. So, not only are you supporting your gut health, you might also be able to tamp down some bodily inflammation. That's always a good thing!

PREP TIME: **15 MINUTES**
FERMENTATION TIME: **2–4 DAYS**
TOTAL TIME: **2–4 DAYS 15 MINUTES**
YIELD: **8 CUPS**

EQUIPMENT

Gallon (128oz) jar with
  screw-on lid
pH strips (optional)
Flour sack towel or
  cheesecloth
Colander or fine-mesh
  strainer
Large glass bowl
Narrow-mouth funnel
Approximately 6 (16oz) glass
  bottles with screw-on caps

INGREDIENTS

1 large organic pineapple
  (rind and core only)
½ cup unrefined whole
  cane sugar
1 Ceylon cinnamon stick
  (3–4 inches/7.5–10cm)
8 cups chlorine-free water,
  plus more if needed

1   Cut away the pineapple's top and bottom. Remove the rind and core and chop them into 1- to 2-inch (2.5- to 5-cm) pieces. (Save the fruit of the pineapple to enjoy later.)

2   Place the pineapple rind and core pieces, along with the sugar and the cinnamon stick, into the jar. Fill the jar with water, leaving a 1-inch (2.5-cm) headspace. Place the lid on the jar and tighten.

3   Place the jar in a shallow bowl (to catch any seepage) in an area away from direct sunlight. Allow the pineapple mixture to ferment at room temperature for 2 to 3 days. This ferment is very forgiving and will be able to handle warmer temperatures than what most ferments prefer.

4   After 2 to 3 days, bubbles and foam should begin to form on the top of what is now tepache. It should smell fruity and yeasty, and there should be no signs of mold. You can use a pH strip to check the acidity level to determine if the tepache is at 4.6 or lower, but this is not traditionally done because studies of this beverage have found that the pH drops very quickly on the first day of fermentation, often in the pH range of 3. Taste the tepache. If it is to your liking, it's ready to strain. If you would like it slightly more acidic, you can ferment it for one more day up to a total of 4 days—any longer is not recommended.

5   Take a flour sack towel or cheesecloth and run it under cold water to saturate, then ring it out very well. Line a colander or fine-mesh strainer with the damp cloth and place it over a large bowl. Dump the contents of the jar into the lined colander and strain the tepache into the bowl. You can use the pineapple rind and core again to make a second, slightly weaker batch of tepache. (See **Cook's Notes**.)

6   Use a funnel to decant the tepache into glass bottles with screw-on caps. Leave a 2-inch (5-cm) headspace to allow for any additional minor fermentation. Refrigerate the bottles of tepache. Once chilled, enjoy the tepache straight up or pour over ice. Tepache is best consumed within 3 days of making it.

····················· COOK'S NOTES ·····················

Is there anything more you can do with the pineapple scraps after making a second batch of tepache? You bet! You can put the pineapple scraps into a half-gallon jar along with ¼ cup of sugar. Fill the jar with water, leaving a 1-inch (2.5-cm) headspace. Cover the jar with a paper coffee filter or piece of cheesecloth and secure it with a rubber band or piece of string. Stir this mixture twice daily and in 30 days you will have a pineapple scrap vinegar!

Fermented Cherry Tomatoes with Basil

Maybe I shouldn't play favorites, but truth be told, this is my number one all-time favorite ferment! Something magical happens when you ferment cherry tomatoes with basil. The tomatoes become magnificent little flavor bombs that pop in your mouth. In addition to snacking on them right out of the jar, they are perfect for making bruschetta. You can also try them smashed on a BLT sandwich in place of sliced tomatoes. And best of all, because this is a ferment, the tomatoes become rich in probiotics with all of their benefits.

Living in the intense summer heat of central Texas, it can be challenging to grow a big crop of tomatoes, such as beefsteaks. I am generally limited to Italian plum varieties and an abundance of tomatoes in the cherry family. As far as I am concerned, that is never bad because I can't get enough fermented cherry tomatoes with basil. Once you make these, you will feel the same way, too!

PREP TIME: **10 MINUTES**
FERMENTATION TIME: **14 DAYS**
TOTAL TIME: **14 DAYS 10 MINUTES**
YIELD: **2 POUNDS (907G)**

EQUIPMENT

Toothpick

Half-gallon (64oz) jar with screw-on lid

Fermentation weight or small jar no larger than 4oz (optional)

INGREDIENTS

2 lb (907g) fresh cherry tomatoes, washed

10 leaves fresh basil, washed

1½ rounded tbsp fine-ground sea salt

Chlorine-free water

1 Remove any stems from the tomatoes. Use a toothpick to poke a hole in the tomato where the stem was originally.

2 Layer the tomatoes, basil, and salt in the jar. Pack the mixture as tightly as possible without rupturing the tomatoes. Continue layering the tomatoes, basil, and salt in the jar, leaving a 1-inch (2.5-cm) headspace.

3 Fill the jar with the water, making sure that the tomatoes are completely submerged.

4 If desired, place extra basil leaves and stems at the top of the jar on top of the tomatoes to help keep the tomatoes submerged under the brine. You can also use a fermentation weight or small jar to hold down the tomatoes, but it is usually not necessary. Put the lid on the jar and tighten.

5 Place the jar in a shallow bowl (to catch any seepage) in an area away from direct sunlight. For best results, you should maintain the temperature between 68°F and 72°F (20°C and 22°C). This can be difficult when fermenting tomatoes in the summer when they are in season. Heat rises, so keep your ferment on the floor of a cool, dark pantry if possible.

6 Each day, loosen the lid of the jar to allow carbon dioxide to escape. The good bacteria produce this gas during the fermentation process. Once the gas is released, retighten the jar lid.

7 After about 2 to 3 days, you will begin to see bubbles developing in the jar. At this point, refrigerate the tomatoes in the jar, placing it in the door or on the top shelf. Alternative storage options include a cellar or root cellar if those locations can properly maintain a temperature of approximately 40°F (4°C). The cooler temperature will slow the fermentation process, but it will continue. The lower temperature will also help to prevent the development of mold, which can be a problem with a summertime ferment when temperatures are often warmer than ferments prefer. However, if at any time you do observe mold forming on this ferment or it takes on a foul odor, discard it immediately.

8 The fermented tomatoes will be ready to eat in approximately 2 weeks. They will stay fresh in your refrigerator for approximately 6 months but will be at their peak during the first 3 months. After that, they will begin to soften but will still be very flavorful.

Fermented "Pink" Cauliflower and Pearl Onions

Fermented "Pink" Cauliflower and Pearl Onions are a visually stunning and probiotic-rich treat. The addition of beet juice to the brine gives the cauliflower a beautiful pink hue, making this ferment visually appealing. The juice also adds a delightful sweetness and earthiness to the tangy fermented cauliflower and pearl onions. Add this treat to a charcuterie platter and everyone will be asking where you found the delicious "pink" cauliflower.

PREP TIME: **20 MINUTES**
FERMENTATION TIME: **7–14 DAYS**
TOTAL TIME: **7–14 DAYS 20 MINUTES**
YIELD: **1 HALF GALLON (64OZ)**

EQUIPMENT

Half-gallon (64oz) jar with screw-on lid

Fermentation weight or small jar no larger than 4oz

INGREDIENTS

1 large head cauliflower

1 ½ cups chlorine-free water, plus more if needed

½ cup beet juice (see **Cook's Notes**)

1 ½ rounded tbsp fine-ground sea salt

2 cups pearl onions, peeled

1   Wash and cut the cauliflower into small florets. Also cut the stalk of the cauliflower into bite-size pieces. Set aside.

2   Combine the water, beet juice, and salt in a medium bowl. Mix until the salt is fully dissolved. This is your brine.

3   Layer the cauliflower florets, cauliflower stalk, and pearl onions in the jar, alternating with one layer of cauliflower and then a few onions, ending with cauliflower at the top of the jar. Compact the cauliflower as tightly as possible without crushing the onions. Leave a 1-inch (2.5-cm) headspace.

4   Pour the brine over the cauliflower and onions. Add additional water if necessary to ensure they are completely submerged under the brine. Leave a 1-inch (2.5-cm) headspace.

5   Use a fermentation weight or small glass jar to keep the vegetables under the brine. Place the lid on the jar and tighten.

6   Place the jar in a shallow bowl (to catch any seepage) in an area away from direct sunlight. For best results, you should maintain the temperature between 68°F and 72°F (20°C and 22°C). This temperature should be attainable if you are fermenting cauliflower when it is in season, generally in cooler months.

7   After the first few days of the fermentation process, you should begin to see bubbles form in the jar and float up the sides to the top. This is carbon dioxide, a normal by-product of the fermentation process. Once you see the bubbles forming, loosen the lid of the jar and allow the gas to escape, then retighten the lid. Continue releasing the gas from the jar each day during the fermentation process.

8   After 7 days, open the jar and set the lid aside. Examine the ferment. Since pH strips do not work well with highly colored ferments, you will need to use your eyes and nose to determine success. This ferment should look somewhat effervescent and have a pleasant, somewhat tangy aroma similar to pickled vegetables. If you see any mold or the ferment has a foul odor, it will need to be discarded.

9   If the ferment looks to be progressing nicely, taste one of the florets. If the texture and taste are to your liking, it's time to refrigerate the jar. Keep in mind that initially the brine clinging to the cauliflower may be a bit on the salty side, but once refrigerated, the cauliflower will absorb more of the brine and become more tasty, and the brine clinging to the cauliflower will be less salty. If you want more tang and less crunch to the cauliflower, you can let it ferment for up to 14 days.

10 Once the cauliflower is to your liking, transfer the jar to the refrigerator, placing it in the door or on the top shelf. Alternative storage options include a cellar or root cellar if those locations can properly maintain a temperature of approximately 40°F (4°C).

11 Fermented cauliflower holds up exceptionally well and will stay fresh in your refrigerator for up to 6 months.

Fermented Red Bell Peppers and Onions

Fermented Red Bell Peppers and Onions are a delightful addition to any meal. They offer a tangy, probiotic-rich alternative to traditional marinated peppers. By incorporating a simple fermentation process, you can enjoy these delicious peppers while reaping the benefits of gut-friendly bacteria.

This ferment is a zesty treat that brings a burst of flavor and probiotics to your meals. This recipe combines the natural sweetness of roasted red peppers with the subtle heat of onions, all enhanced through the magic of fermentation. Perfect for adding to salads, sandwiches, or as a simple but elegant topping for sourdough toast, these fermented veggies are both delicious and healthy.

PREP TIME: **20 MINUTES**
FERMENTATION TIME: **7–10 DAYS**
TOTAL TIME: **7–10 DAYS 20 MINUTES**
YIELD: **1 QUART**

EQUIPMENT

Baking sheet

Tongs

Wide-mouth quart (32oz) jar with screw-on lid

Fermentation weight or small jar no larger than 4oz (optional)

pH strips

INGREDIENTS

4 medium red bell peppers

1 medium yellow onion

1 tbsp fine-ground sea salt

½ cup chlorine-free water, plus more if needed

1 tbsp cultured whey (see "Making Whey for Ferments" on page 185) or brine from a vegetable ferment (see **Cook's Notes**)

1. Roast the red bell peppers on a baking sheet under the broiler until the skins are blackened and blistered. Using tongs, flip the peppers to expose their underside and continue to roast under the broiler until the skins are blackened and blistered. Place the peppers in a bowl and cover with a towel to steam for about 10 minutes. Once cooled, peel off the skins and remove the seeds and stems. Slice the peppers into 2-inch (5-cm) wide strips.

2. Peel the onion and slice it in half. Slice each half into ¼-inch (.65-cm) half-moons.

3. Combine the salt and water in a small bowl. Stir until the salt is dissolved. This is your brine.

4. Layer the roasted red pepper strips and onion slices in the quart jar, alternating between peppers and onions, ending with peppers. Since the peppers have been roasted, you do not want to pack these too tightly—we don't want to create mush! Once all the peppers and onions are in the jar, you should have a 2-inch (5-cm) headspace.

5. Pour the brine over the peppers and onions, adding additional water if necessary to ensure the peppers and onions are completely submerged under the brine but leaving slightly more than a 1-inch (2.5-cm) headspace.

6. Add the cultured whey into the jar to end with a 1-inch (2.5-cm) headspace. If necessary, use a fermentation weight or small glass jar to keep the vegetables below the brine. Place the lid on the jar and tighten.

7. Place the jar in a shallow bowl (to catch any seepage) in an area away from direct sunlight. For best results, you should maintain the temperature between 68°F and 72°F (20°C and 22°C). This should be attainable if you are fermenting the peppers at the end of their season in September when temperatures are beginning to cool.

8 After the first few days of the fermentation process, you should see bubbles begin to form in the jar and float up the sides to the top. This is carbon dioxide, a normal by-product of the fermentation process. Loosen the lid of the jar and allow the gas to escape, then retighten the lid. Continue releasing the gas from the jar each day during the fermentation process.

9 After 7 days, open the jar and set the lid aside. Examine the ferment. It should look somewhat effervescent and have a pleasant, somewhat tangy aroma similar to pickled vegetables. Unfortunately, if you see any mold or the ferment has a foul odor, it will need to be discarded. Use pH strips to determine the acidity level. If it is 4.6 or below, taste the ferment.

10 If the texture and taste are to your liking, it is time to refrigerate the jar. Keep in mind that initially the brine clinging to the peppers and onions may be a bit on the salty side, but once refrigerated, the peppers and onions will absorb more of the brine and become more tasty, and the brine clinging to them will be less salty.

11 If you would like more tang to the peppers and onions, you can let them ferment longer, up to 10 days, but not much past that. Since the peppers have been roasted, they are already soft, and you do not want the fermentation process to make them too much softer.

12 Once the peppers and onions are to your liking, transfer the jar to the refrigerator, placing it in the door or on the top shelf. Alternative storage options include a cellar or root cellar if those locations can properly maintain a temperature of approximately 40°F (4°C).

13 Fermented peppers and onions will stay at peak freshness in your refrigerator for up to 3 months. After that, the texture of the peppers may begin to degrade.

.... COOK'S NOTES ....

Why did we use cultured whey or brine from a vegetable ferment with this ferment? Generally, vegetables contain sufficient yeasts and good bacteria to assist with the fermentation process; however, in this ferment, when we roasted the peppers to enhance their flavor, we killed off some of the yeasts and good bacteria. So, to replace what has been lost, we need to add a starter culture. In this case, we added cultured whey or brine from another vegetable ferment, which will assist in the fermentation process.

Fermented Beet Relish

If you are not a fan of beets, this fermented beet relish will change your mind. This nutritious way to enjoy beets tamps down some of the earthiness that can be off-putting to some palates. Plus, probiotics enhance this relish through the fermentation process. These beets are a bit tangy and slightly sweet, with a bit of zesty flavor thanks to some fresh horseradish. You can use this relish to top salads or as a colorful side dish. Mix this relish into some mayonnaise in place of a traditional pickle relish, and you will have a unique sandwich spread or the start of some delicious Thousand Island salad dressing.

PREP TIME: **20 MINUTES**
FERMENTATION TIME: **5–7 DAYS**
TOTAL TIME: **5–7 DAYS 20 MINUTES**
YIELD: **1 QUART (32OZ)**

EQUIPMENT

1 quart (32oz) jar with screw-on lid

Fermentation weight or small jar no larger than 4oz

INGREDIENTS

2 large beets, peeled and grated

1 medium red onion, peeled and grated

1-inch (2.5-cm) piece fresh horseradish, peeled and grated

1 tbsp fine-ground sea salt

½ cup chlorine-free water, plus more if needed

1 Combine the grated beets, grated onion, and grated horseradish in a large bowl. Mix well to combine.

2 Pack the beet mixture tightly into a quart jar leaving a 1-inch (2.5-cm) headspace.

3 Dissolve the salt in the water. This is your brine.

4 Pour the brine over the beet mixture, adding additional water if necessary to ensure the beets are completely submerged under the brine. Leave a 1-inch (2.5-cm) headspace. Use a fermentation weight or small glass jar to keep the beets under the brine. Place the lid on the jar and tighten.

5 Place the jar in a shallow bowl (to catch any seepage) in an area away from direct sunlight.

For best results, you should maintain the temperature between 68°F and 72°F (20°C and 22°C). This temperature should be attainable if you are fermenting beets in the late fall when they are still in season.

6 After the first day or two of the fermentation process, you should see bubbles begin to form in the jar and float up the sides to the top. This is carbon dioxide, a normal by-product of the fermentation process. Once you see the bubbles forming, loosen the lid of the jar and allow the gas to escape, then retighten the lid. Continue releasing the gas from the jar each day during the fermentation process.

7 Grated beets tend to ferment quite quickly. After 5 days, open the jar and set the lid aside. Examine the ferment. Since pH strips do not work well with highly colored ferments, you will need to use your eyes and nose to determine success. This ferment should look somewhat effervescent and have a pleasant, somewhat tangy aroma similar to pickled vegetables. If you see any mold or the ferment has a foul odor, it will need to be discarded.

8 If the ferment looks to be progressing nicely, taste the relish. If the texture and taste are to your liking, it is time to refrigerate the jar. Keep in mind that initially the brine clinging to the relish may be a bit on the salty side, but once refrigerated, the relish will absorb more of the brine and become more tasty, and the brine clinging to the relish will be less salty.

9 If you want the relish to have more tang and less crunch, you can let it ferment for up to 7 days, but no longer. Grated beets left at room temperature can become overly tangy if fermented too long and begin to develop the flavor of alcohol.

10 Once the relish is to your liking, transfer the jar to the refrigerator, placing it in the door or on the top shelf. Alternative storage options include a cellar or root cellar if those locations can properly maintain a temperature of approximately 40°F (4°C).

11 This fermented relish will stay fresh in the refrigerator for up to 3 months.

Spiced Preserved Lemons

Spiced Preserved Lemons are a flavorful and versatile condiment that adds a zesty kick to many dishes and is a perfect staple for a traditional foods kitchen. This traditional preservation method enhances the lemons' flavor and prolongs their shelf life. The addition of spices like allspice berries, cardamom, cinnamon, cloves, and coriander infuses the lemons with a warm, aromatic flavor, making them perfect for adding to Moroccan tagines, adding very thinly sliced as a garnish for salads, topping a cracker with a dollop of ricotta cheese for an easy hors d'oeuvre, or adding to sparkling water for a different twist on lemon with water.

PREP TIME: **15 MINUTES**
FERMENTATION TIME: **30 DAYS**
TOTAL TIME: **30 DAYS 15 MINUTES**
YIELD: **1 QUART**

EQUIPMENT

Wide-mouth quart (32oz) jar
  with screw-on lid

INGREDIENTS

8 medium organic lemons
¼ cup sea salt
1 tsp allspice berries
1 (3- to 4-inch/7.5- to 10-cm)
  Ceylon cinnamon stick,
  broken into pieces
6 cardamom pods,
  cracked open
6 whole cloves
½ tsp coriander seeds
½ tsp cumin seeds
½ tsp black peppercorns
Freshly squeezed lemon juice
  (optional)

1   Wash the lemons thoroughly. Cut each lemon into quarters, leaving the base intact so the quarters remain attached. Remove the seeds.

2   Open the lemons slightly and place them, cut side up, into the quart jar, then sprinkle some sea salt inside the lemon quarters. Add a few of each of the spices.

3   Continue this process of adding lemons to the jar, sprinkling salt into the lemons, and adding in some of the spices. Pack everything tightly into the jar after each addition to release the juices from the lemons, stopping when you come within a 1-inch (2.5-cm) headspace. If needed, add additional lemon juice to cover the lemons completely. The lemons should be wedged so tightly into the jar that they do not float above the lemon juice. (It's okay if some of the spices float to the top of the lemon juice.) Place the lid on the jar and tighten.

4   Place the jar in a shallow bowl (to catch any seepage) in an area away from direct sunlight. Preserving lemons with this heavily salted lemon brine is very forgiving. Even a warm room temperature on a kitchen counter is fine. If you never see bubbles appear, do not worry. The brine is so highly salted that the lemons are being cured (preserving food with salt) and will cure exceptionally well. The salt and the acid of the lemon juice create an environment that is extremely inhospitable to the development of bad bacteria.

5   The preserved lemons will be ready to use in recipes in 30 days. Some home cooks leave their preserved lemons at room temperature and use them as needed. I recommend refrigerating the preserved lemons after 30 days of room temperature–curing fermentation. This prevents the lemon peel from becoming overly soft and possibly mushy.

6   Preserved lemons can be stored on the top shelf of your refrigerator or refrigerator door. Alternative storage options include a cellar or root cellar if those locations can properly maintain a temperature of approximately 40°F (4°C). The preserved lemons will stay fresh in the refrigerator for 6 months.

--------------------- COOK'S NOTES ---------------------

How to use the preserved lemons:

Rinsing: It's a good idea to rinse preserved lemons in cool water to remove some of the excess salt before using them. This helps balance the flavor so the saltiness doesn't overpower your dish.

Using the peel: The peel is the most commonly used part of the preserved lemon. After rinsing, cut the lemon into quarters or smaller pieces, depending on your recipe. You can either use the peel as is or finely chop it. The peel adds a lovely, concentrated lemon flavor with a slight saltiness and a subtle fermented tang.

Using the pulp: The pulp is also edible and can add a burst of intense lemon flavor to a variety of dishes. However, it's much saltier and more bitter than the peel. If you decide to use it, use it sparingly and chop it finely, then mix it into marinades, stews, or sauces for a punch of lemony flavor.

Sweet Fermented Radishes

When my son, Ben, was little, we often grew French breakfast radishes in our kitchen garden. We would harvest them, scrub them in the kitchen sink, slice them, slather them with butter and a sprinkle of sea salt, and enjoy to our hearts' content. But since we usually had an abundance of radishes, we would ferment them, too. This recipe is probably one of our tastiest forays into the world of fermented radishes. Radishes hold up beautifully to the fermentation process. They retain their crisp nature but take on a piquant pickled flavor. They are perfect for layering onto sandwiches in place of lettuce and pickles or relish. Different varieties of radishes are in season at different times of year. This recipe is best made with the radishes that come into season in the spring or fall.

PREP TIME: **20 MINUTES**
FERMENTATION TIME: **7–14 DAYS**
TOTAL TIME: **7–14 DAYS 20 MINUTES**
YIELD: **1 QUART (32OZ)**

EQUIPMENT
Quart (32oz) jar with
  screw-on lid
Small bowl
Fermentation weight or small
  jar no larger than 4 ounces
pH strips

INGREDIENTS
2 bunches fresh radishes
  (Approximately 18 medium
  or 24 small)
1 tsp mustard seeds
1 tsp black peppercorns
Handful of fresh dill sprigs
  (optional)
1 tbsp fine-ground sea salt
2 tbsp raw honey
½ cup chlorine-free water,
  plus more if needed

1. Remove the green tops from the radishes, wash the radishes, and slice them into thin rounds, approximately ¼ inch (0.65cm) to ½ inch (1.25cm).

2. Layer the radishes in the quart jar, periodically sprinkling in the mustard seeds and peppercorns. Tuck the dill sprigs (if using) down the sides of the jar. Pack everything very tightly so you leave a 1-inch (2.5-cm) headspace.

3. Combine the salt, honey, and water in a small bowl. Stir until fully dissolved. This is your brine.

4. Pour the brine over the radishes, ensuring they are completely submerged. Add additional water if needed to fully cover the radishes, leaving a 1-inch (2.5-cm) headspace. Use a fermentation weight or small glass jar to keep the radishes below the brine. Place the lid on the jar and tighten.

5. Place the jar in a shallow bowl (to catch any seepage) away from direct sunlight. For best results, you should maintain the temperature between 68°F and 72°F (20°C and 22°C). This temperature should be attainable if you are fermenting radish varieties that are generally in season in the spring or fall.

6. After the first few days of the fermentation process, you should see bubbles begin to form in the jar and float up the sides to the top. This is carbon dioxide, a normal by-product of the fermentation process. Once you see the bubbles forming, loosen the lid of the jar and allow the gas to escape, then retighten the lid. Continue releasing the gas from the jar each day during the fermentation process.

7. After 7 days, open the jar and set the lid aside. Examine the ferment. This ferment should look somewhat effervescent and have a pleasant, somewhat tangy aroma similar to pickled vegetables. If you see any mold or the ferment has a foul odor, it will need to be discarded.

8 Use pH strips to determine the acidity level. If it is higher than 4.6, keep fermenting the radishes for up to 14 days (if you want more tang and less crunch). If the pH is 4.6 or below and the texture and taste are to your liking, it is time to refrigerate the jar. Keep in mind that initially the brine clinging to the radish may be a bit on the salty side, but once refrigerated, the radish will absorb more of the brine and become more tasty, and the brine clinging to the radish will be less salty.

9 Once the radishes are to your liking, transfer the jar to the refrigerator, placing it in the door or on the top shelf. Alternative storage options include a cellar or root cellar if those locations can properly maintain a temperature of approximately 40°F (4°C).

10 Fermented radishes hold up exceptionally well and will stay fresh in your refrigerator for up to 6 months.

Fermented Chipotle Mayonnaise

Fermented Chipotle Mayonnaise is a fabulous way to add a tangy, spicy twist to your dishes while reaping the benefits of probiotics. This homemade mayonnaise is enhanced with chipotle peppers for a smoky kick and fermented to boost its health benefits, making it perfect for sandwiches, dips, and salads. But I will share that this recipe may not be for the faint of heart. As the recipe name implies, this is a fermented mayonnaise, which means that prior to refrigeration, we will be leaving the mayo at room temperature. It's not a long fermentation— just long enough to extend the life of the mayonnaise from 1 week to 2 weeks once refrigerated. If you prefer not to ferment this mayo but want to enjoy the chipotle flavor, you can skip the fermentation and pop it right into the fridge after making it.

PREP TIME: **40 MINUTES**
FERMENTATION TIME: **8 HOURS**
TOTAL TIME: **8 HOURS 40 MINUTES**
YIELD: **ABOUT 1 CUP**

EQUIPMENT

Medium heatproof glass bowl

Blender or food processor

Quart (32oz) jar with screw-on lid

Immersion blender

INGREDIENTS

1 chipotle pepper, thoroughly washed

¼ cup chlorine-free water, plus more if needed

1 very fresh large egg (preferably room temperature) (see **Cook's Notes**)

1 tsp Dijon mustard

1 tsp fine-ground sea salt

1 tsp lemon juice

½ tsp raw apple cider vinegar

⅛ tsp cayenne pepper (optional)

½ cup extra-virgin olive oil

½ cup sesame oil (not toasted sesame oil)

2 tbsp cultured whey (see "Making Whey for Ferments" on page 185), or brine from a vegetable ferment

1 Thoroughly wash the chipotle pepper, then place it in a medium-size heatproof glass bowl and cover it with boiling water. Keep the chipotle submerged in the water by weighing it down with a small plate. Let it soak for 30 minutes.

2 After 30 minutes, drain the chipotle and discard the soaking water. (It can be bitter.)

3 Remove the stem and add the chipotle to a blender or food processor with the water. Whirl the chipotle until it begins to turn into a paste.

4 Scrape down the sides of the blender or the food processor and add additional water, if necessary, to make a paste. Set aside.

5 Dip the egg in boiling water for 10 seconds while still in the shell. (This cleans the shell and prevents the introduction of bad bacteria into the mayo.)

6 Crack open the egg and add it to the quart jar. Add the chipotle paste, mustard, salt, lemon juice, apple cider vinegar, and cayenne pepper (if using) to the jar. Pour the olive oil and sesame oil into the jar.

7 Place the immersion blender at the bottom of the jar and turn it on. Blend for 30 to 45 seconds, slowly lifting the blender as the mixture emulsifies and thickens.

8 Once the mayonnaise has formed, add the whey or ferment brine and blend again until well incorporated. Even if you do not want to ferment the mayo, adding the whey or brine will keep it fresh for up to 1 week as opposed to just a few days.

9 Place the lid on the jar and tighten. Leave the jar of mayonnaise to sit, out of direct sunlight, at room temperature under 75°F (24°C) for 8 hours to ferment. This step enhances the probiotic content and flavor.

10 After fermenting, refrigerate the mayonnaise. It will continue to thicken as it chills and can be stored in the refrigerator for up to 2 weeks.

> ···················· COOK'S NOTES ····················
>
> *Is it safe to eat foods made with raw eggs?* The USDA recommends that no one should eat raw eggs. However, traditional cultures have eaten raw eggs for centuries. So, use common sense to determine what is best for you. That said, if you are pregnant, immune compromised, or you are feeding a child, raw eggs are best avoided.

Fermented Steak Sauce

Fermented Steak Sauce is a rich and tangy condiment that adds depth and complexity to any steak. This sauce combines the robust flavors of traditional steak sauce ingredients with the probiotic benefits of fermentation, enhancing both its taste and nutritional profile. But best of all, this recipe includes tamarind paste—an ingredient once common in steak sauce but now often replaced with a raisin paste, which, for me, is just not the same. So search out tamarind paste that can be found reasonably priced at most specialty grocery stores or online.

If the word tamarind is new to you, it is the pod-like fruit of the tamarind tree, prized for their uniquely tangy-sweet flavor that adds a rich depth to sauces, chutneys, and marinades. The fruit's pulp is naturally high in tartaric acid, which gives it that signature tang, while also providing a boost of essential vitamins and minerals like potassium, magnesium, and B vitamins. When transformed into a paste, tamarind becomes a powerhouse ingredient that enhances both the taste and nutritional value of your favorite dishes. And let me tell you, whenever I grill up a steak for Ted and me, you can bet this steak sauce is on the table—its bold, complex flavor takes every bite to the next level!

PREP TIME: **15 MINUTES**
FERMENTATION TIME: **12 HOURS**
TOTAL TIME: **12 HOURS 15 MINUTES**
YIELD: **SLIGHTLY LESS THAN 1 QUART**

EQUIPMENT

Large bowl

Whisk

Quart (32oz) jar with screw-on lid

INGREDIENTS

1 cup Spicy Texas-Style Ketchup (p. 172)

¼ cup Worcestershire sauce

¼ cup apple cider vinegar

¼ cup soy sauce, preferably naturally fermented

¼ cup chlorine-free water

2 tbsp molasses

1 tbsp Dijon mustard

1 tbsp tamarind paste

1 tbsp raw honey

1 small yellow or red onion, peeled and finely grated

1 tsp smoked paprika

1 tsp freshly ground black pepper

½ tsp cayenne pepper

2 tbsp cultured whey (see "Making Whey for Ferments" on page 185) or brine from a vegetable ferment

1   Add all the ingredients to a large bowl. Whisk until combined. (You can also use a wooden spoon, but a whisk helps to thoroughly distribute all the ingredients, especially the grated onion.)

2   Pour the mixture into the quart jar. The mixture will not fill the jar, so you can easily leave more than a 1-inch (2.5-cm) headspace. Place the lid on the jar and tighten.

3   Place the jar in an area away from direct sunlight for 12 hours to ferment at a temperature between 68°F and 72°F (20°C and 22°C). This ferment is very forgiving, so the room temperature during fermentation is not crucial.

4   After 12 hours, refrigerate the steak sauce. It will stay fresh, refrigerated, for up to 1 month.

Sweet-and-Sour Fermented Dipping Sauce

This Sweet-and-Sour Fermented Dipping Sauce offers a delightful combination of tangy and sweet flavors with the added benefits of probiotics. Perfect for dipping crispy appetizers in, drizzling over stir-fries, or even adding to marinades, this sauce is versatile and enhances any dish with its complex flavor profile.

PREP TIME: **15 MINUTES**
FERMENTATION TIME: **12 HOURS**
TOTAL TIME: **12 HOURS 15 MINUTES**
YIELD: **SLIGHTLY LESS THAN 1 QUART**

EQUIPMENT

Large bowl

Quart (32oz) jar with screw-on lid

INGREDIENTS

¼ cup pineapple juice

¼ cup raw apple cider vinegar

1 cup raw honey

2 tbsp soy sauce, preferably naturally fermented

2 tbsp ketchup, preferably homemade and naturally fermented

1-inch (2.5-cm) piece of fresh ginger, peeled and finely grated

½ tsp red pepper flakes (optional)

2 tbsp cultured whey (see "Making Whey for Ferments" on page 185) or brine from a vegetable ferment

1 Combine the pineapple juice, apple cider vinegar, honey, soy sauce, ketchup, ginger, and red pepper flakes (if using) in a large bowl. Mix until well combined.

2 Stir in the whey or brine.

3 Pour the mixture into a quart jar. (This mixture will only fill the jar about halfway full.)

4 Place the lid on the jar and tighten. Let the sauce sit in an area away from direct sunlight at room temperature for 12 hours to ferment. This ferment is very forgiving, so the room temperature during fermentation is not crucial.

5 After 12 hours, refrigerate the sauce. It will stay fresh, refrigerated, for up to 1 month.

Apricots and Vanilla Fermented in a Honey Brine

Fermented Apricots and Vanilla in a Honey Brine is a wonderfully simple and delicious way to preserve the sweet, juicy flavors of fresh apricots. This recipe combines the natural sweetness of honey with the fragrant warmth of vanilla, turning a simple fruit into a treat that's perfect for adding to yogurt or oatmeal, as a snack all on its own, or even as a delightful topping for desserts, including ice cream or pound cake. The fermentation process enhances the flavor and infuses the apricots with beneficial probiotics, making them a healthy and tasty addition to our diets.

PREP TIME: **15 MINUTES**
FERMENTATION TIME: **4 DAYS**
TOTAL TIME: **4 DAYS 15 MINUTES**
YIELD: **1 QUART**

EQUIPMENT

Wide-mouth quart (32oz) jar with screw-on lid

Small bowl

Fermentation weight or small glass jar no larger than 4oz (optional)

INGREDIENTS

Approximately 12 fresh medium apricots, halved and pitted

¼ cup raw honey

¼ tsp fine-ground sea salt

¼ cup chlorine-free water

1 vanilla bean pod, split and seeds scraped

2 tbsp cultured whey (see "Making Whey for Ferments" on page 185)

1 Place the apricot halves into a quart jar, cut sides down. Pack them tightly, leaving a 1-inch (2.5-cm) headspace.

2 Dissolve the honey and salt in the water in a small bowl. Add the vanilla bean seeds and mix well until distributed throughout the honey water. This is your brine.

3 Cut the scraped vanilla bean pod in half and push each halfway down opposite sides of the jar.

4 Pour the honey brine into the jar and over the apricots, ensuring the apricots are fully submerged in the brine. Leave a little more than a 1-inch (2.5-cm) headspace.

5 Add the whey to the jar, leaving a 1-inch (2.5-cm) headspace. If necessary, use a fermentation weight or small glass jar to keep the apricots below the brine. Place the lid on the jar and tighten.

6 Place the jar in a shallow bowl (to catch any seepage) in an area away from direct sunlight. For best results, you should maintain the temperature between 68°F and 72°F (20°C and 22°C). Apricots fermented in a honey brine can withstand slightly cooler and slightly warmer temperatures. Overall, this is a good ferment for the last of your apricot harvest in the early fall when temperatures are beginning to cool into the lower 70s (F) or lower 20s (C).

7 Apricots in a honey brine begin to ferment very quickly. Within 24 hours, you should see bubbles begin to form in the jar and float up the sides to the top. This is carbon dioxide, a normal by-product of the fermentation process. Loosen the lid of the jar and allow the gas to escape, then retighten the lid.

8 After 2 days, transfer the jar to the refrigerator, placing it in the door or on the top shelf. Allow the fruit to continue to ferment for 2 more days in the refrigerator. After a total of 4 days (2 days at room temperature and 2 days in the refrigerator), the fruit is ready to enjoy.

9 Stored in the refrigerator, the fermented apricots will stay at peak freshness for up to 1 month.

End-of-Season Fruit Ferment

As the growing season comes to a close, it's the perfect time to capture the essence of the harvest with an End-of-Season Fruit Ferment. This easy recipe allows you to preserve the sweet and tangy flavors of a variety of fruits, turning them into a nutritious and probiotic-rich treat. Perfect for adding to your breakfasts or desserts, or simply as a snack, this fruit ferment is both delicious and healthful.

PREP TIME: **15 MINUTES**
FERMENTATION TIME: **4 DAYS**
TOTAL TIME: **4 DAYS 15 MINUTES**
YIELD: **1 QUART**

EQUIPMENT

Quart (32oz) jar with a
  screw-on lid

Fermentation weight or small
  jar no larger than 4oz

INGREDIENTS

Mixed seasonal fruits, such as
  apples, pears, grapes, and
  berries (you'll need enough
  for about 3 cups)
  (see **Cook's Notes**)

¼ cup raw honey

¼ tsp fine-ground sea salt

¼ cup chlorine-free water

1 vanilla bean, split and seeds
  scraped (optional)

1 Ceylon cinnamon stick
  (optional)

2 tbsp cultured whey
  (see "Making Whey for
  Ferments" on page 185)
  (see **Cook's Notes**)

1 Wash and chop the fruits into bite-size pieces. If using berries, keep them whole unless they are strawberries, which should be quartered. Pack the mixed fruits into the quart jar, leaving a 1-inch (2.5-cm) headspace.

2 In a bowl, dissolve the honey and sea salt in the water. Add the vanilla bean seeds (if using) and mix well until distributed throughout the honey water. This is your brine.

3 Break the cinnamon stick (if using) into 2 pieces and slide each piece down opposite sides of the jar.

4 Pour the brine over the fruits, ensuring they are completely submerged. Add the whey to the jar, leaving a 1-inch (2.5-cm) headspace. Use a fermentation weight or small glass jar to keep the fruits below the brine. Place the lid on the jar and tighten.

5 Place the jar in a shallow bowl (to catch any seepage) in an area away from direct sunlight. For best results, you should maintain the temperature between 68°F and 72°F (20°C and 22°C). Fruits fermented in a honey brine can withstand slightly cooler and slightly warmer temperatures. Overall, this is a good ferment for your end-of-season fruit harvest in the early fall when temperatures are beginning to cool into the lower 70s (F) or lower 20s (C).

6 After 24 hours, loosen the lid of the jar and allow the gas to escape, then retighten the lid. (Mixed fruits in a honey brine begin to ferment very quickly. Within 24 hours, you should see bubbles begin to form in the jar and float up the sides to the top. This is carbon dioxide, a normal by-product of the fermentation process.)

7 After 2 days, transfer the jar to the refrigerator, placing it in the door or on the top shelf. Allow the fruit to continue to ferment for 2 more days in the refrigerator.

8 After a total of 4 days (2 days at room temperature and 2 days in the refrigerator), the fruit is ready to enjoy.

9 Stored in the refrigerator, the fermented end-of-season fruits will stay at peak freshness for 1 month.

······················· COOK'S NOTES ·······················

What is the best combination of end-of-season fruits for this recipe? If you have a variety of fruits ready for an end-of-season mix, stone fruits such as peaches, nectarines, and apricots work great together. Apples and pears are another ideal mix, while berries of any variety work well together.

Why do we use cultured whey in this recipe? Fruit ferments very quickly, but the natural sugars in fruit can allow bad bacteria to take over in the ferment before the good bacteria can get a foothold. Using cultured whey introduces good bacteria, giving the ferment a great start to thwart any bad bacteria lurking in the shadows!

End-of-Season Vegetable Ferment

As the growing season winds down, it's the perfect time to make an End-of-Season Vegetable Ferment, which will allow you to harness the rich flavors and nutrients of a variety of vegetables. The simple fermentation process enhances the vegetables' natural taste. It adds beneficial probiotics, making it a nutritious and delicious addition to your meals in place of the more commonly pickled veggies. Best of all, you can make this ferment with vegetable scraps left over from other fermentation or home canning projects. Pretty much any combination of nonstarchy vegetables will work in this recipe.

PREP TIME: **20 MINUTES**
FERMENTATION TIME: **7–14 DAYS**
TOTAL TIME: **7–14 DAYS 20 MINUTES**
YIELD: **1 QUART**

EQUIPMENT

Quart (32oz) jar with a screw-on lid
Small bowl
Fermentation weight or small jar no larger than 4oz (optional)
pH strips
1 tsp mustard seeds
1 tsp black peppercorns
Small bunch of fresh herbs, such as chives, dill, parsley, or tarragon (optional)
1 tbsp fine-ground sea salt
¼ cup chlorine-free water, plus more if needed

INGREDIENTS

Mixed end-of-season nonstarchy vegetables, such as asparagus, beets, carrots, bell peppers, spicy peppers, yellow squash, and zucchini (see **Cook's Notes**)

1   Wash and chop the vegetables into bite-size pieces.

2   Place the mixed vegetables into the quart jar, alternating layers with a few mustard seeds and peppercorns and the fresh herbs (if using). Pack everything tightly, leaving a 1-inch (2.5-cm) headspace.

3   In a small bowl, dissolve the salt in the ¼ cup water. This is your brine.

4   Pour the brine over the vegetables, ensuring they are completely submerged. Add additional water, if needed, leaving a 1-inch (2.5-cm) headspace. If necessary, use a fermentation weight or small glass jar to keep the vegetables below the brine. Place the lid on the jar and tighten.

5   Place the jar in a shallow bowl (to catch any seepage) in an area away from direct sunlight. For best results, you should maintain the temperature between 68°F and 72°F (20°C and 22°C). This temperature should be attainable since this is an end-of-season ferment when temperatures start to cool.

6   After the first few days of the fermentation process, you should see bubbles begin to form in the jar and float up the sides to the top. This is carbon dioxide, a normal by-product of the fermentation process. Once you see the bubbles forming, loosen the lid of the jar and allow the gas to escape, then retighten the lid. Continue releasing the gas from the jar each day during the fermentation process.

7   After 7 days, open the jar and set the lid aside. Examine the ferment. It should look somewhat effervescent and have a pleasant, somewhat tangy aroma similar to pickled vegetables. Use pH strips to determine the acidity level. If it is 4.6 or below, taste the ferment. (If you see any mold or the ferment has a foul odor, it will need to be discarded.)

8   If the texture and taste are to your liking, it is time to refrigerate the jar. Keep in mind that initially the brine clinging to the vegetables may be a bit on the salty side, but once refrigerated, the vegetables will absorb more of the brine and become more tasty, and the brine clinging to them will be less salty. If you want the vegetables to have more tang, you can let them ferment for up to 14 days.

9   Once the vegetables are to your liking, transfer the jar to the refrigerator, placing it in the door or on the top shelf. Alternative storage options include a cellar or root cellar if those locations can properly maintain a temperature of approximately 40°F (4°C).

10 Fermented end-of-season vegetables will stay at peak freshness in your refrigerator for up to 6 months.

Can you include green beans in your end-of-season vegetable ferment?

Unfortunately, there is some disagreement over this. I side with the camp that believes green beans should generally not be fermented raw because they contain naturally present toxins called lectins. To deactivate these substances, the green beans need to be blanched first. The drawback to blanching them before fermenting them is that the blanching process will kill the natural yeasts and good bacteria that are present on all raw vegetables. Will there still be some yeasts and good bacteria from the other vegetables in the mix? Yes, and those might be sufficient to foster a successful fermentation. You also have the option of adding some cultured whey or a bit of the brine from a previous ferment to help the fermentation process get off to a good start. However, all of that said, I simply prefer to home can green beans or blanch them and then pickle them.

Chapter Seven
ALL ABOUT FROZEN FOOD PRESERVATION

GETTING STARTED WITH FROZEN FOOD PRESERVATION

When my sweet son, Ben, was a little boy, he was fascinated with being able to freeze things. Now, keep in mind, this didn't necessarily mean freezing food. He was more inclined to freeze various items in water, which, after a few hours, were now suspended in ice. After all, how can you really play Star Wars if you can't have a Han Solo action figure suspended in carbonite? We often joke that some kids think inside the box, others think outside the box, and some never saw the box. Ben definitely fell into the latter category when improvising for various ingredients he didn't have at his disposal. No carbonite? No problem. Water mixed with different food colors to create gray before freezing will do just fine!

Ben also enjoyed having a bit of fun when his friends would come over to play. I am a big fan of making bone broth. One of the secrets to a gelatinous bone broth is chicken feet. If you have never seen them frozen, they look rather odd. Some might even say they're a bit creepy. To my son, they were an opportunity for amusement. Ben would open the freezer and show his buddies the shelf of frozen chicken feet, proclaiming them to be alien hands, and bragging that the secretive Area 51 had nothing better!

All kidding aside, the freezer can be your ally when it comes to food preservation. When stored properly in a freezer, you can extend your food's shelf life considerably. You just want to keep in mind that when it comes to freezing food as a form of preservation, you can get the best bang for your buck by freezing ingredients that can be turned into hors d'oeuvres, quick meals, or desserts; or better yet, complete dishes that can be easily heated on the stovetop or in the oven.

The Convenience of Freezing: Simple and Effective Food Preservation

The beauty of freezing food as a form of preservation is that it is easy and convenient. Depending on the food or foods being frozen, there is a bit of pre-freezer prep that may take some time on the part of the home cook. However, once that's done, the freezer takes over the job.

What Foods Are Best Frozen?

When it comes to freezing foods, there are lots of options. And the truth is that you can freeze pretty much any food, with few exceptions. However, certain foods definitely freeze and defrost better than others. Once frozen, some foods change considerably in texture when defrosted, and this is not considered a good change. Foods whose texture changes considerably when frozen are better off being preserved through other methods. Still, you'll find a wide variety of foods that freeze and defrost well. A sampling of these foods include:

- Baked goods, including breads, cakes, and muffins
- Casseroles and other prepared foods
- Egg whites, raw
- Fish, meat, and poultry
- Fruits
- Herbs and spices
- Nuts and seeds
- Sourdough starter
- Unbaked pie crust
- Vegetables
- Whole eggs, cooked (best frozen as part of a dish like scrambled eggs or a frittata)
- Whole grains and whole-grain flours

What Foods Are Best Not Frozen?

Some foods should not be frozen because their consistency, taste, and texture can change—not for the better—when frozen. Some of those include:

- Avocados, which tend to brown as they defrost, and lose their buttery taste and texture.

- Certain condiments, including mayonnaise and salads mixed with mayonnaise; as mayonnaise thaws, the emulsion can separate or become clumpy and unappetizing.

- Coffee beans or ground coffee can lose flavor if frozen. These are both best stored in an airtight container in a cool, dry, dark pantry.

- Some dairy products, including milk, cream, yogurt, buttermilk, sour cream, cream cheese, and soft cheeses. Once frozen, these foods may have varying degrees of separation and curdling. If you decide to freeze some of these dairy foods, they are best reserved only for recipes in which they will be cooked. However, butter freezes exceptionally well and once defrosted will appear and act the same as butter that has never been frozen.

- Most unblanched vegetables. However, not all vegetables lend themselves to being frozen even when blanched, including cabbage, celery, cucumbers, and radishes. Because of their high water content, they become mushy when defrosted.

- High-water foods frozen whole, such as a head of lettuce and other greens. These should be blanched and puréed prior to freezing.

- Pasta will become somewhat mushy once defrosted. No-Boil-Noodle Freezer Lasagna (p. 246) and other pasta casseroles are the exception.

- Raw potatoes become soft once defrosted. Once cooked, potatoes can be frozen.

CAN YOU FREEZE CANNED FOODS OR FOODS PACKAGED IN BOTTLES OR JARS?

You should never freeze canned food or food packaged in bottles or jars that are not intended for freezing. Liquid in food expands when frozen. If prepackaged food is not intended for freezing, the packaging can burst once frozen.

SHOULD YOU FREEZE EGGS?

Another food you want to avoid freezing are eggs in the shell, especially raw eggs. The shells will crack, and the eggs will then spoil. You can freeze a raw egg removed from the shell, but I would try freezing one egg first and seeing what you think. When eggs are frozen, the yolks can become quite thick. Once defrosted, these yolks do not blend well with the white of the egg, nor do they blend well with other ingredients. When it comes to eggs, it may be best to use your yolks fresh and freeze your egg whites for later use—such as making a meringue.

How to Freeze Food Correctly

If you have ever frozen food and found that it lost its quality either while in the freezer or upon defrosting, it often has to do with how the food was prepared for freezing and packaged for storing in the freezer in the first place. In each freezer recipe I share with you, I will explain step by step exactly what to do to ensure that your foods will freeze and defrost successfully.

When freezing fruits and vegetables, there will be some change in texture. You can't avoid this. When foods are frozen, their cell walls rupture to some extent. The secret is to keep this rupturing to a minimum. You minimize cell rupture by making sure that the food can be frozen as quickly as possible. You can do this by ensuring the food you are freezing has already been chilled and that you allow room for sufficient air to circulate around the food once placed in the freezer. These two simple steps will ensure that when you defrost your food, especially fruits and vegetables, the texture will be as intact as possible.

Before you forge ahead with freezing food, make sure that your freezer is operating efficiently to prevent possible problems. The correct temperature for a standard household freezer (either as part of your refrigerator or a stand-alone unit) is 0°F (−18°C). This temperature means that your ice cream should be rock hard!

When it comes to freezing food to maintain good taste, texture, and quality, specific common problems can thwart even the best efforts. However, knowing about these troublemakers ahead of time will provide you with the knowledge to prevent them. Common problems when freezing food include:

- Too much water being left on washed food, which may lead to the development of large ice crystals. These large crystals cause the cells in food to rupture excessively and cause the food to become mushy. Dry off your food!

- Too much air surrounding the food caused by improper sealing of the packaging, which may lead to a loss of moisture and cause freezer burn.

- Freezing food when it is hot. Food must be chilled before freezing; otherwise, the heat from hot food will create steam, introducing moisture and delaying freezing time. This will lead to the formation of large, damaging ice crystals.

- Putting too much unfrozen food in the freezer at once and raising the temperature of the freezer.

- Not remembering to repackage foods from the butcher or fishmonger. Their packaging is often not airtight and will lead to the food degrading quickly, most likely from freezer burn, once frozen.

- Packing too much food into your freezer so the cold air can't circulate around the food.

- Freezing stone fruits with the pit. This will impart a bitter flavor to the fruit.

- Not properly blanching most vegetables in boiling water for approximately 30 seconds prior to freezing will lead to a very unsatisfactory end product once defrosted. Blanching most vegetables prior to freezing will slow down the enzymes responsible for the ripening process and improve the flavor, color, texture, and nutrient retention of the food.

HOW DO YOU FREEZE ALLIUMS?

Even though most vegetables are best blanched prior to freezing, commonly used foods in the allium family, including garlic, onions, leeks, chives, and scallions, do not need to be blanched before freezing. They can be chopped or sliced and immediately frozen in a ziplock bag or vacuum-sealed bag.

HOW DO YOU PREPARE TOMATOES FOR FREEZING?

When freezing tomatoes, always blanch them first and then remove the skins. Defrosted tomato skins are tough and often unpalatable. Cut an X into the top, or stem end, of a tomato and boil it for 30 seconds. Remove the tomatoes with a slotted spoon and transfer them to a bowl of cool water large enough to hold them. Once cool, remove the skins, then cut out the core.

The Best Storage Options for Freezing Food

The best container for freezing food will be determined by what food you are freezing. It may be something as simple as ziplock bags or reusable silicone storage bags. If you decide to use plastic bags, make sure they are made for the freezer. If not, you will need to double them.

Solid-sided freezer containers include BPA-free reusable plastic containers or glass containers with snap-on lids, as well as more elaborate glassware with snap-on lids. Wide-mouth canning jars with lids and bands or with plastic screw-on storage lids also make great ways to freeze food, as do Weck jars and French working glasses with plastic storage lids.

When it comes to freezing food in plastic bags, the secret is to make sure you can eliminate as much air as possible from the bag. You can do this best manually by laying the bag on a flat surface and physically pressing down on the bag with one hand to release air while sealing the bag with the other hand. Another way of sealing food in plastic bags is by using a food vacuum sealer. These come in makes and models today to fit every budget. If you find that you like storing food in plastic bags in your freezer, investing in a vacuum sealer will be money well spent.

If what you are freezing lends itself to be stored in jars, such as bone broth, soup, or stew, thick-walled glass jars are ideal options. As with the plastic bag system, there is a secret to successfully freezing food in jars—actually, two secrets. First, choose a glass jar with a wide mouth. As the frozen liquid expands, it is less likely to crack wide-mouth jars as opposed to regular mouth jars. By wide-mouth jar, I mean a jar that has an inner diameter of approximately 3 inches (7.5cm), like the typical wide-mouth canning jar.

The second secret to freezing food successfully in jars is to make sure that you leave a good amount of headspace—at least 1 inch (2.5cm)—from the rim of the jar to allow the frozen liquid room to expand and prevent the glass jar from cracking. For this reason, one of my favorite ways to store bone broth in the freezer is in French working glasses (sometimes called French jelly jars or storage jars). These thick-walled glasses with a rolled rim allow plastic lids to attach to the rim by simply pressing down on it. Note that the lid is not a screw-on lid or a lid that is clamped down. If, for any reason, I underestimate the headspace and my bone broth expands past the rim of the glass, the lid pops up and off.

Other ways to store food in the freezer include:

- Casserole dishes with lids, or covering the dish with heavy-duty aluminum foil
- Ice cube trays with lids
- Silicone freezer molds with lids
- Wrapping food in plastic wrap plus heavy-duty aluminum foil and then placing it into a freezer-proof container or storage bag

It's important to remember that whatever way you choose to store your various frozen foods, you should make sure that the method is as close to airtight as possible. Keeping air out of containers protects foods from absorbing off-flavors and odors while in the freezer.

How Long Can Food Be Stored In the Freezer?

Different frozen foods will have different best-used-by dates, but the bottom line is that frozen food is technically never good or bad; it just degrades in quality. The same holds true for most preserved

foods and your typical shelf-stable foods from the grocery store. They may become stale, tasteless, and degrade in nutrition, but they rarely spoil. The biggest enemy of freezer food is freezer burn. Even the best frozen food may eventually fall prey to it. However, with each recipe I share, I will also include a time frame for how long the food will be at peak quality while in the freezer.

As a general rule, most frozen foods will stay at peak quality for a minimum of 2 months to a maximum of 12 months. I realize this is a huge spread! Foods that have been prepared in some way, such as a casserole, will tend to have a shorter frozen shelf life, being at their peak quality for approximately 2 to 3 months. Liquids, including bone broth, soups, and stews, may vary but can often be frozen for up to 6 months. However, they might be at their peak a bit sooner. Fruits usually do well frozen for up to 6 months, and vegetables for up to 12 months. A raw beef chuck roast or whole chicken may remain at their peak up to 12 months frozen. The exceptions to these ranges are foods such as lunchmeat and hot dogs, which may remain at peak quality for only 1 month.

Just remember that whenever you repackage food and then freeze it, you should label and date the food. And don't just put the date when you put the food into the freezer; also put your own best-used-by date based on general recommendations from the USDA or the NCHFP.

How to Properly Defrost Food

The phrase you always want to remember when preserving food through freezing is "Freeze Fast; Defrost Slow!" Frozen food is best defrosted in the refrigerator. Yes, defrosting in the fridge takes a bit more time than defrosting on the counter, but the quality of the defrosted food will be significantly better. This is because frozen food loses its ability to hold on to moisture. If you allow food to defrost on the counter, the water that leaches out of the frozen food evaporates. The loss of water and subsequent evaporation lowers the quality of the food, especially the texture. When you defrost the same food in the refrigerator, the process of the food losing water and that water evaporating goes at a much slower rate. So once the food in the refrigerator defrosts, it has retained more water and will have a better texture.

The USDA concurs that the best way to thaw food is in the refrigerator. Thawing food on the counter can make it unsafe to eat. Freezing food to 0°F (−18°C) inactivates microbes present on food, including bacteria, yeasts, and molds. When food thaws and becomes warmer than 40°F (4°C), bacteria (including other microbes) that may have been present before freezing can start to multiply. The bacteria on the food, especially the outer layer, can multiply quickly. So stick with defrosting food in the refrigerator. It will be of better quality and food safe. Once defrosted, be sure to handle the food as you would any perishable food.

As a general rule, most baked goods, fruits, and vegetables defrost relatively quickly in the refrigerator. However, what if you are in a rush and are tempted to defrost large frozen pieces of food, such as meats or poultry, on the counter to speed up the process? I understand completely. But if you take this route, you need to follow some very specific rules so you can try to maintain the quality of the food as it defrosts and, at the same time, be conscious of maintaining food safety. Defrosting food on the counter is best reserved for food in its original packaging. For example, what if you forgot to defrost your Thanksgiving turkey, and you're expecting guests for dinner? No problem, here is what you need to do:

Start this process as early in the day as possible:

1   Place the turkey (or other food in its original packaging) into a leakproof plastic bag large enough to hold it. This bag is to protect the food in case the original packaging is damaged in any way.

2   Determine how many pounds your turkey weighs. The packaging should state this information.

3   Once you know the weight of the turkey, calculate how much time you will need to defrost it using this method: Allow 30 minutes of defrosting time per pound.

4   Submerge the frozen turkey in its original packaging and sealed in the outer plastic bag in a sink or container of cold water.

5   Change the water every 30 minutes.

For example, the defrosting time for a 10-pound turkey will be 5 hours.

What about Refreezing Food?

Frozen food that you have thawed and kept in the refrigerator can be refrozen without cooking it first. However, the refreezing process may cause some loss in texture of certain foods. This is caused by the fact that during the first thaw, the frozen food lost some internal moisture. It's now going back into the freezer in this somewhat compromised state. Make sure that whatever the food is, it is well wrapped to protect it from the air and further drying out. Air and the lack of internal moisture damage food and will decrease the texture and taste of the food once you defrost it. The second time you defrost and cook that food, you can store any cooked leftovers in the refrigerator or frozen.

General Guidelines for Freezing Food

1   Make sure that your freezer can maintain a temperature setting of 0°F (−18°C).

2   Choose a food or foods that freeze well.

3   Choose the appropriate bag or container for the food you will be freezing.

4   Follow the recipe by preparing the food you will be freezing.

5   Keep any external moisture to a minimum.

6   Make sure that the prepared food is chilled before packaging.

7   Once you've placed the prepared food into the container, try to eliminate as much air as possible.

8   Mark the container with the food it contains, the date it was placed in the freezer, and a best-used-by date. Also include any specific defrosting/cooking instructions, where appropriate.

9   Place the packaged food in the freezer, allowing air to circulate around it.

10 When ready to defrost the frozen food, do so in the refrigerator.

Let's Get Started with Freezing Food

Now that you understand the basics of how to freeze food, start with the simple recipes that follow for freezing fruits and vegetables. Afterward, advance to learn how to make a variety of freezer-ready foods, from gravy to main meals to desserts. Your freezer will now be a well-organized and efficient source of preserved foods.

How to Freeze Fresh Fruit

When I can acquire a bounty of fresh fruit from the farmer's market or a local farm, there are so many things I can create with it, including a variety of jams, preserves, desserts, and more! But sometimes it's nice to have frozen fruit stashed away to use when making baked goods, smoothies, or simply to top a bowl of oatmeal.

Freezing fresh fruit is a quick and easy way to preserve the bounty of the season when you may be overwhelmed with so much produce that you can't process everything while it is still fresh. This is when your freezer will become your best friend so you will be able to enjoy your favorite fruits all year long. One of the best things about freezing fresh fruit is that it helps maintain its flavor and nutritional value.

PREP TIME: **20 MINUTES**
FREEZING TIME: **2–4 HOURS**
TOTAL TIME: **2–4 HOURS 20 MINUTES**
YIELD: **VARIES**

EQUIPMENT

Small bowl

Baking sheet

Parchment paper or silicone mat

Freezer-proof bags or airtight containers

INGREDIENTS

Fresh fruit (e.g., berries, peaches, bananas, apples, pears, grapes, etc.)

1 tbsp lemon juice (for light-colored fruits)

1 cup water

1 Wash the fruit thoroughly. For fruits like bananas, peaches (and nectarines), apples, and pears, peel and slice them. Berries and grapes can be left whole.

2 For light-colored fruits including bananas, peaches (and nectarines), apples, and pears, combine the lemon juice and water in a small bowl. Dip the fruit slices in the lemon juice solution to prevent browning.

3 Line a baking sheet with parchment paper. Spread the fruit on the baking sheet in a single layer, ensuring the pieces do not touch each other. Gently pat the fruit dry to absorb any extra moisture from washing or being dipped in the lemon juice solution.

4 Place the baking sheet in the freezer for 2 to 4 hours or until the fruit is frozen solid.

5 Transfer the frozen fruit to labeled and dated freezer-proof bags or airtight containers. Remove as much air as possible before sealing to prevent freezer burn.

6 Frozen fruit can be stored in the freezer for up to 12 months. Use frozen fruit as is in smoothies or in baked goods. For other uses, defrost the fruit in the refrigerator overnight.

How to Freeze Fresh Vegetables

There is something so rewarding about growing your own vegetables and then freezing them for later use. It's the perfect option if you only have a small kitchen garden like me and you're tight on time. Freezer space is valuable, so when it comes to freezing vegetables, pick those you know you will want to use in various recipes. Some of my favorites to freeze are a traditional mixture of peas and carrots, which is getting harder to find at my local grocery store, plus sweet bell peppers, corn (if I am lucky enough to grow some), and onions. Freezing a small variety of vegetables ensures you can enjoy your garden-fresh produce all year long!

PREP TIME: **30 MINUTES**
FREEZING TIME: **2–4 HOURS**
TOTAL TIME: **2–4 HOURS 30 MINUTES**
YIELD: **VARIES**

EQUIPMENT

Large (10- to 12-quart)
  stockpot for blanching
Slotted spoon or
  spider strainer
Bowl of ice water
Baking sheet
Parchment paper or
  silicone mat
Freezer-proof bags or
  airtight containers

INGREDIENTS

Fresh vegetables
  (e.g., broccoli, carrots,
  green beans, peas, bell
  peppers, etc.)
Water
Ice

1 Wash and chop the vegetables into desired sizes. (For example, cut carrots into rounds, chop bell peppers into strips, and break broccoli into florets. Peas should be left whole.)

2 Bring a large stockpot of water to a boil over high heat. Add the vegetables in small batches. Blanch tender vegetables for 1 minute and sturdier vegetables for 2 minutes. (Blanching helps preserve color, flavor, and nutrients.)

3 Using a slotted spoon or spider strainer, immediately transfer the blanched vegetables to a bowl of ice water to stop the cooking process. Let them sit in the ice water for a few minutes to chill.

4 Using the slotted spoon or spider strainer, transfer the vegetables to a clean, lint-free kitchen towel and pat them dry to remove excess moisture.

5 Arrange the vegetables in a single layer on a parchment paper–lined baking sheet. Place the baking sheet in the freezer for 2 to 4 hours or until the vegetables are frozen solid.

6 Transfer the frozen vegetables to labeled and dated freezer-proof bags or airtight containers. Remove as much air as possible before sealing to prevent freezer burn.

7 Blanched frozen vegetables can be stored in the freezer for up to 12 months. When using frozen vegetables in a recipe, follow the directions for whether the vegetables can be used frozen or need to be defrosted. If the vegetables need to be defrosted, do so by transferring them to the refrigerator overnight.

COOK'S NOTES

What about corn? Fresh corn can be blanched on the cob and then frozen on the cob, or the blanched kernels can be cut off the cob.

Can leafy greens be frozen? Yes, but for best results start with fresh, young, tender greens; give them a good wash to remove any dirt or sand; remove tough stems; chop the greens; then blanch them for no more than 1 minute. Then proceed with the main recipe.

Ginger-Garlic Paste Ice Cubes

Ginger-garlic paste is a flavorful addition to many savory dishes but is also an ideal staple to have on hand for preparing a variety of natural remedies. Making this paste in bulk and freezing it in ice cube trays ensures you'll always have it on hand. The ice cubes make it easy to portion and use, and freezing preserves the flavor and nutritional benefits of the ginger and garlic without any preservatives. Add a cube or two to a cup of honey and store in the refrigerator so you can take a teaspoon or two whenever you feel the sniffles coming on.

When mixed with honey, this paste becomes a powerful Healing Pantry staple—one that's ready to support your wellness whenever needed. Just like with my Thyme and Honey Pickled Cough Syrup (p. 280) that should be kept chilled in the refrigerator, this is one of those special remedies that should be kept in the fridge, rather than in your designated Healing Pantry within your Extended Pantry. Keeping it cold ensures that the fresh, immune-boosting properties of the ginger and garlic stay intact while making it easy to scoop out a spoonful when you need a natural boost.

I suppose my love for garlic as a remedy is in my blood—literally! My sweet mom, Gloria, was a firm believer that garlic could cure just about anything that ailed you, and she raised me to believe the same. But let me tell you, both my dad and my dear husband, Ted, always knew when Mom and I had been driving the car during our cold January weather. That eau de parfum of garlic we left behind was unmistakable! And honestly, we wore it like a badge of honor. After all, if a little extra garlic could keep us healthy during the winter, we were all in!

PREP TIME: **20 MINUTES**
FREEZING TIME: **2–4 HOURS**
TOTAL TIME: **2–4 HOURS 20 MINUTES**
YIELD: **APPROXIMATELY 2 CUPS**

EQUIPMENT

Blender or food processor

Ice cube tray

Freezer-proof bags or airtight containers

INGREDIENTS

2 (5-inch/12.75-cm) pieces fresh ginger, peeled and chopped into small pieces

1 cup fresh garlic cloves, peeled

Water, as needed

1 Combine the ginger and garlic in a blender or food processor. Blend until a smooth paste forms, adding water, if necessary, in small amounts.

2 Spoon the paste into the ice cube trays, filling each compartment about ¾ full to allow for expansion as the mixture freezes. Smooth the tops with the back of a wet spoon and cover the ice cube tray with a lid, aluminum foil, or plastic wrap.

3 Place the ice cube trays in the freezer and freeze until solid. This may take about 2 to 4 hours.

4 Once frozen, transfer the cubes to labeled and dated freezer-proof bags or airtight containers. Store in the freezer for up to 6 months.

···················· COOK'S NOTES ····················

Can you use less garlic and more ginger to make these ice cubes? Definitely! Home cooks have altered this traditional combination to their liking for centuries, so please make this your own.

Quick-and-Easy Freezer Marinade

Marinating is a simple yet delightful way to add flavor to your food before cooking. Essentially, it's the process of soaking foods in a well-seasoned liquid, which we call a marinade. Marinades can be acidic, enzymatic, or even neutral, depending on the ingredients you choose. In this recipe you'll find a mix of oil, herbs, and spices that will give the marinated food a wonderful depth of flavor and make it all the more delicious when it's time to cook!

A freezer marinade is a convenient way to prepare a flavorful meal in advance by marinating your food while it is freezing. This saves you time when you are ready to make a meal that calls for marinated meats or poultry. Just pull a bag out of your freezer the night before, let it defrost in the refrigerator, and you will be ready to cook the marinated food when dinnertime rolls around.

PREP TIME: **10 MINUTES**
TOTAL TIME: **10 MINUTES**
YIELD: **APPROXIMATELY ¾ CUP (1 BATCH OF MARINADE FOR 1 GALLON-SIZE BAG)**

EQUIPMENT
Gallon-size freezer-proof bag
Measuring cups
Measuring spoons

INGREDIENTS
¼ cup olive oil
¼ cup apple juice or apple cider
2 tbsp Worcestershire sauce
1 tbsp honey or maple syrup
1 tsp fine-ground sea salt
1 tsp mixed herbs, such as Italian seasoning or herbes de Provence
¼ tsp freshly ground black pepper
¼ tsp red pepper flakes (optional)
3–5 lb (1.35–2.25kg) beef, chicken, or pork

MARINATING AND FREEZING THE MEAT:

1   Add all the ingredients except for the meat to a labeled and dated gallon-size freezer-proof bag. Mix well until all ingredients are thoroughly combined.

2   Add your choice of meat (e.g., cut-up whole chicken; pork chops; or tougher cuts of beef, preferably on the bone, such as a chuck roast). Seal the bag, removing as much air as possible.

3   Gently massage the marinade into the meat, ensuring it is evenly coated.

4   Flatten the bag as much as possible and then lay the bag flat in the freezer. The marinated meat can be stored in the freezer for up to 3 months.

COOKING THE MEAT:

1   When ready to cook, thaw the meat in the refrigerator overnight.

2   Cook using your preferred method, depending on the particular cut of meat. Marinated meats can be slow cooked in a slow cooker or Dutch oven, pressure cooked, grilled, baked, broiled, or pan fried.

> ··········· COOK'S NOTES ···········
>
> ***Do you need to discard the marinade, or can you use it in some way?*** You can use the marinade to make a sauce to be served along with the final dish, but you will first need to heat the marinade on the stovetop by bringing it to a boil on high heat, stirring it for 1 minute, then turning the heat down to low and allowing the marinade to simmer for 10 minutes.

Einkorn Chive and Cheese Freezer Biscuits

These Einkorn Chive and Cheese Freezer Biscuits are a delightful savory treat and perfect for any meal. These are drop biscuits, so they couldn't be easier to make. No rolling dough, no cutting out shapes—just mix, drop, and freeze! Best of all, when you're ready to bake, these biscuits will taste as though the dough was just mixed. No one will ever suspect you pulled these out of the freezer!

PREP TIME: **20 MINUTES**
FREEZING TIME: **2–4 HOURS**
TOTAL TIME: **2–4 HOURS 20 MINUTES**
YIELD: **12 DROP BISCUITS**

EQUIPMENT

Large mixing bowl

Whisk

Wooden spoon

Baking sheet

Parchment paper or
   silicone mat

Freezer-proof bags or
   airtight containers

INGREDIENTS

2 cups all-purpose einkorn
   flour, sifted (alternatively,
   all-purpose spelt flour
   can be used)

1 tbsp baking powder

½ tsp fine-ground sea salt,
   plus more for sprinkling

1 cup grated sharp
   cheddar cheese, loosely
   packed

¼ cup chopped fresh chives

1–1½ cups heavy cream

MAKING AND FREEZING THE DOUGH:

1   Add the einkorn flour (or spelt flour), baking powder, and sea salt to a large bowl. Whisk until well combined.

2   Add the cheese and chives to the bowl and toss well in the flour mixture.

3   Pour 1 cup cream into the bowl and mix gently using a wooden spoon. (If using the einkorn flour, 1 cup of cream may be sufficient. If using spelt flour, you might need a bit more cream. You are looking for a dough with a wet, sticky texture, often referred to as "shaggy.")

4   Scoop equal portions of the dough from the bowl and drop them on a parchment paper–lined baking sheet. You should have 12 portions. Sprinkle the top of each drop biscuit with additional salt, if desired.

5   Transfer the baking sheet to the freezer and freeze the drop biscuits until solid, about 2 to 4 hours.

6   Transfer the frozen drop biscuits to a labeled and dated freezer-proof bag or container. The drop biscuits may be stored in the freezer for up to 3 months.

BAKING THE BISCUITS:

1   When ready to bake the drop biscuits, preheat your oven to 425°F (220°C). Arrange the frozen biscuits on a parchment paper–lined baking sheet and place on the middle rack of the oven.

2   Bake for 10 to 15 minutes or until golden brown and cooked through the center.

No-Cook Berry Freezer Jam

Making No-Cook Berry Freezer Jam is a splendid way to capture the flavors of summer and enjoy them all year round. And best of all, if you are new to making jam, this version is a breeze. This simple method requires no cooking, no canning, and best of all, it preserves the fresh taste of berries like no other form of jam-making. Freezer jam is perfect for spreading on toast, stirring into yogurt, or even gifting to friends and family.

One of the best things about this jam—besides its vibrant, just-picked flavor—is how quick and easy it is to make. With just a few simple ingredients and a little mixing, you'll have a beautifully fresh jam ready to enjoy in no time. Since it's stored in the freezer rather than canned, there's no need to worry about special equipment or long cooking times. Just thaw a jar when you need it, and you'll have a taste of summer sunshine ready to brighten up everything from breakfast to desserts.

PREP TIME: **15 MINUTES**
RESTING TIME: **30 MINUTES**
TOTAL TIME: **45 MINUTES**
YIELD: **5–6 CUPS**

EQUIPMENT

Large mixing bowl
Potato masher or fork
Small mixing bowl
Whisk
5–6 (8oz) freezer-proof containers or jars with lids

INGREDIENTS

4 cups fresh berries (frozen berries can be used but must be thawed)
2 tbsp fresh lemon juice (optional)
1½ cups superfine sugar
1 (1.59oz/45g) package no-cook freezer jam pectin (about 11¼ teaspoons or slightly less than ¼ cup)

1 Wash the berries thoroughly. Gently crush them in a large mixing bowl using a potato masher or fork. Keep the berry mixture somewhat chunky.

2 Add the lemon juice (if using) and stir. (The lemon juice can provide a bit of tanginess to the jam if the berries are exceptionally ripe and sweet.)

3 In a small mixing bowl, combine the sugar and the no-cook freezer jam pectin and whisk them together well.

4 Whisk the sugar mixture into the berry mixture and continue to whisk well for approximately 3 minutes.

5 Ladle the jam into clean freezer-proof containers or jars, leaving about ½ inch (1.25cm) headspace to allow for expansion during freezing. Place the lids on and allow the jam to sit at room temperature for 30 minutes so the jam can thicken.

6 Label and date each container and transfer them to the freezer. This jam can be stored in the freezer for 1 year.

7 When ready to use, transfer the jam to the refrigerator and use within 3 months. After 3 months, the jam may begin to crystallize.

········· COOK'S NOTES ·········

Will the consistency of a freezer jam be different than other types of jams? Yes, freezer jams set up looser than other jams. However, this consistency makes them versatile for use on toast and drizzling over waffles, pancakes, or ice cream. Plus, the intense fruit flavor is well worth any sacrifice in consistency.

What is superfine sugar? Superfine sugar is granulated sugar that has been ground into smaller crystals, making it dissolve more easily than regular granulated sugar. It's also known as baker's sugar, caster sugar, or extra-fine sugar and is generally available in the baking aisle of most grocery stores.

PREP TIME: **1 HOUR 20 MINUTES**
REFRIGERATION TIME: **UP TO 24 HOURS**
TOTAL TIME: **UP TO 25 HOURS 20 MINUTES**
YIELD: **2 PIE CRUSTS (DISKS) SUFFICIENT FOR A 9-INCH (23-CM) REGULAR PIE PAN, DEEP-DISH PIE PAN, OR TART PAN**

EQUIPMENT

Large mixing bowl

Small mixing bowl

2 butter knives or a pastry cutter

Wooden spoon

Plastic wrap

Freezer-proof bags

Rolling pin (when ready to roll out disks)

INGREDIENTS

2 ½ cups all-purpose einkorn flour, divided, plus more for dusting

12 tbsp unsalted butter, cut into ½-inch (1.25-cm) cubes

1 tsp fine-ground sea salt

1 tsp sugar, optional (see **Cook's Notes**)

1 cold large egg, lightly beaten (see **Cook's Notes**)

¼–½ cup cold 100% hydration sourdough discard made with any variety of all-purpose flour (you can also use an active sourdough starter, but chill it first), divided

Einkorn Sourdough Pie Crust

Baking with all-purpose einkorn flour is more nutritious than common all-purpose flour milled from modern-day wheat. Even though the bran and germ have been removed from einkorn flour, what remains contains more vitamins and minerals than other all-purpose flours. If you are new to baking with ancient grains, of which einkorn is considered the most ancient, you will like using its all-purpose form as opposed to its whole-grain form, which has more of a learning curve.

This particular einkorn sourdough crust is perfect for sweet and savory dishes, full-size pies, hand and toaster pies, quiches, tarts, galettes, and more. It freezes beautifully and makes any type of pie-making a breeze! Best of all, it uses your sourdough discard. If the term sourdough discard is new to you, it is the small amount of sourdough starter you remove from your starter before you feed the remaining starter with fresh flour and water.

MAKING AND FREEZING THE PIE DOUGH:

1   In separate plastic bags, place the flour and the cubed butter in the freezer for 1 hour.

2   Remove the flour and butter from the freezer. Set the butter aside. In a large mixing bowl, combine the cold einkorn flour, sea salt, and sugar (if using). Whisk well to completely distribute the salt and sugar throughout the flour.

3   Add the cold butter pieces to the flour mixture and use your fingers (run under cold water and dried), two butter knives, or a pastry cutter to blend until the mixture resembles coarse crumbs with some pea-size bits of butter still intact.

4   In a small mixing bowl, mix the egg and ¼ cup sourdough discard (or starter) together and then add this mixture to the large bowl and mix with a wooden spoon until all the flour is moistened. Do not overmix. You should be able to see bits of butter throughout the dough. The dough should come together in the shape of a loose ball.

5   If, after adding the sourdough discard or starter, the dough appears dry and crumbly and can't

form into a ball, you can gradually add additional sourdough discard (or starter), 1 tablespoon at a time (up to ¼ cup more), while mixing until the dough begins to come together. Einkorn flour, even the all-purpose version, absorbs liquid and fats differently than modern-day all-purpose wheat flours, so go very slowly if you need to add discard (or starter).

6 Turn the dough out onto a floured surface, divide it into 2 equal pieces, and shape each piece into a disk. Wrap each disk in plastic wrap, then place the wrapped disks in the refrigerator overnight or for up to 24 hours for a slow fermentation. This will create a very flaky crust when baked.

7 After the refrigeration fermentation, place each wrapped disk of dough into a labeled and dated freezer-proof bag and store it in the freezer. The dough can be frozen for up to 3 months.

USING THE PIE DOUGH:

1 When you are ready to use the dough, transfer it, still wrapped in plastic, to the refrigerator and allow it to defrost overnight or at least 8 hours.

2 Once fully defrosted, remove 1 disk of dough from the refrigerator, unwrap it, place it on a floured surface, and use a rolling pin to roll the disk into a circle approximately ⅛ inch (0.3cm) thick and approximately 12 inches (30.5cm) around.

3 Place the rolled-out dough into a 9-inch (23-cm) pie plate. Add the pie filling. Remove the remaining disk of dough from the refrigerator, unwrap it, place it on a floured surface, and use a rolling pin to roll the disk into a circle approximately ⅛ inch (0.3cm) thick and approximately 12 inches (30.5cm) around. Drape the second rolled-out dough over the pie filling and crimp the edges. Bake the pie according to the recipe instructions.

4 If you're using a single crust and a wet filling, you will need to parbake the crust. (See **Cook's Notes**.)

········· COOK'S NOTES ·········

Why does this pie crust recipe call for optional sugar? Adding sugar to this recipe makes the dough more tender because it interferes with gluten development, plus it helps give the crust a golden color.

Why does this pie crust recipe call for an egg? If you have ever struggled with rolling out a pie crust, you will find that once you add an egg to your dough, this problem will magically disappear! When added to a pie crust dough, an egg acts as a special type of binder, helping to hold the dough together better than adding additional water. This can make the dough easier to handle and roll out without cracking. Plus, the egg also offers other benefits, including enhanced flakiness, better browning, and a touch of richness that is not present in eggless crusts.

Do you ever need to parbake this crust, and is that different than blind baking the crust? Yes, if you are adding a wet filling to the pie crust, such as when making a quiche, you will need to parbake the crust in a preheated 425°F (220°C) oven for approximately 15 minutes or until the crust is a light golden color. Once the dough is rolled out and placed into the pie pan, use a fork to poke the bottom of the dough in multiple places. Then, place a piece of parchment paper on top of the dough and add pie weights to the center before placing the pie dough on the middle rack of the oven. If you do not have pie weights, you can use dry beans. (Going forward, you will want to reserve these beans as your pie weights, as they will not be palatable if they are cooked.) Once the crust is a light golden color, remove it from the oven. Remove the parchment paper and the pie weights, and allow the parbaked crust to cool completely before filling.

Parbaking partially bakes the pie crust, while blind baking fully bakes a pie crust or pastry without a filling. Sometimes, people will use these terms interchangeably today, which can make things confusing; but technically, parbaking and blind baking are two different things. Parbaked crusts are intended for fillings that require further cooking, such as the quiche I mentioned previously, while blind-baked crusts are used for fillings that don't need to be baked further and will be filled and served, such as a pudding-based pie.

On which oven rack should you bake your pie? I prefer to bake my pies on the bottom rack of the oven because it's closer to the heat source and helps ensure the bottom crust is fully baked and golden brown. Other bakers may advise that the middle rack is a good option because it allows air to circulate evenly around the pie and prevents the bottom from burning. However, if you are new to baking pies, I highly recommend using a glass pie plate, which allows you to monitor your pie's baking to ensure you reach a beautiful golden brown on the bottom of the pie (without burning). No matter what rack you bake your pie on, if you are baking a double-crust pie and the top crust is browning too quickly but the pie is not fully baked, you can tent the pie with aluminum foil.

Can you use lard in this pie crust? Lard, specifically leaf lard (free of any pork aroma), is very helpful for creating a flaky pie crust, especially for a beginner baker who may inadvertently overwork the pie dough. If you want to use lard for making this crust, reduce the butter to ½ cup and add ¼ cup leaf lard.

Einkorn Sourdough Toaster Hand Pies

These scrumptious toaster oven pies are perfect for any time of the year. Using the versatile Einkorn Sourdough Pie Crust (p. 236), you can make these pies in a snap filled with your favorite fruits—fresh or frozen. If you prefer, you can substitute your favorite pie crust in place of the einkorn version used here.

PREP TIME: **1 HOUR**
REFRIGERATION TIME: **1 HOUR**
BAKE TIME: **25 MINUTES**
TOTAL TIME: **2 HOURS 25 MINUTES**
YIELD: **8 (4-INCH × 3-INCH/10-CM × 7.5-CM) PIES**

EQUIPMENT

Mixing bowls

Rolling pin

Sharp knife

Baking sheet

Parchment paper or
  silicone mat

Flat metal spatula

Pastry brush

Plastic wrap

Freezer-proof bags
  or airtight containers

Toaster or toaster oven
  (for toasting)

INGREDIENTS

Approximately 2 cups mixed
  berries, fresh or frozen
  (e.g. blueberries, diced
  strawberries, raspberries)

¼ cup unrefined whole cane
  sugar, maple sugar, or
  coconut sugar

1 tbsp cornstarch, arrowroot
  powder, or tapioca powder

1 tsp lemon juice

½ tsp vanilla extract

2 refrigerated Einkorn
  Sourdough Pie Crust
  disks (p. 236)

1 large egg

1 tbsp water

Demerara sugar, for topping
  (optional)

MAKING THE TOASTER PIES:

1   Combine the mixed berries, sugar, cornstarch, lemon juice, and vanilla extract in a large mixing bowl. Mix well, slightly mashing the berries. Set aside to allow the berries to macerate in the sugar mixture.

2   On a well-floured surface, roll each disk of pie dough into an 8-inch × 12-inch (20.25-cm × 30.5-cm) rectangle, approximately ⅛ inch (0.3cm) thick. Using a sharp knife, start on the 12-inch (30.5-cm) side of the dough and cut 4 rectangles. Each rectangle will be 3 inches (7.5cm) wide and 8 inches (20.25cm) long. Repeat this process with the second disk of dough.

3   Place approximately 2 to 3 tablespoons of the macerated fruit in the middle of the lower half of each rectangle, leaving a ½-inch (1.25-cm) border. Using a clean finger dipped in water, brush the entire ½-inch (1.25-cm) border of the rectangle. Carefully lift the top part of the rectangle and fold it over the lower part. Press all four sides of the dough using a fork, sealing it to create a toaster pie. Using the tip of a sharp knife, make a small ½-inch (1.25-cm) incision on the top of the toaster pies.

4   Using a flat metal spatula, carefully transfer the toaster pies to a parchment paper–lined baking sheet and use a fork to make one set of puncture marks on top of each pie, then transfer the baking sheet to the refrigerator for 1 hour.

5   Preheat the oven to 425°F (220°C) for 15 minutes prior to removing the toaster pies from the refrigerator.

6   After the pies have chilled for 1 hour, whisk the egg and water together until well mixed. Then brush the top of each pie with the egg wash using a pastry brush or the back of a spoon. Sprinkle each pie with demerara sugar (if using).

7   Transfer the baking sheet with the pies to the middle rack of the preheated oven. Lower the temperature to 375°F (190°C) and bake until golden brown, about 25 minutes.

8   Allow the pies to cool for a few minutes on the baking sheet, then transfer them to a cooling rack to cool completely.

9   Once completely cooled, tightly wrap each pie in plastic wrap. Place the wrapped toaster pies in labeled and dated freezer-proof bags or airtight containers. Store the toaster pies in the freezer for up to 3 months.

HEATING THE TOASTER PIES:

1   When ready to serve, reheat the frozen toaster pies in a toaster or toaster oven until warmed through.

Einkorn Ready-to-Bake Yeast Freezer Rolls

These rolls make any meal special, offering a lighter texture due to the ancient grain einkorn. They will be frozen together and ready to bake up into delicious and tender pull-apart rolls whenever you need them. Simply bake them straight from the freezer for a convenient and delightful treat.

PREP TIME: **30 MINUTES**
RISING TIME: **1 HOUR 30 MINUTES**
FREEZING TIME: **2 HOURS**
TOTAL TIME: **4 HOURS**
YIELD: **12 ROLLS**

EQUIPMENT

Large mixing bowl or stand mixer with a dough hook

Kitchen towel

9-inch (23-cm) cake pan (this is a standard-size cake pan)

Pastry brush (optional)

Plastic wrap

Freezer-proof bag or airtight container

10-inch (25.5-cm) cast-iron skillet (for baking)

Baking sheet lined with parchment paper or silicone mat (for baking)

INGREDIENTS

1–1¼ cups whole milk, room temperature

3 tbsp unsalted butter, melted and cooled, plus more for greasing the cake pan

¼ cup honey

1 tsp fine-ground sea salt

2¼ tsp (1 packet) instant yeast

4 cups all-purpose einkorn flour, plus additional flour for dusting (alternatively, you can use all-purpose spelt flour)

1 tbsp olive oil

1 egg (for egg wash)

1 tbsp water (for egg wash)

MAKING AND FREEZING THE ROLLS:

1 Combine 1 cup milk along with the melted butter, honey, salt, and yeast in a large mixing bowl. Gradually add the einkorn flour, mixing with a wooden spoon until a sticky dough forms. If you're using all-purpose spelt flour, you will need to add 1¼ cups milk to achieve a sticky dough. (Alternatively, you can use the bowl of a stand mixer and a dough hook.)

2 Transfer the dough to a lightly floured surface and knead the dough by hand for about 10 minutes. (Avoid adding too much flour to the surface as you knead the dough as this may create a dense roll. [See **Cook's Notes**.]) (Alternatively, you can use the dough hook on the stand mixer to knead the dough for approximately 5 minutes.) Whether kneading by hand or with a stand mixer, you want the dough to look smooth.

3 Grease a clean bowl with the olive oil. Transfer the dough to the bowl and roll it around in the bowl until it is completely coated with the olive oil. Cover the bowl with a damp, lint-free kitchen towel and let the dough rise in a warm place for about 1½ hours or until approximately doubled in size. (Just eyeball this. It does not have to be exact.)

4 Punch down the dough and divide it into 12 equal pieces. Shape each piece into a ball and place the balls into a greased 9-inch (23-cm) cake pan. Cover the rolls with the damp kitchen towel and let them rise for approximately 30 minutes or until they appear puffy and touch each other on the sides.

5 Mix the egg and the water together with a fork and use a pastry brush or the back of a spoon to coat the tops of the rolls.

6 To freeze the rolls, place the cake pan, uncovered, into the freezer. Freeze the unbaked rolls until solid, approximately 2 hours.

7 Once the rolls are frozen solid, remove the cake pan from the freezer, turn it upside down, and pop out the frozen rolls, which should now all be attached into one piece. Wrap the attached rolls tightly in plastic wrap and transfer them to a labeled and dated freezer-proof bag or airtight container. These rolls may be stored in the freezer for up to 3 months.

BAKING THE ROLLS:

1 When you're ready to bake the rolls, preheat the oven to 350°F (180°C).

2 Unwrap the frozen rolls and place them on a parchment paper–lined baking sheet or into a 10-inch (25.5-cm) cast-iron skillet.

3 Bake on the middle rack of the oven for approximately 25 minutes or until golden brown and heated through the center.

.... COOK'S NOTES ....

When kneading the dough, it appears very sticky.
What should you do? Einkorn flour and other ancient grain
flours (even in their all-purpose forms) have a different gluten
structure, which can make the dough slightly stickier than those
made with modern-day wheat. If necessary, you can wet your
hands instead of using additional flour to knead the dough.
Wet hands are excellent at preventing the dough from sticking.

Freezer-Friendly Simple Brown Gravy

This simple brown gravy recipe is rich, flavorful, and perfect for freezing. Made with a basic roux and beef broth, this gravy is ideal for enhancing mashed potatoes, meatloaf, and various other dishes. By freezing it in portion sizes, you can enjoy homemade gravy anytime without the hassle of starting from scratch. Just warm and serve!

This freezer-friendly gravy is an absolute game changer during the holidays—especially for Thanksgiving when every minute in the kitchen counts! Instead of whisking up a last-minute gravy while juggling side dishes and a turkey, you can have this rich, velvety brown gravy ready to go in minutes. Simply thaw and warm it on the stovetop while your turkey rests, and you'll have a perfectly smooth, flavorful sauce to drizzle over stuffing, and, of course, those tender turkey slices. It's also a lifesaver for repurposing leftovers—just heat up a portion and pour it over hot turkey sandwiches or mix it into a pot pie filling for a next-day feast.

PREP TIME: **5 MINUTES**
COOK TIME: **10 MINUTES**
TOTAL TIME: **15 MINUTES**
YIELD: **APPROXIMATELY 4 CUPS**

EQUIPMENT

Small (2- to 4-quart) saucepan
Whisk
4 (8oz) freezer-proof containers with lids

INGREDIENTS

4 tbsp unsalted butter
¼ cup all-purpose flour
4 cups beef broth, stock, or bone broth
½ tsp fine-ground sea salt

MAKING AND FREEZING THE GRAVY:

1   Melt the butter in a small saucepan on medium heat.

2   Sprinkle the flour over the melted butter and whisk continuously for 2 minutes to cook the flour until it takes on a slight golden color.

3   Gradually add the broth and salt while whisking constantly to prevent lumps. Once all the broth is added, bring the mixture to a boil on high heat, continuing to whisk for 1 minute to prevent scorching.

4   After 1 minute, reduce the heat to its lowest setting and simmer the gravy for approximately 5 minutes, whisking occasionally until the gravy thickens slightly. Taste and add more salt, if desired.

5   Remove the gravy from the heat and cool completely.

6   Once cooled, pour 1 cup of gravy into a labeled and dated freezer-proof container, leaving at least a ½-inch (1.25-cm) headspace to allow for expansion. Put the lid on the container. Repeat with remaining gravy.

7   Transfer the containers to the freezer. This gravy can be frozen for up to 3 months.

USING THE GRAVY:

1   When ready to use this gravy, remove a container from the freezer and allow it to defrost for a few minutes so you can loosen the gravy out of the container.

2   Transfer the gravy to a saucepan on low heat. The frozen gravy will begin to defrost. Once completely defrosted, bring it to a boil on high heat, stirring continuously, then immediately turn the heat down to low and simmer the gravy for a few minutes until heated through. The total heating time will be about 20 minutes.

3   If necessary, you can thin the gravy with additional broth, stock, or bone broth until you reach the desired consistency. In a pinch, you can also thin the gravy with water.

Einkorn Frozen Crêpes

Einkorn Frozen Crêpes are a distinctive and versatile addition to any traditional foods kitchen. These delicate, thin pancakes are made from the ancient grain einkorn; it offers a nutty, hearty flavor and is easier to digest than modern wheat. By preparing and freezing them in advance, you can enjoy these delicious crêpes anytime with minimal effort.

PREP TIME: **15 MINUTES**
REST TIME: **30 MINUTES TO 12 HOURS**
COOK TIME: **35 MINUTES**
TOTAL TIME: **1 HOUR 20 MINUTES TO 12 HOURS 50 MINUTES**
YIELD: **12–15 CRÊPES**

EQUIPMENT

Blender or mixing bowl

Whisk

Nonstick skillet or crêpe pan

Spatula or pancake spatula

Baking sheet

Parchment paper

Plastic wrap

Freezer-proof bags or airtight containers

INGREDIENTS

½ cup all-purpose einkorn flour

½ cup whole-grain einkorn flour

1¼ cups whole milk

2 tbsp unsalted butter, melted and cooled, plus 1 tbsp, divided, for cooking the crêpes

2 large eggs

2 tbsp unrefined whole cane sugar

¼ tsp fine-ground sea salt

PREPARING THE BATTER:

1   In a blender or mixing bowl, combine the einkorn flours, milk, melted butter, eggs, sugar, and salt. Blend or whisk until the batter is smooth and well combined. This is easiest done in any standard blender (you do not need a high-speed blender), but it can also be mixed by hand.

2   Cover the batter and let it rest in the refrigerator for at least 30 minutes or up to 12 hours.

COOKING AND FREEZING THE CRÊPES:

1   Preheat a nonstick skillet or crêpe pan over medium heat. Lightly grease the pan with butter. Pour about ¼ cup of the batter into the center of the pan, tilting and swirling the pan to spread the batter into a thin, even layer.

2   Cook the batter for approximately 1 to 2 minutes until the edges begin to lift, and the underside appears a golden brown.

3   Flip the crêpe and cook for an additional 30 seconds to 1 minute. (Flipping the crêpe can be done with a regular spatula, but a rounded pancake spatula works even better.)

4   Remove the cooked crêpe from the pan and place it on a parchment paper–lined baking sheet. Repeat with the remaining batter, stacking the crêpes with parchment paper placed in between each crêpe to prevent sticking.

5   Allow the crêpes to cool completely. Once cooled, keep them stacked with parchment paper between each crêpe to prevent sticking, and wrap the stack tightly in plastic wrap. Transfer the wrapped crêpes to a labeled and dated freezer-proof bag or airtight container. The crêpes can be frozen for up to 3 months.

REHEATING AND SERVING THE CRÊPES:

1   To reheat the crêpes, remove the desired number of crêpes from the freezer, separate them, and let them thaw at room temperature for a few minutes.

2   Place a nonstick skillet or crêpe pan over medium heat. Warm each crêpe, one at a time, for about 30 seconds on each side, then place on a plate and fill with sweet or savory options (see **Cook's Notes**) and serve.

COOK'S NOTES

What can you fill the crêpes with? You can fill crêpes with a variety of sweet fillings, such as fresh fruit, jam, marmalade, or a chocolate hazelnut spread with a dollop of whipped cream. Alternatively, you can fill crêpes with savory fillings, such as a combination of ham, scrambled eggs, and grated Swiss cheese; cooked chicken and sautéed mushrooms; or smoked salmon with a light smear of cream cheese along with a sprinkling of capers, red onions, and fresh dill.

Slice-and-Bake Spelt Freezer Cookies

These freezer cookies made with whole-grain spelt flour are delicious and convenient! You can slice and bake them whenever you want a fresh batch. Customize the dough with your favorite flavors and mix-ins and store the dough logs in the freezer for later use. They're perfect for any occasion with a wholesome twist. This recipe will create a rich, buttery cookie with just the right touch of subtle sweetness.

PREP TIME: **30 MINUTES**
REFRIGERATION TIME: **1 HOUR**
TOTAL TIME: **1 HOUR 30 MINUTES**
YIELD: **APPROXIMATELY 24 COOKIES**

EQUIPMENT

2 large mixing bowls
Handheld electric mixer (optional)
Parchment paper
Plastic wrap
Freezer-proof bags or airtight containers
Baking sheet (for baking)

INGREDIENTS

1 cup unsalted butter, room temperature
¾ cup unrefined whole cane sugar, coconut sugar, or maple sugar
1 large egg
2 tsp vanilla extract (see **Cook's Notes**)
2 cups whole-grain spelt flour
½ tsp baking powder
¼ tsp fine-ground sea salt

MIX-INS (OPTIONAL)

Chocolate chips
Chopped nuts
Chopped dried fruit
Grated citrus zest
Chopped fresh herbs (mint or lavender work well)
Shredded coconut
Spices (these can be added individually or all together)
¼ tsp ground allspice
¼ tsp ground cardamom
¼ tsp ground cloves
1 tsp ground cinnamon

MAKING AND FREEZING THE DOUGH:

1 Add the butter and sugar to a large mixing bowl and cream together until light and fluffy. (You can do this by hand with a wooden spoon or with a handheld electric mixer.)

2 Beat in the egg and vanilla extract until well combined.

3 In a separate bowl, whisk together the flour, baking powder, and sea salt. (If you plan on adding in any grated citrus zest, chopped herbs, shredded coconut, or spices, it is easiest to do so at this point, but if you want to divide the dough first, it will just take a little more thorough blending.) Gradually add the dry ingredients to the wet mixture, mixing until just combined. Do not overmix.

4 Divide the dough into multiple portions if you want to make a variety of cookies. Gently mix in any desired additions such as chocolate chips, chopped nuts, or dried fruit. Wrap the dough in plastic wrap and chill until firm—approximately 1 hour.

5 Once the dough has been chilled and is firm, place it on a piece of parchment paper and shape it into a log approximately 2 inches (5cm) in diameter. Wrap the dough tightly in the parchment paper, then wrap tightly in plastic wrap. Place the wrapped dough into a labeled and dated freezer-proof bag or airtight container. The dough can be frozen for up to 3 months.

BAKING THE COOKIES:

1 When ready to bake, preheat the oven to 350°F (180°C). Line a baking sheet with parchment paper or a silicone mat. Unwrap the frozen dough, slice the dough into ½-inch- (1.25-cm-) thick rounds, and place them on the prepared baking sheet, spaced about 2 inches (5cm) apart.

2 Bake for 10 to 12 minutes or until the edges become lightly golden. Let the cookies cool on the baking sheet for 5 minutes, then transfer them to a wire rack to cool completely.

3 Stored in an airtight container at room temperature, these cookies will stay fresh for up to 1 week. Baked cookies can also be frozen, well wrapped, for up to 3 months. Unwrap and defrost at room temperature when ready to eat. Cookies that have been frozen and thawed will have a softer texture but can be re-crisped in a 200°F (95°C) oven for 5 to 10 minutes.

No-Boil-Noodle Freezer Lasagna

This lasagna is a convenient and delicious way to prepare a classic dish without the hassle of precooking the noodles. This method uses regular lasagna noodles, allowing them to soften during freezing and thawing. This ensures the lasagna turns out perfect every time, making it a superb option for meal prep and busy weeknights.

PREP TIME: **1 HOUR**
TOTAL TIME: **1 HOUR**
YIELD: **6 SERVINGS**

EQUIPMENT

Large skillet
Large mixing bowl
9 × 13-inch (23 × 33-cm) baking dish
Plastic wrap
Aluminum foil

INGREDIENTS

1 lb (454g) lean ground beef or Italian sausage (sweet or spicy), or a combination of both

3 cups marinara sauce (homemade or store-bought)

1 (14.5oz/411g) can diced tomatoes, drained

1 tsp dried oregano

1 tsp dried basil

1 tsp fine-ground sea salt

¼ tsp freshly ground black pepper

⅛ tsp red pepper flakes (optional)

1 (15oz/425g) container ricotta cheese

2 cups shredded mozzarella cheese, divided

1 cup grated Parmigiano Reggiano cheese, divided

2 large eggs

2 cups baby spinach, cooked, squeezed dry, and chopped (optional)

1 (16oz/454g) box regular lasagna noodles

PREPARING AND FREEZING THE LASAGNA:

1   Add the ground beef or sausage (or combination of both) to a large skillet over medium heat. Fully cook, then drain the excess fat from the skillet.

2   Add the marinara sauce, diced tomatoes, oregano, basil, salt, pepper, and red pepper flakes (if using). Stir to combine. Simmer over medium heat for 10 minutes, stirring occasionally. Taste and adjust seasonings, if desired. Remove from the heat and set aside.

3   Combine the ricotta cheese, 1½ cups mozzarella cheese, ¾ cup Parmigiano Reggiano cheese, and the eggs in a large mixing bowl. Stir until well combined. Add the baby spinach (if using).

4   Spread a thin layer of the meat sauce into the bottom of the baking dish. Layer uncooked lasagna noodles over the sauce. (If needed, you can break the noodles to make them fit in the baking dish.)

5   Spread a layer of the cheese mixture over the noodles, followed by another layer of meat sauce. Repeat the layers until all ingredients are used, ending with a layer of meat sauce. Sprinkle the remaining ¼ cup Parmigiano Reggiano cheese and remaining ½ cup mozzarella cheese over the top.

6   Cover the assembled lasagna tightly with plastic wrap and then with aluminum foil. Label and date the lasagna and freeze for up to 3 months.

BAKING THE LASAGNA:

1   Remove the baking dish with the lasagna from the freezer and let it defrost in the refrigerator, still completely wrapped, overnight or for up to 24 hours. (The lasagna must be completely defrosted before baking.)

2   When you're ready to bake the lasagna, preheat the oven to 375°F (190°C). Remove the plastic wrap and aluminum foil from the baking dish. Discard the plastic wrap, but reserve the foil.

3   Re-cover the lasagna with the aluminum foil. Bake for 45 minutes, then remove the foil and bake for an additional 15 minutes or until the cheese is bubbly and begins to turn a light golden brown.

4   Allow the lasagna to cool for approximately 10 minutes before slicing and serving. (This will allow the slices to come out clean.)

Freezer-Ready Chicken Pot Pie

This Freezer-Ready Chicken Pot Pie uses our Einkorn Sourdough Pie Crust (p. 236) for a nutritious twist on a classic comfort food. By preparing and freezing the pie, you can enjoy a hearty, homemade meal any time with minimal effort. The method ensures the filling is flavorful and the crust remains perfectly flaky.

PREP TIME: **15 MINUTES**
COOK TIME: **30 MINUTES**
COOLING TIME: **30 MINUTES**
FREEZING TIME: **4 HOURS**
TOTAL TIME: **5 HOURS 15 MINUTES**
YIELD: **6 SERVINGS**

EQUIPMENT

Medium (6- to 8-quart) saucepan

8- to 10-inch (20-cm to 25.5-cm) pie plate, regular or deep dish

Rolling pin

Plastic wrap

Aluminum foil

INGREDIENTS

For the filling:

1 tbsp extra-virgin olive oil

1 tbsp unsalted butter

1 medium yellow onion, diced

3 medium carrots, peeled and diced

2 celery ribs, diced

½ cup all-purpose flour

1 tsp poultry seasoning

4 cups chicken broth or bone broth

1 cup whole milk or heavy cream

2 cups cooked, cubed chicken (white or dark meat or a combination)

1 cup frozen corn

1 cup frozen peas

1 tsp fine-ground sea salt

¼ tsp freshly ground black pepper

For the crust:

2 disks Einkorn Sourdough Pie Crust (p. 236)

PREPARING THE FILLING:

1   Add the olive oil and butter to a medium saucepan on medium heat. Add the onion and sauté until soft and translucent, about 2 minutes.

2   Add the carrots and celery to the saucepan and cook until tender, about 5 minutes.

3   Sprinkle the flour and poultry seasoning into the saucepan and stir well to combine with the onions, carrots, and celery. Cook for about 2 minutes more.

4   Gradually whisk in the broth, then whisk in the milk or cream. (Cream will create the creamiest filling.)

5   Bring the mixture to a boil on high heat, whisking continuously to prevent scorching. Once the mixture comes to a boil, immediately reduce the heat to low and simmer for approximately 10 minutes to thicken. You can test if the mixture

has thickened sufficiently by dipping a wooden spoon into the mixture. Pull out the wooden spoon and use your finger to draw a line down the middle of the back of the spoon. If the mixture stays separated and does not come back together, it has achieved the correct thickness.

6   Once the mixture has thickened, stir in the cubed chicken, corn, and peas and season with the salt and pepper. Stir well, taste, and add more salt and pepper, if desired.

7   Remove the pan from the heat and allow the mixture to cool completely.

ASSEMBLING AND FREEZING THE POT PIE:

1   Use a floured rolling pin to roll out 1 disk of the pie crust into a 12-inch (30.5-cm) round and place it into the pie plate. Pour the cooled filling into the crust.

2   Roll out the second disk of dough into a 12-inch (30.5-cm) round and place it over the filling. Trim any excess dough and crimp the edges to seal. Cut a few slits in the top crust.

3   Place the uncovered pot pie in the freezer and allow it to freeze until firm, about 4 hours.

4   Once completely frozen, remove the pot pie from the freezer and wrap it tightly in plastic wrap, then wrap it in aluminum foil. Label and date the pot pie and freeze for up to 3 months.

BAKING THE POT PIE:

1   When you're ready to bake the pot pie, preheat the oven to 375°F (190°C).

2   Unwrap the frozen pot pie and cover the edges with foil (or a pie crust protector shield) to prevent overbrowning.

3   Bake for approximately 90 minutes or until the crust is golden brown and the filling is bubbling out through the slits in the top crust. Allow the pie to cool for 10 minutes before serving.

Freezer-Marinated Chicken Legs

Freezer-Marinated Chicken Legs are a clever way to prepare a ready-to-go meal for busy days when time is really tight. By marinating the chicken and then freezing it, you lock in the savory and slightly sweet marinade flavors, making for a delicious meal and, most importantly, guaranteeing that the chicken won't dry out under the fast-cooking high heat of the oven broiler.

This dish became a staple in our home when Ben was little. On Saturday nights, when we'd hunker down for a cozy family movie night, these marinated chicken legs were the perfect homemade alternative to a store-bought TV dinner. I'd pair them with home fries and a side of buttery peas, and we'd all gather around, filled plates on our tray tables, ready for the feature film. The best part? With the chicken already marinated and ready to go, all I had to do was pop them under the broiler while the previews rolled. To this day, it's still one of our favorite easy, comforting meals for a laid-back evening together.

PREP TIME: **15 MINUTES**
TOTAL TIME: **15 MINUTES**
YIELD: **8 MARINATED CHICKEN LEGS**

EQUIPMENT
Gallon-size freezer-proof bag
Aluminum foil
Baking sheet (for broiling)

INGREDIENTS
8 skin-on chicken legs
¼ cup olive oil
2 tbsp soy sauce
2 tbsp Worcestershire sauce
2 tbsp honey
1 tsp smoked paprika
½ tsp onion powder
1 tsp fine-ground sea salt
¼ tsp freshly ground
   black pepper
⅛ tsp red pepper flakes
   (optional)

MARINATING AND FREEZING THE CHICKEN LEGS:

1 Label and date a gallon-size freezer-proof bag, then add all the marinade ingredients to the bag.

2 Add the chicken legs to the bag, seal it (removing as much air as possible), and massage the bag so all the chicken legs are coated thoroughly with the marinade.

3 Flatten the bag as much as possible and then lay the bag flat in the freezer.

4 The marinated chicken legs can be frozen for up to 3 months.

BROILING THE CHICKEN LEGS:

1 When you're ready to broil the chicken legs, remove the bag from the freezer and thaw it in the refrigerator overnight.

2 Place the thawed chicken legs on a baking sheet lined with aluminum foil (for easy cleanup).

3 Place the baking sheet on the middle rack of the oven and set the oven to broil. Broil the chicken legs for 10 to 12 minutes on one side. Open the oven door and, using tongs, carefully flip the legs over. Close the oven door and continue to broil for an additional 10 to 12 minutes until the chicken legs are golden brown with skin that has a crispy appearance.

4 Make sure that the juices run clear when the chicken legs are sliced, or use a food thermometer to make sure the internal temperature of the chicken legs has reached at least 165°F (74°C).

> ·········· COOK'S NOTES ··········
>
> **Batch and freeze for later:** This recipe is perfect for meal prepping. Make a few batches with different marinades. It's easy to do. Omit the smoked paprika and switch out the soy sauce for lemon juice and herb seasoning, or a tangy barbecue sauce, or even make them with an Italian twist with tomato sauce and oregano. With these tweaks, you'll always have variety on hand for busy nights.

Freezer-Ready Individual Salisbury Steaks

Salisbury steaks are one of my husband's favorite meals, so having them freezer-ready to pop into the oven allows me to surprise him with a delicious meal, even on busy weeknights. These individual "steaks" or patties can be frozen on a baking sheet, stored in a freezer-proof bag or airtight container, and cooked from completely frozen for a quick dinner option. This method ensures the patties maintain their shape and texture.

I have a fun fact to share about these Salisbury steaks, named after Dr. James Henry Salisbury from the 1800s. If he were alive today, he would be hailed as a true traditional foods cook! Not only did he realize the importance of meat in one's diet, he was also one of the first physicians to recognize that animal fats were also necessary for good health. Today, many people have come around to agree with him, bringing tallow and lard back into their kitchens.

Another reason I love making these freezer-ready Salisbury steaks is how easy they are to turn into a complete, comforting meal that feels straight out of an old-fashioned diner. It has long been a classic, served up on top of fluffy mashed potatoes all covered in brown gravy, and a buttered roll on the side for good measure. It's the kind of stick-to-your-ribs meal that reminds us of home-cooked meals from decades past—simple, satisfying, and made with love.

PREP TIME: **20 MINUTES**
COOK TIME: **20 MINUTES (FOR THE GRAVY)**
FREEZING TIME: **4 HOURS**
TOTAL TIME: **4 HOURS 40 MINUTES**
YIELD: **6 SERVINGS**

EQUIPMENT

Large mixing bowl
Baking sheet
Parchment paper
2 gallon-size freezer-proof bags
Large skillet

INGREDIENTS

For the Salisbury steaks:

2 lb (907g) ground beef (preferably an 85%/15% mix)
1 cup seasoned breadcrumbs
¼–½ cup whole milk
1 large egg
1 medium yellow onion, peeled and grated
1 tbsp Worcestershire sauce
1 tsp fine-ground sea salt
½ tsp freshly ground black pepper
¼ tsp red pepper flakes (optional)

For the gravy:

2 tbsp unsalted butter
1 large yellow onion, peeled, cut in half, and sliced thin
½ lb fresh white button mushrooms, sliced
2 tbsp all-purpose flour
2 cups beef broth or bone broth
1 tbsp Worcestershire sauce
1 tsp fine-ground sea salt
½ tsp freshly ground black pepper

PREPARING AND FREEZING THE SALISBURY STEAKS:

1   In a large mixing bowl, combine the ground beef, breadcrumbs, milk, egg, grated onion, Worcestershire sauce, salt, black pepper, and red pepper flakes (if using). Mix until well combined.

2   Shape the mixture into 6 individual rounded but slightly rectangular patties.

3   Place the patties on a parchment paper–lined baking sheet and freeze for 4 hours or until frozen solid.

4   Label and date a gallon-size freezer-proof bag and transfer the frozen patties to the bag, removing as much air as possible. Freeze the patties for up to 3 months.

PREPARING THE GRAVY:

1   Add the butter to a large skillet on medium heat. Heat the butter until it's melted and sizzling, then add the onions and mushrooms. Cook until the onions are translucent and the mushrooms are tender.

2   Stir in the flour and cook for **approximately 2 minutes or until the mixture is lightly golden brown.**

3   Gradually add the broth, Worcestershire sauce, salt, and black pepper. Bring to a boil over high heat, stirring continually to prevent scorching. When the mixture comes to a boil, immediately reduce the heat to low and simmer for 10 minutes or until the gravy thickens. Taste and season with additional salt and pepper, if desired.

4   Remove the gravy from the heat and allow it to cool completely. Label and date a gallon-size freezer-proof bag and pour the gravy into the bag, carefully removing as much air as possible while preventing the gravy from oozing out of the bag. Freeze the gravy for up to 3 months.

COOKING THE SALISBURY STEAK PATTIES:

1   Remove the gravy from the freezer and place it on the countertop to defrost slightly.

2   When you are ready to cook the Salisbury steak patties, heat 2 tablespoons tallow or 1 tablespoon olive oil and 1 tablespoon butter in a large skillet on medium-high heat.

3   Add the frozen patties and cook for approximately 2 to 3 minutes per side until they are lightly brown but not yet cooked through. Turn the heat down to low.

4   Loosen the gravy from the bag, it may still be slightly frozen, and add it in chunks to the skillet along with the patties. Cover, and allow the gravy to defrost slowly on low heat.

5   Once the gravy appears to be fully defrosted, turn the Salisbury steaks over using tongs, then turn the heat up to medium and allow the patties to simmer in the gravy until cooked through. This will take approximately 10 minutes or until the steaks are no longer pink in the center.

6   If desired, serve the Salisbury steaks atop mashed potatoes, then cover them with gravy.

Traditional Italian Carrot Cake

This Italian carrot cake, known as torta di carote, was one of my mom's favorite cakes to make and enjoy. It is a tender, moist cake that freezes beautifully without drying out. Unlike American carrot cakes, this version does not have frosting and is simply dusted with powdered sugar before serving. It's perfect for preparing ahead and enjoying a flavorful, homemade treat anytime or when company arrives unexpectedly, since you can pop this cake into a warm oven and thoroughly defrost it in minutes.

PREP TIME: **30 MINUTES**
BAKE TIME: **35–45 MINUTES**
TOTAL TIME: **1 HOUR 5–15 MINUTES**
YIELD: **8 SERVINGS**

EQUIPMENT

2 large mixing bowls
Handheld electric mixer (optional)
9-inch (23-cm) straight-sided tube pan or springform pan
Parchment paper
Plastic wrap
Aluminum foil

INGREDIENTS

1¼ cups almond flour (or finely ground almonds)
1 cup all-purpose flour or whole wheat flour (see **Cook's Notes**), plus more for dusting the pan
2 tsp baking powder
Pinch of fine-ground sea salt

3 large eggs
½ cup granulated sugar or unrefined whole cane sugar
½ cup unsalted butter, melted and cooled, plus more for greasing the pan
¼ cup whole milk
1 tsp vanilla extract
Zest of 1 well-scrubbed medium lemon or small orange
2 cups finely grated carrots (about 4 medium carrots, peeled)
Confectioners' sugar (also known as powdered sugar or icing sugar), for dusting (see **Cook's Notes**)

MAKING AND FREEZING THE CAKE:

1   Preheat your oven to 350°F (180°C). Grease a 9-inch (23-cm) tube pan very well and then dust the pan with the additional flour. If you want to be extra diligent about the cake not sticking to the bottom of the pan, you can cut a piece of parchment paper with a hole in the middle and place it on the bottom of the tube pan. (In a pinch, you can use a springform pan but will have to bake the cake slightly longer.)

2   In a large mixing bowl, whisk together the almond flour, all-purpose flour (or whole wheat flour), baking powder, and a pinch of salt. Set aside.

3   In a second large mixing bowl, beat the eggs and sugar until light and fluffy. You can do this with a wooden spoon or use a handheld electric mixer. Add the melted butter, milk, vanilla extract, and lemon or orange zest. Mix until well combined. Set aside.

4   Gently toss the finely grated carrots with the dry ingredients.

5   Gradually add the dry ingredients to the wet mixture, stirring until just combined. Be careful not to overmix, which will result in a dense cake.

6   Pour the batter into the prepared tube pan and work your way around the tube, smoothing the top of the batter. If using a springform pan, make sure to spread out the batter evenly and then smooth the top.

7   Place the cake on the middle rack of the oven and bake for 35 to 40 minutes. The top of the cake should turn a lovely golden brown and be firm to the touch. If it is not firm to the touch, this cake can be baked for an additional 5 minutes. If you are using a springform pan, insert a toothpick into the center of the cake at 40 minutes. If it comes out clean, the cake is baked; if not, bake the cake for an additional 5 minutes.

8   Allow the cake to cool in the pan for about 10 minutes, then unmold and transfer it to a wire rack. The cake should still be warm. Shake a generous amount of confectioners' sugar on top of the cake and rub it in with your hand.

9 Once the cake has cooled completely, wrap the cake tightly in plastic wrap and then wrap it in aluminum foil. Label and date and freeze for up to 6 months. (This moist cake will hold up well in the freezer.)

DEFROSTING AND SERVING THE CAKE:

1 When you are ready to serve this carrot cake, remove it from the freezer, unwrap it, place it on a wire rack, and let it defrost completely at room temperature. If you are in a rush, defrost the cake in a warm oven, set at 200°F (95°C) for approximately 30 minutes. Place the cake directly on to the oven rack.

2 Once fully defrosted, again dust the cake heavily with confectioners' sugar. Since this cake does not have any icing and is made with a relatively small amount of sugar, the powdered sugar provides a welcome touch of sweetness. Slice and serve.

································· COOK'S NOTES ·································

Why use whole wheat flour in this recipe? You can certainly use all-purpose flour in this recipe, but my mom always used whole wheat flour, which created a rustic cake that was also more nutritious—something she always focused on when making sweet treats. You can also use the ancient flours einkorn or spelt in place of modern-day whole wheat flour. However, if you make this switch, you will need to decrease the butter by 2 tablespoons if using spelt flour and 4 tablespoons if using einkorn flour.

What can you use in place of confectioners' sugar in this recipe? If you don't have confectioners' sugar, it's easy to make your own if you have granulated sugar. Just whirl 1 cup of granulated sugar in a blender or food processor. This will create approximately 1⅔ cups of powdered sugar. This will provide you more than enough to dust the cake and have some leftover for dusting other cakes. (Yes, it does seem counterintuitive that after grinding granulated sugar, you would have more powdered sugar, but this is correct thanks to all the air pockets created between the tiny sugar particles when ground finely.)

French Nougat Apple Tart

This French Nougat Apple Tart combines the scrumptious flavors of caramelized apples and a crunchy nougat topping, all tucked into our versatile Einkorn Sourdough Pie Crust (p. 236). (But if you prefer, you can substitute your favorite pie crust in place of the einkorn version used here.) This sophisticated dessert hails from the Alsace region of France, and it's perfect for preparing in advance and freezing. You'll be able to quickly defrost and share this treat when company stops by or anytime you feel like being a little fancy, such as when enjoying a hot cup of afternoon tea on a chilly fall day.

PREP TIME: **45 MINUTES**
COOK TIME: **15 MINUTES**
BAKE TIME: **45–50 MINUTES**
FREEZING TIME: **4 HOURS**
TOTAL TIME: **5 HOURS 50 MINUTES**
YIELD: **8 SERVINGS**

EQUIPMENT

9-inch (23-cm) tart pan with
  a removable bottom or a
  springform pan
Rolling pin
Parchment paper or
  silicone mat
Pie weights or dried beans
  (see **Cook's Notes**)
Large skillet
Whisk or handheld
  electric mixer
Spatula
Cooling rack
Baking sheet
Plastic wrap
Aluminum foil

INGREDIENTS

For the crust:

1 disk Einkorn Sourdough
  Pie Crust (p. 236)

For the filling:

2 tbsp unsalted butter
3 large apples (Fuji, Braeburn,
  or Granny Smith work
  best), peeled, cored, and
  chopped
¼ cup unrefined whole cane
  sugar or maple sugar
  (see **Cook's Notes**)
1 tsp vanilla extract
Zest and juice of
  1 well-scrubbed
  medium lemon

For the nougat topping:

2 large egg whites
¼ cup granulated sugar
⅔ cup chopped hazelnuts
  (also known as filberts)

MAKING AND FREEZING THE TART:

1 Preheat the oven to 350°F (180°C).

2 Flour a flat surface and roll out the pie crust dough to fit a 9-inch (23-cm) tart pan. Press the dough into the pan and trim the edges. Use a fork to poke a few holes across the bottom of the dough.

3 Line the dough with parchment paper and fill it with pie weights. Parbake the crust for 15 minutes, remove the pie weights and parchment paper, and bake the crust for another 5 minutes until lightly golden. Leave the oven on and set the crust aside to cool completely.

4 Add the butter to a large skillet on medium heat. Add the chopped apples, sugar, vanilla extract, and lemon zest and juice. Cook, stirring occasionally, until the apples are tender and caramelized, about 15 minutes. Remove from the heat and allow to cool.

5 In a bowl, whisk the egg whites until frothy. Gradually add the sugar, continuing to whisk until soft peaks form. Gently fold in the chopped hazelnuts.

6 Spread the cooled apple mixture evenly over the parbaked crust.

7 Spoon the nougat topping over the apples, spreading it out to cover the filling.

8 Bake the tart on the middle rack of the oven for 25 to 30 minutes or until the nougat topping is golden brown.

9 Place the tart on a cooling rack so air can circulate under the tart pan. Allow the tart to cool completely in the pan.

10 Once cooled, carefully loosen and remove the tart from the ring of the tart pan. Use a spatula to remove the bottom of the tart pan from the tart and transfer the tart to a parchment paper–lined baking sheet. Place the tart into the freezer, uncovered, and allow to freeze completely. This may take up to 4 hours.

11 Once completely frozen, remove the tart from the freezer and wrap it tightly in plastic wrap, then wrap it in aluminum foil. Label and date and freeze for up to 3 months.

DEFROSTING AND SERVING THE TART:

1 When ready to serve, unwrap the tart and place on a cooling rack to defrost at room temperature. (This will prevent the bottom crust from becoming soggy.) Defrosting the tart will take anywhere from 2 to 4 hours.

2 If you would prefer to serve the tart warm, you can place the frozen tart directly on the middle rack of the oven, with a baking sheet placed on the lower rack to catch any potential drips, and warm it at 200°F (95°C) until heated through. This can take up to 30 minutes.

······· COOK'S NOTES ·······

If you use beans as pie weights, do you need to discard them after the first use? No. Allow the beans to cool and then store them in a jar or container to use the next time you need pie weights. But keep in mind, the beans can be only used as pie weights and can't be cooked and consumed.

Which sugar is best for the filling? I know it can be a bit pricey and sometimes challenging to find, but it's worth keeping a bit of maple sugar tucked away in your pantry for baked goods such as this apple tart. This is an exceptional dessert—almost a bit gourmet. And for recipes like this, I like to use an extra-special ingredient or two.

Serving suggestion: Although not required, adding a light dusting of powdered sugar—looking like snow—on each slice of the tart before serving can make a lovely presentation when served during the wintertime.

Toaster Gingerbread Waffles

These gingerbread waffles bring the warm, spiced flavors of gingerbread into a convenient breakfast treat perfect for the holiday season. Using the famous Sue Gregg whole-grain blender batter method, these waffles become a highly digestible, soaked whole-grain waffle that can be made ahead and frozen—providing a Christmas morning breakfast that is both nutritious and quick.

PREP TIME: **15 MINUTES**
SOAK TIME: **12 HOURS**
COOK TIME: **30 MINUTES**
FREEZING TIME: **2 HOURS**
TOTAL TIME: **14 HOURS 45 MINUTES**
YIELD: **APPROXIMATELY 6 WAFFLES**

EQUIPMENT

Blender

Waffle iron

Cooling rack

Baking sheet lined with parchment paper or silicone mat

Additional parchment paper

Freezer-proof bags or airtight containers

Toaster or toaster oven (for reheating)

INGREDIENTS

1 cup whole-grain berries (whole wheat, spelt, emmer, einkorn, or kamut berries)

1½–2 cups buttermilk or plain kefir

½ tsp apple cider vinegar

¼ cup molasses

2 tbsp honey

2 large eggs

4 tbsp butter, melted and cooled

1 tsp vanilla extract

1 tsp ground ginger

1 tsp ground cinnamon

¼ tsp ground cloves

½ tsp fine-ground sea salt

1 tsp baking powder

½ tsp baking soda

MAKING AND FREEZING THE WAFFLES:

1   In a blender, combine the whole grain of your choice along with 1½ cups buttermilk or kefir. Blend until the grains are completely pulverized, adding more liquid as needed so there is always a clearly defined vortex in the middle of the mixture while whirling in the blender. Blend until the mixture is completely smooth. Let the mixture soak in the blender at room temperature overnight or for up to 12 hours. (See **Cook's Notes**.)

2   After soaking, add the vinegar, molasses, honey, eggs, melted and cooled butter, and vanilla extract to the blender. Blend until well combined.

3   Add the ginger, cinnamon, cloves, and salt to the blender. Blend until the spices are well distributed throughout the batter.

4   Add the baking powder and baking soda to the blender. Blend briefly until incorporated.

5   Preheat your waffle iron according to the manufacturer's instructions. If recommended, grease the waffle iron prior to pouring the batter.

6   Pour the batter into the preheated waffle iron, using the recommended amount of batter for your specific waffle iron. Cook until the waffles are crisp.

7   Transfer the cooked waffles to a wire rack to cool completely.

8   Once cooled, place the waffles in a single layer on a parchment paper–lined baking sheet and freeze, uncovered, until frozen solid— approximately 2 hours.

9   Transfer the frozen waffles to labeled and dated freezer-proof bags or airtight containers with parchment paper placed between each waffle. Freeze the waffles for up to 3 months.

REHEATING THE WAFFLES:

1   When ready to serve, reheat the frozen waffles in a toaster or toaster oven until heated through and crisp, about 3 to 5 minutes.

2   Serve with your favorite toppings.

COOK'S NOTES

What are whole-grain berries? Grain in its whole form (as opposed to cracked or turned into flour) is referred to as berries, as in whole wheat berries, spelt berries, einkorn berries, etc.

Can you refrigerate this batter in Step 1? Yes, you can put the blender right into your refrigerator for up to 24 hours in advance of making the waffles.

Frozen Syllabub (Nonalcoholic)

Welcome to a uniquely refreshing twist on a classic dessert whose origins date back to sixteenth-century England. Historically, a syllabub was a frothy dessert of cream, sugar, and usually wine or cider, all whipped together. This recipe takes a traditional syllabub and turns it into a frozen treat similar to ice cream. This creamy, tangy treat is perfect for warm weather and offers any meal a lovely, light finish—and a rather historically elegant one at that! This version is made without alcohol, so it's a family-friendly option that everyone can enjoy.

What makes this frozen syllabub so special is its delicate balance of flavors and textures. The combination of rich cream, a hint of citrus, and just the right amount of sweetness creates a dessert that is simple, yet luscious, and perfect to serve when entertaining. This treat makes a delightful way to end a patio dinner party on a warm day. Serve it in elegant stemmed glasses for a simple yet stunning presentation that feels straight out of an old-world feast.

PREP TIME: **15 MINUTES**
FREEZING TIME: **2–3 HOURS**
TOTAL TIME: **2 HOURS 15 MINUTES TO 3 HOURS 15 MINUTES**
YIELD: **4 SERVINGS**

EQUIPMENT

Whisk or a handheld electric mixer

Mixing bowl

Shallow rectangular freezer-proof container with lid

INGREDIENTS

1 ½ cups heavy whipping cream (also known as double cream)

¼ cup superfine sugar (caster sugar) or confectioners' sugar

Zest and juice of 1 well-scrubbed large lemon (see **Cook's Notes**)

½ tsp vanilla extract

Fresh berries, for garnishing (optional)

1 Combine the heavy cream and sugar in a large mixing bowl. Using a whisk or handheld electric mixer, beat the mixture until soft peaks form.

2 Gradually add the lemon zest, lemon juice, and vanilla extract to the whipped cream mixture. Continue whisking or beating until all ingredients are well combined and the mixture holds its shape.

3 Transfer the syllabub mixture to a shallow rectangular freezer-proof container. Smooth the top with a spatula, then put the lid on the container.

4 Place the container in the freezer for 2 to 3 hours or until the syllabub is firm and frozen.

5 Before serving, let the syllabub sit at room temperature for about 5 minutes to soften slightly. Scoop into serving glasses and garnish with fresh berries, if desired.

6 Serve immediately. (Frozen syllabub is best enjoyed the day it is made.)

COOK'S NOTES

What citrus zest and juice can I use in place of the lemon? For this recipe, a tasty substitute for the lemon is the zest and juice of a small orange. Using this in place of the lemon creates a creamsicle flavor that is quite enjoyable. For a Christmastime twist on this recipe, you can omit the citrus zest and juice and the vanilla extract. In their place, you can add ¼ cup apple juice and ½ teaspoon peppermint extract. Top the frozen syllabub with crushed red-and-white peppermint candies!

Can you make this dairy-free? Yes, indeed! Just substitute the heavy cream with coconut cream.

Chapter Eight
ALL ABOUT PICKLING

GETTING STARTED WITH PICKLING

During the years when I was homeschooling our son, Ben, we usually took summers off from school, following the schedule of most brick-and-mortar schools. We would send Ben to a variety of different camps where he learned how to ride horses, train dogs (with his dog Obi in tow), swim, paint and draw, play various sports, and do a whole host of other activities. However, some of the best memories Ben has shared with me as he has grown into an adult are the downtimes he shared with me. When there was no camp to attend, Ben and I would rise early in the morning, get into the car, and drive out into the Texas Hill Country for a day of looking for assorted treasures at little hole-in-the-wall stores that sold used items. Since it wasn't quite antiquing, we called it junking!

There was so much more to our adventures than just hunting down special little items to bring home. Our day also included stopping at a roadside stand and making purchases, such as farm-grown beefsteak tomatoes and homemade ciabatta bread. Halfway through our day, we would sit in the car, tear off pieces of bread, and take big bites out of the tomatoes that would dribble with juice down our chins. To this day, Ben and I can still taste those delicious tomatoes!

Probably the most fun we had was stopping at a large farm outside of a town named Marble Falls. This farm offered a variety of activities, including picking your own fruits, flowers, herbs, and vegetables. We would fill bushels—and our arms—full of whatever looked best. One day, we came home with so much food that we got to work in the kitchen the minute we returned home. We put beautiful flowers in Mason jars, whipped up batch after batch of homemade pesto with fresh basil, and best of all, we pickled a wide variety of fresh vegetables—a few of which we quick pickled so that we could enjoy them a few hours later. By evening, we had lots of pickled vegetables tucked away on the shelves of our refrigerator that we would enjoy over the coming months. Once our school days resumed, we often enjoyed those pickled vegetables with our lunch and reminisced about our summer adventures. Wonderful memories indeed!

Beyond Cucumbers: The Endless Possibilities of Pickling

When you think of pickling food, probably the first thing that comes to mind is traditional pickles. But the world of pickled food is much broader than that. The beauty of making pickled foods is that it's easy to do and, in many cases, after a few hours of refrigeration, you can enjoy your pickles to your heart's content.

Even though pickled food is referred to as "pickled" or "pickles," you can pickle and enjoy a whole host of foods beyond cucumbers! On its most basic level, pickling is a simple way to preserve food by soaking the food in a brine made of salt and water along with an acid such as vinegar. Additions to this basic pickling brine can include herbs and spices, plus a bit of added sweetness, especially when pickling fruits and vegetables. Pickling is probably one of the most creative ways to preserve food because of the variety of foods that can be pickled, from meat to fish to eggs to fruits and vegetables. They all have their own taste profile, and each one is delicious!

One of the best things about learning how to pickle food is that it can help cut down on food waste, especially when it comes to fruits and vegetables. For example, if you have a variety of vegetable bits and bobs in your refrigerator, such as part of a carrot, half an onion, or one lone beet, all of these can be pickled together. You'll create a tasty treat, and you'll save these odds and ends from going into the garbage or the compost pile.

What Foods Are Best to Pickle

An easy place to start when making pickled foods is with vegetables. Pickling offers the ability to keep the texture of vegetables firm with a delightful crisp. And the often sweet-and-sour flavor that comes with pickled vegetables is unbeatable. The best thing about pickling your own vegetables, as opposed to buying pickled vegetables from the grocery store, is that you can create your own unique flavor blends while making the best use of abundant in-season food from the farmer's market or your kitchen garden bounty. But this doesn't stop with vegetables. Here is a list of foods you can successfully preserve through pickling:

- **Aromatics:** Herbs, horseradish, leeks, garlic, ginger, onions (all varieties), shallots, spices.

- **Beef:** Specifically brisket when pickled with a salted brine called "salt curing" or "corning."

- **Eggs:** Hard-boiled only.

- **Fish:** Although herring is especially popular, almost any type of fish may be pickled.

- **Fruits:** Some of the best to pickle (as well as to turn into relishes and chutneys) include apples, blueberries, citrus peel, citrus slices, citrus supremes, cherries, cranberries, cantaloupe, figs, grapes, honeydew, nectarines, peaches, pears, strawberries, and watermelon rind.

- **Vegetables:** Some of the best to pickle (as well as to turn into relishes and chutneys) include artichokes, asparagus, beets, carrots, cauliflower, celery, corn, cucumbers, fennel, green beans, jicama, mushrooms, okra, parsnips, peppers (sweet, bell, and spicy varieties), radishes, summer squash and zucchini, tomatoes (fully ripe as well as green), tomatillos, and turnips.

.... **WHAT IS CORNING?** ....

Corning has nothing to do with corn. It refers to the size of the grain of salt that was originally used to preserve meat. The grains of salt were about the size of a kernel of corn and were rubbed into the meat. This was one method of preserving dried meat with salt. Today, we usually brine brisket in a salty brine—and the salt grains don't have to be the size of a kernel of corn. However, we still call the process corning, and the end product is the corned beef we know today and often serve to celebrate St. Patrick's Day.

.... **WHAT ARE CITRUS SUPREMES?** ....

Supremes are sections of citrus fruit with the pith and peel removed and the membranes around each segment removed to expose the flesh. This technique is also referred to as segmenting or sectioning. Supremes are perfect for adding to a salad and benefit from being pickled in a sweet and sour brine.

What Foods Should *Not* Be Pickled

Even though pickling is well suited for a wide variety of foods, some foods are not suitable for pickling. These include:

- **Dairy products:** Pickling causes curdling.

- **Leafy greens:** Tender greens like lettuce become a slimy mess when pickled.

- **Heavily waxed foods from the grocery store:** The wax prevents even absorption of the brine, creating an unsatisfactory end product.

How to Successfully Pickle Food

You will want to follow some general rules when you begin to pickle foods. Many of the foods you will be pickling likely fall into the fruits and vegetables category. If so, you want to make sure that the produce you pick is at its peak freshness and does not show signs of spoilage. As you graduate to pickling beef or fish, freshness is crucial. If you try to pickle meat or fish past its prime, you will not be pleased with the end product, and you could also risk foodborne illness.

As with ferments, foods that are going to be pickled prefer plain, clean water as free of chemicals and chlorine as possible. If you have highly chlorinated water, you can leave some out overnight in a pitcher, allowing some of the chlorine to dissipate. You can also boil the water and allow it to cool, which may eliminate some of the chlorine as well. Bottled spring water can be a terrific option for making a pickling brine, and I recommend it.

When you prepare your pickling brine, make sure you use canning and pickling salt or some other type of salt without additives. Using table salt that may contain anticaking agents will create a very cloudy brine and potentially affect the flavor of the pickled food. And even more importantly, make sure you do not use iodized salt when making a pickling brine. It may darken the food to the point of looking very unappetizing. Sea salt is an option, but because of its high mineral content, it might affect the brine's clarity. Note this is not necessarily a problem and should not affect the flavor of the pickled food, but remember that you might notice a cloudiness develop in the brine.

In addition to water, you'll make a pickling brine with vinegar. You have many options when choosing vinegar, but the common denominator is that you want a vinegar with 5% acidity. White vinegar and apple cider vinegar are two popular choices and are guaranteed to create a flavorful brine that adds the right amount of tang but also allows the flavor of the food to shine through.

When making the recipes that follow, do not decrease the amount of vinegar called for. A pickled product's acidity level is critical for taste, texture, and food safety. Too little vinegar might cause your food to not be pickled safely and may cause foodborne illness. If you prefer a less tangy or sour pickled food, add a sweetener instead of decreasing the vinegar.

Speaking of a sweetener, white granulated sugar is the typical choice, but I understand if you want to pull back on using this type of sugar. Although sugar does act as a preservative, there is such a significant amount of vinegar in a pickling brine that sugar's role in preserving food can take a back seat. So, if you want to reduce the sugar in a pickling recipe, it's fine to do so.

As traditional foods cooks, we are always looking for healthier alternatives when it comes to sweetening our food. Unrefined whole cane sugar is an option, but it can darken the end product. Plus, it will create a stronger flavor. A mild honey, like a simple clover honey, can be a good choice. You can also choose raw honey or pasteurized honey. It doesn't matter. A mild honey tends not to darken a pickling brine to the same extent as the unrefined whole cane sugar. And if you like honey, it can provide a pleasant flavor to the brine.

Herbs and spices added to a pickling brine can considerably boost the flavor. Most pickling recipes call for at least one aromatic addition. Keep in mind that you want to use fresh herbs and whole spices when adding herbs and spices to a pickle brine. Dried herbs (other than bay leaves) and ground spices may cause the pickle brine to darken or become cloudy.

Depending on the recipe, pickled food may be sliced, chopped, diced, or left whole. Once you decide on how you want your food to be prepared, all you need to do is mix the food with the brine in the way the recipe specifies. Always make sure that the food is completely submerged in the brine. Next, you'll pop it in your fridge and wait the required amount of time until your pickled food is ready.

TANNINS TO THE RESCUE!

Certain pickled foods, such as actual pickles, might require some extra care if you want to maintain their crunch. Slipping a few bay leaves into each jar of cucumbers can do the trick. Bay leaves are rich in tannins, and these compounds prevent pickles from turning soft and mushy. If you are making a quart of pickles, be sure to add 5 to 6 bay leaves to the jar as you add your cucumbers.

No bay leaves? No problem! If you have a black tea bag—caffeinated or decaf is fine—pop it into the bottom of your jar and then add your cucumbers and brine. Like bay leaves, tea is loaded with tannins and will keep your pickles crisp! Be sure to leave the bay leaves or tea bag in the jar when you refrigerate your pickles.

Pickling vs. Quick Pickling

You may hear the terms pickling and quick pickling used when referring to pickled food. There are differences between the two ways to prepare pickled foods that easily accommodate the home cook's schedule.

PICKLING

Pickling is when you put fresh food into a vessel and cover it with a brine that has been brought to a boil, either kept hot or cooled, and then poured over the food. Next, you tuck your vessel into the refrigerator to steep, allowing the food to soak in the brine and take on the flavor over the course of a week or two.

Alternatively, you can cook fresh food on the stove in a brine, ladle the food and the brine into a jar, and then refrigerate the jar. Allowing the food to mellow in the fridge over a week or two will help the flavors meld to create a delicious pickled food. This is also referred to as pickling.

IS IT REALLY PICKLING IF IT'S NOT WATER BATH CANNED?

There is a little controversy over what I describe as pickling. This comes down to whether the food is refrigerated or home canned with the water bath method. I consider pickled foods stored in the refrigerator to be a nice contrast to pickled foods that have been water bath canned. If you are busy home canning other foods, it's nice to know you can pickle foods and pop them in the refrigerator without tying up your stove with water bath canning equipment. Plus, I find some variation in texture and taste between pickled foods that have been refrigerated versus those that have been water bath canned, making both options desirable. Variety is always welcome at mealtime!

QUICK PICKLING

In addition to traditional pickling, there is a fast and easy technique that is also a form of pickling: it's the quick version—or quick pickling. This technique is a terrific way to pickle fresh vegetables. You cut them up, add them to a clean jar, bring a brine to a boil, and then pour the hot brine over the vegetables in the jar, leaving some headspace but making sure all the veggies are covered with the brine. Pop a lid on the jar and refrigerate it. These quick-pickled vegetables—or what some would call refrigerator pickles—can be ready to eat within 1 hour. They'll have lots of crunch to them, and the brine will improve their flavor. These quick-pickled vegetables are a flavorful addition to any last-minute dinner of hamburgers and hot dogs.

Best Kitchen Equipment for Pickling Food

When it comes to pickling food, the equipment and tools you need are quite basic. A good cutting board and a sharp knife will come in handy, as they do for pretty much any form of food preservation prep, but the main piece of equipment will be a vessel in which your food can be pickled and stored. This should be an appropriately sized vessel made of glass or a high-quality enameled stockpot or baking pan. These vessels are sturdy and can hold a highly acidic brine without being damaged or leaching any chemicals into the brine.

Can you use food-safe plastic? Yes, but I prefer something less porous because pickle brine is usually a 1:1 ratio of water to vinegar. Vinegar's high acidity can eat away at plastic if it is not of a heavyweight construction, such as a five-gallon storage bucket. I generally prefer to rely on glass or enamel when it comes to pickling because I question whether or not the plastic, even if food-safe, may leach chemicals into the brine.

In addition to the vessel in which you will be pickling your food, also have a saucepan or additional stockpot on hand that is made of a nonreactive metal such as enamelware or stainless steel. You do not want the high acid content of the brine, which may need to be heated, to react with your cookware. Materials such as copper, brass, iron, or aluminum may react with the acids in the brine when heated. (Make sure the utensils you use that may come in contact with the brine are also not made of these metals.) The reaction will cause undesirable color in the brine. Using the wrong cookware may even form toxic compounds in the pickle mixture.

How Long Can Pickled Food Be Stored in the Refrigerator?

You should refrigerate pickled foods during the pickling process and continue to keep them refrigerated once they are pickled. Similar to fermented foods, pickles like to be stored at about 40°F (4°C). The top shelf or the door of your refrigerator is a perfect place for them. According to the USDA, pickled foods can stay fresh in the refrigerator for approximately 3 months. After that point, the pickling brine might become cloudy, and the texture of the pickled foods may not be at its peak.

Always remember, as with any food, to use your eyes and nose. If a picked food appears to have developed mold, discard it. And if any pickled food takes on a foul odor, discard it.

General Guidelines for Pickling Food

1 Prepare the vessel and any other cookware and utensils you may need.

2 Start with the freshest food possible.

3 Wash and prepare the food as specified in the recipe.

4 Prepare the brine as specified in the recipe.

5 Use a 5%-acidity vinegar.

6 Use pure water that is low in chlorine.

7 Do not alter the vinegar-to-water ratio.

8 When making the brine, use only salt that contains no anticaking agents and is not iodized.

9 Add fresh herbs or whole spices to the brine, if desired.

10 Mix the prepared food and the brine together as called for in the recipe.

11 Refrigerate the food and brine and allow for the pickling time as specified in the recipe.

Let's Get Started with Pickling

Pickled foods are easy to whip up with little effort and are great for adding a flavor boost to any meal! These foods come in a variety of forms including seasonings, condiments, salads, main entrées, and even sweet and tangy fruits that make for a tongue-tingling topping for ice cream! Besides being delicious, many pickled foods, especially fruits and vegetables, add fiber and a whole host of antioxidants to our diet.

Onion and Herb Vinegar

You'll welcome this delightful addition to your homemade pantry! This Onion and Herb Vinegar is simple to make and bursts with flavor to elevate your dishes. It's perfect for salads, marinades, and even as a tangy twist in your nonalcoholic syllabub.

PREP TIME: **15 MINUTES**
COOK TIME: **15 MINUTES**
PICKLING TIME: **2 WEEKS**
TOTAL TIME: **2 WEEKS 30 MINUTES**
YIELD: **APPROXIMATELY 3 CUPS**

EQUIPMENT

2 wide-mouth pint (16oz) jars with lids

Small skillet

Small (2- to 4-quart) saucepan

Slotted spoon

Ladle

Wide-mouth funnel (optional)

Large bowl

Narrow-mouth funnel (optional)

Bottle with tight-fitting cap sufficient to hold approximately 24 ounces

INGREDIENTS

1 tsp mustard seeds

1 tsp black peppercorns

1 tsp coriander seeds

1 cup water

2 tbsp unrefined whole cane sugar

1 tsp pickling salt

2 small yellow or red onions, peeled and thinly sliced

2 cups raw apple cider vinegar (homemade or store-bought)

2 bay leaves

2 sprigs fresh thyme

2 sprigs fresh rosemary

.... COOK'S NOTES ....

How can you give this vinegar a spicy kick? To spice up this vinegar, add ¼ to ½ teaspoon red pepper flakes to each pint jar. Or you can crush a few dried chili peppers of your choosing and add 2 or 3 to each pint jar.

Can you make this vinegar in a quart jar? Yes, but I have found that dividing the ingredients between two pint jars creates a better-tasting end product. I discovered this once when I was out of quart jars and made this vinegar using two pint jars. I can't explain why it tasted better, but it did. As the saying goes, necessity is the mother of invention. I needed to make this vinegar and I discovered a new and more flavorful way to do it!

1 Wash the pint jars and lids in warm, soapy water. Rinse them well and set them aside to dry.

2 Heat a small skillet over low heat. Add the mustard seeds, black peppercorns, and coriander seeds to the skillet and toast them until they become fragrant, no more than 5 minutes. Keep a close eye on them—they can burn easily. Once the ingredients are toasted, remove the skillet from the heat.

3 Add the water, sugar, and salt to a small saucepan along with the toasted spices and the sliced onions. Bring the mixture to a boil over high heat, stirring continuously until the sugar and salt are dissolved. Turn the heat down to low, cover the saucepan, and simmer the mixture for 10 minutes. Remove from the heat, and let the mixture cool completely.

4 Once the mixture is cooled, add the raw apple cider vinegar and stir. Set aside.

5 Add 1 bay leaf, 1 thyme sprig, and 1 rosemary sprig to each pint jar.

6 Using a slotted spoon, divide the onions and spices evenly between each pint jar and then use a ladle to fill each jar with the vinegar mixture. (Optionally, you can use a wide-mouth funnel placed over the pint jars as you ladle in the vinegar mixture.) Leave approximately a ½-inch (1.25-cm) headspace.

7 Wipe the rims of the jars with a clean, damp cloth and seal with the lids. Transfer the filled jars to the refrigerator.

8 After 2 weeks, remove the jars from the refrigerator, strain the contents of each jar over a large bowl, and decant the vinegar into a bottle sufficient to hold approximately 24 ounces. You can use a narrow-mouth funnel to make the decanting process easier and neater.

9 The vinegar can be stored in a cool, dark pantry. Due to its highly acidic nature, vinegar can have an indefinite shelf life, but a homemade flavored vinegar is probably best used within 5 years. You can use this vinegar in the recipes in this chapter that call for raw apple cider vinegar if you want to introduce a new flavor.

Pickled Ginger

If you have ever eaten at a sushi restaurant or purchased sushi at your local grocery store, it was probably accompanied by a small portion of pickled ginger, also known in Japanese cuisine as gari. It is considered a palate cleanser you can enjoy between each different taste of food so the flavor of the previously consumed food does not overshadow the taste of the new food.

Even if you do not make sushi at home, having some pickled ginger on hand can make a tasty accompaniment to sandwiches or to a charcuterie board. Plus, all on its own, it can help as a home remedy when taken at the first sign of the sniffles. Whether raw or pickled, ginger is rich in antiviral properties that can support our bodies when we feel a bit under the weather.

PREP TIME: **45 MINUTES**
COOK TIME: **10 MINUTES**
TOTAL TIME: **55 MINUTES**
YIELD: **2 PINTS**

EQUIPMENT

2 wide-mouth pint (16oz) jars
  with screw-on lids
Vegetable peeler (optional)
Sharp paring knife or
  mandoline
Colander or mesh strainer
Medium bowl
Small (2- to 4-quart)
  saucepan
Wide-mouth funnel
  (optional)
Ladle

INGREDIENTS

1 lb (454g) fresh ginger
2 tsp pickling salt, divided
1 cup rice vinegar
1 cup water
½ cup granulated sugar

1   Wash the pint jars and lids in warm, soapy water. Rinse them well and set them aside to dry.

2   Peel the ginger using a spoon (a serrated grapefruit spoon works well) or a vegetable peeler. Thinly slice the ginger using a sharp paring knife or a mandoline.

3   Place the sliced ginger into a colander or mesh strainer placed over a medium bowl. Sprinkle the ginger with 1 teaspoon pickling salt, and let it sit for about 30 minutes. This will help soften the ginger and pull out some of its liquid.

4   Add the vinegar, water, sugar, and remaining 1 teaspoon pickling salt to a small saucepan over high heat. Bring the mixture to a boil, stirring continuously until the sugar and salt are dissolved completely, then immediately put a lid on the saucepan and remove it from the heat. This is your pickling brine.

5   Toss the salted ginger in the colander or mesh strainer a few times, then pat it dry with a lint-free kitchen towel or paper towels. Divide the ginger slices evenly between the 2 pint jars.

6   Remove the lid from the saucepan and ladle the hot pickling brine over the ginger, ensuring the slices are fully submerged. If you need additional liquid, you can add equal parts rice vinegar and water. Leave about a ½-inch (1.25-cm) headspace. (Optionally, you can use a wide-mouth funnel placed over the pint jars as you ladle in the pickling brine.)

7   Wipe the rims of the jars with a clean, damp cloth and seal with the lids. Transfer the filled jars to the refrigerator. The ginger will be ready to use after 1 week. It should be stored in the refrigerator and will stay fresh for up to 3 months.

··············· COOK'S NOTES ···············

How can you make the pickled ginger taste milder?
For a milder flavor, blanch the ginger slices in boiling water for 2 to 3 minutes before salting.

Pickled Hot Cherry Peppers

If you have not had Pickled Hot Cherry Peppers, you are in for a treat! Once pickled, they retain their vibrant red color and take on a tongue-tingling tang that is perfect for adding to salads, sandwiches, or even as a snack on their own. Our area has a small Italian restaurant that serves these pickled cherry peppers sliced in half and stuffed with the soft cheese chèvre. These stuffed peppers are placed on a charcuterie platter along with some thinly sliced meats, cheeses, and toast points. It's a delicious array of goodies, but those stuffed peppers keep us coming back. The good news is that these peppers are easy to make in our kitchens!

PREP TIME: **20 MINUTES**
COOK TIME: **10 MINUTES**
TOTAL TIME: **30 MINUTES**
YIELD: **1–2 PINTS**

EQUIPMENT

1–2 wide-mouth pint (16oz) jar(s) with screw-on lid(s)

Small (2- to 4-quart) saucepan

Wide-mouth funnel (optional)

Ladle

INGREDIENTS

1 lb (454g) hot cherry peppers, washed (10–15 peppers, depending on size)

1 cup 5%-acidity white vinegar

1 cup water

1 tbsp granulated sugar

1 tsp pickling salt

1 tsp black peppercorns

1–2 bay leaves

1 Wash the pint jars and lids in warm, soapy water. Rinse them well and set them aside to dry.

2 Remove the stems from the cherry peppers. Slice the peppers in half and remove the seeds and membranes. Set aside. (See **Cook's Notes**.)

3 Add the vinegar, water, sugar, salt, and black peppercorns to a small saucepan. Bring the mixture to a boil over high heat, stirring continuously until the sugar and salt are completely dissolved, then immediately turn the heat down to low and simmer the mixture for 10 minutes. Cover the saucepan, remove from the heat, and allow to cool. This is your pickling brine.

4 If you have large cherry peppers, divide the halved peppers evenly between the 2 pint jars. If you have small cherry peppers, the halves may fit in 1 jar. Nestle 1 bay leaf into the jar(s) alongside the peppers.

5 Using a ladle, pour the cooled pickling brine over the peppers, ensuring they are fully submerged. If you need additional liquid, you can add equal parts vinegar and water. Leave about a ½ inch (1.25cm) of headspace. (Optionally, you can use a wide-mouth funnel placed over the pint jars as you ladle in the pickling brine.)

6 Wipe the rims of the jars with a clean, damp cloth and seal with the lids. Transfer the filled jars to the refrigerator.

7 The peppers will be ready to use after 1 week. They should be stored in the refrigerator and will stay fresh for up to 3 months.

···················· COOK'S NOTES ····················

What should you do with the seeds and membranes you removed from the cherry peppers? Instead of discarding the seeds and membranes, you can dry them in an oven on its lowest setting. Once dry, you can whirl them in a spice grinder or blender to make a homemade chili powder. Seal the powder in a jar with a tight-fitting lid and store it in a cool, dark pantry.

What can you do with extra pickling brine? With any of the pickling recipes in this chapter, when you find yourself with extra pickling brine, you do not need to discard it unless the recipe specifically tells you to discard it. If you can keep the pickling brine, strain out the solids and decant the brine into a bottle, put on a tight-fitting cap, and then refrigerate it. You can use this brine for future pickling projects, to marinate meat, or in place of vinegar when making a salad dressing.

Sweet-and-Sour Pickled Baby Carrots

Sweet-and-Sour Pickled Baby Carrots are a delightful treat to tuck into a lunch box or serve alongside a simple soup and sandwich for a Saturday night supper. Their tangy and sweet notes create a perfect balance, which, combined with a satisfying crunch, make them irresistible.

PREP TIME: **10 MINUTES**
COOK TIME: **10 MINUTES**
TOTAL TIME: **20 MINUTES**
YIELD: **2 PINTS**

EQUIPMENT

2 wide-mouth pint (16oz) jars with screw-on lids

Small (2- to 4-quart) saucepan

Wide-mouth funnel, optional

Ladle

INGREDIENTS

1 lb (454g) fresh baby carrots

½ cup water

¼ cup granulated sugar

1 tbsp pickling salt

1 tbsp pickling spice (found in the spice aisle of most grocery stores)

1 (3- to 4-inch/7.5- to 10-cm) Ceylon cinnamon stick

½ tsp red pepper flakes, for a spicy brine (optional)

½ cup raw apple cider vinegar (homemade or store-bought)

2 bay leaves

1 Wash the pint jars and lids in warm, soapy water. Rinse them well and set them aside to dry.

2 Fill a small saucepan halfway full with water and bring to a boil over high heat. Add the baby carrots and blanch for 2 minutes, then drain, and rinse the carrots under cold water until they feel cool to the touch.

3 Add the water, sugar, salt, pickling spice, cinnamon stick, and red pepper flakes (if using) to the saucepan. Bring the mixture to a boil over high heat, stirring continuously until the sugar and salt are dissolved, then remove from the heat. Allow to cool completely. Once cooled, add the raw apple cider vinegar to the saucepan and stir. This is your pickling brine.

4 Divide the blanched baby carrots between the 2 pint jars, leaving about a ½ inch (1.25cm) of headspace. Nestle 1 bay leaf into each jar alongside the carrots.

5 Using a ladle, pour the cooled pickling brine over the carrots, ensuring they are fully submerged. If you need additional liquid, you can add equal parts of vinegar and water. Leave about a ½ inch (1.25cm) of headspace. (Optionally, you can use a wide-mouth funnel placed over the pint jars as you ladle in the pickling brine.)

6 Wipe the rims of the jars with a clean, damp cloth and seal with the lids. Transfer the filled jars to the refrigerator.

7 The carrots will be ready to use after 1 week. They should be stored in the refrigerator and will stay fresh for up to 3 months.

.... COOK'S NOTES ....

Can you add more salt to these pickled carrots? Definitely! Although I like these with 1 tablespoon pickling salt, if you find your palate generally prefers a bit more saltiness, you can use 1½ tablespoons pickling salt when making these carrots.

Simple Pickled Tomatillo Relish

Simple Pickled Tomatillo Relish is a tangy, slightly spicy condiment that's perfect for adding a spicy kick of flavor to tacos, quesadillas, burgers, hot dogs, and sandwiches. Be sure to try it in your next batch of tartar sauce for a pleasant change of flavor, or in any other recipe calling for traditional pickle relish.

PREP TIME: **15 MINUTES**
COOK TIME: **10 MINUTES**
TOTAL TIME: **25 MINUTES**
YIELD: **3 PINTS**

EQUIPMENT

2 wide-mouth pint (16oz) jars with screw-on lids

Food processor or blender

Rubber spatula

Small (2- to 4-quart) saucepan

Ladle

Wide-mouth funnel (optional)

INGREDIENTS

2 lb (907g) large tomatillos, husked and quartered (approximately 14 tomatillos)

4 cloves garlic, peeled and rough chopped

2 jalapeños or Serrano peppers, rough chopped (remove seeds and membranes for less spice)

1 cup rough chopped fresh cilantro or flat-leaf Italian parsley

1 cup 5%-acidity white vinegar

1 cup water

1 tbsp unrefined whole cane sugar

1 tsp pickling salt

1 tsp whole cumin seeds

1 tsp whole coriander seeds

1 tsp black peppercorns

Zest and juice of 1 small lime

1 Wash the pint jars and lids in warm, soapy water. Rinse them well and set them aside to dry.

2 Add the tomatillos, garlic, peppers, and cilantro or parsley to a food processor or blender. Pulse or blend a few times until well chopped and still chunky, but not puréed. Periodically scrape down the sides of the food processor or blender with a rubber spatula to make sure the mixture is evenly chunky.

3 Evenly divide the tomatillo mixture between 2 pint jars and set aside.

4 Add the vinegar, water, sugar, salt, cumin seeds, coriander seeds, and peppercorns to a small saucepan over high heat. Bring the mixture to a boil, stirring continuously until the sugar and salt are dissolved, then turn the heat down to low, cover the saucepan, and simmer the mixture for 5 minutes. Remove from the heat. Remove the lid, stir in the lime zest and lime juice, and put the lid back on the saucepan. This is your pickling brine.

5 Using a ladle, pour the hot pickling brine over the tomatillo mixture, ensuring it is fully submerged. It shouldn't be necessary, but if you need additional liquid, add equal parts of vinegar and water. Leave about a ½ inch (1.25cm) of headspace. (Optionally, you can use a wide-mouth funnel placed over the pint jars as you ladle in the pickling brine.)

6 Wipe the rims of the jars with a clean, damp cloth and seal with the lids. Transfer the filled jars to the refrigerator.

7 Leave the tomatillo relish to pickle in the refrigerator for at least 2 weeks before using. During that time, the tomatillos will absorb the brine, creating a highly flavorful relish. This relish should be stored in the refrigerator and will stay fresh for up to 3 months.

Pickled Cornichons

When my son was a little boy, he loved growing "Parisian" Pickling Cucumbers, which, once pickled, are commonly referred to as cornichons. These tiny cucumbers are perfect for holding in small hands and pack a punch of tangy flavor in a brine with just a modest touch of sweetness. They are ideal for introducing small children to a flavorful yet less sweet food. These delightful little pickles are a staple in French cuisine, often enjoyed as an accompaniment to pâtés, terrines, and charcuterie boards because they help aid in digestion when served along with rich foods. They also make a delightful addition to sandwiches when sliced in half lengthwise, particularly when added to the classic French jambon-beurre sandwich (a baguette with ham and butter), which my husband and I recently enjoyed at our local grocery store cafe.

PREP TIME: **1 HOUR 35 MINUTES**
COOK TIME: **10 MINUTES**
TOTAL TIME: **1 HOUR 45 MINUTES**
YIELD: **2 PINTS**

EQUIPMENT

2 wide-mouth pint (16oz) jars with screw-on lids

Large glass or stainless steel bowl

Colander

Small (2- to 4-quart) saucepan

Ladle

Wide-mouth funnel, optional

INGREDIENTS

1 lb (454g) 2–3-inch (5–7.5-cm) gherkin-type small cucumbers (can vary from 20–30 cucumbers, depending on size)

¼ cup plus 1 tbsp pickling salt, divided

1 cup white wine vinegar (or 5%-acidity white vinegar)

1 cup water

1 tbsp granulated sugar

1 tsp mustard seeds

½ tsp whole black peppercorns

6 peeled pearl onions (optional)

2 sprigs fresh tarragon (optional, but traditional in French recipes)

1 Wash the pint jars and lids in warm, soapy water. Rinse them well and set them aside to dry.

2 In a large bowl, toss the cucumbers with ¼ cup salt. Let the cucumbers rest in the bowl for 5 minutes, then transfer them to a colander placed in the sink or over a bowl. Allow the cucumbers to drain for 90 minutes. This step will remove moisture from the cucumbers, increasing their crispness and allowing them to absorb more of the flavorful brine.

3 After 90 minutes, rinse the cucumbers thoroughly. Set aside.

4 Add the vinegar, water, sugar, mustard seeds, peppercorns, and remaining 1 tablespoon pickling salt to a small saucepan. Bring the mixture to a boil over high heat, stirring continuously until the sugar and salt are dissolved, then cover the saucepan and remove it from the heat. This is your pickling brine.

5 Divide the onions (if using) between the 2 pint jars. Next, divide the cucumbers between the 2 pint jars, leaving about a ½ inch (1.25cm) of headspace. Nestle a sprig of fresh tarragon (if using) along with the cucumbers into each jar.

6 Using a ladle, pour the cooled pickling brine over the cucumbers, ensuring they are fully submerged. If you need additional liquid, you can add equal parts of vinegar and water. Leave about a ½ inch (1.25cm) of headspace. (Optionally, you can use a wide-mouth funnel placed over the pint jars as you ladle in the pickling brine.)

7 Wipe the rims of the jars with a clean, damp cloth and seal with the lids. Transfer the filled jars to the refrigerator.

8 Let the cornichons pickle in the refrigerator for at least 2 weeks before enjoying them. The flavor will develop best during this time. They should be stored in the refrigerator and will stay fresh for up to 3 months.

> ···················· COOK'S NOTES ····················
>
> **Will the cornichons remain crisp?** When prepared according to this recipe, the cornichons should remain crisp for up to 3 months while refrigerated. However, if you are concerned about this, you can place a black tea bag (caffeinated or decaffeinated) in the bottom of each pint jar before adding the cucumbers. The tannins in the tea will ensure your cornichons will remain quite crisp.

Sweet Pickled Red Onions

Our town has a restaurant that serves pickled red onions with many of their traditional Mexican dishes. They are scrumptious, and it's not uncommon for my son and I to gobble them up before eating anything else! These Sweet Pickled Red Onions are as close as I have been able to get to those restaurant onions. They make a versatile condiment that adds a tangy-sweet crunch to a variety of home-cooked meals. With just a few simple ingredients, you can quickly prepare a batch to have ready in your fridge to add to pretty much anything you want. You can't go wrong when adding these onions to salads, sandwiches, grilled meats, and even as a topping on tortilla soup.

PREP TIME: **15 MINUTES**
COOK TIME: **10 MINUTES**
TOTAL TIME: **25 MINUTES**
YIELD: **2 PINTS**

EQUIPMENT

2 wide-mouth pint (16oz) jars
  with screw-on lids
Small (2- to 4-quart)
  saucepan
Slotted spoon
Ladle
Wide-mouth funnel
  (optional)

INGREDIENTS

1 cup 5%-acidity
  white vinegar
1 cup water
½ cup unrefined whole cane
  sugar (or finely grated
  piloncillo)
1 tsp pickling salt
2 (3- to 4-inch / 7.5- to 10-cm)
  sprigs fresh Mexican
  oregano (or ½ tsp dried
  Mexican oregano)
  (see **Cook's Notes**)
½ tsp black peppercorns
½ tsp cumin seeds
½ tsp coriander seeds
½ tsp whole cloves
½ tsp whole allspice berries
1 Ceylon cinnamon stick
2 large red onions, peeled
  and thinly sliced
Zest and juice of 1 small lime

1 Wash the pint jars and lids in warm, soapy water. Rinse them well and set them aside to dry.

2 Add all the ingredients except the onions and lime to a small saucepan over high heat. Bring the mixture to a boil, stirring continuously until the sugar and salt are dissolved. Add the onions and stir well to combine. Put the lid on the saucepan, turn the heat down to low, and simmer for 5 minutes.

3 Remove from the heat and add the lime zest and juice. This is your pickling brine.

4 Use a slotted spoon to evenly divide the onions into the 2 pint jars.

5 Using a ladle, pour some of the hot brine over the onions ensuring they are fully submerged. If you need additional liquid, you can add equal parts of vinegar and water. Leave about a ½ inch (1.25cm) of headspace. (Optionally, you can use a wide-mouth funnel placed over the pint jars as you ladle in the pickling brine.)

6 Wipe the rims of the jars with a clean, damp cloth and seal with the lids. Transfer the filled jars to the refrigerator.

7 Let the onions pickle in the refrigerator for 2 to 3 days, allowing them to absorb some of the brine before using. They should be stored in the refrigerator and will stay fresh for up to 3 months.

COOK'S NOTES

Can you use Italian oregano instead of Mexican oregano in this recipe? Although these two herbs contain the same name, their flavor profile differs since they are from different plant families. So, when making these onions, be sure to search for Mexican oregano. You will be pleased with the hints of citrus and anise flavor it lends to these onions.

Homemade Tartar Sauce with Sweet Pickled Relish

Tartar sauce is a classic condiment that pairs wonderfully with seafood dishes, providing a creamy and tangy complement to fried fish, shrimp, and even sandwiches. Making it at home allows you to customize the flavors to your liking, and adding a homemade sweet pickled relish imparts a delightful sweetness and crunch that elevates the sauce to new heights.

TARTAR SAUCE
PREP TIME: **5 MINUTES**
CHILL TIME: **30 MINUTES**
TOTAL TIME: **35 MINUTES**
YIELD: **APPROXIMATELY 1¼ CUPS**

SWEET PICKLED RELISH
PREP TIME: **1 HOUR 30 MINUTES**
CHILL TIME: **24 HOURS**
COOK TIME: **15 MINUTES**
TOTAL TIME: **25 HOURS 45 MINUTES**
YIELD: **1 PINT**

TARTAR SAUCE EQUIPMENT

1 (12oz) jar with screw-on lid

Medium mixing bowl

INGREDIENTS

1 cup mayonnaise (homemade or store-bought)

¼ cup homemade Sweet Pickled Relish (recipe follows)

1 small shallot, peeled and finely minced

1 tsp lemon juice

1 tsp Dijon mustard

1 tsp dried dill or 1 tbsp minced fresh dill

1 tsp fine-ground sea salt

¼ tsp freshly ground black pepper

SWEET PICKLED RELISH EQUIPMENT

Wide-mouth pint (16oz) jar with screw-on lid

Large bowl

Colander

Ladle or spoon

Small (2- to 4-quart) saucepan

Wide-mouth funnel (optional)

INGREDIENTS

2 cups finely chopped unpeeled English or hothouse cucumber

½ cup finely chopped red bell pepper

½ cup finely chopped onion

1 tbsp pickling salt

1 cup 5%-acidity white vinegar

1 cup water

½ cup unrefined whole cane sugar

1 tsp fine-ground sea salt

1 tsp mustard seeds

½ tsp ground turmeric (also known as turmeric powder)

TARTAR SAUCE RECIPE:

1   Wash the jar and lid in warm, soapy water. Rinse them well and set them aside to dry.

2   Add all the ingredients to a medium bowl. Mix well to combine.

3   Transfer the tartar sauce to the jar. Wipe the rim of the jar with a clean, damp cloth, and seal with the lid.

4   Transfer the filled jar to the refrigerator and chill for at least 30 minutes to allow the flavors to meld before serving. The tartar sauce should be stored in the refrigerator and will stay fresh for 5 to 7 days.

SWEET PICKLED RELISH RECIPE:

1   Wash the pint jar and lid in warm, soapy water. Rinse them well and set them aside to dry.

2   Combine the chopped cucumber, red bell pepper, and onion in a large bowl. Sprinkle with the pickling salt, mix well, and let sit for about 1 hour. After 1 hour, transfer the mixture to the colander and drain over the sink, then rinse under cold water for 1 minute to remove excess salt.

3   Add all the remaining ingredients and the drained vegetable mixture to a small saucepan over high heat. Bring the mixture to a boil, stirring continuously until the sugar and sea salt are dissolved, then turn the heat down to low and simmer, uncovered, for 10 minutes or until the mixture has thickened.

4   Once thickened, use a spoon or a ladle to fill the pint jar with the relish, leaving about a ½ inch (1.25cm) of headspace. (Optionally, you can use a wide-mouth funnel placed over the pint jar as you add the relish.)

5   Wipe the rim of the jar with a clean, damp cloth and seal with the lid. Transfer the filled jar to the refrigerator.

6   Let the relish chill in the refrigerator for at least 24 hours to allow the flavors to meld. This relish should be stored in the refrigerator and will stay fresh for up to 3 months.

Honey-Pickled Orange Slices

Honey-Pickled Orange Slices are a delightful and versatile treat. The combination of sweet honey and tangy vinegar enhances the natural flavors of the oranges, creating a unique pickled delicacy. You can use these pickled orange slices in various dishes, including chopped into salads or stir-fries, as a showstopping topping for pancakes and waffles, or as a base for a dollop of vanilla ice cream. In a pinch, they make a great stand-in for orange marmalade at teatime.

PREP TIME: **20 MINUTES**
COOK TIME: **30 MINUTES**
TOTAL TIME: **50 MINUTES**
YIELD: **3 PINTS**

EQUIPMENT

2 wide-mouth pint (16oz) jars with screw-on lids
Small (2- to 4-quart) saucepan
Colander
Ladle
Wide-mouth funnel (optional)

INGREDIENTS

Water to cover, plus 1 cup, divided

4 medium thin-skinned oranges (e.g. Valencia, Seville), washed and thinly sliced with pips removed
1 vanilla bean pod, cut in half crosswise and split (optional)
1 cup 5%-acidity white vinegar
1 tsp whole allspice berries
1 tsp whole cloves
2 Ceylon cinnamon sticks
4 cardamom pods, crushed
1 cup raw honey

1 Wash the pint jars and lids in warm, soapy water. Rinse them well and set them aside to dry.

2 Add the orange slices to a small saucepan and cover with water. Bring the mixture to a boil over high heat, then immediately turn the heat down to low, cover the saucepan, and simmer for 15 minutes. Drain the orange slices in a colander in the sink.

3 Divide the orange slices between the 2 pint jars, packing them in the jars tightly. Nestle one half of the vanilla bean pod (if using) into each jar alongside the orange slices.

4 Return the saucepan to the stovetop and add the vinegar, allspice berries, cloves, cinnamon sticks, and cardamom pods along with 1 cup water. Bring the mixture to a boil over high heat, then immediately turn the heat down to low, cover the saucepan, and simmer for 5 minutes. Remove the lid and simmer, uncovered, for an additional 5 minutes on low. Remove from the heat and allow to cool completely, then stir in the honey. This is your pickling honey brine.

5 Using a ladle, pour some of the cooled honey brine from the saucepan over the orange slices, ensuring they are fully submerged. You should not need additional brine, but if you do, simply add a bit of honey poured on top of the orange slices. Leave about a ½ inch (1.25cm) of headspace. (Optionally, you can use a wide-mouth funnel placed over the pint jars as you ladle in the honey brine.)

6 Wipe the rims of the jars with a clean, damp cloth and seal with the lids. Transfer the filled jars to the refrigerator.

7 Let the oranges pickle in the refrigerator for 2 to 3 days, allowing them to absorb some of the honey brine before using. They should be stored in the refrigerator and will stay fresh for up to 3 months.

Thyme and Honey Pickled Cough Syrup

Homemade cough syrup is a targeted remedy for soothing sore throats and relieving coughs while helping to fight off bacteria and viruses, too! This Thyme and Honey Pickled Cough Syrup combines the soothing properties of honey with the herbal benefits of thyme (specifically thymol contained in thyme), creating a natural and effective remedy. Thymol has antimicrobial, antioxidant, and anti-inflammatory properties. And thanks to the raw apple cider vinegar to top it off, giving the cough syrup a pickled effect, it adds some probiotics (good bacteria) to help keep our digestive systems humming. Every year in late summer, I snip some thyme from my kitchen garden to make this syrup. It brings me so much peace of mind knowing that I have this tucked away in the back of my fridge if anyone in the family starts coughing during cold and flu season. Thyme is an easy herb to grow that does it all in the kitchen, and it's a great addition to your Healing Pantry—just remember that some remedies, like this one, belong in the fridge rather than in your designated Healing Pantry within your Extended Pantry!

PREP TIME: **10 MINUTES**
COOK TIME: **1 HOUR 10 MINUTES**
TOTAL TIME: **1 HOUR 20 MINUTES**
YIELD: **SLIGHTLY LESS THAN 1 PINT**

EQUIPMENT

1 pint (16oz) jar or bottle with screw-on lid

Small (2- to 4-quart) saucepan

Fine-mesh strainer

Medium bowl

Wide-mouth or narrow-mouth funnel (optional)

INGREDIENTS

2 cups water

1 tightly packed cup fresh thyme sprigs (or ⅓ cup dried thyme)

Zest and juice of 1 large lemon

¼ cup raw apple cider vinegar (homemade or store-bought)

1 cup raw honey

1   Wash the jar and lid in warm, soapy water. Rinse them well and set them aside to dry.

2   Add the water, thyme, and lemon zest to a small saucepan over high heat. (The thyme may not be completely submerged, but this is okay. The steam from the water will help to release the essential oils from the thyme.) Bring the mixture to a boil, then immediately turn the heat down to low, cover the saucepan, and simmer for 30 minutes. Periodically remove the lid and stir the thyme around in the water.

3   Remove the lid and continue to simmer the thyme water on low until reduced to about ½ cup. This will take approximately 20 to 30 minutes.

4   Strain the thyme water through a fine-mesh strainer placed over a bowl. Discard the thyme solids or add them to your compost.

5   Allow the thyme water to cool to room temperature, then stir in the lemon juice, vinegar, and honey. Continue to stir until the honey is completely dissolved.

6   Using a ladle, pour the thyme cough syrup into the pint jar, leaving about a ½ inch (1.25cm) of headspace. (Optionally, you can use a wide-mouth funnel placed over the pint jar as you ladle in the cough syrup.)

7   Wipe the rim of the jar with a clean, damp cloth and seal with the lid. Transfer the filled jar to the refrigerator.

8   The cough syrup is ready to use anytime and should stay fresh for approximately 6 months in the refrigerator.

> ·········· **COOK'S NOTES** ··········
>
> **How do you use the cough syrup?** Take 1 tablespoon as needed to ease a cough. This syrup is effective for dry and productive coughs and can also soothe a sore throat.
>
> **A word of caution!** As with any natural remedy, always check with your health care professional before using, especially if you are pregnant, nursing, or taking medication (either prescription or over the counter), have a compromised immune system, or may be allergic to certain herbs. This syrup is not suitable for children under 1 year old due to the risk of botulism from honey.

Pickled Corn and Jalapeño Relish

If you love a bit of sweet and spicy in your dishes, this Pickled Corn and Jalapeño Relish is the perfect addition to your pantry. This versatile condiment brings a delightful crunch and a kick of heat to anything from salads to tacos to grilled meats. Since we live in Central Texas, jalapeños are a staple in our kitchen, and this relish is a family favorite—especially for my husband and son, who enjoy it mixed with black beans and served with tortilla chips!

One of the things I love most about this relish is how it lets you savor the bright flavors of summer all year long. The sweetness of the corn balances perfectly with the jalapeño's gentle heat, creating a harmony of flavors that only gets better as it marinates. Whether you're spooning it over a juicy burger, layering it onto a sandwich, or simply enjoying it as a dip, this relish is sure to add a burst of color and zest to your meals. And let's be honest—any excuse to enjoy more jalapeños is a good one in our house!

PREP TIME: **20 MINUTES**
COOK TIME: **10 MINUTES**
TOTAL TIME: **30 MINUTES**
YIELD: **2 PINTS**

EQUIPMENT

3 wide-mouth pint (16oz) jars with screw-on lids

Large bowl

Medium (6- to 8-quart) saucepan

Ladle or spoon

Wide-mouth funnel (optional)

INGREDIENTS

3 cups fresh corn, cooked (from about 4 large ears), or frozen corn

2 jalapeños, seeded and finely diced (for more heat, retain the seeds and membranes)

1 medium red onion, finely diced

1 medium red bell pepper, finely diced

2 cloves garlic, minced

1 cup 5%-acidity white vinegar

1 cup water

½ cup unrefined whole cane sugar

1 tsp fine-ground sea salt

½ tsp ground cumin

½ tsp ground coriander

¼ tsp freshly ground black pepper

1. Wash the pint jars and lids in warm, soapy water. Rinse them well and set them aside to dry.

2. Combine the corn, jalapeños, onion, bell pepper, and garlic in a large mixing bowl. Mix well. Set aside.

3. Add the vinegar, water, sugar, sea salt, cumin, coriander, and pepper to a medium saucepan over high heat. Bring the mixture to a boil, stirring continuously until the sugar and salt dissolve, then turn the heat down to low. Cover the saucepan and simmer the mixture for 5 minutes.

4. Remove the lid from the saucepan and add all the ingredients from the bowl. Stir well to combine. Bring the mixture to a boil over high heat, then immediately turn it down to low. Simmer, uncovered, for a minute or two. (The mixture should have a thick consistency similar to a relish. If not, simmer it a little longer.)

5. Once the proper thickened consistency is reached, use a spoon or a ladle to fill the pint jars with the relish. Leave about a ½ inch (1.25cm) of headspace. (Optionally, you can use a wide-mouth funnel placed over the pint jars as you add the relish.)

6. Wipe the rims of the jars with a clean, damp cloth and seal with the lids. Transfer the filled jars to the refrigerator.

7. Let the relish chill in the refrigerator for at least 24 hours to allow the flavors to meld. This relish should be stored in the refrigerator and will stay fresh for up to 3 months.

Bread-and-Butter-Style Pickled Yellow Summer Squash

Bread-and-butter pickles are a beloved classic, and this tasty twist is an ideal way to use up an abundance of squash from your garden. For those of us in the Texas Hill Country where summer squash is abundant, this recipe is an excellent way to preserve your bounty. But chances are, no matter where you live, if you grow summer squash, you know how plentiful it can be! If you grow zucchini, too, or find a bumper crop at the farmer's market, you can alternate yellow squash with green zucchini for a pretty jarred end product. Use this pickled squash just as you would traditional bread-and-butter pickles.

PREP TIME: **1 HOUR 30 MINUTES**
COOK TIME: **10 MINUTES**
TOTAL TIME: **1 HOUR 40 MINUTES**
YIELD: **6–8 PINTS**

EQUIPMENT

6–8 wide-mouth pint (16oz) jars with screw-on lids

Large glass or stainless steel bowl

Colander

Medium (6- to 8-quart) saucepan

Slotted spoon

Ladle

Wide-mouth funnel (optional)

INGREDIENTS

4 lb (1.81kg) yellow summer squash (or a mix of yellow squash and zucchini), sliced into ¼-inch (0.65-cm) rounds

2 large yellow onions, thinly sliced

2 jalapeño peppers, sliced into rings (optional)

¼ cup plus 1 tbsp pickling salt, divided

Crushed ice

2¼ cups granulated sugar

2¼ cups 5%-acidity white vinegar

2 tsp mustard seeds

1 tsp black peppercorns

1 tsp ground turmeric (also known as turmeric powder)

6–8 black tea bags, caffeinated or decaffeinated (optional)

1 Wash the pint jars and lids in warm, soapy water. Rinse them well and set them aside to dry.

2 Combine the sliced squash, onions, and jalapeño peppers (if using) in a large bowl. Add ¼ cup pickling salt and mix well. Cover the mixture with crushed ice and let it sit for about 1 hour. (This helps to crisp the vegetables.) After 1 hour, drain the mixture in a colander placed in the sink and rinse the vegetables under cold water for 1 minute. Set aside to drain thoroughly.

3 Combine the sugar, remaining 1 tablespoon salt, vinegar, mustard seeds, peppercorns, and turmeric in a medium saucepan over high heat. Bring the mixture to a boil, stirring until the sugar and salt are dissolved. This is your pickling brine.

4 Add the drained squash mixture to the saucepan, stir, and return to a boil, then reduce the heat and simmer for 5 minutes. Remove the pan from the heat.

5 Before filling the pint jars, if desired, you can place a tea bag in the bottom of each jar. (The tea's properties can help the squash retain a crisp texture. But this is not required. The salted ice treatment also helps retain a texture to the squash similar to bread-and-butter pickles.)

6 Using a slotted spoon, transfer the squash mixture to the pint jars. As you transfer the squash, try to place one slice on top of the other to create an attractive pattern in each jar. Leave about a ½ inch (1.25cm) of headspace. Then use a ladle to fill each jar with the remaining brine in the saucepan, once again leaving about a ½ inch (1.25cm) of headspace, but making sure that the squash is submerged under the brine. (Optionally, you can use a wide-mouth funnel placed over the pint jars as you ladle in the brine.)

7 Wipe the rims of the jars with a clean, damp cloth and seal with the lids. Transfer the filled jars to the refrigerator.

8 Let the squash pickle in the refrigerator for 2 to 3 days to allow it to absorb some of the brine before using. The squash should be stored in the refrigerator and will stay fresh for up to 3 months.

Prepared Horseradish

Prepared Horseradish is a powerful and pungent condiment that adds a sharp, spicy kick to many dishes. My sweet husband loves it paired with roast beef when mixed with a bit of sour cream. You will find making your own prepared horseradish quite rewarding because your homemade version will ensure you have a fresher, more potent product— a little goes a long way!

PREP TIME: **15 MINUTES**
TOTAL TIME: **15 MINUTES**
YIELD: **APPROXIMATELY 1 CUP**

EQUIPMENT

Half-pint (8oz) jar with screw-on lid

Vegetable peeler

Food processor or blender

Small bowl

INGREDIENTS

1 (8- to 10-inch-/20.25- to 25.5-cm-) long piece of fresh horseradish root

2–3 tbsp water, divided

1 tbsp raw apple cider vinegar (homemade or store-bought)

Pinch of fine-ground sea salt

1. Wash the jar and lid in warm, soapy water. Rinse them well and set them aside to dry.

2. Peel the horseradish root using a vegetable peeler. Chop the root into approximately 1-inch (2.5-cm) pieces. (Before starting this next step, be advised that horseradish, when processed, will emit pungent fumes, so be cautious.)

3. Place the chopped horseradish pieces into the food processor or blender. Add 2 tablespoons water. Process until the horseradish is finely ground, adding more water, a teaspoon at a time, if needed, to reach the desired consistency. (Remember to be cautious of the pungent fumes.)

4. Transfer the horseradish into a bowl and add the vinegar and sea salt. Mix well to combine. The vinegar will help preserve the pungency of the grated horseradish.

5. Transfer the prepared horseradish to the clean jar. Wipe the rim of the jar with a clean, damp cloth, and seal with the lid. Transfer the filled jar to the refrigerator. The prepared horseradish should be stored in the refrigerator and will stay fresh for up to 3 months.

Pickled Italian Salsa Verde

Pickled Italian Salsa Verde is a vibrant green sauce made with fresh herbs, capers, and a touch of anchovy. Traditional Italian salsa verde is best consumed the day it is made, but I am sharing a version that my mom would make to preserve her homemade Italian salsa verde longer. She would simply add it to a vinegar brine. This approach gives this green sauce a more intense, tangier flavor and extends its refrigerator life. This versatile condiment is perfect for enhancing the flavors of meats, vegetables, and sandwiches, and as a zesty dip for crudités. It's bold, herbaceous, and brings a touch of Italy to any dish!

PREP TIME: **20 MINUTES**
TOTAL TIME: **20 MINUTES**
YIELD: **APPROXIMATELY 1 ½ CUPS**

EQUIPMENT

12 ounce jar with screw-on lid
Medium bowl

INGREDIENTS

1 cup finely chopped flat-leaf Italian parsley

2 tbsp capers, drained and finely chopped

2 anchovy fillets, finely chopped

2 cloves garlic, minced

1 small shallot, finely chopped

½ cup extra-virgin olive oil

½ cup white wine vinegar (optional)

1 tsp granulated sugar (optional)

Fine-ground sea salt, to taste (optional)

Freshly ground black pepper, to taste (optional)

1 Wash the jar and lid in warm, soapy water. Rinse them well and set them aside to dry.

2 In a medium bowl, combine the parsley, capers, anchovies, garlic, and shallot. Stir in the olive oil until the mixture is well combined. Use immediately or move on to the next step to preserve the Italian salsa verde for more than 1 day.

3 To preserve the Italian salsa verde, combine the white wine vinegar and sugar in a small bowl and stir until the sugar is dissolved. The sugar should dissolve in the vinegar without needing to be heated.

4 Pour the vinegar mixture over the salsa verde in the bowl and stir well to combine. Taste the mixture and adjust the seasoning if necessary, adding salt and pepper to taste and a pinch more sugar to balance the acidity.

5 Transfer the salsa verde to the jar. Wipe the rim of the jar with a clean, damp cloth, and seal with the lid. Transfer the filled jar to the refrigerator. This version of Italian salsa verde should be stored in the refrigerator and will stay fresh for up to 1 month.

Quick Pickle Cucumber Salad

This Quick Pickle Cucumber Salad is a delightful blend of sweet and sour flavors with a refreshing crunch. It's a perfect side dish for any meal, but especially great during the hot summer months. And best of all, since it is a "quick" pickle, it's ready in no time at all. Just give it about an hour to chill and you are ready to enjoy it!

PREP TIME: **10 MINUTES**
COOK TIME: **10 MINUTES**
CHILL TIME: **1 HOUR**
TOTAL TIME: **1 HOUR 20 MINUTES**
YIELD: **4 SERVINGS**

EQUIPMENT

Wide-mouth quart (32oz) jar
  with screw-on lid
Large bowl
Wooden spoon
Small (2- to 4-quart)
  saucepan
Ladle
Wide-mouth funnel
  (optional)

INGREDIENTS

2 large English or hothouse
  cucumbers, thinly sliced
1 large red onion, peeled and
  thinly sliced
1½ cups 5%-acidity
  white vinegar
1½ cups water
½ cup granulated sugar
1 tsp pickling salt
¼ tsp freshly ground
  black pepper
2 sprigs fresh dill, minced

1 Wash the jar and lid in warm, soapy water. Rinse them well and set them aside to dry.

2 Place the cucumbers and onion in a large bowl. Toss to combine, then fill the quart jar with the cucumbers and onions. Tamp them down with a wooden spoon, if necessary, to come within ½ inch (1.25cm) of the rim of the jar. Set aside.

3 Add the vinegar, water, sugar, salt, and black pepper to a small saucepan over high heat. Bring the mixture to a boil, stirring continuously until the sugar and salt are dissolved, then turn the heat down to low, cover the saucepan, and simmer for 5 minutes. Remove from the heat. Stir in the fresh dill. This is your pickling brine.

4 Use a ladle to fill the jar with the pickling brine, making sure the cucumbers and onions are completely submerged in the brine. Leave about a ½ inch (1.25cm) of headspace. (Optionally, you can place a wide-mouth funnel placed over the jar as you ladle in the brine.)

5 Wipe the rim of the jar with a clean, damp cloth and seal with the lid. Transfer the filled jar to the refrigerator.

6 Let the cucumber salad chill for about 1 hour before serving. If you can wait, let this pickled salad marinate in the brine for 2 to 3 days. This pickled cucumber and onion salad should be stored in the refrigerator and will stay fresh for up to 3 months.

Sweetly Spiced Pickled Eggs with Beet Juice

These Sweetly Spiced Pickled Eggs are a flavorful classic snack. The addition of beet juice gives the white of the eggs a beautiful red color, making them delicious and visually appealing. These eggs are perfect for slicing and adding to salads or simply enjoying on their own. The beet juice adds a subtle earthiness that balances beautifully with the vinegar and the combination of cinnamon, cloves, and peppercorns to infuse the eggs with a warm, aromatic flavor that's sweet and tangy.

Pickled eggs in beet juice have a long history as a beloved old-fashioned snack, especially in Pennsylvania Dutch country and other rural communities where resourceful home cooks found ways to preserve eggs before refrigeration was common. The vibrant magenta hue from the beets and the tangy-sweet brine made them both a visual delight and a flavorful treat. Whether enjoyed at a roadside diner or straight from a jar in the family kitchen, pickled eggs were a simple pleasure from a time when nothing went to waste, yet every bite carried a bit of deliciousness.

PREP TIME: **15 MINUTES**
COOK TIME: **30 MINUTES**
MARINATING TIME: **3 DAYS**
TOTAL TIME: **3 DAYS 45 MINUTES**
YIELD: **12 PICKLED EGGS**

EQUIPMENT

Wide-mouth half gallon (64oz) jar with screw-on lid

Medium (6- to 8-quart) saucepan

Slotted spoon

Ladle

Wide-mouth funnel (optional)

Bottle with tight-fitting cap (optional)

INGREDIENTS

1 dozen large eggs

1 cup beet juice (from canned beets or fresh beets)

1 cup water

1 cup 5%-acidity white vinegar

½ cup unrefined whole cane sugar

1 tsp pickling salt

1 small red onion, peeled and thinly sliced

1 Ceylon cinnamon stick

6 whole cloves

6 black peppercorns

1. Wash the jar and lid in warm, soapy water. Rinse them well and set them aside to dry.

2. Add the eggs to a medium saucepan and cover with water. Bring to a boil over high heat, then immediately remove from the heat and cover. Let the eggs cook in the hot water for 15 minutes. Using a slotted spoon, transfer the eggs to an ice bath to cool, and then peel them under cold running water. Place the peeled eggs in the half-gallon jar. Set aside.

3. Return the saucepan to the stovetop and add all the remaining ingredients. Bring to a boil over high heat, stirring continuously until the sugar and salt are dissolved, then reduce the heat to low, cover the saucepan, and simmer for 5 minutes. Remove from the heat. This is your pickling brine.

4. Using a ladle, pour the hot pickling brine over the eggs, ensuring they are fully submerged. If you need additional liquid, you can add equal parts of vinegar and water. Leave about a ½ inch (1.25cm) of headspace. (Optionally, you can use a wide-mouth funnel placed over the jar as you ladle in the pickling brine.) If you have extra brine, do not discard it. Refrigerate it in a bottle with a tight-fitting cap.

5. Wipe the rim of the jar with a clean, damp cloth and seal with the lid. Transfer the filled jar to the refrigerator. Refrigerate for at least 24 hours before serving. For best results, let the eggs marinate for 2 to 3 days to fully absorb the brine. If, during this marination time, you notice that the top eggs are no longer completely covered by the brine, add the reserved brine to the jar. If you do not have any reserved brine, you can add equal parts of vinegar and water. These pickled eggs can be stored in the refrigerator for up to a month.

COOK'S NOTES

Do you leave the pickled eggs in the brine for the entire month? Yes, they will absorb a bit more of the brine every day and become more and more flavorful!

Natural Home-Cured Corned Beef

If you have ever wanted to learn how to naturally cure meat to make your own corned beef, this recipe is for you! Best of all, this process is completely natural and does not include sodium nitrate, commonly referred to as pink curing salt. This recipe relies on sea salt and a combination of flavorful spices to achieve a classic corned beef. Once you see how easy it is to cure your own beef brisket using a salty brine, this will become your go-to recipe every St. Patrick's Day—or any day!

If you have ever wondered why a cured beef brisket is called corned beef, it is because the term corned comes from the large grains of salt, known as corns—similar in size to a kernel of corn—that were used in the traditional curing process. We may not have that exact type of salt in our home kitchens, but the good news is that coarse-ground sea salt is a great substitute.

PREP TIME: **20 MINUTES**
CURE TIME: **7 DAYS**
TOTAL TIME: **7 DAYS 20 MINUTES**
YIELD: **1 (5LB/2.25KG) CORNED BEEF**

EQUIPMENT

Very large (10- to 12-quart) stockpot

INGREDIENTS

1 (5 lb/2.25 kg) beef brisket, preferably a flat cut

1 gallon water

1 tbsp raw apple cider vinegar (homemade or store-bought)

2 cups coarse-ground sea salt

½ cup unrefined whole cane sugar or coconut sugar

1 tbsp black peppercorns

1 tbsp mustard seeds

1 tbsp coriander seeds

1 tbsp allspice berries

1 tsp whole cloves

1 tsp red pepper flakes

4–6 bay leaves

1 Ceylon cinnamon stick

1 tsp ground ginger (also known as powdered ginger)

1 Unwrap the brisket and rinse well with cool water. Pat it dry with paper towels. Rub the salt all over the brisket and then wrap it tightly in plastic wrap or place it in a large sealable plastic bag, removing as much of the air as possible. Refrigerate overnight.

2 The next day, add all the remaining ingredients to a very large stockpot over high heat. Bring the mixture to a boil, stirring continuously until the sugar is fully dissolved, then immediately remove from the heat, and allow it to cool completely. This is your curing brine.

3 Remove the brisket from the refrigerator, unwrap it, and place it in the stockpot, making sure that it is fully submerged in the brine. If needed, add additional water. Weigh the brisket down with a plate to keep it submerged.

4 Cover the stockpot and transfer it to the refrigerator. Allow the brisket to cure in the refrigerator for 7 days. Turn the brisket over once a day to ensure even curing.

5 After the curing period is complete, remove the brisket from the brine and rinse it thoroughly under cold water. Discard the brine.

6 To cook the corned beef, see the recipe that follows.

Traditional Corned Beef and Cabbage

When Irish immigrants arrived in the United States, they couldn't find the exact ingredients they used to make their traditional St. Patrick's Day meal back in Ireland. But these new Americans discovered beef brisket, and the classic Irish-American dish of corned beef and cabbage was born. This classic dish is a staple in our home that Ted and Ben always look forward to. It's a hearty combination of tender beef, flavorful cabbage, and perfectly cooked potatoes and carrots. This recipe ensures a delicious and festive meal that everyone will love.

PREP TIME: **20 MINUTES**
COOK TIME: **4 HOURS**
TOTAL TIME: **4 HOURS 20 MINUTES**
YIELD: **4–6 SERVINGS**

EQUIPMENT

Very large (10- to 12-quart) stockpot

Slotted spoon

INGREDIENTS

4–5 lb (1.81–2.27kg) corned beef brisket (preferably flat cut), home-cured or store-bought

1 tbsp whole black peppercorns

2 bay leaves

4 medium yellow onions, peeled and quartered with core intact

2 lb (907g) small, thin-skinned potatoes (quartered if large)

2 lb (907g) carrots, peeled and cut into 3-inch (7.5-cm) pieces

2 heads green cabbage, quartered with core intact

1. Place the corned beef brisket in a large stockpot and cover with water. Bring to a boil over high heat, then reduce the heat to low and simmer, skimming off any foam that rises to the top.

2. Add the peppercorns and bay leaves, or use the seasoning packet (if included with the store-bought brisket). Next, add the onions. Cover and simmer for about 3 hours.

3. Add the potatoes, carrots, and cabbage to the stockpot. Cover and continue to simmer for an additional hour or until the vegetables and meat are tender.

4. Remove the pot from the heat. Remove the brisket from the stockpot and transfer it to a cutting board. Let it rest for a few minutes before slicing it against the grain.

5. Place the sliced corned beef on a serving platter and use a slotted spoon to transfer the vegetables from the stockpot to the serving platter. Enjoy with a grainy mustard or horseradish, if desired.

Potted Pickled Corned Beef Topped with Clarified Butter

Making potted meat has been a beloved culinary practice for centuries. This traditional method of preserving meat involves cooking meat until tender, blending it into a paste, and sealing it with a layer of clarified butter. This process was historically used to preserve meat without refrigeration. Using leftover corned beef from our corned beef dinner makes this recipe quick, economical, and delicious. Adding cornichons or other pickled cucumbers adds a welcome taste that helps lighten an otherwise rich dish. It's perfect spread on toast or crackers.

PREP TIME: **15 MINUTES**
COOK TIME: **10 MINUTES**
TOTAL TIME: **25 MINUTES**
YIELD: **4 (2-OZ/60-G) RAMEKINS**

EQUIPMENT

Food processor or blender
4 (2-oz/60-g) ramekins or small jars
Small (2- to 4-quart) saucepan
Ladle

INGREDIENTS

½ lb (227g) leftover cooked corned beef, cubed

½ cup beef broth, stock, or bone broth, plus more if needed

½ cup cornichons or other pickled cucumbers

½ tsp fine-ground sea salt

½ tsp freshly ground black pepper

¼ tsp freshly grated nutmeg

1 cup clarified butter

1   Place the cubed corned beef into a food processor or blender. Add the beef broth, cornichons, salt, black pepper, and nutmeg. Blend, periodically scraping down the sides of the food processor or blender, until the mixture forms a smooth paste. If the mixture is too dry, add more broth 1 tablespoon at a time, until you reach the desired consistency.

2   Transfer the beef paste into ramekins or small jars, packing it tightly to remove any air pockets.

3   Melt the clarified butter in a small saucepan over low heat, skimming off any foam that may form on the top. Remove from the heat and let it sit for a few minutes to cool slightly.

4   Carefully ladle the melted fat over the top of each potted meat, ensuring that the meat is completely covered. This fat layer acts as a seal to preserve the meat.

5   Allow the potted meat to cool to room temperature, then cover and refrigerate. Generally, potted meat sealed with clarified butter will stay fresh in the refrigerator for 2 to 3 months. Once the fat seal is broken, you should consume the potted meat within 3 to 5 days.

End-of-Season Quick Fruit Pickles

End-of-Season Quick Fruit Pickles are a unique way to preserve the last of the summer's fruit bounty from your kitchen garden or the farmer's market. This method is simple, versatile, and perfect for adding a burst of flavor to your meals. Whether you're snacking straight from the jar, topping your salads, or adding to a charcuterie board, these quick fruit pickles are sure to be a hit in your home.

PREP TIME: **15 MINUTES**
COOK TIME: **10 MINUTES**
TOTAL TIME: **25 MINUTES**
YIELD: **1 QUART**

EQUIPMENT
1 wide-mouth quart (32oz) jar with screw-on lid

Small (2- to 4-quart) saucepan

Ladle

Wide-mouth funnel (optional)

INGREDIENTS
1 cup water

1 cup 5%-acidity white vinegar

½ cup granulated sugar

1 tsp pickling salt

4 cups mixed fresh fruit (washed, peeled, and cubed apples, nectarines, peaches, or plums work best)

1 cinnamon stick

1 tsp whole cloves

1 tsp black peppercorns

1 vanilla bean pod, split, and/or 1 star anise (optional)

1. Wash the quart jar and lid in warm, soapy water. Rinse them well and set them aside to dry.

2. Add the water, vinegar, sugar, salt, cinnamon stick, whole cloves, and peppercorns to a small saucepan over high heat. Bring to a boil, stirring continuously, until the sugar and salt are dissolved, then reduce the heat to low, cover the saucepan, and simmer for 5 minutes.

3. Remove the pan from the heat. This is your pickling brine.

4. Pack the fruit tightly into the quart jar, leaving about a ½ inch (1.25cm) of headspace. If desired, you can add a vanilla bean pod, star anise, or both to the jar. (The star anise will add a flavor similar to licorice.)

5. Using a ladle, pour the hot pickling brine over the fruit, ensuring it is fully submerged. If you need additional liquid, you can add equal parts of vinegar and water. Leave about a ½ inch (1.25cm) of headspace. (Optionally, you can use a wide-mouth funnel placed over the jar as you ladle in the pickling brine.)

6. Wipe the rim of the jar with a clean, damp cloth and seal with the lid. Transfer the filled jar to the refrigerator. The quick-pickled fruits will be ready once cooled, approximately 1 hour. They should be stored in the refrigerator and will stay fresh for up to 3 months.

End-of-Season Quick Vegetable Pickles

Quick pickling is an excellent way to preserve the last of your summer and fall vegetables. As with making quick-pickled fruits, this method is simple and incredibly versatile. Whether you want to add a tangy crunch to your sandwiches, a flavorful bite to your salads, or enjoy a delicious snack, this quick pickle recipe is perfect.

PREP TIME: **15 MINUTES**
COOK TIME: **10 MINUTES**
TOTAL TIME: **25 MINUTES**
YIELD: **1 QUART**

EQUIPMENT

Wide-mouth quart (32oz) jar with screw-on lid

Small (2- to 4-quart) saucepan

Ladle

Wide-mouth funnel (optional)

INGREDIENTS

1 cup water

1 cup 5%-acidity white vinegar

1 tsp pickling salt

2 tbsp pickling spice mix, homemade (see recipe below) or store-bought

1 tsp red pepper flakes, to add spiciness (optional)

2 tbsp granulated sugar, to add a mild sweetness (optional)

4 cups mixed vegetables (washed, peeled, and cubed carrots, cucumbers, and bell peppers work best)

BASIC PICKLING SPICE MIX

8 whole cloves

2 tbsp mustard seeds

1 tbsp allspice berries

2 tsp coriander seeds

1 tsp dill seeds

1 tsp black peppercorns

1 Ceylon cinnamon stick, broken into pieces

1 Wash the quart jar and lid in warm, soapy water. Rinse them well and set them aside to dry.

2 Add the water, vinegar, salt, pickling spice, red pepper flakes (if using), and sugar (if using) to a small saucepan. Bring the mixture to a boil over high heat, stirring continuously until the salt and sugar are dissolved, then reduce the heat to low, cover the saucepan, and simmer for 5 minutes. Remove the pan from the heat. This is your pickling brine.

3 Pack the vegetables tightly into the quart jar, leaving about a ½ inch (1.25cm) of headspace.

4 Use a ladle to pour the hot pickling brine over the vegetables, ensuring they are fully submerged. If you need additional liquid, you can add equal parts of vinegar and water. Leave about a ½ inch (1.25cm) of headspace. (Optionally, you can use a wide-mouth funnel placed over the jar as you ladle in the pickling brine.)

5 Wipe the rim of the jar with a clean, damp cloth and seal with the lid. Transfer the filled jar to the refrigerator.

6 The quick-pickled vegetables will be ready once cooled, approximately 1 hour. They should be stored in the refrigerator and will stay fresh for up to 3 months.

I want to share my sincerest thank you and gratitude to those who made this second book possible:

My wonderful husband, Ted, for all you do for me every day. This book—and pretty much everything I do in life—would have never been possible without you. Your name translates to "Gift from God," and that you are indeed!!

My amazing son, Ben, you have been such a joyful support to me through the entire process of writing this second book. Your smile, hugs, and, most of all, the love you show me and dad every day make us the most blessed parents in the world.

The Dream Team: Senior Editor Brook Farling, Photographer Kimberly Davis, Food Stylist Susan Gebhard, and Designer Lindsay Dobbs. Once again, you have all created a book more beautiful than I ever imagined. You four make my dreams come true!

Publisher Mike Sanders and the entire team at DK Publishing, thank you for all your support throughout the entire process of creating this second book.

Thom England and Susan Gebhard for testing such an array of recipes to ensure each one would come out perfectly. You both did an amazing job!

Lauren Cornman and the marketing and publicity team at DK, and book publicist Carrie Bachman, for helping to make this second cookbook an amazing success!

Jamie O'Hara, for helping bring *The Modern Pioneer Cookbook* curriculum to life with engaging lesson plans that teach K-12 students traditional foods and lifelong kitchen skills—and for proofreading my latest book.

My best friend forever, Michele Pryse, for virtually holding my hand every day through the writing of this book. The Good Lord may not have given me a sister by birth, but He sent you into my life just at the right time!

Father David Leibham, for your amazing support and friendship, and especially all the prayers you said for us as we navigated the "Holy Chaos" of writing this second book. You're officially family now!

All my Sweet Friends around the world who make Mary's Nest possible. You have made my life such a joy by joining me on this traditional foods journey!

And as always, to the Dear Lord above, thank you for all the gifts you have given me: my life, my family, the knowledge to write this second book, and the opportunity to share my talents to help others.

THANK YOU, ALL!

Love and God bless,
Mary

Index

.... ABOUT THE AUTHOR ....

Mary Shrader is the founder of the Mary's Nest website and the Mary's Nest YouTube channel. With over one million subscribers, 67 million views and counting, her over 600 in-depth videos teach traditional cooking skills to those longing to be modern pioneers. Her detailed recipes provide step-by-step instructions on how to make nutrient-dense foods, including bone broth, cultured dairy, ferments, and sourdough. She also shares a video series showing how to stock a pantry with a wide variety of homemade staples.

Mary learned how to make traditional foods from her loving and patient mother, who lived through the Great Depression and was skilled in all the gentle domestic arts. Eventually, when Mary married and became a mom, she discovered her passion for teaching other moms how to make traditional foods. Over 20 years ago, she started sharing simple lessons as moms and nursing babies gathered around her kitchen island. Then in 2018, she launched her YouTube video channel and discovered that millions of people worldwide longed to learn how to become modern pioneers and make traditional foods!

Since then, she published her first bestselling book, *The Modern Pioneer Cookbook*, to show how anyone can begin their traditional foods journey and become a modern pioneer in the kitchen by creating nutritious and delicious foods. And now she is thrilled to be able to bring this, her second cookbook, *The Modern Pioneer Pantry*, to you!

Through her gentle and encouraging manner, Mary shares traditional recipes with whole ingredients that make use of every last kitchen scrap, with the goal of creating a no-waste kitchen, just like our ancestors. She also published *The Modern Pioneer Cookbook Curriculum* to provide lesson plans to accompany her first cookbook and teach students in grades K–12 how to make traditional foods and gain lifelong skills in the kitchen.

Mary lives in the Texas Hill Country outside of Austin with her sweet husband, Ted, and their lovable yellow lab, Indy. Their son, Ben, is just a drive away and often visit for holiday celebrations, board games, and cozy family meals by the kitchen fireplace.

Find out more about Mary at marysnest.com and @MarysNest.